Rechtspolitisches Symposium
Legal Policy Symposium

Herausgegeben im Institut für Rechtspolitik an der Universität Trier
von Bernd von Hoffmann und Gerhard Robbers

Band 14

PETER LANG
Frankfurt am Main · Berlin · Bern · Bruxelles · New York · Oxford · Wien

Islam and State in the EU

Juan Ferreiro

Islam and State in the EU

Church-State Relationships, Reality of Islam, Imams Training Centres

PETER LANG
Internationaler Verlag der Wissenschaften

Bibliographic Information published by the Deutsche Nationalbibliothek
The Deutsche Nationalbibliothek lists this publication in the Deutsche Nationalbibliografie; detailed bibliographic data is available in the internet at http://dnb.d-nb.de.

ISSN 1610-8906
ISBN 978-3-631-61565-2

www.peterlang.de

To all those unknown heroes who have shed their blood in Europe victims of intolerance.

TABLE OF CONTENTS

FOREWORD

As this research could be framed within the issue of the relationship between politics and religion, I thought it might be useful if this foreword contained the testimony of two very symbolic political and religious authorities. Even though they are well known I wanted to highlight the fact that Juan Fernando Lopez Aguilar, currently Chair of the Committee on Civil Liberties, Justice and Home Affairs of the European Parliament and former Spanish Minister of Justice, has long been fighting for the protection and implementation of human rights in Europe. For his part, Mustafa Cerić, Grand Mufti of Bosnia and Herzegovina, is one of the most representative Islamic Faith leaders in the Old Continent

I

Over 3 years between 2004 and 2007, I had the honor to serve as Minister of Justice of the Government of Spain. Traditionally, the Ministry of Justice has held the role of exercise the dialogue with religious communities through the General Department of Religious Affairs.

Ours has been a country with a history of long hegemony of the Catholic Church. The system of a Confessional State has been a constant in our history - i.e. the establishment of the Catholic Church as the State official Church, as the "only true religion" of the Spanish people, as stated the fundamental principles of the national movement law of 1.958 which ruled until the entry into force of the 1978 Constitution.

The legal system based on democracy and respect for freedoms established in Spain with the Constitution has led to a cycle of civic and social deep transformations, with profound consequences in our core values and a progressive setting up of religious pluralism, a necessary corollary of religious freedom, that becomes a fundamental right along with religious equality, as it is enshrined in articles 9. 2, 14 and 16 of the Constitution.

The transformation of Spain into a society open to immigration and to the integration of diversity has gone in parallel with a growing presence of Islam in Spain, in a volume unknown since the expulsion of the "*moriscos*" by the absolute monarchy of the Habsburg in 1609.

In this context I started, as Minister of Justice, a process of dialogue with religious communities aimed at updating the institutional cooperation with the religious factor and the growing religious pluralism in Spanish society.

Not without difficulties or resistance, through subtle diplomacy displayed by Mercedes Rico as head of the General Department of Religious Affairs, we launched the Foundation pluralism and coexistence, in which Professor Contreras played the role of deepening and extending the horizon of equality in the exercise of freedom of religion. This led - among other measures and initiatives – to active policies aimed to the recognition Islam in a variety of social levels in which, hitherto, was barely visible on the grounds of prejudice, mistrust and perplexity caused by the fear of the different or unknown.

With the recognition of the presence of Islam in those public spaces where Muslims could exercise their fundamental rights and duties - education, health, welfare benefits, armed forces, prisons – a step forward was taken towards a an arena traditionally dominated by the inertia that encouraged the recognition of the Catholic religion as the only true religious creed which could dialogue with the State.

Let us say it clearly: the social context that explains these steps forward and progress is not reversible. Spain will not be anymore a homogenous society neither regarding to religion nor in other human dimensions (ethnic, axiological) where we have gone beyond the threshold and there is no turning back. These social and legal transformations are here to stay, if they not prelude other larger changes.

In order to frame properly the Spanish situation, we should appreciate the effort displayed by a demanding group of experts on religious freedom.

The painstaking work of Professor Juan Ferreiro is part of this itinerary of normalization of Islam in a country long accustomed to religious reductionism, when not exclusion, to marginalization, and even to the demonization and political persecution, of all forms of heresy, dissent, heterodoxy or agnosticism. Thus, this itinerary includes a strong commitment in the preservation of freedom in equality, and the active fight against all forms of discrimination.

Juan Ferreiro´s research regarding to relations between State and Islam in the European Union, with particular reference to the Imams training centers, constitutes a valuable contribution to update the Spanish situation to the binding compromises within our comparative international context: the integration of Spain in an area of freedoms, regional integration i.e. a EU governed by the law, founded on values and anchored in the respect of human dignity.

The entry into force of the Treaty of Lisbon (December 1, 2009), represents a crucial and certainly enormous step. Finally, it includes the European Charter of fundamental rights as annex with full normative force. It consolidates an area of freedom, security and justice in Europe. And, also a European policy subject to the ordinary legislative procedure (i.e. co-decision) and subject to judicial review by the Court of justice. The Treaty of Lisbon also underlines a European citizenship as the main engine of the European construction and also as civil context supported by rights and freedoms shared in a space of free movement of people.

As a consequence of all this, the protection of religious freedom and the banning of discrimination on religious grounds –and its necessary corollary, religious pluralism- pose many challenges to local, regional, national and European political powers.

In my opinion, this well informed, well structured and rigorous research helps to address the first of these challenges: an analytic and accurate of the experiences within other State Members of the European Union, in the terms of a comparative approach very useful to set up the shared minimum guarantees and standards for the protection of religious freedom in a shred legal and political system where the respect for human dignity is the core value.

I am convinced that the international cooperation in order to guarantee the right of denominations to form their clergy –in this case the imams- can find in this research a useful tool to a better knowledge of the reality of Islam in Europe, of the efforts that Muslims are doing to integrate into the various constitutional systems of the EU State Members and into the constitutional traditions and principles on which European Union law lays, that can be summarized in the respect to human dignity which –with grater eloquence than the internal market of the Euro- explain the idiosyncrasy of Europe as a legal institution.

Researches like this one, refresh us the evidence that Europe will not only be constructed by the euro and competence rules, but by citizens able to exercise their rights within their limits and respecting the freedom of others, attitudes that make the EU a remarkable model, a civilization itself.

Juan Fernando López Aguilar
Professor of Constitutional Law
Chair of the committee on Civil Liberties, Justice and Home Affairs of the European Parliament.
Former Minister of Justice of the Spanish Government

II

All three Abrahamic faiths – Judaism, Christianity, and Islam, have originated in the East and have come to Europe at various times for different reasons. The arrival of Islam in Europe is as natural and as important for European history and culture as the arrival of Judaism and Christianity. It is a fact that none of the messengers of God are of European origin. Hence, no one has the right to claim the priority in terms of nativity of his faith in Europe. But all these three religions belong to Europe and thus Europe has the right, nay, the obligation to treat them as its own. No one should feel as a guest, let alone ghost in Europe. Nuances aside, we are all hosts in Europe in one way or another.

My colleague the chief mufti of Serbia likes the metaphor which likens the contemporary return of Islam to Western Europe to a return of a long missing brother home. Irrespective of how dear to the family, his comeback inevitably causes problems. The family needs to make some space for him after its members accustomed to life without him, distributed his property etc. In the case of Islam this return is accompanied by some problems. One of them is the fear of Muslim unruliness in the administration of their affairs, education of their religious leaders being an important aspect of that. The best antidote to this fear is institutionalization of imam training which will give European governments and non-Muslim citizens a sense of control of the system.

For those educational institutions to be successful and fulfil their mission they ought to be accepted by Muslims themselves as well. To be credible and legitimate in the Muslim eyes they need to be a result of partnership between local European authorities and legitimate representatives of Muslim communities. As in any partnership compromises are unavoidable. Muslims should understand that like in any case of institutionalization they will have to give away some of their current 'freedom', which often amounts to nothing more but anarchy. That was the case with the establishment of schools of Islamic law, *madhahib* and the major Islamic learning institution, *madrasa* in the early centuries of Islam in its heartland. The standardization of Islamic learning into schools of law reduced somewhat academic freedom of Islamic scholars – *ulama'* - but established the conditions for the maintenance of stability and necessary unity of the Muslim Community. Similarly, the *madrasa* was established when the Muslim government needed to gain some control over both the teaching and learning process in Islam.

However the institutions are so important to warrant such a sacrifice. Bosnian Muslims, as one of the indigenous European Muslim nations, have made this compromise over a century ago probably because they understood well that while nothing in human history can be generated without individual men and women, nothing can last without institution. In exchange for submitting some of their religious autonomy European Muslims are right to expect that their legitimate voices be included, heard and respected. They will also need administrative and financial support of European institutions. We wish them and their governments all the best.

The Islamic Community in Bosnia and Herzegovina with its long history of institutional interpretation and administration of Islam in secular state as well as its rich tradition of Islamic education and ambitions in this field is capable of and willing to contribute significantly to this process. It is our hope that eventual institutionalization of imam training in the European Union will be a win-win situation for all and that the work of Professor Juan Ferreiro Galguera is a step forward.

May God help us all to work together for a permanent peace and security in Europe, our common motherland.

Dr. Mustafa Cerić
Grand Mufti of Bosnia and Herzegovina

III

Islam today is, after Christianity, the second largest religion in Europe with more than 15-20 million adherents. This number is expected to double by 2025.[1] Muslims in Europe are a diverse population of citizens, as well as recently arrived migrants. But Islam is still a rather unknown religion amongst non-Muslim citizens. And this lack of knowledge is, among others, one of the causes of Islamophobia. In many opinion polls people that recognize themselves as having prejudices against Muslims admit at the same time that they hardly know anything about Islam. Therefore their feelings and attitudes towards anything or anyone related to Islam are fed essentially by clichés, sometimes disseminated by the media.

One of the unknown things about Islam referred to is the Muslims' religious leaders: who are the Imams in Europe? Where do they come from? Where have they been trained? How many imam training centres are there in the European Union? What kind of education do they offer? Answering these

---

[1] *Muslims in Europe. A report on 11 EU cities.*Open Society Institute, 2009 (At home in Europe Project), p. 22

questions is the objective of this project: to make a map of the Imam training centres present in the 27 EU Member States.

We have chosen the term *Imam* because it is a more established term than *Muslim faith leaders*, even though, we consider that the latter term to be more inclusive than the former. So when we refer to imams we are thinking in a wider sense: Muslim faith leaders. For Sunni Islam, the imam is the religious leader who leads prayers in a mosque, full-time or part-time. However, faith leadership is exercised not only at mosques but also at schools, universities, courses, conferences, youth settings etc., and by a wide range of religious scholars (*alims and alimahs*)[2], teachers, instructors, youth workers, chaplains, writers and opinion leaders, including many women. To focus only on imams would be to miss the important leadership roles exercised by many members of Muslim communities.

The issue of Imam training centres, especially those that can give official certification, deals with the broader concept of relations between State and religion. According to the Spanish constitutional framework, relations between public authorities (at national, autonomous and municipal level) and religious groups, should be developed within two juridical principles that functions if they were two juridical coordinates: the principle of secularism (or non-confessional state) and the principle of cooperation:

a) Secularism, or the non-confessional State, is a legal principle established, with certain nuances, in the constitutional law of all European Union countries. Secularism is a concept based on two principles: the separation between churches and State and the neutrality of public powers regarding religious matters.
b) The principle of cooperation, also observed by some European Constitutions (Austria, Germany, Italy…), is a peculiarity of the Spanish Constitutional system. Because of the constitutional duty of the public powers to take into account religious beliefs of Spanish society and to maintain cooperation relations with Catholic Church and others religions,[3] the Spanish Constitutional Court has qualified its Church-State relations system as "positively secular".

This Cooperation mandate has been basically developed throughout the adoption of Cooperation Agreements both with the Catholic Church (1979), under the juridical form of international treaties, and with the other three relig-

---

[2] A scholar of Islam who is well-versed in the Qur'an and the Islamic sciences. The term is derived from the word *ilm*, meaning knowledge, usually of a religious or spiritual nature. The plural in Arabic is *ulama*. The feminine of *alim is Alimah*

[3] Art. 16.3 Spanish Constitution: "No religion shall have a state character. The public authorities shall take into account the religious beliefs of Spanish society and shall consequently maintain appropriate cooperation relations with the Catholic Church and other confessions".

ions that, at the moment that those agreements were signed (1992), had been declared by the administration as "deeply rooted" denominations (Muslims, Jews and Protestants). Afterwards, those agreements were validated by the Parliament as ordinary laws.

Concerning the training of faith leaders, Spanish laws (basically the cooperation agreements mentioned above) recognise the right of the four denominations that have signed a cooperation agreement with the State to create training centres for faith ministers at the university level. Although up to now, only the Catholic Church has developed training centres of this kind officially recognized by the State, the Spanish Organic Law on Universities (LOU) makes the government responsible for regulating the conditions for the creation of training centers by the other three denominations having signed Cooperation Agreements (Jews, Muslims, and Protestants) for faith ministers at the university level[4].

Considering that the Spanish legal model could be inspiring to the project of legally normalizing faith leader training centres, in 2008 the Council of Europe proposed that I conduct research on the training of faith leaders in Europe. The proposal was backed by my superiors in the Ministry of Justice at the time.[5] First, we discussed on whether to focus this research on faith leaders in general or to concentrate on religious leader training of a specific denomination.

I suggested then to concentrate on Islamic faith leaders, for two reasons. The primary reason is that according to the number of its adherents, Islam is currently the second largest religion in Europe after Christianity. The second reason is that unfortunately Islam is still very much unknown in Europe and people's knowledge about it is still to a large extent based on false clichés. As I said before, one of the main causes of Islamophobia is ignorance, but the most effective medicine to combat ignorance is knowledge. Thus, the challenge of

---

[4] Organic Law 4/2007, of 12 April, amending Organic Law 6/2001, of 21 December, on Universities.ELEVENTH ADDITIONAL PROVISION Recognition of civil effects. "The government, at the request of the competent ministries dealing with justice and university matters, in application of the provisions adopted in the Cooperation Agreements signed between the Spanish State and the Federation of Evangelic Denominations in Spain, approved by Law 24/1992, of 10 November, the Federation of Israeli Denominations in Spain, approved by Law 25/1992, of 10 November, and the Islamic Commission in Spain, approved by Law 26/1992, of 10 November, shall regulate the conditions for recognising civil effects to the academic degrees regarding theological and faith training teaching at university level, imparted in educational institutions of higher education accountable to the above mentioned religious denominations".

[5] When we first discussed this Project, the Ministry of Justice was Juan Fernando López Aguilar.

promoting knowledge about Islam requires knowing more about a core issue: who teaches Islam in the EU and where are those teachers trained?

Getting to know the real face of "academic Islam" in our countries (their methods, their inner thoughts, their problems...) could be of great interest not only to those European Imams who want to improve their religious education in Europe but also for the whole of European society. This is true above all for people interested in learning more about this religion, in other words, those who are attracted to Islam not only from a faith point of view but from a thirst for knowledge.

This commitment was a daunting one but a very exciting challenge for me because it was also closely connected to my research work as a professor of Law at the University of A Coruña. So, in July 2008 I accepted this project, proposing a very simple but clear strategy consisting of three steps. In general terms, we wanted to answer to three important questions:

1) What kind of Islamic faith leader training centres are there in the EU? (In other words, what was our starting reality);

2) What problems (juridical, sociological, linguistically…) have arisen within those imam training centres?

3) Given the reality with its difficulties and obstacles, what are possible solutions for those problems?

1. Existing Imam training centres in Europe

The first step of the strategy consisted in mapping out Islamic faith leader training centres in the European Union. The idea was to draw up a map-report showing the different kinds of Imam Training centres existing in each EU Member State. This book is the result of this first step.

How did I proceed? I started drawing up a questionnaire which I sent to the pertinent authorities in all EU Member States. When I received their answers I compared the data and undertook further research.

At this point I thought it would be interesting to widen the scope beyond imam training centres. This was for two reasons. First, it couldn´t be ignored that such centres existed in countries where Islam was a reality. Second, it was obvious that the countries where those centres are located had their own particular system of relations between churches and the state. So we decided to enrich the picture of imam training centres with two prerequisite pieces of information about each EU Member State: a) relations between church and state in each country, b) the "face of Islam" in those states via statistics related to the real presence of that religion.

Consequently, following in the mode of the general to the specific, we have dedicated a chapter to each of the 27 Member States, and in each chapter we have tried to respond to three questions,

a) Regarding State-Church relationship, we wanted to have a clear idea about two issues:

- Which are the administrative bodies that deal with denominations in each country?
- What kind of legal forms do denominations adopt in each State Member (religious entities, civil associations, foundations, charities…?)

b) The second part of each chapter, dedicated to a Member State, aims at showing the reality of Islam in each country in terms of general features such as:

- How is Islam recognized from a legal point of view?
- Which is the estimated number of Muslims?
- Which are the main organizations that represent Islam in each country?
- What is the estimated number of imams and mosques?
- How many Islamic faith leaders work as chaplains in prisons, in the army, in hospitals or in similar public institutions?
- Figures about Islam in schools: whether it is taught in public schools, if there are private Muslim schools etc.

c) After those two introductory parts in each MS, I focused on drawing up a map-report on Imam training centres in each country. We took into account differences between:

- Centres mainly concerned with theological teaching
- Centres mainly dedicated to teaching Islamic religious leaders about the country´s culture in terms of integration (laws and juridical principles, language, history, political system, human rights…)
- Centres which offer a combination of both.

We have also distinguished between courses linked to a university from those which are from private institutions, and also courses which deliver official certificates from those that so far do not any kind of legal recognition from State educational authorities.

2. Diagnosis of the existing shortcomings and legal problems

As, it has been said, this book is the result of the first step of a long term strategy. Once the map of the existing Imams training centres in the EU has been prepared, the time will come to consider the problems and needs that arise from each of these centres.

We can presume that some problems are linked to the lack of publicity for these courses (sometimes even a lack of transparency), as well the lack of official recognition for their diplomas in the education system. But there can be other problems too, such as the excessive presence of *ad hoc* contracted foreign teachers or the fact that some courses are delivered in languages not spoken in the country where the centre is located.

Maybe this challenge will require organizing some seminars. I think it might be useful to gather officials from EU countries (preferably those that belong to the administrative bodies that are qualifaid to mantain relationship with churches). They could provide a general view of the problems of Imam training centres from a "public powers' perspective. But, at the same time, it would be also necessary to summon up the representatives of the Imam training centres themselves -starting for example with those we have identified through our mapping- together with persons who play an important role in teaching Islam in Europe. At this point we should definitely include the Islamic leaders of the Balkans, an indispensable area not only to take into account but also to play a leading role in this project.

Dialogue within Islamic Faith leaders would be essential not only to receive a view of these centres from inside, but also to advance in the important task of creating a network of Islamic religious leaders connected with the European Imam training centres; a network thaw could show the starting draft of the academic face of Islam in Europe.

It would be useful that these meetings, gatherings and seminars could lead to drawing a report on the real problems the Imam training centres face in their respective countries.

3. Solutions

After identifying the Imam training centres existing in Europe and having analyzed the legal and sociological problems or shortcomings, the time will come to suggest possible solutions to the diagnosis previously done.

The main objective at this future stage will be to put forward recommendations in order to solve the problems regarding European Imam Training centres. We can foresee that suggestions may be located within two areas:

a) The easiest and most feasible recommendation would be to draw up general guidelines relating to aspects such as providing legal advice with regard to the legal recognition of those studies.
b) A more ambitious objective would be to start a debate about the possibility of establishing a European Institute or University of Islamic Studies. This would be a university or institute of academic nature, something similar to *Al-Azhar* University in Cairo, but in Europe. This debate could possibly be developed within the framework of a cooperation project between European Islamic faith leaders and the EU institutions

Such an institution would be of assistance not only for Imams but likewise any other European citizen looking for solid theological Islamic training. They would subsequently not be forced to go to centres located outside of their geographical environment to receive that type of education. Such a European Institute or University might work in close collaboration with other prestigious Islamic Universities all over the world. The closer these collaborations are the better it would be for conveying knowledge and a sense of transparency about Islam. This could also be a platform where all imam training centres and Islamic curricula from one common European context could converge somehow as an example of tolerance and intercultural dialogue.

Such a project would contribute to transparency and open the way for Islam, which is a religion of love and peace, to respond in an academic manner to the misunderstandings and false hoods disseminated by the media and public opinion and to stop the manipulation of minorities by undesirable groups who justify indiscriminate violence in the sacred name of Islam.

If this project is to be established according to the principle of cooperation between political and religious authorities for the sake of promoting religious freedom it would, naturally, require the agreement of European public authorities and Islamic religious leaders. We should take into account that a project of this kind cannot be achieved if European Muslim representatives do not request it themselves. Everybody is aware of the difficulties involved in creating a representative Islamic voice in Europe; the network of leaders in European imam training centres would be a useful tool in forming one. Once initiated by a representative academic Islamic authority, the project would also need the consensus of the pertinent political representatives in the European Union if they are willing to participate in this endeavour for the promotion of religious freedom

Whether this project is feasible or not, this book has managed to map out the existing imams training centres in Europe from a wider juridical and sociological context. I really hope this book could be of some help for the second and third step to come: analyzing the problems of the Imam training centres and proposing solutions.

We have already identified some of the difficulties and challenges of the steps which follow. In any case, the next stage should be approached within the spirit of dialogue, cooperation, and union. The lesson that the world has learned from the recent events in Tunisia and Egypt truly applies here: United we stand. This is epitomized in the old but wise saying: "If you want to walk fast, you walk alone. If you want to walk far, you walk together."

Last but not least, I want to express my deepest thankfulness to Erika Cerrolaza. Her extremely intellectual -and also human- generosity was crucial for me in order to carry out this research.

I would also like to underline my gratitude to the 27 Embassies of Spain in the EU State Members for their help with data, to all the people that have helped me in editing and correcting this book, and a special mention to the Faculty of Islamic Studies of the University of Sarajevo for the support and the enlightenment I received from them in a delicate and decisive moment.

Juan Ferreiro
Full Professor of Law (University of A Coruña)

AUSTRIA

I. RELIGION AND STATE

1. Administrative bodies that have contact with denominations.

The Ministry of Education, Art and Culture (*Bundesministerium für Unterricht, Kunst und Kultur*) is responsible for relations between the State and religious societies. The special department is the "Office of Churches and Religions." (*Kultusamt*)[6].

2. Recognition of religions.

Austria is a non confessional State. This means that the State and churches (or religious communities) are institutionally separated and that State protects religious freedom of individuals and communities and maintains neutrality before religious dogmas. The Constitution does not refer to any particular church. It includes comprehensive guarantees concerning freedom of religion and belief (*Weltanschauung*). The constitutional provisions in Austrian law relating to religion are contained in the "*Staatsgrundgesetz über die allgemeinen Rechte der Staatsbürger*" (Constitutional Act on the Fundamental Rights of Citizens of 21 December 1867 - StGG), which was declared a constitutional law of the Federal State by Article 149 sect.1 of the Austrian *Bundes-Verfassungsgesetz* (Federal Constitutional Act - B-VG) 1920[7]. According to the article 15 of this law:

"Every Church and religious society recognized by the law has the right to joint public religious practice, to arrange and administer its internal affairs autonomously, and to retain possession and enjoyment of its institutions, en-

---

[6] www.bmukk.gv.at

[7] Art. 9 of the European Convention on Human and Fundamental Rights is also of importance within the Austrian constitutional system because it has constitutional status.

dowments and funds devoted to worship, instruction and welfare, but is like every society subject to the general laws of the land".

The essential point of reference is the self-understanding of the religious community concerned.

So the legal system of the relations between state and church in Austria is based on three main principles:

- The fundamental right to individual freedom of religious and philosophical beliefs;
- The fundamental rights of religious communities to celebrate acts of cult in the public sphere,
- A system of two special legal forms for religious communities:
  1) "Legally recognized Churches and religious societies", which enjoy public law status;
  2) "State-registered religious denominational communities", which obtain legal entity under private law.[8]

Religious communities can also obtain legal status on the basis of the Law on Associations of 2002 (*VereinsG* 2002), if they do not fulfil the conditions for legal recognition or state-registration, or if the requirements to acquire legal personality are not accepted because of their doctrine. These organisations enjoy equal status to other ideological private associations. Contrary to the other two categories, religious communities established as non-profit associations are not identified by state bodies as being 'religious'[9].

- Legally recognised churches and religious societies

Among this first category of religious communities, there are two different ways for getting recognition.

1. Churches and religious societies that benefit from special laws on religion (or a concordat) in force regulating their external affairs: Catholic Church, Protestant Churches, Greek-Oriental Church, Oriental-Orthodox Churches, Hebrew Religious Community and Islamic Religious Community.

---

[8] Cf. B. SCHINKELE, Religious Entities as Legal Persons Austria, in L. Friedner (ed.) Churches and other religious Organisations as Legal Persons, Proceedings of the 17th Meeting of the European Consortium for Church and State Research Höör (Sweden), 17./20. November 2005, Leuven-Paris-Dudley/MA 2007.

[9] The Association Law of 2002 does not apply to those associations constituted under other legal provisions or which have adopted a different legal form under other appropriate legislation SCHINKELE, B.(2007): "Religious entities as Legal Persons" in *Churches and other organisations as legal persons,* Peeters 2007, pp. 37-44

2. Churches and religious societies, which are recognised by ministerial ordinance according to the Law concerning the recognition of religion (*Anerkennungsgesetz – AnerkG*) of 1874 (RGBI Nr 68), which contains the legal principles for these communities. On the basis of the *AnerkG* the following denominations have been recognised by ordinance: The Old Catholic Church (1877), the Methodist Church (1951), the Church of Jesus Christ of the Latter Day Saints (Mormons) (1955), The New Apostolic Church in Austria (1975), the Austrian Buddhist Religious Association (1983), and Jehovah Witnesses (2009).

The *AnerkG* provides some preconditions for recognition. According to sect. 1, recognition will be granted to the followers of a previously legally unrecognised denomination under these conditions,

"*(1) religious teaching, service, statutes, and chosen name do not contain anything illegal or morally offensive*

(2) The creation and continuous existence of at least one cult community according to the requirements of this law is guaranteed."

This Act has been complemented by sect. 11 *Bekenntnisgemeinschaftengesetz* 1998 (Law on Registration of Religious Denominational Communities – BekGG). Other requirements for recognition are:

- A number of followers equal to at least 2/1000 of the population of Austria according to the most recent census (that is according to 2001 Census: 16.066),
- Twenty-year period of existence in Austria, including ten years being a registered religious community,
- Use of income and assets for religious purposes,
- A positive attitude both toward the society and the State,
- No illegal disturbance of relations with existing legally recognised churches and religious societies or any other religious communities.

- **- State-registered religious denominational communities**

This second category was introduced in 1998 by the BekGG. The acquisition of a legal personality for a religious community – not for a philosophical community (*Weltanschauungsgemeinschaften*) – principally follows the system of the Law on Associations.

Therefore a religious denominational community can acquire legal personality if it has at least 300 followers. Once the application for register has been presented, the Administration has six-month to answer. If it doesn´t answer within that period the community will get legal personality as a registered denomination.

The application must contain a description of the religious doctrine, which must be different from the doctrines of other existing religious communities. Referring to the name and to the doctrine, the "principle of exclusivity" applying for the recognized churches and religious societies has also been extended to the registered religious communities. The Minister is obliged to deny acquisition of legal personality if the statutes are not in accordance with the requirements of the law or if its doctrine is against public safety, public order, health, morals or the rights and freedoms of others; especially in the case of incitement to crime, or when psychological integrity of others is damaged, for example using psychotherapeutic methods for indoctrination.

At the time being, there are 10 state registered religious communities: Baha'i Religion, Federation of Baptist Communities in Austria, Federation of Evangelical Communities in Austria, Christian Community – Movement for religious Revival in Austria, Free Christian Community/Pentecostal Community, Hindu Mandir Society, Church of Seventh Day Adventists, Mennonite Free Church of Austria, Pentecostal Church-Community of God in Austria, and Elaia Christian Community. In future this category of religious communities could be a choice for some Islamic traditions that don't belong to the already recognized Islamic Community in Austria, for instance the Alevis.

The "*Bundesstelle für Sektenfragen*" (Federal Office for Sect Issues)

Under the Federal Act on the Establishment of an Office on Documentation and Information about Sects 1998, a legal basis for state informative action was created in relation to new religious movements. The law does neither apply to recognised churches and religious societies nor to their institutions.

The "*Bundesstelle für Sektenfragen*" is structured as an independent institution under public law. Its tasks comprise the documentation and information about dangers that can arise from programmes or activities of sects or sect-like activities. There must be a well founded suspicion and a danger to certain legal values. The range of tasks of the Federal Office for Sect Issues is equivalent to the limits stated in Art. 8 (2) and Art. 9 (2) of the ECHR. Protected values to which these dangers can be related to are explicitly mentioned: life and physical or psychological well-being of human beings, the free unfolding of human personality including the freedom to enter or leave religious or philosophical communities, integrity of family life, property, financial independence of people and the free mental and physical development of children and juveniles (Section 4(1)). To fulfil its tasks the Federal Office is especially entitled to collect, analyse and forward information, advise people affected, co-operate and exchange information with internal and foreign authorities and to develop, supervise and co-ordinate research projects.[10]

II. ISLAM IN AUSTRIA

1. Legal recognition of Islam

In 1878, the former Ottoman provinces of Bosnia and Herzegovina were occupied by Austrian troops and were annexed in 1908. After this year Bosnia and Herzegovina became formal part of the Hapsburg Empire, and for the first time the Habsburgs assumed authority over a large Muslim population. Therefore Islam in 1912 got the status of a legally recognized religious society in Austria and Hungary. The Act on the Recognition of the Adherents of Islam following to the Hanafite Rite raised the Hanafite Muslims to the legal position of the other legally recognised churches and religious societies and thus entitled them to manifest their religion in public, administer their internal religious affairs independently; establish foundations for religious, educational and charitable purposes, and have the Act on the Inter-Confessional Relations applied for their affairs.

In 1979 the Federal Minister of Education and Art approved the constitution of the Islamic Religious Community in Austria (*Islamische Glaubensgemeinschaft in Österreich – IGGiÖ*). This approval was renewed by a Decree of 2nd August 1988, which summarises in seven points the elements that must be contained "in particular" in the constitution of the Religious Community with respect to its external legal circumstances.[11]

---

[10] R. POTZ, "State and Church in Austria" in *State and Church in the European Union*, 2nd Edition, Ed Nomos, Baden-Baden 2005, 391-418.
[11] *Ibid* p. 399.

2. Muslim population

The history of the Muslims' presence in Austria is closely related to its relations with the Islamic populations in the Balkans. In the 20th century, above all after the World War II, migration movements from the former Yugoslavia and Turkey and from Arab countries such as Egypt contributed to create a heterogeneous Muslim community within Austrian soil.[12]

According to the 2001 Census (8.032.926 inhabitants), the religious and denominational structure of the population of Austria presents the following picture: Roman Catholics 73.66 %, Protestants 4.68 %, Muslims (339.000) 4.30 %, Orthodox 2.17 %, Old Catholics 0.18 %, Buddhists 0.13 %, Jewish 0.10 %, Oriental-Orthodox 0.06 % and 11.99 %.belonging to no denomination. In 2010, out of a population of 8,355,260 inhabitants, approx. 6, 2 % are Muslims (about 516.000[13]) from whom 49 % are Austrian citizens, 21% have Turkish citizenship, and 10% are Bosnian.

The highly industrialized Federal State of Vorarlberg and Vienna account for most of the Muslim population in Austria, whereas the Eastern and Southern Federal States are the less Muslim populated.

3. Muslim representative organizations

The official representation of the Muslim community in religious affairs is the "Islamic Religious Community in Austria (*Islamische Glaubensgemeinschaft in Österreich* (IGGiÖ).[14] The IGGiÖ is an entity under public law which was constituted in 1979, based on the Law on Islam of 1912. It is a corporation with public law status and acts officially as the highest religious representation of the Austrian Muslims especially vis-à-vis the State and public institutions.

The IGGiÖ has established a set of organs for the –currently four– local communities: the local council, the regional committee, the First Imam, the spiritual counsellors; and for the parent body, the Islamic Religious Community

[12] S. KROISSENBRUNNER: "Islam in Austria" in HUNTER, S. (ed.): *Islam, Europe's second religion. The new social, cultural and political landscape*, Preaeger 2002, pp. 141-155.

[13] Österreichischer Integrationsfonds, "Islam in Österreich", Feb. 2010.

[14] www.derislam.at.

of Austria: the Shura Council, the Supreme Council, the President of the IG-GiÖ, the Advisory Committee, the Mufti, and the Court of Arbitration.

The Shura Council is the legislative body. It consists of a minimum of sixteen members who are elected by the six chairmen of the regional communities, which are elected by the local councils in the provinces of Austria. The Supreme Council, consisting of 12 members elected by the Shura Council every five years, is the executive organ mainly dealing with religious, cultural and financial matters. Not more than one third of the members both of the Shura Council and the Supreme Council may stem from the same ethnic and linguistic group. The president, elected every five years, is at the same time the chairman o the Supreme Council (Executive Body) of the IGGIÖ. Financial affairs are regulated by the Shura Council and the income of the IGGIÖ is a combination of donations, membership fees and fees paid by teachers of Islam.

Like everywhere in Europe, the social, cultural, and religious life of the majority of Muslims is shaped by a number of federations and organisations. The IGGiÖ on the one hand is a kind of an umbrella organisation for these federations and organisations. But there are also some small groups outside the IG-GiÖ.

In 2009 a new Statute required official acknowledgement by the competent Ministry. It shall guarantee a stronger involvement of the different associations in the work of the IGGiÖ. The establishment of nine regional Communities and new regulations for the elections are also foreseen.

The IGGiÖ is regarded as a "clear and secure basis, which gives Muslims in Austria the possibility to enter in dialogue with different social and public organizations" (Report on the Protection of the Constitution 2006 by the Ministry of Interior). The Austrian State regards the organs of the IGGÖ "contact persons representing and negotiating the interests of the Muslims".

There are other Muslim associations throughout Austria, while approximately 270 being registered. The Alevis are represented by the Alevi Federation in Austria (*Föderation alevitischer Kulturverbände*), the Shi'ites are united under the *Ahl-ul-Bayt Österreich* and the Sunnis are represented by the IG-GiÖ[15].

Turkish organizations also play an important role. The Federation of Turkish-Islamic Associations, linked to the *Diyanet*, is one of the main umbrella or-

[15] EDNAN, A.-HEINRICH, P.: "Austria" in V.V.A.A. *Yearbook of Muslims in Europe* Edited by NIELSSEN, J.S.; AKAGÖNÜL, S.; ALIBASIC, A; MARECHA,B.; MOE,C; Leiden-Boston, (2009) pags. 27-28.

ganizations. The number of Turkish speaking associations is presumably the highest[16]. Among them, the *Millî Görüş* – lit. "Denominational vision" a movement registered as an alliance of mosques which manages several of them-, and the Suleymancis, a Sufi brotherhood with Turkish background. There are also Arab Associations[17], Bosnian Muslims[18], and a number of supra-regional Muslim associations[19].

4. Mosques and imams

At present there are more than 300 Muslim worship places in Austria.[20] There are four big mosques: the biggest one, with a minaret 32 m. high, was built in Vienna in 1980, financed by the King of Saudi Arabia. The others are in Saalfelden (Salzburg), in Telfs (Tirol) and in Bad Vöslau (Lower Austria, near Vienna). Recently, two Federal States, Kärnten and Vorarlberg, modified their legislation hardening the requirements to build mosques in their regional territory. The establishment of an Islamic Cultural Centre is planned in Vienna-(Brigittenau district).

The first Islamic cemetery in the country has been opened in Vienna in November 2008 (23th district). The second one was opened in Voralberg.

Muslim worship places comprise a broad range of facilities usually run by non-profit associations. Some associations cannot afford paying an imam. There are no reliable figures about the exact number of imams, but according to some statistics, there are around 250 imams in the whole Republic.[21] In 2006 Vienna hold the second Conference of European Imams, following the first one organised in Graz in 2003, with the support of the federal government and the

---

[16] E.g., *Islamische Föederation in Osterreich (MillîGöurus); Turkisch Islamische Unionfür Klturelle und soziale Zusammenarbeit in Ostereich –ATIB* (www.deutsch.atib.at.) *Union Islamischer Kulturzentren* (www.uikz-org) *Dachorgnisation Türkischer Kultur un Sportgemeinschaft Ibidem.*

[17] www.aawleague.org , eg. *Gesellschaft für Zusammenkunf der Kulturen; Liga Kultur; Schur Moschee*

[18] represented by the *"Dachverband der Bosniaken in Österreich* and *Verein Bosnischer Muslime der hamefitischen Rechtsschule Gazi Husrevbeg.*

[19] E.g. *Initiative muslimische ÖsterreicherInnen IMÖ* (www.islaminitiative.at), Kulturverein Al-Andalus (www.andalus.at.) *Liga Kultur Verenin für Multi-Kulturellen Bückenbau* www.alnur.at EDNAN, A.-HEINRICH, P.: "Austria" in V.V.A.A. *..op. cit.* pag. 28

[20] Source: Spanish Embassy in Vienna

[21] *Ibid.*

European Commission and the city of Vienna. The conference brought together some 130 imams from more than 40 countries focusing on integration and the role of imams in helping their communities integrate into society.

5. Chaplains

Special religious counselling may be organised for public hospitals, medical institutions, nursing homes, prisons, and community homes with the consent of the competent church authority (the Catholic diocesan bishop; the governing body of the Protestant Church). Local pastors of all denominations - including those not legally recognised - have the right of free access to proved religious assistance to members of their denomination in state institutions.

The Islamic chaplaincy service is provided and governed by IGGiÖ. The chaplains are selected by the Supreme Council of this organization. Islamic chaplains are required to have a qualification from an Islamic higher education establishment or adequate practical experience in chaplaincy work recognized by this association. In 2000, the IGGiÖ organised an Islamic Visiting and Social Service (IBS) to provide for social services to Muslims patients. In January 2010 an agreement between the government and the IGGiÖ has been signed in order to regulate the job framework of chaplains

There are around 8,600 prisoners in the 28 existing prisons in the Republic of Austria and around 1160 of these prisoners are Muslims (13,5%).[22] Muslim volunteers who are certified and coordinated by the IGGiÖ are engaged in religious counselling services for Muslim prison inmates. They receive allowances from the Prison administration.

There are 38 Muslim chaplains within all the Federal States, except for Burgenland and Oberösterreich where there are none23. Depending on the Federal State, chaplains are appointed by the Islamic Religious Community in Austria, the Islamic Cultural Centres Union, the Turkish General Consulate (Bregenz) or by different regional associations.

There is no permanent imam for the army, but volunteer imams work in Vienna and Salzburg. In 2004, the first prayer room for soldiers was opened in the "Casern of Maria Theresia".

[22] *Ibid.*
[23] *Ibid*

There are two permanent IBS in the Franz Josef Hospital and in Vienna General Hospital and other medical institutions are visited by request. According to the 2006 census, 6.160 patients in Vienna General Hospital received religious services from Islamic chaplains[24].

6. Islam in public schools, Islamic private schools

Providing religious instruction in state schools is an exclusive right of legally recognized churches and religious societies. In state schools, all children belonging to a legally recognized church or religious society receive religious education in their confession. The expenses for such an education are borne by the State. The Religious Education Act 1949 (*Religionsunterrichtsgesetz)* establishes that the State pays for Islamic education in public schools. Religious education is conducted in cooperation with and under the supervision of the specific recognised religious community (art. 2.1). The curricula for religious education (hours of teaching and content) are announced by the federal minister but recognised religious communities have responsibility for content.

According to the IGGiÖ, 50.000 pupils study Islam in 2.110 of the 2.700 schools existing in the Republic. There are around 400 teachers of Islam in public and private schools.

The Islamic community has the following educational centers or institutions: eight nursery schools, three primary schools, one secondary school, and a vocational training centre, all of them located in Vienna.[25]

---

[24] EDNAN, A.-HEINRICH, P.: "Austria" in V.V.A.A. ..*op. cit.* pag. 30.
[25] Source: official data from the Austrian Ministry of Education provided by the Spanish Embassy in Vienna.

III. TRAINING CENTRES FOR TEACHERS AND IMAMS[26]

According to the Austrian constitutional and legal system, the responsibility for any training of Muslim faith leaders, such as imams, is part of the "internal autonomy" of the Muslim community.[27]

The Islamic Religious Community in Austria is currently preparing a project for setting up an Islamic Faculty at the University of Vienna in order to provide imams with high level training in theological studies including subjects such as German language, and the history of Austria and Europe.

A special program for Turkish imams coming to work in Austria through the *Avusturya Türk Islam Kültür ve Sosyal Yardimlasma Birligi* (Turkish Islamic Union in Austria for Social and Cultural Cooperation, ATIB), was also set up in 2009 by the Austrian Ministry of European and International Affairs in cooperation with the *Diyanet*. In the case of Austria, such as in other countries, the Turkish government sends Turkish imams to serve its communities abroad. To ease the start and the work of these imams, a one week long course was established. The course comprises topics such as socio-political and cultural aspects of Austria, Islam and the inter-faith situation, and gender and migration.

1. Training courses for teachers of Islam in public and private schools

The *Federal Law on the Organisation of the Pedagogical Colleges and their Studies* 2005 (HochschulG) provides for an independent incorporation of the Teachers' Training Academies into the tertiary sector of education including Bachelor's degree for teaching appointments. Until that time the Religious Education Teachers' Training Academies (Religious-pedagogical Academies) had been established as denominational private schools pursuant to the *Law on Private Schools* and had been conferred public law status on this legal basis.

---

[26] There is no known specific research on imam training in Austria, although one of the conclusions of the Austrian Imam Conference held in Vienna in April 2005 was the need for developing imam's training in Austria.

[27] The right of "legally recognised churches and religious communities" to arrange and administer their internal affairs autonomously is guaranteed under Article 15 of the Basic Law on the General Rights of Nationals of 1867.

The Islamic Religious-pedagogical Academy (IRPA[28]), an institution of the IGGiÖ, began its activities in the academic year 1998/99 according to the *Law on Private Schools.* The curriculum last six semesters, leading to a Bachelors degree, and the course can be attended by primary school teachers. The number of students In October 2007 this Academy was transferred into a University College of teacher education according to the *HochschulG* 2005. It comprises also an Institute for Advanced Vocational Training and the facilities and courses of this institute can be used by imams too. Now its name is Private Course for the teaching of Islamic religion in compulsory schools (*Privater Studiengang für das Lehramt für Islamische Religion an Pflichtschulen*).

The legislator has taken into account that the subject matters of religious instruction as well as the training of teachers fall within the ambit of the "internal affairs" of the legally recognised churches and religious societies. Thus, the right to religious freedom comes to an effect, primarily as far as the curricula are concerned. With respect to the fact that denominational Colleges are private institutions, the legal relationship with their students is based on a contract under private law. Regarding the structure and organisation of the Colleges the same quality and academic level as it is given at the public institutions must be guaranteed.

As a consequence, the denominational Pedagogical Colleges are obliged to observe the general provisions concerning qualification of the teaching staff including performance review, the academic autonomy, and co-determination of the students, the allowance of previous studies, personal staff, and material equipment. Among the general leading principles, the development of a social competence in connection with imparting social, ethic and religious values is explicitly mentioned. In order to ensure the comparability of these studies and degrees with those of the public Teachers' Training Colleges, the law provides for recognition proceedings.

2. Postgraduate Programs: Muslims in Europe

In 2006, the Faculty for Philosophy and Educational Sciences of the University of Vienna offered a Masters degree in Islamic Religious Pedagogy (IRP) and this will be a required qualification for teaching religious education in Austrian high schools.

---

[28] *Islamische Religionspädagogische Akademie*

Apart from educating teachers for religious instruction the department has the aim of scientific research of the situation of Muslims in Europe. This includes also the development of teaching materials that support the imparting of Islamic-European identity to the pupils.[29] The course lasts four semesters and is currency attended by 50 students, six of whom are preparing to present their Master thesis. Most of the students are alumni of the former IRPA and there are also students who had attended high school in Austria or Germany or students with who come from abroad (mainly Turkey, Bosnia and Egypt)[30].

Although until now there was no general program for imam's training, the University of Vienna offered in the academic year 2009-2010 a Master degree. The target group are Imams or Islamic religious leaders, who have already trained in their homeland and want to go to Austria to work in a religious community, and Muslim chaplains. This one-year program is called "Imams in Europe". In cooperation with the IGGiÖ, it offers courses on the Austrian political and juridical system, notably fundamental rights, mosque management, financial and educational skills and the challenge of teaching Islam in a European context. The program is taught over four semesters (60 ECTS) and is accessible by full-time study or through evening classes. It accommodates 30 students which are required to have studied Muslim theology in advance. The requirements are:

- Bachelor, Master degree or PhD in Islamic theology from an approved university in Austria or abroad
- If no required degree can be provided the Islamic Religious Community will prepare an expert opinion for the selection process.
- Proof of employment in Austria
- Applicants whose mother tongue is not German have to possess a good knowledge of German, at least level B2 according to the Common European Framework of Reference for Languages

Women are preferred among candidates with equal qualifications[31].

[29] http://islamische-religionspaedagogik.univie.ac.at/index.php?id=24164&L=2
[30] EDNAN, A.-HEINRICH, P.: "Austria" in V.V.A.A. ..*op. cit.* pag. 30.
[31] http://mie.univie.ac.at/en/admision

BELGIUM

I. RELIGION AND STATE

1. Administrative bodies that have contact with denominations.

Belgium is a constitutional, popular monarchy and a parliamentary democracy. Belgium is a Federal State made up of communities and regions. There are three communities: the French Community, the Flemish Community and the German Community and the three regions are: the Wallon Region, the Flemish Region (both of them divided in provinces and municipalities), and the Region of Brussels.

At the federal level, the Ministry in charge of relations with denominations is the Ministry of Justice but since the law of 13th of June of 2001, regions have been increasingly assuming more competences regarding the issue of religion.

2. Recognition of religions.

The constitution of a church or a religious denomination in Belgium does not require any approval by the government. They can enjoy legal personality and so participate actively in legal life if they organise themselves as an association. The ideal form is a V.Z.W./A.S.B.L. (*Vereniging zonder winstoog-merk* /Association sans but lucrative), a legal form which has existed since 1921[32] and allows for active participation in legal life.

Religions are not required to register. Nevertheless, there is a specific status of recognised religion (*culte reconnu)* which is given by a Law. So any religion can enjoy of legal personality being simply an association or a "recognised religion" if they have got that status by a law of the Federal Parliament. The no-

[32] Article 4 of the Law of 13 July 2001, *Moniteur Belge,* 3 August 2001. In theory, religious groups are not forbidden to use other legal forms in order to participate in legal life. The formula of a company can be chosen, as long as all requirements (including a profit, and not a non-profit orientation) are fulfilled TORFS, R.: "Religious entities as Legal Persons –Belgium-" in *Churches and other organisations as legal persons p. 45-48.* Peeters, 2007.

tion of recognition comes from the law of the 4th of March 1870 on the organisation of the temporal needs of the religions. The main basis for such recognition is the social value of the religion as a service to the population.

Currently, six denominations enjoy the status of recognized religions: Catholicism, Protestantism, Judaism, Anglicanism (Law of 4th of March 1870)[33], Islam (Law of 19th of July 1974 amending the said law of 1870) and the Greek and Russian Orthodox Church (Law of 17th of April 1985) amending the same law of 1870. A change to the Constitution on 5th of June 1993 specified that groups of non-religious believers (non-denominational Ethics Movement) were also to be financed. Their representative bodies are the *Centrale Vrijzinnige Raad* (Conseil Central Laïque).

If a new group wants to obtain the recognition of the authorities they have to submit an application to the Ministry of Justice and to attach documents to prove that they fulfil the administrative jurisprudential criteria for recognition. There are no formal requirements in written law, just informal guidelines. The religious or ideological group must send the application to the Minister of Justice and the administration will then examine the file and eventually ask for complementary information, if necessary.

The conditions for recognition (as we have just said, they are not in any law but consist of administrative jurisprudence) are the following:

a) An important number of adherents (the figure is not fixed and it is to the religious group that has to determine who they consider as adherents): at least a number of 15,000.

b) The capacity to organise themselves into a single representative body that will deal with the public authorities (this body must encompass a majority of the civil society in that religion or conviction).

c) Being present in the country for a certain amount of time. There must be certain stability in the presence and also certain organisation.

d) Presenting a social interest (it is examined if the religious group can contribute to society and if they really respond to the need for that religion or conviction of the population or of a sufficient part of it).

---

[33] This law is not the only source. The recognition of Catholicism is a direct result of the Concordat of 1801, confirmed by the law of 18th Germinal X (8th April 1802). Protestantism also obtained recognition as a result of the law of I8th Germinal X. Judaism found its recognition through the decrees of 17th March 1808. Finally Anglicanism obtained recognition through the decrees of 18th and 24th April 1835. All this was confirmed by the law of 4th March 1870.

e) Not being involved in activities that are contrary to social order (generally public order and security are the focus of the criteria).

The examination will not make a judgment on that particular religion or conviction, nor assert its rules. If the results of that examination are positive, a bill of law will be submitted to Parliament in order to enact the recognition. If the request or application is rejected by the Minister of Justice, this decision can be appealed to the Council of State (administrative Court in Belgium).

Regionalisation has affected religion since the law of 13 July 2001. From then on, the regions (and not the federal state) are responsible for the organisation of the recognised religions. According to a Cooperation agreement of 27th of May 2004 between the federal Government and the different regional governments (Flanders, Wallonia and Brussels capital region) there will be previous consultation among them.

This gradual evolution towards greater competence for the regions does not affect the requirements and conditions for obtaining legal personality, which remain a federal matter. Recognition of religious or ideological groups and payment of salaries and pensions of ministries of cult, including the chaplains in the prisons and the army, are competence of the federal government while the establishment of religious local communities, the upkeep of religious buildings and the legislation that implement those matters is competence of the municipalities or regions.

Once the federal law of recognition is passed, the particular religion or conviction is recognised and that decision is binding to all regional authorities. Nowadays Catholicism, Evangelism, Orthodox Judaism and Anglicism as well as Islam are recognised religions in Belgium. The non-denominational Ethic Movement is also recognised while the recognition of Buddhist philosophy is under examination.

Consequences of the recognition[34]:

- **At Federal level.**

a) Salaries and pensions of ministers of recognised religions.

The recognition implies that the salaries and later the pensions of the ministers of that religion or conviction will be paid by the federal state. The salaries will be decided by law. The law of the 2nd of August 1974 enlists all

---

[34] TYSEBAERT, M.(2008): "Administrative and Financial Maters. The situation in Belgium" in *Legal Aspects of Religious freedom* (International Conference, 15-18 September 2008), Ljubljana, pp. 286-304.

the functions that exist in the different religions and convictions and the according wages.

When a new religion is recognised, the salaries and functions of their ministers will be integrated in that law and the negotiations will be conducted with the representative body. The recognition will not automatically take effect and therefore salaries will not be paid immediately. In order to keep the budget within certain limits, a multiannual scheme can be agreed between the State and the religious authorities. Moreover, the payment is only granted for those minsters that serve the public, and not, for example, priests who are in a convent.

Payment of salaries depends on the previous recognition of religious local entities (parishes) by the regional authorities. When the local structure is recognised by the region, a number of places will be fixed but the payment of the religious ministers of these worship places will be paid by the federal state. So, negotiations are conducted on two levels within the framework of the co-operation agreement mentioned above: between the civil and religious authorities on one side and between the federal and regional authorities on the other.

Although the salaries are paid by the Federal Government, there is no working relationship between those religious ministers or delegates of the laic movement and the State. Their labour link remains between them and the religious/philosophic authorities (which are their employers). The only exceptions are the chaplains in the army who have the status of officials and report to the Minister of Defence.

Normally the number of ministers paid by the Federal State is fixed, after a negotiation with the representative body of the recognised religion, upon the number of adherents. An exception was made with Catholicism. As compensation for the concordat under Napoleon, it was assumed the fiction that the total population was Catholic. For the others, the number of followers was calculated according to the real figures. The number of delegates of the non-denominational Ethic Movement has been determined by separate negotiations: it was fixed in the bill of law in 2002 (maximum 354).

Federal government would pay ministries and delegates according to these criteria:

- Catholic Church: a priest per 600 parishioners, a second one for each portion of 1.400 believers, and further ones per 3.000 followers[35].

- Protestant –Evangelic: the Federal State will pay the first pastor per 600 adherents and a second place for each 1000 followers.

---

[35] Around 1.100 euros a month for a Catholic priest.

- Anglican: 1 place per 250 adherents.
- Jews: 1 rabbi per 600 adherents and further ones for every 1000.
- Orthodox: 1 priest for each parish with at least 200 adherents;
- Islam: 1 imam for each mosque between 250 and 500 adherents, 2 imams if the mosque congregates between 500 and 1500 adherents and 3 imams for mosques with more than 1500 worshipers.
- The laic movement has 50 delegates for the federal secretariat; 7 per provincial establishment (12 establishments) and 5 per local service (44 services).

b) Chaplains.

Recognised religions and non-denominational Ethic Movement have the right to have a chaplain, paid by the State, in prisons (salaries paid by the Ministry of Justice), in the army (salaries paid by the Ministry of Defence), in hospitals (salaries paid by Social Security, unless if it is done on a voluntary basis) and in ports, airports and the fishing industry (salaries paid by the Ministry of Transport or Agriculture).

c) Tax advantages.

Recognised religions have the following tax benefits at the federal level:

- exemption from taxes on property transfers
- reduced taxes on donations made by people
- reduction for legacies received
- Exemption from tax on goods used for the exercise of religious (or philosophic) purposes.

In any case, if non-recognised religious organisations adopt the form of a non-profit association, they may obtain, by decision of the Ministry of Finance, the same benefits.

- **At regional level.**

As it has been said, since the law of 13th of July 2001, the regional level has gained a lot of competence regarding religious activities. As the regions are autonomous, they also have different legislation on religious matters.

The regional authorities are competent to recognise local entities (e.g. parishes) but this recognition will only take place once the concerned denomination has established a local structure (administrative board).

Even if there are differences between regional laws, all of them recognise some financial consequences:

a) The structure mentioned above (board of administration) obtains legal personality with the recognition.

b) Depending on the organisational structure of the religion (provincial or community level) either the province or the municipality is obliged to cover the budget deficit of the religious local community whenever this deficit is considered normal (if it has been necessary for the normal exercise of the religion or philosophy). Local authorities are also obliged to cover the costs of the maintenance of the buildings used by the denominations or non denominational groups for its religious or ethical purposes.

c) The province or the commune has to provide appropriate[36] housing for the principal minister of that religion. This does not apply to the delegates of the laic movement.

d) Religious or non denominational ethic movements may request regional subsidies for construction, restoration or maintenance of the buildings used by the denominations or non denominational groups for its religious or ethical aims[37].

e) The regional authority has to approve the budget and the accounts of the local religious or philosophical entity. Eventually they can make observations but not questioning the necessary expenses for the normal exercise of that religion or ethic philosophy. According to this, the local authorities also supervise a number of decisions made by the local religious groups, such as: buying or selling property, renting land, accepting legacies, investing money, construction or renovation works. (The Ministry of Justice is the competent authority for supervising the laic movement).

Furthermore, recognised religions and philosophies get **free public radio and television broadcasting time**. In Belgium, public broadcasting time is available for Catholic and Jewish services, but there was a negative response to proposals to give time to Muslims[38]. There are several Islamic publishing houses and book stores in Belgium which sell mostly traditionalist or Salafi publications[39]. There are also several Muslim websites like http://www.islamic-events.be/ or http://www.hadith.be/. .

---

36 'Appropriate' means: in accordance with his social status. See e.g. Council of State, 2nd April 1953, *Rechtskundig Weekblad*, 1952-1953, 1691

37 The legal sources are: Article 92,3° of the Imperial Decree of 30th December 1809 ; the law of 4th March 1870 (*Moniteur belge*, 9th March 1870) and the law of 7th August 1931 (*Moniteur belge*, 5th September 1931), as well as the Royal Decree of 2nd July 1949 and lst July 1952.

38 *Muslims in Europe. A report on 11 EU cities*. Open Society Institute, 2009 (At home in Europe Project), pág. 216

39 They include *Al Imen* (Brussels), *Editions al-Hadith, Al Iqra, etc.* Some French publishers also distribute publications such as *Editions le Savoir, Editions Tawid* or *Maison d'Ennour* in French speaking areas. *Vid.* MANÇO, U.-KANMAZ, M.: "Belgium" in V.V.A.A. *Year-*

Regarding **schools and universities**, it has to be noted that the education system in Belgium is in generally divided in public schools and universities and those held by a religion or a non denominational ethic group. Recognised religions and philosophies have the right to set up their own schools and universities as far they respect the legal provisions concerning the education laws and programmes. They can also get subsidies for their centres. Catholic Church education institutions are by far the most numerous and are attended by a majority of scholars. **Public schools** must provide **religious education** in the recognized religions. So, the six recognised denominations can also teach their doctrine in public schools. Religious teachers are paid by the regional Minister of Education

The law of 2nd of June 1998 (modified by the law of 12th of April 2004) created the *Centre d'information et d'avis sur les organisations sectaires nuisibles*[40] (Centre of information and advice over destructive sects, CIAOSN) whose members are appointed by the Chamber of Representatives among prestigious experts in these issues. It is somehow similar to the interdepartmental *Miviludes*[41] in France. Both *Miviludes* and CIAOSN have received critics over the criteria they have used to distinguish between religious groups and the so called sects.

book of Muslims in Europe Edited by NIELSSEN, J.S.; AKAGÖNÜL, S.; ALIBASIC, A; MARECHA,B.; MOE,C; Leiden-Boston, (2009) pag. 46.

[40] http://www.ciaosn.be

[41] *Mission interministérielle de vigilance et de lutte contre les derives sectaires*

II. ISLAM IN BELGIUM

1. Legal recognition of Islam

Islam was recognised in Belgium in 1974 by the Law of July 19th of 1974 amending the law of 1870. Islam is therefore entitled to obtain financial state support. But, the fact that there's no organisation that can claim to represent the Muslim communities as a whole and serve as a legitimate interlocutor to the State has played an important role in the delay of the institutionalisation of Islam in Belgium.

2. Muslim population

Most of the Muslim population of Belgium comes from the different migrant inflows that began to arrive to the country in the 20th century. The first Muslim communities to settle in Belgium were labour force related to the French colonisation of the Magreb. In the 1960s, economic migrants arrived through bilateral labour agreements signed with Morocco and Turkey (1964), Tunisia (1969) and Algeria (1970) to work mainly in the coal and steel industries, and the construction sector[42]. As in other European countries, the 1970s brought a diversification of the Muslim population with the arrival of the workers families through reunification procedures and the creation of new families. Changes in the law in 1991 regarding naturalisation made it easier for foreigners to acquire the nationality and today half of the Muslim population is naturalised[43].

Attending to the countries of origin, the Muslim population in Belgium is estimated in around 500.000 people[44] out of a total population of 10.5 million inhabitants. The bigger Muslim communities are the Moroccan and the Turkish ones. The majority of Muslims are Sunnis but there is a minority group of Shi'is. The Sunnis with Moroccan background belong to the Maliki rite, whereas the Turkish Muslim are Hannafis (although some Kurds follow the Shafi'i school). There are also some Alevi Turks and Kurds.

Muslim communities are mainly located in the urban areas of Brussels and Antwerp. Moroccans prefer the French speaking region of Wallonia and Brussels whereas half of the Turkish population is to be found in the Flemish

---

[42] BOUSETTA, H. and BERNES, L.A. (2007): *Muslims in the EU: Cities Report. Belgium. Preliminary research report and literature survey*, Open Society Institute.
[43] *Ibid.*
[44] *Ibid.*

speaking regions of Ghent and Antwerp. More than 40% of Belgium´s Muslims live in the Brussels Capital Region and 17% of Brussels Region´s population are Muslims. This makes Brussels, which is the capital of both Belgium and The European Union, one of the cities in the Western world with the largest Muslim population[45].

3. Main Muslim organizations

As Islam is not structured in the same hierarchical fashion as other religions, it faces some organisational problems in providing a representative body to deal the Government. Discussions about the setting up of an official representation of Muslims in Belgium went on for years until 1995, when it was decided to hold a general election amongst the Muslim community in Belgium in order to elect a representative body. However, the election, which took place in 1996, did not succeed.

In 1998 the Muslim community in Belgium made a proposal to the Government that was accepted: every Muslim in the country should be inscribed in a register as a voter indicating the national community they belonged to according to their national background. Candidates should also inscribe themselves in one of those communities-categories.

The election of the representative body was to take place in two steps. First, a General Assembly of 68 members would be elected. Then the General Assembly would appoint the Executive of the Muslims of Belgium (*Executif des Musulmans de Belgique,* EMB), which would be formed by 17 delegates: 7 of Moroccan origin, 4 Turks, 3 from other nationalities and 3 representing the converted Belgians. The General Assembly would present these members to the Ministry of Justice and they would present them to the King to be passed by a Royal Decree[46].

The elections were held in 1998 and around 40,000 registered voters participated. Due to internal disputes, the first Executive was not very efficient and a transitional Executive was appointed in 2003. But, as no agreement could have been reached between them and the Government, a bill of law was passed to enable a Commission to organise new elections (20 July 2004).

---

[45] MANÇO, U.-KANMAZ, M.: "Belgium" in V.V.A.A. *Yearbook of Muslims... op. cit* pag. 36.

[46] *Arrêté Royal portant reconnaissance de l´Exécutif des Musulmanes de Belgique 3 mai 1999*

So, at the instance and supervision of the Ministry of Justice, new elections were held on 20th of March 2005 with the participation of over 45,000 voters, and the opposition of the Moroccan community.

The new representative body was appointed by royal decree on 7th of October 2005, but already in 2006 there were problems with the administration of the body that was investigated by the judiciary. Some members of the Executive lost the confidence of the General Assembly and others resigned leading to the appointment of a new Executive in March 14th 2008.

The tasks of the Muslim Executive Board include providing religious education at schools as well as educational training for imams and the appointment of Muslims chaplaincies in hospitals and prisons. The EMB has been receiving state subsidies since 2001.

Besides the official body EMB[47] Muslim Executive Board, there are many other associations and federations[48]. The Islamic and Cultural Centre of Brussels (*Centre Culturel et Islamique de Belgique*[49]), attached to the Great Mosque of Brussels. It is a creation of World Muslim League, controlled by Saudi Arabia. It has played an important role in Belgium until 1996. Even if it is no longer the official body for the Islamic faith in Belgium it has religious authority within some Muslims sectors (converts included).

The most influential Turkish Islamic movement is the Belgian branch of the Presidency of Religious Affairs of the Republic of Turkey[50], known as *Diyanet* (*Belçika Turk Islam Diyanet Wakfi* -BTIDV-)[51]. It unites close to 2/3 of the Turkish mosques in Belgium and receives imams and Islamic teachers trained and financed by Turkish government. The second Turkish Islamic group is the religious political movement *Millî Görüş* represented by the Islamic Federation of Belgium (*Belçika Islam Federasyonu*)[52]. It gathers a third of the Turkish mosques in Belgium. The other Turkish Islamic communities are smaller. For example the Gülen movement[53] that runs six primary or secondary

---

47 http://www.embnet.be/

48 MARÉCHAL, B.: « Courants fondamentalistes en Belgique» in Journal d'étude des relations internationales au Moyen-Orient, *Middle Est Review of International Affairs* (MERIA) Vol. 3, No.1 (mars 2008) avaible at http://meria.idc.ac.il/journal_fr/2008/issue1/5.pdf (accesed 18 December 2010)

49 http://www.centreislamique.be

50 The presidency was founded in 1923 to promote a modern, national vision of Hanafi Sunni Islam.

51 http://www.diyanet.be

52 http://www.fibif.be/tr/

53 It is a transnational civic society movement inspired by the teachings of Turkish Islamic theologian Fethullah Gülen. His teachings about *hizmet* (altruistic service to the "common

schools, boarding schools and religious training centers and the Belgian or the Federation of Alevi Associations (*Belçika Alevi Birlikleri Federasyonu*), a heterodox Shi'i variant of Turkish Islam that presents a humanist culture.

Regarding to Belgium's immigrants from Morocco and their descendents, quite a lot of them feel close to the Moroccan monarchy and the traditional Islam they defend. Some Moroccan follow the principles of the pietistic *Tabligh* movement, and some others identify with the reformist branch of the Muslims Brotherhood[54]. The Moroccan religious associations and mosques have formed federations by province. For example, the Antwerp Union (*Unie des Moskeeën en Islamitsch Verenigingen van Antwerpen* (UMIVA) for the Duthc speaking part and the Brussels-Brabant Union (*Union des Mosquées de Bruxelles-brabant Wallon* (UMBB). IN 2002, the provincial Unions came together to form the Federation of Mosque Unions (FUM).

Among many other Muslim organizations, we can mention the Arab European League or the *Mouvement des Jeunes Musulmans*, both of whom have also created political parties

4. Mosques and cemeteries

The oldest mosque in the country is the Islamic Centre in Brussels, founded in 1968. There are only four mosques with the classical architecture. The others are more prayer houses type. In total there are 333 mosques and prayer houses in Belgium generally organized along ethnic and national criteria. Most of them having the formal legal status of non-profit association. Flanders accounts for half of them with 167 mosques or prayer houses. There are 89 in Wallonia and 77 in Brussels Region. About 52% of the mosques are ruled by Moroccans, 42% by Turkish and the remaining 10% belong to Albanian, Bosnian, Pakistani and other Muslim groups[55].

In 2005 some regions published certain criteria for the official recognition of mosques so that salaries to imams attached to those mosques could be paid[56]. To be eligible for state support, for instance, a mosque should have at

---

good") have attracted a large number of supporters in Turkey and Central Asia and increasingly in other parts of the world.

[54] MARÉCHAL, B. (2008) *The Muslim Brothers in Europe: Roots and Discourse* Ed. Brill

[55] MANÇO, U.-KANMAZ, M.: "Belgium" in V.V.A.A. *Yearbook...op.cit* pag. 41.

[56] In 2002, the government had recognized 75 mosques and began paying salaries to imams assigned to these mosques. Source: *International Religious Freedom Report 2002: Belgium*, US Department of State. http://www.state.gov/g/drl/rls/irf/2002/13924.htm (accessed 26/07/2009)

least 250 members, observe human rights and Belgian laws and receive a favourable report from Belgian security services. In Jun 2007, the Walloon regional government recognized 43 mosques (27 Turkish and 17 Moroccan) out of a total of 48 applications. The Brussels-Capital Region accepted 9 out of 28 applications and in early 2008, the Flemish government, recognized 7 of the 32 admissible applications. The Flemish recognition criteria are the strictest in the country. For example, to get paid by the State, imams should take courses in "citizenship building" organized by the regional authorities and Dutch must be the official language in the mosque´s administration[57].

There are no Islamic cemeteries in Belgium. Still most of the bodies of Muslims who die in Belgium are sent back to their homelands for burial, which is quite expensive. Cemeteries are under the competence of the municipalities. Some municipal cemeteries have plots reserved for Muslim burials. There are eleven such cemeteries en Flandes[58], three in Wallonia and two in the Brussels region.

5. Imams

We cannot present an exact number of imams but they are estimated in around 300. They majority of Turkish imams are appointed and sent to Belgium through the *Diyanet* to work in mosques managed by the *Belçika Turk Islam Diyanet Wakfi* (BTIDV). They have a degree in Islamic theology and have done a vocational training for 4 years. Many second generation imams begin their studies in local mosques and afterwards they travel to Arab countries to continue their education in well known universities such as *Al Azhar* and Medina.

Imams from Magreb background have usually been educated in Islamic universities such as *Al Zeitouna* or *Al Qarawiyyin*, in Islamic institutes or have received other kinds of less institutionalised education as the one provided by sufi sheikhs[59].

The *Ligue des Imams* (*Rabitat al Ulama*) is an organization formed mainly by Moroccan imams though there are also religious leaders with Bos-

---

[57] *International Religious Freedom Report 2008*: *Belgium*, US Department of State. http://www.state.gov/g/drl/rls/irf/2008/108437.htm (accessed 26/07/2009) and MANÇO, U.-KANMAZ, M.: "Belgium" in V.V.A.A. *Yearbook...op.cit.* pag. 43.

[58] http://www.flw.ugent.be/cie/archief/docu3.htm (accessed 19 December 2010)

[59] HUSSON, J.F. (2006): *Pour une formation des imams en Belgique. Points de références en Belgique et en Europe*, Brussels, *Fondation Roi Baudouin*.

nian and Somali backgrounds. It is focused on theological issues but it also tries to play a lobby role regarding imams working conditions.

6. Chaplains

Following a 2005 Law and Royal Decree, there are currently 18 imams paid for by the Minister of Justice in the 33 prisons of the State. Muslim counsellors in the Army and prisons are paid by the state. Religious assistance in hospitals is allowed but no subsidized by the state.

7. Islam in schools

Public primary and secondary school offer the possibility of taking two hours per week for religious classes or non denominational ethic classes and the teachers are paid by the State. Islamic religion have been organised in public schools since 1975 both in French and Dutch. For some time, teachers of Islam came mainly from Turkey or Morocco and they didn't have neither proper teaching training nor Dutch or French language skills. Specific teams of inspectors were not appointed until 2003.

Islamic religious classes are given in approximately 850 public primary and secondary schools. These courses are taken by an estimated 30.000 pupils, more or less half of the existing Muslims students in Belgium schools.

Private denominational school can receive subsidies from the State provided they fulfil certain conditions established in the laws. The first Muslim school in Belgium (Al-Ghazali School) was opened in 1989 and run by the Cultural and Islamic Centre of Brussels. The second one, opened in September 2007, was the Avicenne Islamic Secondary School in Molenbeek (Brussels)[60].

---

[60] MANÇO, U.-KANMAZ, M.: "Belgium" in V.V.A.A. *Yearbook... op.cit.* pág 43.

III. TRAINING CENTRES FOR IMAMS

1. Public initiatives or those supported by public authorities.

Although already in 2006 the government of Belgium announced plans to open an imam school, no concrete measures have been implemented yet.

The amendment of the decree of 28 February 2003 on civic integration states that ministers of religion coming from non EU countries will be required to take a training course of individual support that includes Dutch language classes, introduction to citizenship and integration at work. Not complying with this obligation would involve a fine[61].

In 2007, the Catholic University of Louvain, through the Centre for Interdisciplinary Research on Islam in the contemporary World (CISMOC)[62], launched a pilot project to train any (non-) Muslim university graduates anxious to gain a better understanding of Islamic sciences or, more generally, any person interested in Islam as a religious and civilization reality included in contemporary European society. It was organised in partnership with the *Facultés Universitaires Saint-Louis* and the *Institut Supérieur Pédagogique Galilée*, in cooperation with the Inspectorate of Islamic Teaching of the French Community of Belgium (which manages and supervises half of the 700 professors of Islamic faith in Belgium). The initiative had a strong inter-culturally and cultural diversity approach. The programme provided intensive university instruction relating to Islam, in respecting that faith, and taught in a spirit of critical openness, in an exchange with the human sciences, in an approach that is comparative vis-à-vis other religions and philosophies. This course imparts educational contents via an active learning approach. Openness and a spirit of debate, as well as a positive respect among all speakers and participants, are promoted. In a context regularly fuelled by various polemics, the role of this instruction proves itself crucial in learning how to question arguments in-depth.

Within the framework of the *Fonds d'Impulsion pour la Politique des Immigrés* (Kick-Start Fund for Immigrant Policy) and the support of the Ministry of the Walloon Region, a training course for the administrators of the mosques of Namur and Charleroi was organised in 2006 at the Inter-University Centre for Ongoing Education (CIFoP) [63] in partnership with the Observatory

---

[61] HUSSON, J.F. (2007): *Training imams in Europe. The current status*, Brussels, Foundation Roi Baudouin.

[62] Centre Interdisciplinaire d'Etudes de l'Islam dans le Monde Contemporain (CISMOC). http://www.uclouvain.be/cismoc.html

[63] Centre Interuniversitaire de Formation Permanente

of Relations between Religions, Organised Secularity and the State (ORACLE)[64]. This course was intended to mosque's staff and people involved in the mosques management. Topics dealt with in the course included the organisation and funding of religions in Belgium and the administration of a recognised religious establishment. A second edition for foreign ministers of religion was held in 2007. This time the course also comprised modules of language, sociology and Church-State relations.

In Flanders, the Minister of education commissioned research from Antwerp University's Centre for Migration and Intercultural studies (CeMIS) into theological training as well as for imams abroad.

2. Initiatives by the Muslim community

The Islamic Centre of Brussels organises seminars, conferences and courses with the participation of religious scholars and leaders as well as academic experts wishing to contribute to the continuous development of Islam in Belgium. The Centre, funded by the Muslim World League, also manages the European Institute of Theology, where education on Islamic sciences is provided. A non-recognised BA degree on Islamic studies is delivered.

Executive of the Muslims of Belgium presented a draft bill in November 2006 regarding the recognition of ministers of the Muslim religion and of their training with the proposal of introducing a 4-5-year imam education course that comprises both a theological and a civic component. The precise content of the training would be determined in collaboration with a Council of Theologians (to be created) and the universities that would be associated with the project. For already-serving imams, the Executive recommends a top-up course at the end of which they could receive an official degree.

Several Muslim associations have organised imam training courses in order to train their own staff both in Arabic and Turkish-speaking circles, but none of those initiatives has received so far official recognition. The *Cemaat-i Nur* mouvement, a Turkish Sufi brotherhood, has several training centres in Anvers, Gand and Brussels and a private institute called Lucerna 42; the *Académie Européenne de la Culture et des Sciences Islamiques en Belgique* (Al Khayriya Belgian School)[65]; the European Islamic University-Ghent

---

[64] Observatoire des Relations Administratives entre les Cultes, la Laïcité organisée et l'Etat. http://oracle.cifop.be/

[65] http://www.alkhayria.com/

(*Islamitische Universiteit van Europa-Afdeling Gent*)[66]; and the Faculty of Islamic Sciences (*Facultés des Sciences Islamiques de Bruxelles*)[67],.

The non-profit association *Takâfoul – Culture et Société* opened its *Institut des Etudes Islamiques de Bruxelles* (Brussels Institute of Islamic Studies, IEIB) in 2006 with the aim of "propagating the Islamic culture and sciences among young Muslim university students and graduates of Belgian universities" by dispensing university education in Islamic studies and Arabic language. The Institute has 3 departments: the French-speaking Department, the Arabic-speaking Department and the Department of the Holy Koran. It offers a BA and a Master´s on Islamic Sciences and provides a preparatory year of Arabic language but none of their degrees are officially recognized. The Department of Holy Koran studies was inaugurated in 2007 under the direction of Sheikh Fathi Saddem and Sheikh Zakaria Fadlaoui, with the objective of training imams and Koranic specialists in a 4 year program in Arabic. The number of places offered is limited and only students recommended by an imam or a sheikh can be admitted[68].

---

[66] http://www.ifeg.be/

[67] http://www.faculte-islamique.be/fr/index.html

[68] HUSSON, J. F. (2007) *Training imams in Europe. The current status*. Brussels, King Baudouin Foundation.

BULGARIA

I. RELIGION AND STATE

By 1989 Bulgaria starts a series of changes in its political system that include re- establishing relations between state and religious communities, long time restricted by the communist regime (1944-1989). The process of creating a legal framework that regulates the place of religious denominations within the public space and their relation with the State lasts until today.

Relations between State and religions in Bulgaria are bound by the 1991 Constitution and the Law of the Religions of 2002. This law came to solve the problems caused by a number of provisions of the Law of the Religions of 1949 which became unconstitutional with respect to the Constitution adopted in 1991. The new Law of the Religions (2002) not only establishes freedom of religion and its limits but also the procedures by which denominations can be recognised by the State.

1. Administrative bodies that have contact with denominations.

According to article 34 of the Law of the Religions, the Council of Ministers of the Republic of Bulgaria is the institution which shall implement the state policy in the field of religious freedom. The Religions Directorate within the Council of Ministers is a specialised administrative body which regulates the interaction of the state with religious denominations. Among other things, the Religions Directorate:

- Coordinates the relations between the executive power and denominations;
- Supports the Council of Ministers in implementing the state policy of maintaining tolerance and respect between the different religions;
- Organizes and manages the work of an expert consultative commission on religious denomination issues;
-Provides expert conclusions and statements, where is envisaged in this Law;
-Provides opinions on requests for residence permit for foreign religious officials who have been invited by registered religious denominations;

-Checks signals and complaints of citizens concerning violations of religious freedom or illegal religious activities and, if necessary, notify these complaints to public prosecution bodies;
-Makes proposals to the Council of Ministers on the draft state budget about the distribution of the state subsidy, designated for the registered religions

In 2008, the National Council of the Religious Communities was created on the initiative of the Religious Directorate. This National Council, which includes the leaders of the main churches[69], pledges to represent the Bulgarian model of tolerance and to develop interreligious dialogue

2. Recognition of religions: Register in the Sofia city Court.

According to the decrees of the Religions Act (2002), "separate creeds are free, equal in rights and disestablished from the State" (art 4. Paragraph I). The Bulgarian Constitution (art. 13) emphasizes the historical role of the Bulgarian Orthodox Church as the traditional religion of the Republic of Bulgaria, endorsing the Orthodox Christianity but not the Orthodox Church as a legal person. Equality among all religions is implicitly expressed not only in the Bulgarian Constitution but also in the preamble of the Religions Act (2002).

The Religions Act (2002) establishes that religions may have the statute of legal entity through registration. Nevertheless, it is not compulsory to assume a legal statute unless the religious community wants to constitute itself in a legal subject, and therefore act in its own name and establish legal relations with third parts (including the State). In Bulgaria, all religious institutions operate according to the common law in force which presupposes non-interference of the State in the sphere of religions.

The Religions Act (art. 27, paragraph 1) allows the establishment of non profit legal entities following agreement with relevant religious institutions that have obtained the status of a legal entity. Nevertheless, the Religions Act also establishes that "not-for-profit legal entities under paragraph 1 shall not conduct activities amounting to public practice of a religious confession".

---

[69] The Council includes the leaders of the Bulgarian Orthodox Church, the Armenian Apostolic Church, the Islamic Community, the Central Israeli (Jewish) Spiritual Council, the Catholic Church and the United Evangelical Churches. MERDJANOVA, INA.: "Bulgaria" in V.V.A.A. *Yearbook of Muslims in Europe* Edited by NIELSSEN, J.S.; AKAGÖNÜL, S.; ALIBASIC, A; MARECHA,B.; MOE,C; Leiden-Boston, (2009) pp. 27-28.

3. Registration of religious communities.

The registration of religious communities is made by Sofia City Court in the public register of religions following the procedure of Chapter 49 "General Rules" of the Code of Civil Procedure. The Sofia City Court may ask for an expert opinion from the Religions Directorate of the Council of Ministers although it is not a necessary prerequisite for registration and it is for the court to decide whether to take into account the opinion of the Directorate or not. The Sofia City Court keeps a public register of the religions with status of legal entities.

The registers of local religious institutions are managed by municipalities in accordance with their residence. Religions can have local divisions according to their statutes. Registration of local divisions has to be conducted by the mayors of the municipalities according to the location of the institution's offices. Registration is carried out after the religious group representative has submitted an application and also present statutes containing the following information:

- name and seat of the religious denomination
- description of their belief and worship practices
- denomination structure and bodies
- Representative bodies, the way its members are appointed, its faculties and term in office
- Decision making procedures
- Funds and of properties
- Liquidation procedure.

All existing religions under the previous law retain their status of legal entities. There are 31 denominations registered at the moment[70]. Religious groups registered and recognized as legal entitles enjoy several rights, among which:

- to have its own property and the right to use state or municipal property (Art.21)
- to have and maintain cemeteries (Art. 24)
- to get support from the State by tax, financial and other benefits (Art. 25)
- to create and manage charities or humanitarian institutions (Art. 6)
- To open special educative institutions.

---

[70] DIMITROV, I.Z. (2008): "Legal settlement of the relations between the State and religions in Bulgaria today " in *Legal Aspects of Religious freedom* (International Conference, 15-18 Septermber 2008) Ljubljana , pp. 306-308.

- Religious education in public schools: the Bulgarian Ministry of Education and Science is the competent body in this issue.

The economic independence of religions communities is guaranteed with the statute of legal entity: "They are allowed to create or participate in trade relations under commercial law, to create legal entities with non-profit aim and to open medical, social and educational institutions" (Art. 30).

The Religions Act also contains the decrees of restitution that give the possibility of recovering the property of religious lands" after the nationalisations that took place between 1944-1989.

II. ISLAM IN BULGARIA

1. Legal recognition of Islam

Islam is recognised as a denomination registered in the public register of religions of the Sofia City Court.

2. Muslim population

The Ottomans conquered the disintegrating medieval Bulgarian kingdom at the end of fourteenth century. Ottoman rule lasted until 1878, when Bulgaria gained territorial autonomy. A mass exodus of Muslims followed, but a large number of Muslims remained in the country[71].

According to official estimates of the 2001 Census, Muslims make up 12% of Bulgaria's 7.322.858 population. The Census shows a total number of 966,978 Muslims in the country, corresponding to 12.2% of the population[72].

According to the criterion of ethnic group they are divided into the following groups: Turks (713,000) are concentrated in the south –east and north-

---

[71] EMINOV, A.: *Turkish and Other Muslim Minorities in Bulgaria* Ed. Routledge. New York 1997, pag. 79.

[72] Data from the Boston University's World Religion Database (www.WorldReligionDatabase.org). The WRD contains statistics on Muslim affiliation for every country of the world and provides estimates down to the province level for numerous countries. It provides source material, including national censuses, demographic surveys and public opinion surveys, as well as ethnographic 'best estimates'.

east of the country (Shumen and Razgrad and the Black Sea coast) and account for 73, 5 % of the Muslims in Bulgaria. The Bulgarian-speaking Muslims (131,000) are descendants of Slavic Bulgarians who converted to Islam under Ottoman rule). Also Known as Pomaks, they are concentrated in the central and western Rodhope mountain in southern Bulgaria along the border with Greece and they make up 13,5% of the Bulgarian Muslims. The Roma, dispersed throughout the whole country, amount to 10, 5%, some of whom (103,000 -40 %-) are Muslims. and others (20,000)[73].

3. Muslim representative organisations

The Bulgarian Muslim community, officially registered as Muslim Denomination (*Muslmansko* izpovedanie), is represented by the Mufti Head Office (Dar al-Ifta), and the Supreme Muslim Council (*Vissh Duhoven Savet).* Both the Chief Mufti (*Glaven Muftija*) and the Supreme Muslim Council are elected by a conference of Muslims and represent the Muslim communities in the country[74]. The Muslim hierarchy is headed by the Chief Mufti and 18 regional muftis, interpreters of Muslim law, all of whom serve five-year terms.

At the moment there are around 15 Muslim associations and foundations registered in accordance with the Not-for-profit Legal Entities Act.

4. Mosques and imams

There are more around 1300 mosques in Bulgaria[75]. Around 350 mosques have been built in the increase of mosque building after the fall of the Zhivkov communist regime (1989). The largest mosque in Bulgaria is the Tumbul Mosque in Shumen, built in 1774.

There are around 1500 imams in the Muslim community among whom around 900 are employed by the Mufti Head Office (*Dar al-Ifta*), the highest

---

[73] *Bulgaria Census 2001 - Final Results*: *Population by districts and religion group as of 1.03.2001*, National Statistical Institute, published on 05/01/2004. http://www.nsi.bg/Census_e/Census_e.htm (accessed 09/07/2009)

[74] DASSETTO, F., FERRARI, S. and MARÉCHAL, B. (2007): *Islam in the European Union: What's at stake in the future?* Brussels, European Parliament, p. 89.

[75] Islam on line: http://www.islamonline.net/servlet/Satellite?c=Article_C&cid=1221720230322&pagename=Zone-English-News/NWELayout (accessed 12/05/2009).

Muslim religious authority in Bulgaria[76]. According to the same source, the lack of imams in Bulgaria is due to two main reasons: the limited resources of the Fatwa House and the legacy of the communist period when Islamic schooling was forbidden and no imams could be trained in the country. This situation has led to the closure of several mosques.

A small part of the imams studied mainly in Jordan, Saudi Arabia and Egypt. According to official sources, all Muslim faith leaders are Bulgarian citizens.

Foreign preachers including imams can visit the country only if they receive an invitation of the central leadership of the Muslim organizations and after they receive expert approval from the specialized administration (Religions Directorate within the Council of Ministers).

5. Chaplains

In the public sector, Muslim faith leaders are engaged mainly in prisons and they receive no payment from the State. According to the article 167.5 of Execution of Penalties and Detention Act in connection with the Religions Act (2002), "*Ministers of the religious denominations professed by the prevailing number of persons deprived of their liberty who serves a sentence at the respective prison or reformatory may be appointed to a full-time position at the places of deprivation of liberty*".

The main activity of imams in prisons is concentrated in Sofia Prison, where Muslims foreigners serve their sentences. The Directorate "Provision of Assistance for the Religious Needs of the Person Serving Term of Imprisonment" of the Ministry of Justice not only assists the religious needs of the prisoners, but it also has preventive functions.

Chaplains are given access to the penitentiaries as long as they are representatives of an official recognised religion (i.e. registered in accordance with the Religions Act). This practice is related to Art. 7 of the Religions Act (2002), according to which the freedom of the religious faith shall not be used against national security, public order, public health and morality, or against the rights and freedoms of others. Muslim preachers visit the penitentiaries

---

[76] Declarations of Mustafa Hadji, Bulgaria's Grand Mufti, September 24th 2008. Available at the International Islamic News Agency: http://www.islamicnews.org.sa/en/search1.php?misc=search&subaction=showfull&id=946684066&id=1222295147&archive=&cnshow=news&start_from (accessed 12/05/2009)

by request of the Muslim prisoners for the Friday prayer and Muslim religious holidays. The Chief Mufti Office provides Korans for the Muslim prisoners.

Imams (and any other religious ministers) are not allowed in the armed forces, as military law bans any religion activities on military premises as well as ministry to the armed forces.

6. Teaching of Islam in public schools

Since the school year 1999/2000, Islam started to be taught in State and municipality schools in religion class. In October 2005, the new General Education Minimum and Curriculum Act established religion as a separated cultural and educational field, so it has been introduced in the syllabus of the public schools as a compulsory elective[77]. Religion as a school subject can be studied by students from first until twelfth grade. Choice is made by their parents with an application addressed to the school headmaster.

Religion textbooks are prepared on the basis of the curricula approved by the Ministry of Education and Science. The following textbooks are approved for the pupils studying Islam: "Religion Islam" - II grade, "Religion Islam" - III grade, "Religion Islam" – IV grade. The Bulgarian Center of Intercultural Studies and Partnership (CISP) has developed a teachers' handbook for primary-school religion teachers that promotes religious tolerance while working with the Ministry of Education and Science to prepare standards, curricula, and syllabus to guide the teaching of religion in public schools[78]. Free textbooks on Islam following the official curricula are edited for the 2nd to the 4th grades. They are distributed by the Ministry of Education and Science through the Education Inspectorates. Teachers of Islam in public schools must have a degree of the Higher Islamic Institute or an equivalent qualification course.

---

[77] During 2001-2 school year, religious instruction was organized in two forms, namely, compulsory eligible (students must choose a certain number among a list of subjects, and those subjects would become compulsory) and freely eligible (optional). DASSETTO, F., FERRARI, S. and MARÉCHAL, B. (2007): *Islam in the European Union...op.cit.* , p. 91.

[78] As professors Simeon Evstatiev and Plamen Makariev, editors of one of the teacher's books state in their introduction, "it is evident by their curricula that they have a confessional bound character" what makes the purpose of cultivating attitudes of mutual respect among religions most necessary. See: EVSTATIEV, S. ed. (2006): Islam: A Short Handbook, Sofia: Centre for Intercultural Studies and Partnership (CISP) and SMOCK, D. (2005): Teaching about the Religious Other, Special Report nº 143, United States Institute of Peace.

III. TRAINING CENTERS FOR IMAMS

Before the 1940′s, several institutions of Islamic education (such as the Nuvvab local school to train muftis in Shumen or a school for religious teachers created in 1914), existed in Bulgaria, tough all of them were closed when the new regime came to power. After the end of the communist years a process of rebuilding the Muslim community started, and education played a key role.

As it is stated in article 33 of the Religions Act, registered religions can open ecclesiastical schools (secondary general education schools) for their ritual needs in compliance with the Law of the Public Education with permission of the Minister of Education, Youth and Science.

The Islamic education system in Bulgaria consists of three secondary schools, Qur'anic courses and the Higher Islamic Institute in Sofia

Secondary Islamic Schools

By initiative of the Muslim Denomination and by decision of the Ministry of Education, Youth and Science, three secondary religious schools have been established in the towns of Ruse, Shumen and Momchilgrad. These schools, financed jointly by the State and the Mufti Head Office, follow the former Nuvvab model and are supervised by the regional inspectorates of the Ministry of Education, Youth and Science and of the Chief Mufti Office. The graduates from these schools can serve as imams or continue their education.

All three schools are linked to the Turkish administration (*Diyanet*) and also to the Turkish universities of Istanbul, Ankara and Konya. The teachers are mainly Bulgarian citizens but there are also Turkish teachers appointed by Dyanet.

The education provided in these centres is mainly theological and vocational in accordance with the needs of the Muslim denomination. However, the three secondary religious schools (Ruse, Shumen and Momchilgrad) have to grant mandatory degrees of public education within the framework of the general official curricula. The following subjects are taught in the mandatory elective classes and in the optional classes in accordance with the curricula approved by the director of the respective Regional Inspectorate on Education: *Quran* and *Kerim* (Quran Reading), *Fukuh* (Islamic Law), *Tafsir* (Quran Interpretation), *Akaid* (Theology), *Kelyam* (Rhetoric), *Siir* (Mohamed's Life) and *Hitabet* (Preaching Methods). Teaching methodology includes lectures as well as questions and discussions.

Classes are conducted in Bulgarian and textbooks are also in Bulgarian with the exception of those related to the study of the Quran. Men are usually trained separately from women. Some foundations organise Quran courses (not imam trainings) for young women and girls.

The diplomas of the three secondary schools are recognised in the public and private sector on the same basis as secular education. Secondary students can continue their education in the Higher Islamic Institute or in another university. The diploma of the Higher Islamic Institute is recognised only as a qualification within the bounds of the Muslim denomination. Just few graduates from religious schools work as imams. This is due to different reasons like the low salaries they get.

Higher Islamic Institute in Sofia

The Islamic Institute was established in 1991 as a semi-higher institution, and in 1998, upon the proposal of the Chief Mufti Office, was transformed into a higher institute[79]. So, the Higher Islamic Institute of Sofia was established by order of the Deputy Prime Minister and the Minister of Education, Youth and Science with the purpose of training the religious leaders of the Muslim denomination in the country. The Institute was first supported by the Turkish Fetullah Gulen and now operates under a commission regulated by an official protocol signed by the Bulgarian and Turkish States[80].

The Institute's Statute envisages both undergraduate and postgraduate studies but currently only undergraduate program is offered. The main mission of the Institute is to train spiritual leaders (i.e., muftis, imams and religious education teachers). The graduates receive BA in Islamic Theology. There is also a possibility for the graduates to sit for a few additional exams and receive the title of "specialist in History and Culture of Eastern peoples" from the New Bulgarian University in Sofia[81]. Imams, muftiate officials and teachers of religious education can attend the Institute as part time students provided that they are not older than 35 years. Since 1993 the Institute admits female students and currently they constitute more than 30% of all the student population. Around 70% of the students are of Turkish background, there are also Pomaks (30%) and Roma students (10%). After graduation they could teach Islam in the state schools. During the 1991-1998 period the Semi-Higher Islamic Institute produced 123 graduates while 162 students have graduated from the Higher Islamic Institute since its transformation in 1998.

Regarding the curriculum, it resembles very much that in *Ilahiyat* faculties in Turkey. The religious courses are taught by Turkish professors

---

[79] http://islamicinstitute-bg.org/

[80] BADRAN, M., (20 - 26 September 2001): *Finding Islam*, Al-Ahram Weekly Online, Issue No.552.

[81] http://genmufti.net/bg/education/43-vii.html

certified by *Diyanet*. Medium of instruction is Turkish and Bulgarian languages. The curriculum consists of compulsory, elective and facultative courses[82].

Education for full time students is free, as well as accommodation and food. In certain cases students might receive scholarships. During the 1991-1998 period the Institute received aid from a Turkish non-governmental organization. Since the end of 1990s it has been operating under the Commission composed of representatives from the Bulgarian Muslim and Turkish Muslim communities established by an official protocol signed by the Bulgarian and Turkish states.[83] It is currently working towards state accreditation.

It is funded through the Chief muftiate with most funds actually coming from Turkey. State does not finance the Institute[84].

---

[82] ALIBASIC, A.: "Higher education in the Balkans: A Survey" in NILSEN, J.S. (Ed) (2010) *Yearbook of Muslims in Europe* vol. II, Leden: Brill 2010

[83] Badran, M.: "Finding Islam" in *Al-Ahram Weekly Online*, 20-26 Nov. 2001, no. 552.

[84] The institute owns its own premises but does not own a dormitory for its students. However it provides them with rented flats whose expenses are paid by the Institute. ALIBASIC, A.: "Higher education in the Balkans: A Survey"…*op. cit.*

CYPRUS

I. RELIGION AND STATE

1. Administrative bodies that have contact with denominations

A number of Ministries (including the Ministry of Education and Culture, the Ministry of Justice and Ministry of Interior) have in place programs that enhance ethnic community relations.

2. Recognition of religions

According to the Constitution of the Republic[85], everyone has the right to freedom of thought, conscience and religion. Nonetheless, the Constitution states that "the Autocephalous Greek Orthodox Church of Cyprus shall continue to have the exclusive right of regulating and administering its own internal affairs and property in accordance with the Holy Canons and its Charter"[86]. The same article also speaks of the institution of *wakf* ("the Principles and Laws of to, *awakfs – Ahkamül Evkaf-* are recognised by this Constitution"). The *wakf* specifically mentioned in the Constitution, is the Muslim institution that regulates religious activity for Muslims. These religious foundations are among the principle institutions of the Turkish Cypriot community, and historically the *Evkaf* was one of the largest landholders in the island. In the past, the properties of these foundations supported schools and other social places. According to the Constitution (art. 11), the control of these properties belongs to the *Ewkaf* and any laws and regulations shall be enacted by the Turkish Communal Chamber, which from 1960-1963 was comprised of Turkish Cypriot deputies[87].

Furthermore, all religions whose doctrines or rites are not secret are legal. All religions are equal before the law. Every person is free and has the right to profess his faith and to manifest his religion or belief, in worship, teaching, practice or observance, either individually or collectively, in private or in public, and to change his religion or belief.

Regarding the institutional status of the Orthodox Church, it is under dispute if it should be viewed as a legal person under private or under public law. The Su-

---

[85] Article 18, paragraphs 1 and 3 of the Constitution of the Republic of Cyprus

[86] Article 110 paragraph 1 of the Constitution of the Republic of Cyprus

[87] DAYIOGLU, A.-HATAY,M.: "Cyprus" in V.V.A.A. *Yearbook of Muslims in Europe* Edited by NIELSSEN, J.S.; AKAGÖNÜL, S.; ALIBASIC, A; MARECHA,B.; MOE,C; Leiden-Boston, (2009) p. 78

preme Court of Cyprus held that the Orthodox Church was not an authority of the Republic of Cyprus, since it did not function as a governmental body or organ, nor did it exercise any state powers, nor was it subjected to the control of the State. Thus, the Orthodox Church of Cyprus should be considered as a peculiar legal person under private law[88].

The institution of *Wakf*, whose principles and laws are recognized by the Constitution, can therefore be considered as a legal person under private law as well.

The citizens of the Republic of Cyprus belong either to Greek Cypriot Community or to the Turkish Cypriot Community. The religious groups of the Armenians, the Maronites and the Latins (Roman Catholics) have chosen to belong to the Greek Cypriot Community, according to the relevant provision of the Constitution[89]. The Greek community comprises "all citizens of the Republic who are of Greek origin and whose mother tongue is Greek or who share the Greek cultural traditions or who are members of the Greek-Orthodox Church"[90]. Whereas the Turkish community is formed by "all citizens of the Republic who are of Turkish origin and whose mother tongue is Turkish or who share the Turkish cultural traditions or who are Moslems"[91]. Being a member of a religious group determines the community to which each individual belongs (even though any person can choose to change its community regardless of the religious group he/she belongs to[92]).

Other religions like Jehovah's Witnesses, Orthodox Christians Jews and Protestants, do not enjoy the special constitutional privileges of the Orthodox Church and *Wakf* but they are recognised as legal entities under private law if they register.

Religious associations are not required to register. But, if they wish to engage in financial transactions, such as maintaining a bank account, even if the religious purposes are the main ones, they should register as a non-profit-making company. Procedures for registration include an application that must be submitted to the Council of Ministers stating the purpose of the non-profit-making organization and providing the names of the organization's directors. Authorities would refuse to register any religion whose doctrines or rites are secret (Article 18.2 of the Constitution). A religious association can also register as a charitable foundation. For example, the 'Charitable Foundation of the Church of the Grace

---

[88] EMILIANIDES, A. (2007): "Religious entities as legal persons –Cyprus" in *Churches and other organizations as legal* person,s Peeters , pp. 50-51.
[89] Appendix E: article 2 of the Constitution of the Republic of Cyprus
[90] Article 2, paragraph 1 of the Constitution of the Republic of Cyprus
[91] Article 2, paragraph 2 of the Constitution of the Republic of Cyprus
[92] Article 2, paragraph 3 of the Constitution of the Republic of Cyprus

of Jesus Christ' and the 'Charitable Foundation of the Church of the God of Prophecy' registered themselves as private associations.

Once approved, non-profit-making organizations are tax-exempted under certain terms and conditions (Article 8 §13, Law 118 (l)/2002) and if they engage into any commercial activities, then those activities are taxable. They are also required to provide annual reports of their activities. No person shall be compelled to pay any tax or duty the proceeds of which are specially allocated in whole or in part for the purposes of a religion other than his own. (Appendix D: Part 02 – Article 18, paragraph 8). Therefore, Religious groups are tax exempted under certain terms and conditions and if they engage into any commercial activities then these activities are taxable.

The priests or religious ministers of any registered religion may also perform religious marriages according to the rites of their religion, so long as they are also registered with the Ministry of Interior, according to the provisions of the Marriage Law 104(I)/2003 (or if they are registered according to the provisions of the pre-existing Marriage Law, Cap. 279).

Basic law in the area administered by Turkish Cypriots refers to a secular republic and provides for freedom of religion. The *Wakf*, as the institution regulating religious activities for the Muslim community, is the only religious organization to be tax-exempted and receive subsidies. Greek Cypriots and Maronites living in the area administered by Turkish Cypriots are covered by the 1975 Vienna III Agreement that provides for facilities for education and for the practice of these groups′ religions.

II. ISLAM IN CYPRUS

Even when the Muslim presence in Cyprus dates from the seventh century, Islam took root in the island during the Ottoman rule (1571-1878). From 1878 until 1960 Cyprus was a British colony. In 1960, Cyprus gained its independence and the Republic of Cyprus was formed. At the beginning, Turks and Greeks shared the power over the island. But the consensus broke down in 1963 leading to a period of violence over the following decade. The Greek Cypriots controlled the Republic while the Turkish Cypriots established their own administration in armed enclaves.

A Greek-sponsored coup and subsequent Turkish military intervention in 1974 led to the island present division. Greek Cypriots residing in the north moved to the south of the island and Turkish Cypriots living in the south, to the north. The Republic of Cyprus under Greek-Cypriots in the south became the only internationally controlled government of the island. Turkish Cypriots in 1983 proclaimed a State in the north, the Turkish Republic of Northern Cyprus (TRNC), which remains to this day unrecognised by any State other then Turkey. Although the Republic of Cyprus is a bi-communal State, in 2004 it became a member of the European Union without its Turkish Cypriot partners. Even if Turkish Cypriots may belong to the EU via the Republic of Cyprus, the northern part of the island was excluded from the EU[93]

The 2008 Demographic Report estimated the population of Cyprus at 885600 inhabitants, of which 668700 Greek Cypriots (75, 5%), 88700 Turkish Cypriots (10%) and 128200 foreign residents (14, 5%)[94].

Muslims Turkish Cypriots are, since the 1974 Turkish occupation of Northern Cyprus, mainly located in that area although there is also a small Turkish Cypriot community in the Southern part of the island. Turkish Cypriots represent 18% of the island population[95].

Members of the main five religions of the island represent approximately 97.5 % of its population: 83 % are members of the Orthodox Church (which is not under the authority of the mainland Greek Orthodox Church), 13 % are

---

[93] DAYIOGLU, A.-HATAY,M.: "Cyprus" in V.V.A.A. *Yearbook ...op. cit* p. 75-6.

[94] Statistical Abstract 2008, Statistical Service of Cyprus, General Statistics Series II, Report No. 46, November 2009. Note: Illegal settlers from Turkey, which are estimated around 160000-170000 in the Turkish occupied areas, are not included. http://www.mof.gov.cy/mof/cystat/statistics.nsf/All/11DCBB93C796B9F9C22571FE002D5C50/$file/DEMOGRAPHIC_REPORT-2008-301109.pdf?OpenElement.

[95] Statement by the President of the Republic of Cyprus H.E. Mr Tassos Papadopoulos given at the Kennedy School of Government, Harvard University, 1st of June 2004. http://www.hks.harvard.edu/kokkalis/Papadop%20speech%20text.pdf

members of the Muslim religion and 1.5 % are members of other three religious groups[96].

Historically, the two most important Muslim organizations in Cyprus are the *Evkaf,* which manages the affairs of land and business holdings that have been donated for religious purposes, and the Mufti, who is the official spiritual head of the community. The *Evkaf* Administration owns the island's mosques and cemeteries. After the division of 1974, the *Evkaf* lost control of its properties in the south and operates only in the north. Regarding to the Mufti, even if it is the official spiritual head of the Muslim community in Cyprus, after 1974 his office moved to the north and it is effectively without power in the south. In 1980, the Mufti became the Director of Religious Affairs which basically has only authority in the north and is under the control of *Evkaf* Administration.

The number of mosques in the south is estimated in 101[97]. Its maintenance is entertained by the Turkish Cypriot Properties Management Service, under the auspices of the Minister of Interior of the Republic of Cyprus. Since the 1990s, the government of Cyprus has undertaken a policy of restoration of Muslim worship places, cemeteries and monuments in the controlled area. Most mosques are located within the Larnaca, Limassol and Paphos districts. According to the data provided by the Directorate of Religious Affairs in 2007, there are 164 mosques in the north, of which 84 existed before the island's division[98]

Regarding religious education in public schools, primary and secondary students are expected to take instruction in the Greek Orthodox religion unless their parents request to be excused[99].

Regarding prisons, there is a mosque within the only existing prison in Nicosia, where about 200 Muslim prisoners freely exercise their religious duties under the guidance of their imam.

---

96 EMILIANIDES, A., *Op. cit.*

97 Information from the Embassy of the Republic of Cyprus in Doha: http://www.mfa.gov.cy/mfa/embassies/embassy_doha.nsf/ (accessed 03/07/2009). According to a 2006 report prepared by the Turkish Cypriot leadership, 16 of thes mosques have been completely destroyed, only 25 are in good condition, and the rest are partially ruined. Of the 148 existing cemeteries in 1974, 43 have been totally destroyed, 3 are in a good condition and the rest are in a very poor state. DAYIOGLU, A.-HATAY,M.: "Cyprus" in V.V.A.A. *Yearbook op. cit....* p. 80.

98 Fifty two churches have been converted into mosques, and four mosque were previously cinemas or schools.*Ibidem* p. 81

99 *International Religious Freedom Report 2007: Cyprus,* US Department of State http://www.state.gov/g/drl/rls/irf/2007/90170.htm (accessed 03/07/2009)

III.TRAINING CENTRES FOR IMAMS

There are no imam training centers in Cyprus. Besides, the government of Cyprus has not developed any specific policy or subsequent programs concerning training for Muslim faith leaders coming from abroad. The Anadolu University, a Turkish university that has also a Campus in north Cyprus, has an Open Faculty where there is a theology department.

The clergy in north Cyprus are under two authorities, the Directorate of Religious Affairs (under the control of *Evkaf),* which is an institution of the

Turkish Republic of Northern Cyprus, and the Religious Affairs Counselor of the Turkish Embassy in Nicossia.

CZECH REPUBLIC

I. RELIGION AND STATE

1. Administrative bodies that have contact with denominations.

After the 1989 democratic change, the State Office for Churches Matters was dissolved and since then the competence in the field of religious freedom and churches matters was entrusted to the Ministry of Culture. According to its own rules, the agenda of the matters of churches and religious communities is entrusted to the Department of Churches of the Ministry of Culture. In comparison with the totalitarian State Office for Churches Matters, this Department is very small. It has altogether 11 employees. The agenda of the department consists above all of these *activities*:

- proposing the conception of Church-State relations,
- preparing legislative proposals in the area of religious freedom,
- registering new churches and religious societies and listing the legal persons established by churches,
- Providing financial support for the churches and religious societies[100].

2. Recognition of religions.

The freedom of thought, conscience, and religious conviction is guaranteed by the Constitution of 1993 (art.15). Everyone has the right to freely manifest his/her religion or faith, either alone or in community with others, in private or public, through worship, teaching, practice, and observance. Everyone has the right to change his/her religion or faith or not to profess any religious creed.

The Act on freedom of religion and status of churches and religious associations[101] has solved the previous situation where ten thousand of adult be-

---

[100] KRIZ, J.(2008): "Religious Freedom and State in the Czech Republic" in *Legal Aspects of Religious freedom* (International Conference, 15-18 September 2008) Ljubljana, pp. 310-318.

lievers residing in Czech Republic were required for a religious association which is not a member of the World Council of Churches to be legally recognized; therefore many smaller associations could not become legal entities.

There is a difference between religious entities *per se* (churches and religious societies, namely, denominations) and other minor religious entities, whose legal personality is *derived* from the religious entities *per se* (parishes, dioceses, monasteries and priories, church lay organisations, charities or diaconates, etc.). The former, denominations, obtain legal personality by state registration; the latter, by registering the entity created according to its own provisions.

Denominations in the Czech Republic can associate into unions. These unions obtain legal personality by special registration. They do not have the right to establish another legal person.

In the Czech Republic, a denomination can be founded without any approval of the public authorities. They can worship and develop other religious activities even without State registration. But, such organisations acquire legal personality by registration in a State agency (at the moment, in the Ministry of Culture).

Before the churches and religious associations Act of 2002[102] came into force, there were 21 registered denominations with special rights. This law gives new denominations the opportunity to register and so to acquire legal personality as churches or religious societies. The registration procedure contains two steps: requirements for registration and requirements to be entitled to benefit from the so called special rights.

Registration.

A denomination can be registered upon request to the Ministry of Culture, provided that the y fulfils the conditions prescribed by the law. The Ministry of Culture holds a public register of denominations and a public register of the unions of denominations.

When registering, the State agency does not assess the doctrine (it would be contrary to the constitutional law): it only assures that the articles of faith are not contrary to human rights or public order.

The requirements to be registered are the following:

- 300 signatures of believers, residents in the Czech Republic, along with their personal data.
- Religious purposes of the denomination and basic description of its faith.

---

[101] The terms "religious societies" and "religious communities" are also used.

[102] Act nº 3/2002 coll of January 7th 2002 on Freedom of Religious Convictions and legal status of Churches and Religious Societies.

- "Basic Document" containing its staff members and organisation. The religious groups must notify the Register every change on those basic documents. They also have to provide information about individuals who are empowered with statutory powers. Given that, denominations themselves can create places of worship (parishes, monasteries) or charitable institutions (all of them considered 'church legal persons') according to their own provisions, they should also provide information about the legal persons created by them.

A denomination obtains legal personality only by registration. Once it has been registered it can possess property, employ people, and create church legal persons. Enjoying tax benefits is other consequence of registration (for example, exemption from property taxes on religious facilities). Employment of workers in a spiritual sphere is ruled by its own statutes[103]; only employment in a secular sphere (vergers, gardeners, etc.) is ruled by labour law.

But, in order to have special rights, registering is not enough. They must fulfil the following requirements.

- Waiting ten years since being registered.
- Presenting at least one per mil signatures of followers in the Czech Republic, i.e. approximately ten thousand adult believers residing in the country.
- Having published at least an annual financial report for the last ten years.

During recent years, 9 denominations have been registered in the Czech Republic. There are, therefore, 30 registered religious entities, 21 of which enjoy of special rights[104], such as the possibility to officiate marriages, teach religion

---

[103] Just the moment of beginning and termination of the employment. The content of the legal relation is subject to labour law.

[104] Churches and religious societies registered according to the Act No. 308/1991 Coll. (In the brackets yon can find an official Czech name and a date of registration or reception): Apostolic Church (ApoStolská církev. 1989), Brethren Baptist Union (Bratrsküjednota Baplist. 1951), Church of Seventh-day Adventists (Církev advenlistü sedméhо dnc. 1951, Brethren Evangelical Free Church (Církev bratrská, 1951), Czechoslovak Hussite Church (Ceskoslovcnská církev husitská. 1920), The Church of Jesús Christ of Latler-day Saints (Církev Jezíse Krista Svatych posledních dnú, 1990) Greece Catholic Church (Církev feckokatolická. reception from Austria-Hungarian monarchy) Román Catholic Church (Církev fímskokatolická. reception from Austria-Hungarian monarchy) Evangelical Church of Czech Brethren (Ceskobratrská církev evangelická. reception from Austria-Hungarian monarchy) Evangelical Church of Augsburg Confession in Czech Republic (Evangelická církev a.v. v CR, reception from Austria-Hungarian monarchy) Evangelical Methodist Church (Evangelická církev metodistická. 1951) Judaist Federation of Jewish Communities (Federace zidovskych obcí, reception from Austria-Hungarian monarchy) Mo-

in public schools, appointing chaplains to serve in the army and in prisons, the right to establish religious schools or hospitals, the right of receiving State support for the salaries of ministers of cult (a temporary right until the restitution of the property expropriated in the time of the Communist regime).

As we have just said, so far there are 21 registered denominations with so-called special rights, 9 registered denominations and two unions of denominations (The Ecumenical Council of Churches in the Czech Republic and the Military Spiritual Service).

Seventeen of those 30 registered churches and religious societies are financed from the National Budget, pursuant to Act No. 218/1949 Coll. on the Economic Securing of Churches and Religious Societies by the State, and to Act No. 3/2002 Coll. on Churches and Religious Societies; the remaining 11 receive no State funds.

The State contributes to pay the salaries of the clergy and salaries of the administrative staff, their social and health insurance, and also it helps to the maintenance of church property. Other activities of the churches and religious societies (e.g. school activities, social services etc.) are supported in a similar way than other NGOs actions. This support is not considered as a support for churches but as a support for activities of public interest.

Churches and religious societies registered according to Act No. 3/2002 Coll. are: Christian Fellowship Church (2002), Christian Community (2002), Hare Krishna Movement (2002), Czech Hinduism Religious Society (2002), Islamic Centre of Muslim Communities (2004), Russian Orthodox Church (2007), Diamond Way Buddhism of the Karma Kagyu Tradition (2007), Vishwa Nirmala Dharma (2007) and the Living God Church (2007). The precise number of unregistered denominations is not available.

Besides registering, denomination can also acquire legal personality adopting other legal form such as corporation, partnership etc. Civic associations cannot be established for religious purposes. However, many unregistered denominations use the way of civic associations.

---

ravian Church (Jednota bratrská, reception from Austria-Hungarian monarchy) Lutheran Evangelical Church of Augsburg Confession in Czech Republic (Luterská evagelická církev a.v. v CR, 1995) Religious Societly of Czech Unitarians (Nábozenská spolecnost ceskych unitáfu. 1930) Jehovah's Witnesses (Svédkové Jehovovi, 1993) New Apostolic Church (NovoapoStolská církev. 1956) Orthodox Church in Czech lands (Pravoslavná církev v ceskych zemích. Reception from Austria-Hungarian monarchy) Silesian Church Evangelical Church of Augsburg Confession (Slezská evangelická církev a.v., reception from Austria-Hungarian monarchy), Oíd Catholic Church ir» Czech Republic (Starokatolická církev v CR, reception from Austria-Hungarian monarchy). Source: KRIZ, J.(2008): "Religious Freedom and State... *Op.cit.* pp. 315-316.

According to the National Statistics Agency (Census of 2001), 59% of the population doesn't belong to any denomination, 32 %, are adherents to some religion or denomination and 9 % non-respondents[105].

II. ISLAM IN CZECH REPUBLIC

1. Legal recognition of Islam.

Most Czech Muslim organizations are registered with the Ministry of Culture as cultural or social organizations. As such they are not granted any public funding. In 2004 the umbrella organization Islamic Centre of Muslim Communities (*Ustredi muslimskychnabozenskych obci* –UMO-) succeeded in registered.

2. Muslim population

The territory that today is Czech Republic has never been under direct Islamic influence. The Muslim community in the Czech Republic is very small. There is a very small amount of converts, Czech citizens of foreign background (mainly former students from the socialist-oriented countries who went to study to the former Czechoslovakia), and asylum seekers. Estimates of the number of Muslims in the Czech Republic differ but the most probable figure could be 10.000 Muslims out of a total population of 10.5 million of inhabitants.

---

[105] "Out of those 32 % adherents to some religion or denomination, 90 % are Catholics and circa 10 % of the respondents declared themselves as adhering to other denominations. Out of 3,288,000 Czech Christians, pursuant to the last census in 2001, there are 2,740.700 Roman Catholics, 117.200 Czech Brethren. 99.000 Hussites, 22,900 Eastern Christians, 14,800 Evangelic of CR and 14.000 members of Silesian Evangelic Church (of Augsburg conviction), 9,900 Brethren, 9 700 Seventh Day Adventists, 7,600 Greek Catholics, 6,900 Christian Corps, 5.400 Lutheran Evangelic in CR. 4,500 Apostolic and 4,000 Christian Community members. The remaining churches have less than 4.000 members each, except for Jehovah witnesses with 23,000 members" in MEZŘICKY, V.: "Constitutional guarantees f freedom of faith and positions of churches in the Czech Republic" in *Legal Aspects of Religious freedom* (International Conference, 15-18 September 2008) Ljubljana, pp. 56.

3. Muslim representative organisations.

There are several Muslim associations, among which the "Association of Czech Muslim religious communities" (UMC) tends to act as their umbrella organization. ACMRC went through a more complicated recognition process than that of regular foundations or civil associations. In May 1991, when UMC was founded, the Muslim community was not on the list of recognized churches and religious associations. Among their goals were establishing a Muslim publishing house and the construction of a mosque.

As prescribed by law, in 1992 UMC was asked to submit ten thousand signatures of adult believers but UMC refused to do it. The Department for Religion of the Ministry of Culture suspended the recognition process in March 1996. The new "Act on freedom of religion and status of churches and religious associations" came into force in 2001. In March 2004, UMC submitted then a request for the first stage of recognition to the Ministry of Culture. The request was approved in September 2004. For more privileges, such as the right to public funding or running religious schools, there are requirements UMO is still unlikely to fulfill (e.g. establish believers must form at least 0.1% of the total population –around 10.000)

This core of this umbrella organization is an executive council on which every Czech Muslim organization is intended to have a representative. The UMO is now based in the Prague Mosque.

4. Mosques, Imams and cemeteries.

There are two mosques in Czech Republic. The first one was established in Brno in 1998. One year later a mosque was inaugurated in the outskirts of Prague. There around nine prayer houses.

According to available information about 5 imams work currently in the Czech Republic, all of whom come from abroad – Bosnia, Iraq, Turkey and Yemen. These imams do not engage themselves in public sector (prisons, hospitals). Their activities rather consist of management of the mosques and leading the Muslim community.

There are two Muslim cemeteries in the Czech Republic. The older one, with about 50 burial places, was established in 1994 in the town of Trebic, where the UMO had is former headquarters. Ten years later, another burial sector for Muslim burials was established in a section of the Prague cemetery in the suburb Olsany[106].

III. TRAINING CENTRES FOR IMAMS

There are no training centers for imams in the Czech Republic. Contemporary Czech law considers universities to be autonomous institutions that can be founded by State or private bodies. Religious communities are allowed to establish only private universities but they have not yet used this right.

There are currently five theological faculties in the Czech Republic within public universities: three at the Charles University in Prague (Catholic, Protestant and Hussite), and two Catholic theological faculties at other universities[107].

In 2006, the Ministry of Interior proposed and financed the project "Research on the Integration Process of Muslims in the Czech Republic in 2006". The aim was to obtain basic information on the course and current status concerning the integration of Muslims in society in the Czech Republic. The research assessed integration paths and identified several obstacles for the successful integration of Muslims but the integration, education and training of imams was not analyzed. The outcomes of the research were published in July 2007.

Arabic and Islamic Studies programs are offered in some universities. For example, Charles University of Prague (Faculty of Arts), Western Bohemian University in Plzen (Faculty of Art) or Masaryk´s University, in Brno.

---

[106] MACHACEK, S.: "CZECH REPUBLIC" in *Yearbook of Muslims in Europe…op. cit.* p. 92.

[107] TRETERA, J.R. (2005): "State and Church in Czech Republic" in *State and Church in the European Union* Second Edition, Ed Nomos, Baden-Baden, p. 48.

DENMARK

I. RELIGION AND STATE

1. Administrative bodies that have contact with denominations.

The Ministry of Ecclesiastical Affairs, deals mainly with Evangelical Lutheran (National) Church Issues[108] .

Since 2007 the Department of Family Affairs, which is under the Ministry of Justice, has been responsible for considering approval to religious communities according to the Marriage Act

Besides, denominations have contacts with various ministries, according to the item: *hala*l (Ministry of Health), chaplaincy (Ministry of Justice), etc.

In 1999, the Council for Ethnic Minorities was established in accordance with article 43 of the Integration Act. The Council advises the Minister of Refugee, Immigrant and Integration Affairs on issues of importance to immigrants and refugees. Furthermore, the Council comments on any new legal initiatives and, in general terms, make policy recommendations on issues of relevance for refugees and immigrants in Denmark. The Council consists of 14 members who are elected among representatives from the local integration councils in the municipalities.

The Ministry of Refugee, Immigration and Integration Affairs provides secretarial assistance to the Council for Ethnic Minorities and a yearly budget (app. 100.000 Euros). The Council meets with the Minister of Refugee, Immigrant and Integration Affairs every three months to discuss current problems, new initiatives and legislation. The Council also takes part in various working groups that have been set up by the Government to deal with problems of importance to immigrants and refugees.

At a local level, approximately 50 of the existing 98 municipalities have established integration councils which advise municipalities on issues related to local integration policies.

Representatives of the Government meet with the Muslim communities on an *ad hoc* basis, e.g. the Minister for Integration has held dialogue meetings with Muslim women discussing gender issues. The Minister has held several meetings with Muslim faith leaders discussing topics like afternoon classes in

---

[108] The minister, (at the moment I am writing this lines is Mrs. Birth Ronn Hornbeck), is also minister or Refugee, Immigrant and Integration affairs, but she is the head of two separated ministers.

Islam and Quran reading for children, the role of imams as mentors, prevention of radicalisation etc.

2. Recognition and approval of religions.

Denmark enjoys freedom of religion. This principle was explicitly stated in the Constitution of 1849 and remained in all later constitutions, now as article 67, under which citizens have the right to unite in communities in order to worship God the way that corresponds to their convictions, provided that nothing at variance with good morals or public order shall be taught or done. Freedom of religion also means the freedom to change one's religious belonging as well as freedom not to believe in any religious creed

The Danish legal regulation of legal persons in a religious context is essentially determined by four factors.

- The existence of an official Church, namely, the Danish People's Church (*Folkekirken*), with its privileged position guaranteed by the Danish Constitution[109].
- Until 1970, the Danish government granted official status to religious communities by royal decree.
- Since 1970, religious communities are approved under the 1969 Marriage Act, according to which clergy of religious communities other than the Evangelical Lutheran Church may be authorised to perform religious marriage ceremonies. The criteria for approval relate, among others, to the size, organisation and the probability of continued existence of the religious community (stability). Basically, these criteria are the same as those applied under the former recognition scheme (by royal decree).
- Danish law generally does not require any specific official recognition for the establishment of a legal personality. So, religious entities can be freely constituted without any official approval from the State. They could be constituted as companies or foundations but in Denmark the association is generally the preferred model.

Bearing those factors in mind, religious communities in Denmark may be divided into two groups, each governed by specific legal rules:

a) **The Evangelical-Lutheran Church (the National Church of Denmark)**

The official Danish Church is followed by the majority of the Danish population (estimated at about 81, 5 %[110]). Membership is based on baptism

---

[109] FERREIRO GALGUERA, J.: "Reminiscencias del sistema de Iglesia de Estado en los países de la Unión Europea" in *Anuario de Derecho Eclesiástico del Estado* vol. XXVI Madrid 2010, pp. 231 y ss.

[110] Official data, 01/01/2009

and most people have become members as they were baptised as infants.

The local parishes of the Church, represented by the elected parochial church councils, have the status of legal persons, who can be sued and take part in legal transactions. At the national level the Church is represented by the Ministry of Ecclesiastical Affairs. The legal status of the Church might have been different if the Danish Church had had a proper constitution as envisaged by the Danish Constitution (Art. 66)[111]. However this article has not been implemented. Consequently, the Parliament still is the legislative authority of the Church and the Ministry of Ecclesiastical Affairs its highest administrative authority.

Members of the Folk Church pay a church tax, which is collected along with income tax that is paid to the State and to the municipalities. Those who have never been members of the Church or who have cancelled the church membership will not pay that additional amount of money.

About 78% of Folk Church revenues is paid as church taxes by members, state subventions (which are administered by the Ministry of Ecclesiastical Affairs) amounts to 14% and the remaining 8% comes from funds, real property and special contributors

b) Recognised religions:

- Religious communities recognised by Royal Decree (before 1970) and
- Religious communities approved by its adjustment to the requirements of the Marriage Act 1969 (after 1970).

Besides the Official Church, there are religious entities which were recognised by a Royal Decree (administered through the Ministry of Ecclesiastical Affairs) until 1970. Prior to 1970, a total of eleven religious communities were "recognized" by Royal Decree. Such recognition has been given to the Roman Catholic Church, the Jewish community, three reformed congregations, the Methodists, the Baptists, the Russian, Swedish, Norwegian and Anglican communities.

After 1970, the practice of giving recognition by royal decree was substituted by the approval of religious entities. The approval relates to article 16 in the Danish Matrimonial Act that foresees the possibility of weddings being performed within religious entities other than the official Church when one of the parties belongs to a recognised religion and the minister belong to this religious entity has been approved by them to perform weddings. Since then, the State has "recognized" (or acknowledged) more than 100 religious communities under the Marriage Act.

The approval of a religious entity and the competence to authorise specific Ministers from the recognised (or approved) religious communities to perform weddings with legal effects used to be competence of the Ministry of Ecclesiastical affairs, but since November 2007, it is within the competence of the

---

[111] Art. 66: "*The constitution of the Established Church shall be laid down by Statute*".

Ministry of Justice (Department of Family Affairs[112]). Since 1998, a standing advisory committee of experts in religion and law has been appointed to assess whether the conditions for approval as a religious community are fulfilled.

In order to obtain this approval, the religious entity must fulfil certain conditions as to a number of members, doctrine, bylaws, certain organization (e.g. board of representatives in relation to official authorities).

Regarding the number of followers, it may be of importance whether the community asking for approval belongs to an existing religion. In that case, 50 people is normally required, whereas complete independent religious entities based on a faith outside known are required to represent at least 150 persons. Beside the number of followers, a religious group can substantiate its survival or stability through having a system of training and appointing new ministers of cult.

Ministers of the approved or recognised religious communities can formally request the Department of Family Affairs (Ministry of Justice) for a wedding permit, in order to marry people with legal effects. The Department of Family Affairs (under the Ministry of Justice) requires the religious communities to document that marriages celebrated by them do not break the requirements established in the Marriage Act. Those permits can be *ad hoc* (for a specific occasion) or standing permits. Sometimes it is not easy to decide whether required conditions are fulfilled or not. It was the case *Forn Sidr*[113].

Recognised and approved religious communities have special privileges. They are granted property and corporate tax-exempt status, and members may tax-deduct membership fees and donations to the community. As we have just said, after specific consideration, a Minister of a recognised or approved community may obtain authorisation to conduct legal weddings. There are also specific rules for obtaining residence permits for religious preachers.

c) Other religious communities who have not applied for recognition or approval and societies of religious character.

---

[112] http://www.familiestyrelsen.dk/en/englishversion/

[113] *Forn Sidr* is an entity that had defined itself as a religious community aimed at the "gathering of people who worship the old Nordic gods". The belief is called *asetro* and even if the entity does not control "the way in which members practice their faith", it is based on the idea that the old Nordic belief in Thor and other gods never disappeared completely. The entity has its bylaws and ceremonies (*blot*) and believes in divine powers and spirits nature as recorded in old Nordic literature and poetry. It has contacts with similar entities in other Nordic countries. Finally they got the approval in 2003.

II. ISLAM IN DENMARK

1. Legal recognition of Islam

Around 50 Muslim communities have obtained the approved status to date. Among which are 28 communities related to the Danish Turkish Islamic Institution (*Danimarka Türk Diyanet Wakfi*) which is linked to *Diyanet*[114].

2. Muslim population

First Muslims communities in Denmark were constituted by immigrant workers from Turkey, Pakistan, Morocco and former Yugoslavia that began to arrive in the late 1960s. The imposition of much harder requirements to obtain visas from 1973 onwards participated in the definitive settlement of the first generation and their families through family reunification procedures. During the 1980s and the 1990's, a second wave of Muslim population arrived to Denmark: they were mostly refugees from Iran, Iraq, Palestine, Somalia and Bosnia.

The Danish authorities, as the authorities of many State Members of EU, do not register individual religious beliefs. So although there are no official statistics regarding the religious affiliation of residents in Denmark, estimates have been produced on the basis of ethnicity and national origin. These figures suggest that the total number of Muslims is around 210,000 representing 3% of a population of 5.5 million people[115]. Data about the ethnic profile of Muslims in Denmark by country of origin[116] could be summarized as follows:

Turkey	52,500
Iraq	24.700
Lebanon	24.500
Bosnia-Herzegovina and former Yugoslavia	20.600
Pakistan	18.300
Somalia	16.300
Iran	14,500
Afghanistan	11.600
Morocco	9.300
Iran	8,400

[114] Six local Alevi associations were approved as religious communities in 2007.

[115] Estimations from: *Islam and Muslims in Denmark Factsheet*, Ministry of Refugee, Immigration and Integration Affairs, October 2008.

[116] Official data updated provided by the Minister of Refugee, Immigration and Integration Affairs

3. Muslim representative organizations.

Although the first Muslim organizations in Denmark were established following ethnic criteria, second generation organizations have worked to develop a different kind of affiliation using Danish as the common language and encouraging the participation of women on their boards.

Efforts have also been made by the Muslim community to establish a National Muslim Council but no results have been achieved yet. Nonetheless, there are two main umbrella organizations that comprise several groups with different tendencies:

- The *Dansk Muslimsk Union* (Danish Muslim Union), represents six organizations among which are the *Minhaj al-Quran* (Islamic Organisation of Bosnians in Denmark), *Danimarka Müslüman Göcmenler Teşkiláti* (Organization of Danish Muslim Immigrants, from the *Millî Gorüş* movement) and the Danish Islamic Council (member of the Federation of Islamic Organizations in Europe).

- The *Muslimernes Faellesråd*[117] (Muslim Council of Denmark) mainly represents Somalian, Danish, Pakistani and Turkish organizations. It counts among its members the *Danimarka Türk Diyanet Wakfi*, the largest Turkish association in Denmark which manages about 40 mosques linked to the Turkish Directorate for Religious Affairs (*Diyanet*).

During the *Jyllands-Posten* cartoon controversy[118], Naser Khader, founded a Muslim organization called Democratic Muslims[119], but after his founder left, the organization is no longer as active as before[120].

---

[117] Official website:
http://mfr.nu/index.php?option=com_content&task=section&id=27&Itemid=113&language=da

[118] The *Jyllands-Posten* cartoon controversy refers to the publication by the Danish newspaper *Jyllands-Posten* of a series of cartoons of the Prophet Muhamad considered offensive by the Muslim communities. The affair began in September 2005 and rapidly spread reaching the international level. Protests all over the Muslim world and Europe led to riots and the boycott of Danish goods. The *Islamisk Trossamfung* and the Danish-based European Committee for Prophet Honouring (both of them now closed) played a significant role in the affair. Their leaders, Ahmad Abu Laban and Ahmad Akkari, claimed to represent several Danish Muslim organizations campaigning against the *Jyllands-Posten*. *Vid.* FERREIRO GALGUERA, J.: "Las caricaturas sobre Mahoma y las Jurisprudencia del Tribunal Europeo de los Derechos Humanos" in *www.reei.org* pp. 1-8.

[119] Official website: http://www.demokratiskemuslimer.dk/

[120] There are also debate forums like Danish Association of Cybermuslims (DFC).

4. Mosques and imams.

Islamic communities are free to establish mosques in Denmark according to Danish law. There are around 115[121] Islamic worship places in the country, from which three are purpose-built mosques and the rest rented or owned buildings that have been converted into mosques.

Most mosques are located in Copenhagen and in the bigger cities. They great majority are run by Sunni Muslims and 11 by Shiite communities. A third of them are linked to international movements or organizations such as *Diyanet* (28), the *Millî Gorüş* (6) or the Minhaj al-Quran (3)[122].

Mosques tend to be ethnically homogeneous: 60% of them are attended by only one ethnic group[123] such as the Islamic Cultural Centre (mainly Arabic and Pakistani) or the *Kopenhag Kocatepe Camii* (mainly Turkish). Few imams give the Friday sermon in Danish

Most mosques do not have full-time religious leaders with formal education: approximately 15 of them have higher theological education received abroad and around 70 don't have any formal religious education. Imams coming from abroad (approx. 30)[124] are granted a residence and work permit as 'members of the clergy'. In June 2004, the Parliament enacted a law directed at foreign religious leaders seeking residence visas. The so called "Imam Law", which applies to all religious leaders, establishes the amount of visas for religious leaders per religious community depending on its size as well as requiring the applicant to prove his/her association to a recognised or approved religious group in Denmark[125]. Official data shows that some 21 imams were being granted a residence permit as religious preachers in 2007, the majority of whom were related to the *Diyanet* (Turkey), two were from Pakistan and two from Egypt. In April 2007, the Liberal Conservative government passed legislation that required all foreign religious ministers (missionaries, imams, etc) to pass a Danish language test within six months entering the country. Some considered

---

[121] *Islam and Muslims in Denmark Factsheet*, Ministry of Refugee, Immigration and Integration Affairs, October 2008.

[122] *Ibid.*

[123] *Ibid*

[124] *Ibid*

[125] BRIONES MARTINEZ, I.M.(2006): *Religion, Women and Freedom of Speech in Denmark: Three Crucial Factors for a Healthy Society*, paper presented at the Centre for Studies in New Religions 2006 International Conference in San Diego State University; *International Religious Freedom Report 2006: Denmark,* US Department of State. http://www.state.gov/g/drl/rls/irf/2006/71377.htm (accessed 09/07/2009); DASSETO, F., FERRARI, S. and MARECHAL, B. (2007): *Islam in the European Union: What's at stake in the future?* Brussels, European Parliament.

that law as restrictive regarding the entry of Muslim clerics, whose number had already been reduced in by the so called "Imam Law"[126].

5. Chaplaincy.

Danish Prison and Probation service has employed three Muslim chaplains, one of whom -trained in the Saudi University of Medina- is full-time employed. The remaining two are employed on an *ad hoc* basis.

The Prison and Probation Service is currently developing a strategy for future employment of additional imams according to the prisoners' right to practice their religion and follow their beliefs and to attend services or meetings led by approved representatives of their religion. The Service is also working on making specific guidelines and detailed description of chaplains' conditions of appointment, conditions of employment, recruitment procedures etc. It is recommended that newly employed chaplains participate in an introduction training program, corresponding to courses offered to other civilian employees. The first imam in prison financed by the State was appointed in 2002. Today there are about 20 Imams giving spiritual guidance in Danish prisons[127].

Regarding the armed forces, there are only Evangelical Lutheran chaplains, who are full time pastors working part time as chaplains.

A number of Lutheran pastors also serve part of their time in hospitals, but they are paid by the Lutheran Church. Clergy of other denominations are free to serve their fellow believers in hospitals, but they do not hold any specific position in hospitals. Two hospitals in Denmark are working together with the voluntary organisation Ethnic Resource-Team offering spiritual advice and counselling to Muslim patients.

In 2005, the first Muslim prayer room was appointed at the Copenhagen University Hospital (*Rigospitalet*). There is one imam serving in this hospital.

6. Muslim Schools

Religious education in primary and secondary schools is termed "Christian studies" and it has been traditionally taught on an Evangelical Lutheran basis, with the addition of elements about other religions, including Islam. Parents have the right to withdraw their children from Christian studies on religious grounds.

Muslim organizations may found private schools under the private independent school legislation. If the private school fulfils the requirements estab-

---

[126] JACOBSEN, B.A.: "Denmark" in V.V.A.A. *Yearbook ...op. cit* p. 99.
[127] *Ibidem.* P. 106.

lished by the education laws, it will receive state funding equivalent until 75% of their expenditure.

The first private Muslim school was established in Copenhagen in 1978 and nowadays there are around 23 more located in the biggest cities, with approximately 3.600 students[128]. Newer Muslim schools are more heterogeneous and classes are taught in Danish, half of the teachers having a Danish ethnic background.

The majority of Muslim pupils go to public schools.

Although there is no official registration of Quran schools in Denmark, it is known that most mosques and Muslim private schools offer courses on Quran for children and adults.

7. Muslim cemeteries.

Religious groups have the right to acquire land for building a cemetery. Land has been provided in Copenhagen, Aarhus and Odense, among other places, where Muslim cemeteries have been established.

In 2006, the first Muslim cemetery in Denmark was opened after several years of efforts. The *Dansk Islamisk Begravelsesfond* (Danish Islamic Cemetery Fund), a foundation composed by 25 Muslims communities and organisations, is the owner and manager of the cemetery located near Copenhagen.

Fifteen cemeteries of the Evangelical Lutheran Church, which are managed either by parochial church councils or local governments, have special sections for Muslims.

According to some estimates, around 200 Muslims die each year in Denmark, and the bodies of about half of them are flown back to their country of origin to be buried[129]

---

[128] Private schools are not registered in terms of their ideological or religious basis and therefore there's no registration of the number of Muslim schools or pupils. The above-mentioned information is based on information from the *Dansk Friskoleforening* (Danish organisation for independent schools) and on findings from a field study on Muslim private school, HAABER IHLE, A.(2007): *Magt, medborgerskab og muslimske friskoler i Danmark* (Power, Citizenship and Muslim Private Schools in Denmark), Copenhagen University.

[129] *JYLLANDS-POSTEN* 22 September 2006.

III. TRAINING CENTRES FOR IMAMS

1. Programmes concerning training for Muslim faith leaders coming from abroad.

Within the framework of the IOM Helsinki-Initiated pilot project[130], a three-day civic education training course to migrant religious community leaders is offered. The training started in September 2008 and is conducted by the School of Education of Aarhus University. The aim of the course is to provide general information about Danish history, culture, education, political and juridical systems to religious leaders with foreign backgrounds. The course comprises the following subjects: Introduction to Denmark, History of religion in Denmark and Europe, Citizenship in Denmark and Europe – what does it mean, The educational system in Denmark, The labour market and social legislation in Denmark, System of justice and the police, Culture and traditions in Denmark, Life-cycle events in Denmark, Religion and media, Multi-faith and Extremism and keeping society safe.

So far, 23 religious leaders, 10 of whom being Muslim and 13 Christians have attended the course. Permanent and regular courses are also being planned.

2. Imam training centres.

There are no imam training centres in Denmark. Regarding universities, no step has been taken in the direction of establishing confessional education in Islam although according to the Danish Act on Universities, a university is free to decide which research-based degree programmes it wants to offer within its academic scope. The Theological Faculties, which probably would be the most likely to host confessional education, are non-confessional, and training on profession-specific topics is taught outside the university in separate teaching institutions.

Rather than focusing on a specific imam education, several universities in Denmark have recently strengthened their Islamic studies programmes. Within the last three years the following centres or units have been established:

- Arab and Islamic Studies program, in the Faculty of Theology, Aarhus University[131].

In 2005, a new and modernised BA program was inaugurated with an emphasis on modern Arabic and the study of the modern Arab world and Islamic culture. The BA degree in Arab and Islamic Studies is taught predominantly in Danish, though Arabic and English are both also used in certain

---

[130] Funded by the European Commission, "Integration: A Multi-faith Approach" (IAMA)

[131] http://www.teo.au.dk/en/studies/intros/arabic

classes. The MA degree in Arab and Islamic Studies, which will start in 2010, will be taught in English, and so will be suitable for international students.

-Research Unit on the New Islamic Public Sphere, Faculty of Humanities, University of Copenhagen[132]. This unit maps and analyses how new media such as satellite TV and the internet are changing Islamic norms, politics and identity in the contemporary Middle East.

-Centre for European Islamic Thought, Faculty of Theology, University of Copenhagen[133]. The focus of the Centre is on Islamic religious thought in contemporary Europe and on the processes and circumstances in which it is appearing, seeking to locate and understand it in the context both of the history of Islamic religious thought and of contemporary developments in Islamic thinking, and to evaluate it as a response to the European environment specifically and to modernity more generally.

The University also has a research priority area called Religion in the 21st Century. In this framework research about education of Muslim religious leaders in universities has been conducted[134].

3. Other initiatives

Various Muslim organisations have considered different ways of establishing Imam Education programs. The Islamic Faith Society in Copenhagen has been in talks with Al-Azhar University about the possibility of offering specific courses in Denmark to Danish Muslim leaders, but has not implemented any programs so far. Different organisations offer Islamic teaching for ordinary Muslims, mainly targeting young Muslims, but they do not receive a certificate qualifying for a theological position of any kind. None of the Muslim institutions or organisations in Denmark are offering courses with the specific aim of educating Muslim faith leaders.

---

[132] http://islamicpublicsphere.hum.ku.dk/

[133] http://www.teol.ku.dk/english/dept/ceit_eng/

[134] Two reports by B. Schepelern Johansen with the conclusions of the research have been published by the University of Copenhaguen: *Imamuddannelse i Europa – udfordringer og perspektiver* (2005), and *Islam at the European Universities* (2006).

ESTONIA

I. RELIGION AND STATE

1. Administrative bodies that have contact with denominations.

- Department of Religious Affairs, under the Ministry of Interior. According to its statute, this department is responsible for the development of relations between the State and religious associations.
- Registration departments of county courts, under the Ministry of Justice. Previously, under 1993 Churches and Congregations Act (hereinafter the 1993 CCA), religious associations were registered at the Ministry of Internal Affairs. According to the new Churches and Congregations Act (hereinafter the 2002 CCA), religious associations are registered by the registration departments of county courts.

2. Recognition of religions.

a) Legal structure of religious entities according to the fact of being registered:

Estonian Constitution maintains that there is no State church. It also recognises religious freedom of individuals and groups. Therefore it includes the right to found a church or a religious association. A religious association is a legal person of private law.

According to Article 3.2 of the 2002 Churches and Congregations Act (CCA)[135], the objective or main activity of churches, congregations, associations of congregations and monasteries should not be an economic activity. Therefore, if the main target is economic activity this religious association could be dissolved by a court. Nevertheless, it is possible for a religious organization to register itself as a profit-making organization. However, in that case it could be registered as a regular association but not as a religious association or as a religious society as defined in the 2002 CCA. It could not enjoy of legal benefits available to non-profit-making organization either.

Estonian law (2002 CCA) addresses five different types of religious organization and, what is no common in European legislation, defines those cate-

---

[135] As we have said, this Law was passed in 1993 but new revision was adopted in 2002.

gories: Churches[136], Congregations[137], associations of congregations[138], monasteries[139] and religious societies[140].

The first four categories are called religious associations and their activities are regulated by 2002 CCA. On the other hand, the activities of religious societies (social activities included: hospitals, schools, etc) are not regulated by the 2002 CCA (which is as special law) but by the Non-profit Organizations Act[141].

According to CCA, the objective or main activity of churches, congregations, associations of congregations and monasteries must not be earning of income from economic activity.

The legal capacity of a religious association starts as soon as it is registered either in the register of religious associations or in the register of non-profit-making associations and foundations. The process of registration differs according to the register in which the associations are enrolled. Religious associations (churches, congregations, associations of congregations and monasteries) must enrol in the Register of religious associations according to court diction, while religious societies must be registered, also by a court decision, but in the register of non-profit organisations and foundations.

Congregations or association of congregations that belong to a church do not need to have legal personality. It is up to a religious association to decide whether they want it or not. Moreover, a religious association may have depart-

---

[136] A church is an association of at least three voluntarily joined congregations which has an Episcopal structure and is doctrinally related to three ecumenical creeds or is divided into at least three congregations and which operates on the basis of its statutes, is man-aged by an elected or appointed management board and is entered in the register in the cases and pursuant to the procedure prescribed by this Act (Art. 2.2).

[137] A congregation is a voluntary association of natural persons who profess the same faith, which operates on the basis of its statutes, is managed by an elected or appointed management board and is entered in the register in the cases and pursuant to the procedure prescribed by this Act (Art. 2.3).

[138] An association of congregations is an association of at least three voluntarily joined congregations which profess the same faith and which operates on the basis of its statutes, is managed by an elected or appointed management board and is entered in the register pursuant to the procedure prescribed by this Act (Art. 2.4).

[139] A monastery is a voluntary communal association of natural persons who profess the same faith, which operates on the basis of the statutes of the corresponding church or independent statutes, is managed by an elected or appointed superior of the monastery and is entered in the register in the cases and pursuant to the procedure prescribed by this Act (Art. 2.5).

[140] A religious society is a voluntary association of natural or legal persons the main activities of which include confessional or ecumenical activities relating to morals, ethics, education, culture and confessional or ecumenical, diaconal and social rehabilitation activities outside the traditional forms of religious rites of a church or congregation and which need not be connected with a specific church, association of congregations or congregation (Art 4.1).

[141] KIVIORG, M. *Op. Cit.* p. 70, 71.

ments and agencies if this is prescribed in the statutes. However, departments and agencies do not have the status of legal persons[142].

b) Requirements to register a religious association:

-Number of founders: In order to register a congregation at least twelve adult members with active legal capacity should apply for it. Registering a church requires three congregations, in other terms; at least 36 natural persons are needed.

- Memorandum: the founders must present a memorandum of the association including a list of the names and addresses of the founders and those of the members of the management board. Founders have the right to vote in local government elections. At the same time, the Non-profit Organizations Act requires that only half of the board members (including religious societies) need to be resident in Estonia or in another EU country or in Switzerland.

- Statute of a religious association: the statutes of a religious association should describe the objective and doctrinal bases of the association, as well as, obligatory rites. The court will not register a religious association or a religious society if the statutes are not in compliance with the requirements of law or if its activities damage public order, health, morals, or the rights and freedoms of others.

In case of doubt, the chief judge of the court that maintains the register may suspend registration proceedings for two months and request the opinion of a ministry affected with those doubtful activities or of any expert from a competent agency. The refusal to register must indicate the reason.

Registration is not compulsory. Non registered religious groups are also protected by the fundamental right to religious freedom. But, in that case they cannot present themselves as a religious legal entity and, therefore, cannot enjoy of its legal advantages.

c) Advantages of religious legal entities:

Given that sacred church buildings usually have historical, cultural, and artistic value, the State funds registered religions in order to preserve the buildings that belong to them.

Religious associations are automatically exempted from income tax. Other non profit making organizations (including humanist associations and religious societies) have to apply to be included on the list of non taxable organizations.

Religious associations have also certain privileges concerning Value Added Tax (VAT), usually applied as discounts against the ordinary tax rate. They are also exempt from land (property) tax regarding to places of worship such as churches and congregations.

Clergy of registered associations may apply for authorization to perform civil marriages after passing a two day courses. In June 2009 there were 165 clergy-

---

[142] KIVIORG, M. *"Religious entities as legal persons –Estonia"* in *State and Church in the European Union* Second Edition, Ed Nomos, Baden-Baden 2005 p.70-77.

men aloud to perform civil marriages from different religions (twenty of them were women).

Labour law does not apply to persons who conduct religious activities in religious organizations, unless prescribed by their bylaws.

Law also recognises the right of the clergy to keep confessional secrecy, and the exclusive right to wear the professional attire of a minister of religion as prescribed in the statutes. This only affects the clergy to whom a registered religious association has granted the corresponding permission.

Religious societies are treated as regular non-profit-making organizations (thus donations to non profit organizations are deductable for individuals up to 5% of their annual taxable income) and enjoy considerably less autonomy than religious associations (for example, religious associations don't have to fulfil the requirement of being ruled by democratic institutions).

In total, there are nine churches with 330 congregations, nine unions of congregations with 136 congregations. In addition, there are 52 congregations that do not belong to any church. Among these congregations are included non-Christian communities (for example, Buddhists, Jews, Muslims, etc).

In the current law, there is no difference between registration of emerging religious entities and registration of historical majority churches.

Even if in constitutional terms Estonia does not have a State Church, the separation of State and Church has not been interpreted in administrative practice strictly and inflexibly, especially regarding to the Evangelical Lutheran Church. Estonian Evangelical Lutheran Church has, in fact, enjoyed of certain preferential treatment from the State, for example allocations to support a newspaper of the ex-established church, and other forms of preferential treatment of Christian Churches.

Another example of a flexibility in the principle of separation is the economic support given since 1990 to the Estonian Council of Churches[143], an organism which consists of 10 Christian Churches included the three biggest ones (Evangelical Lutheran Church, Estonian Orthodox Church of Moscow Patriarchate and Estonian Apostolic Orthodox Church). This Council of Churches has been very active in determining relations between Churches and State[144].

The State has treated the Council as a partner in decision-making on religious freedom questions in Estonia. The privileged position of the Council is visible, and perhaps most sensitive, in matters of financial support and educa-

---

[143] www.ekn.ee/index.php

[144] The Estonian Council of Churches was established in 1989 and has currently ten member churches including the Estonian Evangelical Lutheran Church, the Estonian Apostolic-Orthodox Church, the Estonian Orthodox Church of Moscow Patriarchate, the Roman Catholic Church, the Union of Evangelical Christian and Baptist Churches of Estonia, the United Methodist Church in Estonia, the Estonian Conference of Seventh-day Adventists Church, the Estonian Christian Pentecostal Church, the Estonian Congregation St. Gregory of the Armenian Apostolic Church, and the Charismatic Episcopal Church of Estonia.

tion. On 17 October 2002 the Government and the Estonian Council of Churches signed the Protocol of Common Concerns: education, chaplaincy, social work, restoration of historical and cultural religious buildings etc.). In the fiscal year 2008 the allocation to this Council was 8,21 million Estonian kroons (526 282 Euros). It has been argued that other religious organisations have the right to seek the same type of cooperation.

II. ISLAM IN ESTONIA

1. Legal recognition of Islam.

Islam is recognised as a religion in Estonia. There are two Muslim religious associations registered at the Register of Religious Associations.

2. Muslim population

The official census in 2000 recorded 1387 Muslim citizens in Estonia, most of them Tatars. The number should have increased as a result of the arrival of immigrants with Muslim background and some conversions. Most of Estonian Muslims are located in and around the capital, Tallin. Over a population of 1.340.935 inhabitants, about 5000 (0, 5 %) are Muslims[145].

3. Muslim representative organizations.

Since the early 1990s, the main representative of the Muslim community in Estonia has been the Estonian Islamic Congregation (*Eesti islami Kogudus*) was established in Tallin. Officially registered in 1994, they have been the most active part of the Muslim community in relation with the Government and the public administrations. The Estonian Islamic Congregation represents Muslims from different ethnic backgrounds (Tatars, Azaris, Kazakhs and Uzbeks) as well as different Muslim traditions (both Sunni and Shiite). It is often consulted by the Government for advice about items related to Islam and intercultural dialogue. In 1995 a small splinter organization, Estonian Muslim Sunni Congregation (*Eesti Muhameedlaste Sunniitide kogudus*) was formed also in Tallin.

---

[145] Source: data from the Islamic Congregation of Estonia.

Alongside these registered organization, there are other informal groups, like the Nur Center of Islamic Religion in Maardu, established in 2001 and also preserving Azeri cultural traditions[146].

4. Mosques and Imams.

There are three Islamic worship places in Estonia: one in Tallinn and the other two in Maardu and Narva. A great part of their congregations have a Russian background.

There are currently two Muslim faith leaders in Estonia[147], both of them with Estonian nationality. One received his religious training in the Ufa Madrasa in the early 1990s. The official supreme leader for the Muslim community in Estonia is of Estonian-Tatar origin and received his religious training in Saudi-Arabia.

5. Chaplains.

Chaplains in the army, prisons and in the police institutions are members of the staff and employed on the same basis as other personnel.

Currently there are 18 chaplains in the 5 prisons where 3.456 prisoners are held. Chaplains in prisons are appointed by the Ministry of Justice and belong to the staff of the penitentiary centre[148].

The inmates have the right to meet the clergy of their denominations. The official supreme leader of the Muslim community (the imam of the Estonian Islamic Congregation) has participated in the training course for military chaplains and is considered to be a military chaplain in reserve. He is occasionally invited to prisons or hospitals to perform rites.

6. Teaching of Islam in schools.

The Estonian school system consists mainly of state schools. There are 573 public schools and only 29 private ones[149]. There are no private primary or secondary schools run by Muslims.

According to the Education Act, the study and teaching of religion in schools is voluntary. In 1999 the Estonian Parliament passed amendments to

---

146 RACIUS, E.: "ESTONIA" *in....Yearbook of Muslims in Europe...op cit.* p. 113.
147 Source: official data from the Estonian Ministry of Justice.
148 *Ibid.*
149 Source: official data from the Ministry of Education of Estonia, 2008: http://www.hm.ee

the Law. Religious education must be offered if at least 15 pupils′ parents demand it. It is mainly a non-confessional education. The content of religious studies is established in a curriculum approved by the Ministry of Education. Teachers of religious studies must have both theological and pedagogical training.

There are not official statistics about the students religion (it is banned by art. 42 of the Constitution), but unofficial statistics show that there might be about a hundred Muslims students.

III. TRAINING CENTRES FOR IMAMS

There are no institutions or organizations providing training for Muslim faith leaders in Estonia but the Estonian Islamic Congregation would like to set up a training centre in the future.

No private research on imam training in Estonia has been developed yet. There is neither a specific policy nor special programs concerning the training of Muslim faith leaders coming from abroad.

According to the Ministry of Education, the existing schools for religious ministries are the following: The Faculty of Theology at the Public University of Tartu, which is fully funded by the State budget, and four private centres (the Theological Institute of the Lutheran Church, the Theological Seminary of the Congregations Union of Evangelical Christian and Baptist Churches, the Theological Seminary of the Methodist Church and the Theological Academy of Tartu).

Academic courses on Islam and the Middle East are offered at the University of Tartu (basically Arabic language and an introduction to Islamic studies, both at the Department of Theology). Tallin University also offers some instruction in Arabic and Turkish languages as well as introduction to Turkish culture.

FINLAND

I. RELIGION AND STATE

1. Administrative bodies that have contact with denominations.

The Ministry of Education administers matters relating to the Churches and other religious communities in Finland and drafts legislation relating to them. The division competent on relations with churches is the Division for Cultural Legislation and Finances, which belongs to the Department for Cultural, Sport and youth Policy under the Ministry of Education.
There is also the National Board on Patents and Registration (NBPR) under the Ministry of Employment and the Economy[150].

2. Recognition of religions.

Freedom of religion was added to the Finish Constitution in 1919 (revised in 1999). Since Finland joined the European Union (1995) the issue of State-Church relations has become a matter of interest in Finland. The Freedom of Religion Act (1992, revised in 2003[151]) provides more regulation on the matter. The Evangelical Lutheran Church and the Finish Orthodox Church enjoy a special status as religious organizations with their own legislation. Nevertheless, with the new Law on Religious Freedom of 2003 the dominant status of the Evangelical Lutheran Church of Finland has decreased. Other religious groups are dealt with under the Freedom of Religion Act as recognised religious bodies or under the Association Act as voluntary associations.
According to Finish laws we can distinguish between not recognised and recognised religious groups. But in the latter we can differentiate three different kinds of legal persons: Lutheran Church, Orthodox Church and other registered religious communities[152].

---

[150] http://www.prh.fi/en/tietoaprhsta.html

[151] Freedom of Religion Act N° 453 of June 6th 2003

[152] Registered religious associations (circa 59000) and number of members (altogether 31.12.2004): Jehovah's Witnesses (18224), The Evangelical Free Church (13471), Catholic Church in Finland (8083), Seventh-day Adventist Church of Finland (4030), The Church of Jesus Christ of Latter-day Saints -The Mormons- (3309), The Baptist community of Finland (1562), Pentecostalic Church of Finland (1240), Orthodox St. Nicolas church in Helsinki (1181), Jewish Community of Helsinki (1072), Finlands svenska baptistsamfund (881), Helsinki Islamic Center (778), The Methodist Church of Finland (644), The Islamic Society of

a) Evangelical Lutheran Church:
Its status of public law entity is ensured in the Constitution, where it says that its organization and administration are laid down by a Church Act. Church's own principal body, the General Synod (a General Assembly of the Lutheran Church) has the exclusive initiative referring to ecclesiastical bill. Only General Synod has the power to introduce bills enacting and changing church law. Parliament, which finally formally enacts the law, can only approve or reject the ecclesiastical bill presented by the General Synod but it can not to amend it.

The Evangelical Lutheran Church of Finland, which has 9 dioceses and 515 parishes, is considered a self-administered body under public law, something like municipalities. Approx. 81% of the Finish population belongs to the Evangelical Lutheran Church.

b) The Finnish Orthodox Church:

Being also a public law entity, the Constitution does not provide that the organization of this church should be regulated by an Act-as it did for the Lutheran Church-. Nevertheless, Orthodox Church is affected by the Orthodox Church Act (521/1969) and its supplementary statute (179/1970).
According to this law, the General Synod has the initiative to introduce new bills to the government on laws and statutes concerning the Church. However, the government is not bound to the content of the bill. Thus the Orthodox Church cannot influence the enacting of laws concerning itself in the same extent than the Lutheran church.

Tampere (615), Finlands svenska metodistkyrka (603), Islamic-congregation of Finland (591), The Evangelical-Lutheran Free Parish Union -Suomen vapaa evankelisluterilainen seurakuntaliitto- (537), Bahai community of Finland (493), The Islamic Society of Finland (446), The prívate Greek-Catholic Church in Vyborg (340), Confessional Lutheran Church of Finland - Suomen Tunnustuksellinen Luterilainen Kirkko- (305), Lutheran Community of Word - Luterilainen Sanan yhdyskunta- (169), The Liberal Catholic Church Province of Finland (132), Jewish Community of Turku (131), The Islamic Society of Savo (115), The Anglican Church in Finland (97), Islamic-congregation of Tampere (85), Anjuman-e-islahul-muslimeen of Turku (83), The Christian Community in Finland (76), Finnish Islamic Center (74), International society for Kríshna Consciousness in Finland (64), The Shiia Muslims of Finland (51), Vórá Frikyrkoforsamling (46), The Islamic Society of Central Finland (41), The Buddish Dharma Center (40), The Islamic Rahma Center in Finland (39), Missionkyrkan Finland (35), The Congregation of God -Jumalan seurakunta- (30), New Apostolic Church of Finland (29), Linkkiseurakunta (28), Finlands svenska pingstsamfund (26), Spaso-Preobrazenskaja (24) and with 20 or less members: Islam and Love, The Islamic Society of Al-Risala, The Islamic Society of Al-Hudaa, The Kimbangu Church (kimbangun kirkkokunta), The Church of Christian Acls (Kristillisten Tekojen Kirkko), The Islamic Society of Northern Finland, Redeemed Christian Church of God, Seventh-day Adventist Church Reformation movement, Friends of the Truth (Totuuden Ystavát). Source: KOTIRANTA, M.: "Status of religious communities" in *Legal Aspects of Religious freedom* (International Conference, 15-18 September 2008), Ljubljana, pp. 64-80.

A new law concerning the Orthodox Church came into force at the beginning of 2007. The basic structure of the church administration would remain, however, largely as it is at present. The status of the central and diocesan administration would be altered to be more independent from the State so that its expenses would not be paid any longer directly by State funds. However, the Church's economic activities would be ensured by State aid. Some internal affairs and administrative matters which until then were competence of the Ministry of Education would be transferred to the Church's own organs.
The Orthodox Church and its parishes would change their employment relationship: civil servants of the Central Church Board and parish clergy would have a contractual relationship[153]. Approximately, 1.1% of the Finnish population belongs to the Orthodox Church.

c) Other Register religious associations:

According to Freedom of Religion Act (2003), other religious communities have the right to register in the National Board of Patents and Registration, under the Ministry of Employment and Economy. Registering is voluntary. But the Freedom Act establishes some requirements that should be fulfilled in order to register:

- Religious associations should apply for registration in the National Board of Patents and Registration in a document signed by a minimum of twenty persons over 18 years old.
- They should also present a Charter of foundation that should include an order of association[154]. This order of association should refer to: Address in Finland and religious purposes.

According to the Religious Freedom Act, "the purpose of a registered religious association is to organise and support individual, corporate and public activities pertaining to religious profession and religious observance, based on confession of faith, Scriptures or other individualized established sacred activities". The bases of the activities of a registered religious association should thus be individualized, established and regarded as sacred by the community.

- The procedure whereby a person may be accepted as a member. The religious association must maintain a register of its members
- The Administrative body (its members and process of decision-making) and also defining the relation between the religious group and its local communities (parishes etc,)
- The fees that must be paid by membership.
- The procedures to modify the order of association, to decide its breaking up and also to distribute the funds in case of dissolution.

---

[153] KOTIRANTA, M.: "Status of religious communities" ...*op.cit* pp. 80-81.
[154] For more details: http://www.prh.ri/stc/lbrms/perusilmoilus_yhdi.slysrekisleriiti.pdf

The National Board of Patents and Registration (previously in the Ministry of Education) must approve the entry of a religious association in the register provided that the order of association is in accordance with the Freedom of Religion Act and the basis of faith and religious observance are not contrary to law.

There is a committee of experts that advises the National Board of Patents and Registration in these matters. This advising body assesses the NBPR whether the religious entity applying for registration is religious or if it represents non-religious worldviews and convictions. They also evaluate the nature of the activities of the organization and their compliance with human rights. The committee also controls if the religious organization is not mainly dedicated to economic activities, is not organised in military fashion and that its purpose is not encouraging illegal activities such as using firearms. The tasks of the committee of experts are limited to assess the purposes and types of activities of an association that has made notification of foundation or has altered the order of association.

A registered religious community may apply for a state subsidy for its activities and for licence to perform marriages with civil effects. Pupils belonging to a registered religious community can receive religious education in comprehensive and upper secondary schools, if there are at least three pupils belonging to the same religious community whose parents request for it. In addition, registration has an effect on taxation and penal protection. At the end of 2008 there were 58 registered religious associations[155]

Some bodies engaging in religious activities have not organized as registered religious association but as ideological associations. For example, Pentecostal assemblies.

II. ISLAM IN FINLAND

1. Legal recognition of Islam.

There are 25 Muslim communities registered in the National Board of Patents and Registration as religious communities. According to the National Centre of Statistic of Finland, those 25 registered Muslim communities represent approximately 5000 to 5.500 of all Muslims in Finland (20% of the overall).

---

[155] KÄÄRIAINEN,K.-FORMAKKA,T "Financinc churches and religious organizations in Finland. *Financing of churches and religious so cities in the 21st Century* Ed. Institute for State-Churches Relations. Bratislava 2010. P.123

2. Muslim population.

Since 1870, Tatar Muslims from the Nizhni Novgorod region started to arrive to Finland. After Finish independence (1917) Muslims were able to organize as a religious community under the Freedom of Religion Act of 1923. But the Muslim population started to grow rapidly at the 1990s due to immigration and refugees and asylum seekers.

Nowadays, from an overall population of 5.300.484 inhabitants[156], there are approximately between 345.000 Muslims[157], that is, 0.8% of the total population.

3. Muslim representative organizations.

The most important organisation representing the Muslim community in the country is the Islamic Council of Finland (*Suomen Islamilainen Neuvosto* – SINE-[158]) was established in 2006 and functions as an umbrella organization for the Muslims in Finland. The Council includes 18 organisations and receives state subsidies for its activities.

SINE also participates in the Advisory Board for Ethnic Relationships[159] (under the Ministry of Interior) altogether with other associations which represent other ethnical and cultural minorities. This organization is also consulted about issues that affect them, for example in the latest amendment of the Religious Freedom Act of 2003.

4. Mosques and Imams.

There are approximately 40 Islamic worship places in Finland, 25 of which belong to registered Muslim communities. Two of them are purpose built an owned by Tatar community. The remaining 24 are prayer halls.

The number of imams is estimated to be the same as mosques (40). Only 30 of them have got a theological training in a University (all of them of foreign Theological Universities: Cairo, Medina, Jartum…).

5. Chaplains.

Chaplaincy in the armed forces is led by a state-financed Lutheran Chaplain General who has 25 full-time, 13 part-time, and five fee-paid army chaplains

---

156 Source: official data from the Finnish National Centre of Statistics
157 Source: official data from the Spanish Embassy in Helsinki
158 http://www.sine.fi/
159 *Etnisten suhteiden neuvottelukunta*

as his subordinates. There are also part-time Orthodox chaplains in the Army but there is no known Muslim chaplain in the armed forces.

Most of the spiritual work carried out in the 26 prisons in Finland is State-funded. In 1999, there were 17 full-time priests working in prisons. Sixteen were Lutherans and one of them was Orthodox. They were appointed by their own churches but their salaries were paid by the state. Additionally, there are some Lutheran deacons working in the prisons paid by the Lutheran church, and volunteers who represent various denominations. There were 3541 prisoners in 2008, 7, 8% of them are foreigners, but there are no figures according to their faith.

Most hospital counsellors are supported by congregations or parish unions. Those persons appointed to be chaplains participate in training courses and work supervision offered by the Church Education Centre to supplement their basic degrees[160].

Muslim organisation have not provided chaplaincy systematically in these institutions. So far some institutions have produced guidelines and information booklet about Islam.

6. Islam in schools.

Religion education in Finish schools is non confessional, but instruction is given in the religion of the pupils. According to the Religious Freedom Act of 2003, Students belonging to a registered religious community are given religious education in comprehensive and upper secondary schools, if there are at least three pupils belonging to the same religious community and their parents request it[161]. Muslim parents, in groups of three or more, are therefore entitled to ask for Islamic religion for their sons or daughters.

The communal school system is responsible for its organisation and funding. Students who do not belong to a church or religious community participate in world view studies (ethics). In the matriculation examination, it is possible to take either a test of one's own religion or of world view studies. The increasing number of the students representing different cultures has created a need to train teachers for Muslim religious education[162].

There are 2.963 schools in Finland, 2.934 of which are public schools and only 29 private (8 Christians and 1 Jewish). The Islamic Society of Finland

---

[160] HEIKKILÄ, M., KNUTILA, J., SCHEININ, M, . "State and Church in Finland" in *State and Church in the European Union.* Second Edition, Ed. Nomos, Baden-Baden 2005. p. 533, 534.

[161] Under the previous Law on Religious Freedom the exemption from Lutheran religious education required a request by the family of students who are members of the Lutheran Church. Instead they are now automatically exempt unless the family wishes to sign up for education in the Lutheran Religion

[162] *Op. Cit.* p. 525-529.

had a private religious school in Helsinki from 2001 to 2005 but the school did not gain official status and was not financially viable[163].

III. TRAINING CENTRES FOR IMAMS

There is not any imam training centre in Finland. Imams living in Finland have studied in foreign universities such as Cairo, Medina, Jartum, Pakistan…[164].

There are 3 Theological Faculties: in Helsinki, Joensuu and Turku. Lutheran and Orthodox priests must have a degree in theology.

Arabic and Islamic studies are offered at the University of Helsinki. Courses on Islam can be found in several disciplines at the universities of Helsinki and Turku and in ABo Akadem University. Since 2007, the Department of Comparative Religion of the University of Helsinki offers a course about training religious teachers. It leads to formal qualification as a Religious teacher in Finland.

In autumn 2008, the International Organisation for Migration has developed a pilot project called *"Integration: A multifaith approach"* in Finland, Denmark, Germany, Latvia and United Kingdom. The project is testing the usefulness of civic education for migrant religious leaders as a tool for the integration of migrants.

---

[163] MARTIKAINEN, T.: "FINLAND" in *Yeearbook of Muslims in Europe...op. cit* p. 121.

[164] Source: official data from the Spanish Embassy in Helsinki.

FRANCE

I. RELIGION AND STATE

1. Administrative bodies that have contact with denominations

The *Bureau central des cultes* (Denominations Central Bureau)[165], is the administrative body in charge of relations with denominations. It is under the *Sous-direction des affaires publiques et de la vie associative* (Sub-Directorate for Public Liberties) which is part of the *Direction des libertés publiques et des affaires juridiques* (Directorate of Public Liberties and Justice Affairs) at the Ministère *de l'Intérieur, de l'Outre-Mer et des collectivités territoriales* (Ministry of Interior, Over-seas and Sub national Entities).

The *Conseiller pour les Affaires Religieuses* (Adviser for Religious Affairs) is under the Ministry of Foreign and Europeans Affaires *(Ministère des Affaires Étrangéres et Européennes)*. This body was created after First Wold War when relations with the Holy See improved after the Catholic Church's refuse of Law of 1905 and also in the context of French mandate in Syria and Lebanon.

Also within the MFA, the *Direction de la Prospective* (Policy Planning Directorate) holds a *Pôle religions* (Religions Team), headed since June 2009 by Joseph Maila, former rector of the Catholic Institute of Paris and former director of the French Centre of Research for Peace and the French Mediation and Negotiation Training Institute. The *Pôle religions* works in coordination with the Adviser for Religious Affairs. The *Pôle* has three fundamental missions: to observe and analyse the evolution of religions in a globalised world; to provide support to the Ministry of Foreign Affairs on various current events and issues which contain a religious dimension; and to help diplomatic personnel hone their understanding of religious questions and to raise awareness of the impact that religion has on major international relations issues.

---

165 Directed by Bertrand Gaume 23/12/2010

2. Recognition of religions

Law of 1905, after recognizing freedom of conscience and guaranteeing free exercise of religion for the individuals (art.1), affirms that the Republic doesn't recognize, fund or subsidize any religion (art. 2). This expression means the end of the status of the "recognised churches" (Catholics, Protestants, and Jews) and the beginning of the Separation between State and churches, which ceased to be public institutions and become part of the private sector.

But even if the Republic is not allowed to fund or subsidize religious groups, it will ensure religious freedom of individuals living in public institutions. That's why the Law of 1905 admits public funding of "chaplaincy services designed to assure the free exercise of religion in public establishments" such as schools, prisons, hospitals… (art. 2). So besides that ban of funding religions, the system provides for support mechanism such as the possibility of creating religious associations as we will see, tax benefits, chaplaincy funded by the State and financial support for the maintenance of places of the maintenance of places of worship.

On the other hand, even if the law of 1905 wanted to make religion a private issue, and therefore public powers shouldn't define *a priori* what a religion is, in practice, even avoiding a general definition, the judges (*Conseil d'Etat, Cour de Cassation, and sometimes also Conseil constitutionel)* ended up deciding if a group is entitled or not to receive one of the legal status that religious groups adopt.

On March 15th 2004 a law was passed which bans pupils in primary and secondary schools to wear symbols which obviously show a religious membership[166]. The headscarf issue emerged in the public arena during the 1980s with the increased visibility of *hiyabs* worn by Muslim girls in public places. The French president set up an investigative committee known as Commission *Stasy* in July 2003. That Commission released a report on December 11th 2003, stating that wearing conspicuous religious symbols violated the secular principle of *laicité* in the French school system. On this basis, the law on secularism and religious symbols in state schools was passed on March 2004.

[166] Art. 1 : « *The wearing of symbols and apparel by which a student conspicuously expresses religious affiliation in public schools is prohibited. The rules of procedure provide for conciliatory dialogue before disciplinary action is taken against an offending student"*

3. Legal structure of religious groups.

a) Religious associations (*associations cultuelles*), under Law of 1905

The law of 1905 suppressed all public church establishments, but it maintained that those religious places might be functioning in the future under a new type of associations: religious associations (*associations cultuelles*) that must have religious targets. As those *associations cultuelles* were capable of receiving the property of the former public church establishments, since 1906, Protestants and Jews created these types of organizations. But Catholic Church did not: they refused to accept the Law of 1905.

While the law of July 1st 1901 on associations required two persons to create an association, according to the law of 1905 the number of followers required to create a religious association (*association cultuelle*) depend on the city: if the village has less than 1000 inhabitants, 7 signatures are required, if it is a town between 1000-20000, 15 citizens are required; and if the town has more than 20.000 inhabitants, 25 persons were necessary to create a "religious association". Those people should be over 18 years old and they must be residents in the place (department or *arrondisment*) where the association is seated.

The agreement or declaration to create an *association cultuelle* must be held before the *prefecture* of the department or before the *sous-préfecture* of the *arrodissment* where the association has its seat. This declaration must contain: the name of the association; its targets, which should be religious; the seat; the names, professions, and addresses of the administrators; the bounds within the religious association is going to act. Besides the declaration, they must present their bylaws.

Within five days, the religious group must be given a receipt. And, in one month, a summary regarding the religious association must be published in the *Journal officiel.* Any modification in the associations bylaw, administrators, addresses, seat etc. must also be declared before those organs of the Public Administration. The *Prefect* or *Sous prefect* don't make any statement of acceptance or assessment of the association believes. They just receive the requirements required.

But, as a matter of fact, the acceptance by public powers of that group as an *association clultuelle* is done *a posteriori* whenever the association demands legal benefits, for example, the reductions over donations in the income tax[167].

---

[167] A.A.V.V. (2005): *Droit des cultes. Personnes, activités, biens et structures,* Paris, Ed. Juris Associations, p.437-438.

In other words, if an association wants to be declared *cultuelle* (religious association) it is up to the Public Powers to decide (normally tax administration[168]).

b) Regular associations (*associations de Droit commun)* under Law of 1901

Catholic Church refused to put the Law of 1905 into practice because of the opposition of the Holy See fearing the emergence of uncontrolled *associations cultuelles,* some of them claiming to be catholic being heretic (according to religious authorities), some of them under control of laity. Even when the same law established that this new kind of religious associations should follow the general organization rules of the religion they claim to belong (art. 4), this formula was not accepted by Catholic Church, who also regretted not being specifically mentioned in the Law.

In order to fill this legal void, Law of January 2th 1907 provided that the public exercise of religion could be held by associations created under the law of 1 July 1901. Law of 1901 allows setting up associations of different purposes (educational, cultural…), religious included.

A lot of Muslim communities have chosen this legal figure and set up cultural associations. Nevertheless, alongside Koranic schools, which normally are cultural associations, there is always a mosque. The difference between religious (*cultuelle)* and cultural associations is not only the law to which they are linked (law of 1905 the first, law of 1901 the latter) but also the tax benefits. Associations are formed by depositing its statutes at the *Préfecture* (or *Sous prefecture)*. As soon as they have been accepted, they acquire legal capacity as associations. They can also be recognised by decree if they are declared as being "of public utility".

c) Diocesan associations (*associations diocésaines*)

After First World War, relations between Church and State improved. France re-established diplomatic relations with the Holy See. In September 13th 1923, the *Conseil d'État,* accepted that Catholic Church could establish diocesan associations (*associations diocésaines*). This idea was also backed by Pius XI.

Since 1924, French bishops have created *associations diocésaines* which are *associations cultuelles*, complying with the Laws of 1901 and 1905, and Canon Law, and are therefore under the authority of the bishop and in communion with the Holy See.

---

168 GARAY, A. (2009): "La reconnaissance des cultes religeux en France au regard de la fiscalité applicable" in *Anuario de Derecho Eclesiástico del Estado*, vol. 25, pp. 490-492.

Regarding ownership of church buildings, the Laws of January 2nd 1907 and of April 3rd 1908 transferred the ownership of existing Catholic churches buildings and the responsibility for their repair to the State. Property of cathedrals and bishops houses should be transferred to the State and property of parish churches and presbyteries should be transferred to the *communes*. By contrast, after 1924, maintenance of new places of worship fell within the responsibilities of the *associations diocésaines*[169].

d) Religious Orders (*congregations*)

It wasn't easy for the religious orders in 19th century; a law or decree was required for their legal existence though most of them existed without such authorisation. The purpose of the Law of 1901 was to abolish religious orders: it declared prohibited all religious orders which had not received this legal recognition, but Parliament systematically rejected every request for recognition. A great part of the religious orders established abroad.

In 1914 the unauthorised orders returned to France. They were illicit but not persecuted. The Law of April 8th 1942 conceived them as licit. The process of authorisation was simplified: a decree of the *Conseil d'État* was required. In 1987 the legal recognition was opened to non-Catholic orders.

e) Companies or foundations.

Assistance and health care are normally State services, but some churches also carry out humanitarian assistance and to this proposal they run out organizations of a religious character dedicated to providing care, such as hospitals, asylums, schools etc

Sometimes they cooperate in this regard with the public authorities. Normally these religious organizations operate in this realm as private sector. Private hospitals of a religious character can adopt the legal form of foundations, declared to be of public utility by decree of the *Conseil d'État* or companies, or associations under Law of 1901.

f) *¿dérives sectaires?*

French law doesn't define what a religion is. Therefore, for long time legislator declined to legislate about the so-called sects. But judges refused to give some groups the tax benefits that entitles to religious entities (*associations cultuelles*). The law of June 12th 2001 introduced in the Penal Code various means to fight against those groups that appear to be religious but don't respect

---

[169] BASDEVANT-GAUDEMET, B. "State and Church in France" in *State and Church in the European Union* Second Edition, Ed Nomos, Baden-Baden 2005. pg. 164

public order or fundamental rights of others. A decree of November 28th 2002 created the Miviludes (*Mission interministérielle de vigilance et de lutte contre les derives sectaires)*: an interministerial commission for surveillance and fight against the so-called *dérives sectaires*

The regime defined by the law of 1905 does not apply neither in the Rhine and Moselle departments (Alsace and Moselle), which were part of Germany in 1905, where recognised denominations are organised within the framework of public law and financed by the public powers (State and towns) nor in the overseas territories.

II. ISLAM IN FRANCE

The presence of Islam in France is the result of different migration waves that started in the second half of the 20th century. Until World War I, Islam was a colonial fact with almost no impact in metropolitan France. In World War I, men from Algeria, Morocco and Tunisia served in the French army and this led to the arrival in France of immigrants from these countries. During the Algerian war of independence, up to 160.000 Algerians were soldiers in the French army. When the war ended (1962) there were reprisals against those soldiers who remained in Algeria and many of them found refuge in France. The number of these ex-soldiers (called *harkis*) and their families who arrived in France between 1962-8 is estimated in 91.000[170]

Policies encouraging migration to a metropolis eager of labour force facilitated the increase of the number of Muslims arriving mostly from Algeria (330.000 in metropolitan France by 1962)[171]. It was a male dominated migration of low skilled work force with tendency to ratatio. Moroccan migration begins to arrive in the sixties consolidating its numbers in the mid 70s (260.000 Moroccans in France by 1975)[172].

The 1973 crisis and the hardening in the requirements to enter the country facilitated the settlement of the so-called "guest workers" who brought their

[170] ZWILLING, A-L.: "France" in V.V.A.A. *Yearbook of Muslims in Europe...op. cit.* p.128.
[171] Report *L'Islam dans la Republique*, Haut Conseil a l'Integration, 2000.
[172] *Op. cit.*

families from their countries[173]. The 70s welcomed the arrival of important numbers of migrants from Turkey[174] and Western Africa who would diversify the scenario of Islam in France. Muslim population in France is currently made up basically of immigrant with North African background (Algeria, Morocco and Tunisia), people from Turkey, Sub-Saharan Africa and their children born in France. There are also South Asians and people from the Middle East and, since the wars in the Balkans (1991-2001), Bosnians and Albanians.

Islam would remain a hidden socio religious reality, what has been called the *Islam des caves* (the Islam of cellars), until the beginning of the 90s, when the French government realized the need of bringing it out and help to support its integration in the Republic. Nowadays, Islam practise seems to be increasing.

1. Legal recognition of Islam.

Islam practice, as for the rest of the denominations, is governed by the 1905 law that states that the Republic guarantees freedom of conscience and free worship but it doesn't recognise neither pay nor fund, any denomination. Muslim institutions representing Islam and funding of worship places fall within this framework.

Most of them usually adopted the form of *associations culturelles* (cultural associations) under the law of 1901. A cultural association may engage in profit-making activity. Although a cultural association is not exempt from taxes, it may receive government subsidies for its cultural and educational operations, such as schools. According to some statistics, approximately 30 of 1,050 Muslim associations have tax-benefits[175].

In the Alsace-Moselle region, the regime pre-1905 law established a system of recognised cults. Islam is not among these recognised denominations. The 1905 law doesn't apply neither in the overseas *departements* nor in the

---

[173] In 1974 the Government passed a law allowing the families of immigrants to join them, so many children and wives moved to France.

[174] After France and the Turkish govenement signed a labour agreement in 1966, a large number of Turks began to migrate to Franc: 18.000 in 1970, 200.000 in the early 90s and 450.000 by 2005 ZWILLING, A-L.: "France" in V.V.A.A. *Yearbook of Muslims in Europe...op. cit.* p.129.

[175] Data from the *France International Religious Freedom Report 2007,* US Secretary for Democracy and Global Affairs, Bureau of Democracy, Human Rights, and Labour. Online edition: http://www.state.gov/g/drl/rls/irf/2007/90175.htm

French Guyana. The first have a concordat regime that allows other religions besides the Catholic to enjoy certain rights, whereas the latter is governed by a royal ordinance of 1828 that assures the funding of the Catholic religion from the public budget.

2. The Muslim population.

Although official statistics on religious affiliation are forbidden in France[176], according to a report from the Ministry of Foreign Affairs[177], the number of Muslims in France was estimated in 2007, 5 million people, making of Islam the second religion of France. Last complete general population census (2010) stated that the total population of France was 64.7 millions[178].

Different polls and surveys that have been carried out by companies on the past years estimate that the number of Muslims in France fluctuates from 5 to 6 million people[179]. These estimates are based on statistics regarding the country of origin of migrants and include second and third generations.

---

[176] Since 1982, it has been forbidden for a cencus to identify people according to religious affiliation. The revised law of January 6th 1978 forbids the collection of any data providing personal information on issues like racial or ethnic origin, philosophical, religious or political opinions or beliefs, union membership, data regarding to health or sexual life of the people (art. 8).

[177] Ministère des Affaires Étrangères *Infosynthese: La France à la loupe. Le culte musulman en France*, March 2007.
http://www.botschaft-frankreich.de/IMG/culte_musulman.pdf

[178] Data available from the Institut national de la statistique et des études économiques: http://www.insee.fr/fr/themes/document.asp?reg_id=98&ref_id=ip1276 (accessed December 24th 2010)

[179] Last SOFRES poll estimated the number of Muslims inhabitants in 2007 in France to be 6-9% out of a population of 64 million people. The same results were published by the *Institut National d'Études Démographiques* survey of 2006. This study showed that Muslim population is primarily located in the Ile de France region and the north of metropolitan France. On the other hand, CIA World Factbook estimates Muslim population to be between 5% and 10% of the total population (*CIA World Factbook*, online edition: https://www.cia.gov/library/publications/the-world-factbook/geos/fr.html#People. Last updated 12/07/2010).

3. Muslim representative organizations

In the beginning of the 1990s, the French government decided "to bring French Islam out of de cave" in reference to the *Islam des caves* that had prevailed until the late 80s. The main objective was creating an institution that could be the interlocutor of the Muslim community before the French State for all questions regarding worship.

The process began with the set up of the *Conseil de Reflexión sur l'Islam* (CORIF) by Pierre Joxe in 1989. Members of the CORIF were appointed by the ministry and their duty was to make proposals to the government (eg: Muslim spaces in cemeteries, *halal* food in the army…). In 1995 the CORIF was dismantled by the interior ministry Charles Pasqua who decided to rely solely in the Great Mosque of Paris, attached to Algeria. In 1999, Jean-Pierre Chevènement, former interior Ministry in Jospin´s government, organised an assembly for a query called *Al Istichâra*, formed by the six big independent mosques[180], six Muslim federations[181] and six Muslim intellectuals[182]. This was the basis of the future *Conseil Français du Culte Musulman* (French Council of Muslim Religion –CFCM-[183]).

In 2001, the members of this consultation came out with a proposal for the election of a representative body of Islam in France. The Ministry of Interior, Nicolas Sarkozy, supported the initiative and in June 2003, the *Conseil Français du Culte Musulman* was established after an election process at the *Conseils Régionaux du Culte Musulman* (CRCM). Elections included 995 worship places that designated 4032 electors based on the worship places area. From the 1500 worship places registered in France, 24,6% refused to participate or didn't have the minimum conditions established for it. Among the electors, 86% voted.

The CFCM is composed of delegates from the 25 CRCMs, representatives of the main mosques in France, and 10 Muslim prominent figures. The 25 CRCMs are formed by representatives of associations managing worship places as well as local religious leaders. The executive bureau of CFCM is composed

---

[180] Centre Culturel islamique d'Évry, Mantes-la-Jolie Mosque, Grande Mosquée de Lyon, Grande Mosquée du sud de la France, Grande Mosquée de Saint-Denis-de-la-Réunion

[181] Grande Mosquée de Paris, Union des Organisations Islamiques de France, Fédération Nationale des Musulmans de France, Invitation et Mission pour la Foi et la Pratique, Tabligh et Daoua Il Allah, Fédération Française des Associations Islamiques d'Afrique, des Comores et des Antilles and Union Turco-islamique d'affaires théologiques en France.

[182] Saada Mamadou BA., Souheib Bencheich, Cheick Khaled Bentounès, Eric Geoffroy, Betoule Fekkar-Lambiote and Mohsen Ismail.

[183] http://www.cfcm.tv/

by 16 members. There's a president and two vice presidents, one of them is in charge of coordinating CRCMs activities and the other's aim is coordinating CFCM's working commissions. The general assembly meets once a year and is integrated by 194 people: 150 of them are elected by the CRCMs, 24 are members of the federations, 10 of them are representatives of the main mosques and 10 persons are qualified figures.

The CFCM has concerns regarding issues such as mosque construction, sections of Muslim burial in cemeteries, halal slaughter, nomination of chaplains for hospitals, prisons and schools, imam's training, organization of the *hajj* etc. Although it has been blocked for a long time due to internal debates and power struggles among the three federations and the ideological and national tendencies they represent, its role in the process of institutionalising Islam in France cannot be overlooked.

In order to fund some of CFCM's activities, a foundation was created in 2007: Foundation for the works of Islam in France (*Foundation pour les oeuvres de l'Islam de France*). The foundation was set up to finance mosque construction and restoration, imam's training and financing the CFCM's through the management of private donations. It is a private institution governed by the 1905 law.

CFCM was set up to represent Islam at a national level, but even if it is recognized by the French government its real capacity to represent French Muslims has been questioned by Muslims themselves. It's formed by the main Muslim federations in France (UOIF, FNMF, GMP and CCMTF)

Mohammed Moussaoui, from the *Rassemblement des musulmans de France* (RMF), associated with Morocco, was elected president of the CFCM in the 2008 elections. The RFM was born in 2005, split from the *Fédération Nationale des Musulmans de France* (FNMF), out of the opposition to the movement headed by Bechari, within the framework of CFCM's 2005 complicated elections. Imam's training and chaplaincies are among the main objectives of the organization. RMF pleads for the emergence of a moderate Islam, tolerant and respectful with the French Republic's laws.

The *Fédération de la Grande Mosquée de Paris* (FNGMP)[184] was created in 2003 depending on the *Grand Mosquée de Paris.* This mosque, funded by the Algerian State, was created after World War I (1916). It gathers more than 250 local associations and has a largely Algerian membership. Its director, Dalil Boubakeur, has been CFCM's president until 2008, when they decided not to participate in the elections on the grounds of the election criteria based

[184] http://www.mosquee-de-paris.org/

on the area of worship places. Seats on the Council are granted according to the ground area of each mosque, which benefits well off communities.

The already mentioned *Fédération Nationale des Musulmans de France* (FNMF), representing mainly Moroccan interests, is headed by Mohamed Bechari. The FNMF was founded in 1985 in opposition to Algerian influenced Paris Great Mosque. It gathers associations related to Morocco and Turkey. The FNMF was the main federation in 2005 CFCM elections. The federation controls several mosques in the Parisian suburbs and the East of France.

The *Union des Organisations Islamiques de France* (UOIF)[185], supported by the Muslim Brotherhood's and the Islamic World League founded by Saudi Arabia, represents an orthodox tendency. The UOIF, presided by Lhaj Thami Breze, has established alliances with other Muslim organizations in France, not only with Comorians and Africans (*Fédération Francaiçe* des *Associations Islamiques de l'Afrique et les Antilles*, created in 1989), but also with the Turks from *Millî Görüş*. The UOIF manages around 30 mosques and 200 associations among which *Ligue Française de la Femme Musulmane*[186], *Jeunes Musulmans de France*[187]and the university union *Etudiants musulmans de France*.

The *Comité de coordination des musulmans turcs de France* (CCMTF) was the third most voted list in 2008 CFCM's elections. Turkish Islam in France is primarily located in the Alsace, Rhône-Alpes, Franche-Comté and Ile de France region, CCMTF is in fact representative of the *Union turco-islamique d'affaires théologiques en France* (controlled by the Dyanet). They have some contacts with other branches of Turkish Islam as the *Milli Görüs* movement (related to Erbakan's islamist party who do not depend on the *Diyanet*) and the Kaplanci radical movement. Franck Frégosi[188] characterises CCMTF message as representing a static and ethnic Islam.

The *Association Tabligh et Dawa ilillah* and the *Association invitation et mission pour la foi et la pratique* belong to the *Tabligh* (the Muslim pietistic movement originated in Pakistan) have their headquarters in Saint Denis (Seine Saint Denis) and in Clichy (Hauts-de-Seine). They were created respectively in 1972 and in 1985 and one of their objectives is to preach for the return of mi-

---

[185] http://www.uoif-online.com/v3/
[186] http://www.lffm.org/
[187] http://jmf-la-courneuve.blogspot.com/
[188] This expert in Islam is the Principal Researcher of the *Centre National de Recherche Scientifique*, PRISME unity, *Université Robert Schuman*, Strasbourg and is in charge of the *Observatoire du religieux*. A great part of his research work deals with the ways of expression and organization of Islam in contemporary Europe.

grant Muslim workers to religious practice. Both of them are part of the CFCM and are managed as religious brotherhoods.

There are also some Sufi orders, including groups such as the Murid Tarikas[189], from Senegal and Mali, the Tarika Naqshbandiyya[190], mostly Turkish, and the Alawiyya Tarika, of Algerian origin[191].

In the beginning of 2009, an attempt to create a new umbrella group to represent secular Muslims is searching for President´s Sarkozy support. Muslim secularists have tried many times in the past to form their own council, but their plans have never materialized[192].

4. Mosques

An official survey[193] about Muslim worship places from 2007 detected 1850 registered mosques and praying rooms. Thirty of which can accommodate 1000 people or more. Two *départements* didn't have any registered praying place: Côtes-d'Armor and la Lozère[194].

In 2008, Didier Leschi[195] presented a study that shows a fast progression in the construction of Muslim worship places: from 500 mosques in 1985, to 1.200 in 1992, 1.600 in 2004 and 1.850 in 2007 (only registered worship

---

[189] http://www.acrim.org/

[190] http://www.naqshbandi.fr/

[191] ZWILLING, A-L.: "France" in V.V.A.A. *Yearbook of Muslims in Europe...op. cit.* p.132.

[192] Information from Euro-islam.net, 19/03/2009: http://www.euro-islam.info/2009/03/19/umbrella-group-to-represent-secular-muslims-creates-divisions/. Euro-Islam.info is an active network of researchers and scholars who conduct comparative research on Islam and Muslims in the West and disseminate key information to politicians, media, and the public. Sponsored by GSRL Paris/CNRS France and Harvard University, the Euro-Islam research network is recognized in political and media circles as the most reliable online reference for Islam in Europe.

[193] Information provided initially by the French Ministry of Interior through the Senate of France. Published in JO Sénat 03/05/1990, page 987, but updated by the *Bereau Central des cultres*

[194] Some defend that attendance to mosques in France is governed by ethnic and national criteria (Interview with F. Frégosi commenting on RFM´s victory in 2008 CFCM´s elections). Le Monde, 10/06/2008.

[195] Didier Leschi was the Chef du Bureau Central des Cultes at the Ministry of Interior, (2004-2008).

places). Among all, the Turkish community appears to be the first in the ownership of worship places in France[196].

The last updated yearbook of Muslim worship places[197]registers 2.415 references, including mosques (1100) and praying rooms (1315).

5. Imams.

There are around two thousands imams in France. According, the percentage of French imams is around 20% from whom roughly 50% speak French. Moroccan imams account for 38% of Muslim preachers, 25% being Algerians, 15 % Turks, 10% Tunisians and 12 % from Africa and Middle East.

In 2004 Parliament passed a law allowing the expulsion of individuals for "inciting discrimination, hatred or violence against a specific person or group of persons." According to the Ministry of Interior, 17 Islamic activists were expelled in 2006, including at least 4 imams, for promoting "propaganda in favour of radical Islam and inciting hate or violence." French law permits the revocation of acquired citizenship and expulsion of individuals that have incited hate or violence[198].

Most imams working in mosques managed by the CCMTF (Turkish origin) are paid by Turkey. As CCMTF´s president, Haydar Demiryurek, explains, their imams are government employees but they don't interfere with the federation's management. Their duties are related mainly to lead worship, religious counselling and children education.

---

[196] LALOUETTE, J. and SORREL C. eds. (2008): *Les lieux de culte en France. 1905-2008*, Éditions Letouzey et Ané, p. 24. Record of the Symposium of the Savoie and Paris 13 Universities (17/11/2006 and 16-17/01/ 2007). The publication collects the papers of the participants preceded by the introduction and two texts of Didier Leschi, director of the Bureau des Cultes (Ministry of Interior) at the moment.

[197] http://www.annuaire-musulman.com (accesed December 25th 2010)

[198] US Secretary for Democracy and Global Affairs, Bureau of Democracy, Human Rights, and Labor *France International Religious Freedom Report 2007* Online edition: http://www.state.gov/g/drl/rls/irf/2007/90175.htm

6. Chaplains.

Article 2 of the 1905 law establishes that chaplain services that assure religious freedom in public institutions such as schools, hospitals and prisons can be paid out of the state budget. The French Council of the Muslim Faith (CFCM) is, since its creation in 2003, the institution in charge of choosing Muslim chaplains. Chaplains are under the supervision of both the administrative authorities of the French state and the religious ones of the CFCM. It's the administrative authorities who may provide the chaplain's salaries although at the moment only part of them are paid by the state and others volunteer. It is the administration who establishes the conditions in which chaplains work.

By 2006, the CFCM *Commission aumônerie* had chosen its three national chaplains: Abdelkader Arbi as *Aumônier National Musulman des Armées* (National Muslim Chaplain for the Army, 2005), Moulay el Hassan El Alaoui Talibi for prisons (2006) and Abdelhaq Nabaoui as *Aumônier Musulman National des Hôpitaux de France* (National Muslim Chaplain for the Hospitals of France in 2006). Among the roles of these General Muslim Chaplains we can mention the following: to evaluate and satisfy the needs of Muslim chaplaincy, to recruit and manage chaplains who master their duties and adhere to republican values, and to answer the questions rose by the administration and the professionals in the exercise of their practice[199].

Military chaplains are responsible for providing religious support to the army staff. They hold the officer grade and need to have French nationality. At the end of 2007, Abdelkader Arbi had already appointed 12 Muslim chaplains with the objective of raising the number up to 40 by 2010.

To become chaplain in hospitals it is compulsory to hold a certificate from the *Aumônerie Nationale*. This National Chaplaincy appoints the regional chaplains who, together with the Regional Councils of the Muslim Faith and the support of the General Chaplain, appoint local chaplains. Among the requirements set up by the *Aumônerie Musulmane des Hôpitaux de France* to become chaplain these requirements are required: to be an upright person with good morality, to have listening and exchange capacities, to have a medium comprehension of Islam far for extremisms and to succeed the training proposed by the *Aumônerie Musulmane*[200].

---

[199] Official blog of the Aumônerie musulmane des Hôpitaux de France: http://aumonerie-musulmane.over-blog.com/

[200] *Op. cit.*

Internal power struggles in the CFCM made it difficult to appoint one National Chaplain for prisons. In 2005 Moulay El Hassan El-Alaoui Talibi, former *Aumônier régional du Nord de la France* for 5 years was appointed for the charge. Data from 2005 showed that out of 185 prisons and 918 chaplains, only 69 of them were Muslims (7, 5%). Taking into account that this surveys estimate 65% of prisoners to be Muslims[201], it appears that Muslim chaplaincy in prisons is still weak. In 2007, the Muslim Chaplaincy for prisons counted 77 chaplains full time and 28, half time.

7. Islam in public schools.

The freedom of education as a constitutional principle established in the 1946 and 1958 Constitutions is governed by a series of 19th century laws. Generally speaking, there are three kinds of school in France:

- Private schools without a contract with the State: they don't receive financial assistance from the State and they can organise themselves as they wish.

- Private schools with a contract with the State: they receive public funding to cover up to a tenth of their costs.

- Public schools

Public education is secular and no religious education is allowed to be taught. In primary schools, no religion course can be organised, whereas in secondary schools religion can be taught by chaplains (not during the school timetable). So, chaplaincies can be created at secondary level (*colleges* and *lycées*) but not in primary schools. Until 2004, no Islamic chaplaincy operated in any public secondary schools[202].

Due to its history, the Alsace-Lorraine region has a different legal system that doesn't include the principle of *laicité*. The region is still under the pre-1905 regime established by the Concordat, which provides for the public subsidy of the Roman Catholic Church, the Lutheran Church, the Calvinist Church

[201] MICHEL, L., BRAHMY B., CANETTI C. and DELBOS V. (2005): *Guide de la pratique psychiatrique en milieu pénitentiaire*, Heures de France, p. 174. There are no official statistics for the number of Muslim prisoners in France. Non official polls and surveys estimate the percentage to be between 60 to 70%, one of the highest in Europe.

[202] Directorate-General for Internal Policies of the Union, Policy Department, Structural and Cohesion Policies, Culture and education: *Study Islam in the European Union: what's at stake in the future*, May 2007

and the Jewish religion as well as public education in those religions. Religion teachers are paid by the public administration as well as the clergy and religious education is part of the general curriculum. The University of Strasbourg offers catholic and protestant theology courses and is planning to open a course on Islamic theology[203].

8. Islamic private schools.

Private confessional education is fully recognised under the December 31st law (Law *Debré*) and also under the Code of Education (L 442). Religion can be taught in these schools. Four private Muslim secondary schools (receiving no public funding) have opened in France in the recent years

The *collège* Réussite was created in 2001 in Aubervilliers as the first secondary Muslim school in France. Its founder is Dhaou Meskine, imam of the Clichy Sous Bois mosque.

The *lycée* Al Kindi has opened 2008 in Lyon. There's also a Muslim kindergarten, the Omar School, located in Bondy.

The *collège* Ibn Khaldoun of Marseille that opened is doors for 2009-2010 courses with two classes of 6th grade.

The Muslim school *Education et Savoir*[204] in Vitry (Val de Marne, Paris suburban region), opened for the course 2009-2010. Regarding to the teaching of Arabic, since 2010 the Muslim School *Institut de Formation de Saint Quentin* in Yveline offers extra curricular teaching of Arabic for children and adults.

As we have just said above, there's a possibility for private education establishments to enter into a contractual relation with the State for the funding of the schools. They can receive public funding to cover up to a tenth of their costs, and possible official recognition of their curriculum and diplomas. According to the Code of Education (art. L141-3), religious education can be given either outside normal hours of schooling, or else as the first or last hours of the day. Religious education is optional for the students and the school cannot discriminate the students because of the option they have made. Contracts can be of two types: either the State pays the school staff (*contrat simple*) or the state pays the staff while local administration also provide funding similar to those given to public schools (*contrat d'association*, the most common).

---

[203] See section III: Training for Imams of this report.
[204] http://www.education-savoir.fr/

There are only two Islamic private schools under a contract of association with the French State. *La Madersa* was the first Muslim school to sign an association agreement with the State in 1990. It is located in *Saint-Denis de la Réunion* (French overseas department) and has 3 kinder garden classes and 2 for primary level. It counts around 130 students. The second place is the *Lycée Averroes* in Lille, opened in 2003. There are others not recognized private confessional schools[205].

III. TRAINING CENTRES FOR IMAMS

There are several institutions dedicated to the study and research on Islamic sciences. We must distinguish between those specifically focused on the training of imams and those who offer a general training with a secular approach.

1. Institutions offering specific training for imams and chaplains

The *Institute de formation des imams et des educateurs* is one of the most well known. This institute belongs to the ***Institut europeen des sciences humaines* (IESH)**, located in Château-Chinon[206]. It was set up by *Département de Dar-alfatwa et de la formation des cadres religieux* of the UOIF in 1991 and has a tight relationship with the *Conseil européen pour la fatwa et la rechérche*, directed by Sheikh Yusuf al Qaradawi who is part of IESH Scientific Board as well[207].

A second branch of this institute was created in 2001 in Paris by Ahmed Jaballah who was the former director of the IESH in Château-Chinon. In contrast to the institute of Château-Chinon, located in a rural area and offering a boarding school system, the Paris centre is an urban institute who proposes training compatible with working duties. Both of them have distance courses. The Paris institute also delivers a certificate on High Theologian Islamic Stud-

[205] Bureau Central des cultes.
[206] http://www.iesh.fr/
[207] The institute has also a branch in the UK (European Institute for Human Sciences, 1997) and another one in the Polish city of Byalstock.

ies (3 years). The imams training program includes two courses on History of the Islam in Europe and Western civilisation. It has signed cooperation agreements with the universities of Rabat and Algiers so that IESH diplomas are recognised in Morocco and Algeria.

In the year 2000, Château-Chinon institute had 120 students, 40% of whom were women and almost 70% French nationals. Training in the UOIF institutes is in Arabic and French. Both institutes are supported by funds coming from the Gulf and Saudi Arabia.

The ***Institut Ghazali*** belongs to the Great Mosque of Paris (GMP) and is linked to Algeria. It offers a four year training for imams and chaplains, delivering a *Diplôme des Sciences Religieuses Islamiques* (4 years studies) and a diploma for chaplains (two years study). The contents of the courses follow the Malikite School. Since 2008 it has established a partnership with the *Institut Catholique de Paris* for complementary training on civil and French law for imams. As a complementary diploma to the one of religious studies organised by Djelloul Seddiki, director of Al Ghazali of the GMP, the course *Religions, laïcité, interculturalité* (400 hours), organised by the Catholic Institute, covers a variety of subjects such as History of the three republican values (freedom, equality and fraternity), Institutions and political life in the French Republic, French Law on religions, Muslim practices in the French Republic, Intercultural practices. The course doesn't include theological aspects. Among the twenty-five students currently enrolled in the first there are 15 military chaplains and 10 foreign imams[208].

The ***Institut superieur de sciences islamiques et de langues*** was founded in 2000 by Sheikh Dhaou Meskine, imam of the Clichy-sous-Bois mosque and General Secretary of the so called *Conseil des imams de France*. As stated by the Sheikh[209], the centre opened with the aim of correcting wrong interpretations and readings of the Sunna. It offers 20 hours per week training for imams and chaplains during the whole year. The academic staff has being trained in Zaitouna (Tunis), al Azhar (Egypt) and Riyadh (Saudi Arabia).

The ***Institut Avicenne des sciences humaines***[210] on Lille was created by Mohamed Bechari, President of the FNMF and Vice president of the CFCM. In 2006 with the support of the city of Lille, it set out a training program for imams including courses of French language and French civilisation.

---

[208] Published in Le Figaro 06/04/2009.

[209] Institut Superieur de Sciences Islamiques et de Langues, official website: http://www.univ-issi.fr/presentation.html.

[210] http://www.avicenne.eu/

The ***Institut Français des Etudes et Sciences Islamiques*** **(IFESI)**[211] is a private centre of Islamic education. It has 3 departments (Arabic Language Department, Quran Department and Islamic Sciences Department) and offers five year studies programs on Doctrine and Thought, Quran and Hadith, Law and Theory of Law, and History of Islam[212].

Until now no Islamic private centre has links with any public institution regarding imam training.

2. Research centres on Islamic sciences

Next to education centres offering specific training courses for imams there are several institutes specialised on Islamic sciences whose aim is to promote intellectual debate and research. They organise seminars, conferences and courses with the participation of religious scholars and leaders as well as academic experts with the aim of contributing to the continuous development of Islamic sciences in Europe.

Among these centres we can mention the ***Institut International de la Pensée Islamique*** **(IIIT)**[213], which was inaugurated in Paris in 2000 as the French branch of the International Institute of Islamic Thought, created in 1981 in EEUU by the Association of Muslim Social Scientists. Its director, Mohamed Mestiri, is specialised on the *laïcité* and the friction between religious authority and religious freedom. In 2002 the IIIT launched the French Forum of Researchers on Islam which have organised several annual congresses since then. It offers a university program on Islamic Interdisciplinary Studies focused on the sources of Islam and has cooperation programs with the University of Marrakesh and Virginia's Fairfax Institute. IIIT´s Education Department proposes two types of training: one represented by the university program mentioned above, and another continuous training course for community leaders, journalists, public officers, imams and chaplains. Subjects of this program cover issues such as Islam and Muslims in Europe: cultural, religious and sociological reference points, Islam sciences, Muslim cultures and contemporary societies, Islamic economy and finance in Europe, Koran sciences, etc…

---

211 http://www.ifesi.fr/

212 HUSSON, J.F. (2006): Pour une formation des imams en Belgique. Points de références en Belgique et en Europe, Brussels, Foundation Roi Baudouin, p. 53.

213 http://www.iiitfrance.net/

The ***Institut des Hautes Etudes Islamiques***[214]was founded in 1994 following the example of its Italian equivalent, the *Comunità Religiosa Islamica* (CO.RE.IS.). Its president, Yahyâ Sergio Yahe Pallavicini, is the son of the well known Italian convert Sufi Shaykh Abd-al-Wâhid Pallavicini. The aim of the institute, created as a study and research group, is to reflect on Islamic tradition and its relation with the contemporary western world. One of its mains concerns is the situation of Islam in the French Republic and the need for the clarification of the principles and practices of Islam.

The ***Centre d'etudes et de recherches sur l'islam* (CERSI)**[215], was created first as the *Université Islamique de France* (1993) and then as the *Institut d'études Islamiques de Paris* (1995). Finally in 2002 it became the CERSI: a centre for the study and research on Islamic sciences which delivers a certificate not recognised by the Ministry of Education. Didier Bourg (member of the FNMF and the Islamic World League) was its founder and Hicham Arafa its current director. Courses in French cover a variety of subjects but they don't offer properly specific training for imams.

In the past years there has been an increasing interest in Islamic Finance that has led to the creation, for the first time in France, of a university diploma in Islamic Finance. The School of Management in Strasbourg offers this *bac +5* which will have 405 teaching hours over a twelve-month period.

The Reims Management School is also launching a specialization program on Islamic Finance called Islamic Banking and Finance. Courses are thought in English and addressed to Master students.

The *Conseil Français de Finance Islamique* (COFFIS) is an organisation that advises financial institutions on Islamic banking according to international standards (AAOIFI, IFRS, IFSB…) based in Paris. It is composed of Shariah Boards from all over the Islamic world and a Fatwa Committee[216].

3. Other projects on imams and chaplains training

There are several projects regarding imam's training, among which the project of a master on Islamology, Religion and Society in Strasbourg which

---

[214] http://www.ihei-asso.org/
[215] http://www.cersi.net/
[216] Its director is Mohamed Nouri, professor of Islamic Economy at the IESH. http://www.coffis.fr/coffis/

have started for the course 2010-2011[217]. Language, law and history aree the three cores of this two year education programme. Although, its objective is not to train imams but to be a research program. As Francis Messner[218] states, the idea is linked with a more ambitious project: to establish a Faculty of Muslim Theology next to those of Catholic and Protestant Theology at Strasbourg's University. The proposal was already launched in the late 80s by Etienne Trocme, former president of Marc-Bloch University, and was taken up again by the Machelon Commission[219] in 2006 with the idea of developing a university education program for religion teachers in Alsace and Moselle.

[217] http://islamologie-strasbourg.fr/

[218] Francis Messner is Director of Research at the CNRS and was a member of the Machelon Comission. In 2006 he deposited (together with other university professors) the statutes of an association for the creation of an education centre of Muslim theology to train chaplains and Muslim religious leaders. The goal was to set up a starting point for a future Institute of Islamic theology financed with public funding.

[219] The Machelon Commission was launched in 2005 by Nicolas Sarkozy as a commission of legal reflection on the relations between religious denominations and public administrations. It was directed by Jean Pierre Machelon, professor at the Rene Descartes University and Studies Director of the Ecole Pratique des Hautes Etudes. A report (*Rapport de la Commission de réflexion juridique sur les relations des cultes avec les pouvoirs publics*) was published in 2006 with a series of guidelines to adapt French laws and administrative procedures regarding the relation State and religions. Some of the recommendations suggested the need to facilitate the construction of worship places, to widen the legal framework within which the *associations cultuelles* work or to assure religious leaders affiliation system to the Social Security.

GERMANY

I. RELIGION AND STATE

1. Administrative bodies that have contact with denominations.

Being a federal State, government tasks of the Federal Republic of Germany are distributed between the Federation and the constituent states *(Länder)*. The German Federal Government does not have a specific state agency competent for religions and their communities.

Under the provisions of the Basic Law of 1949, responsibility for church-state relations primarily lies with the *Länder*[220] and, as a rule, is assigned to the *Länder*'s Ministries of Culture. Nevertheless, other ministries of the *Länder* maintain relations with denominations according to their competence. For example, the Ministry of Social Affairs will deal with chaplaincy in hospitals or the Ministry of Education will attend questions regarding religious teaching in schools or faith schools.

At the federal level, the Federal Chancellery and the Federal Ministry of the Interior have divisions that deal with relations with churches and religious communities, maintain contacts at the working level and prepare political talks.

Other federal ministries, within their sphere of their responsibility, also deal with religious affairs: the Federal Ministry of Defence is in charge of chaplaincy services in the armed forces, the Federal Ministry for Family Affairs, Senior Citizens, Women and Youth deals with minors[221].

---

[220] Article 138 (8) of the Weimar Constitution: "… So far as the execution of these provisions may require further regulation, this is the duty of the Land legislature".

[221] And is also concerned with so-called sects and mind control groups and with the churches' social work KÜSTER, B.: "Administrative and financial matters in the area of religious freedom and religious communities" in *Legal Aspects of Religious freedom* (International Conference, 15-18 September 2008), Ljubljana, 2008, p. 335.

2. Civil recognition of religions in Germany.

The German system allows religious communities to obtain legal status in two ways: under private law[222] or under public law[223].

Under private law, all forms of organization are possible for religious communities. In practice, however, the majority of them opt for the status of a registered association (§§ 21 ss. BGB [Civil Code].

Under public law, a specific feature of German Law is the status of a Public Law Corporation (*Körperschaft öffentlichen Rechts)*. The Basic Law states that those churches and religious communities that were given that status before 1919 may maintain it in the future. But it also declares that such status shall be granted to other religious communities if they guarantee durability by their constitution and the number of their members.

German Law doesn't provide for any register or religious entities as such. There is a Register of Associations (under the competence of Magistrates Courts), that contains all registered associations without any further specification whether they are religious or not. And in respect of Public Law Corporations, the Department of Education of the *Länder* hold registers of all churches and religious communities that have such public status.

Religious communities are not required to be recognized or "registered". Registration is not a condition for being allowed to work in the country as a religious community. Such a requirement would threaten the fundamental right to religious freedom (a fundamental right shouldn't depend on registration to be effective), the right of religious communities to self-determination and also the principle of separation between denominations and the State. There are no stipulated requirements to form a religious community. Nonetheless, the State necessarily cooperates when constituting a church or a religious community as a legal person, for example, when enrolling in the register of associations or granting the status of a Public Law Corporation. That cooperation is limited to the scrutiny of the legal conditions: no margin of discretion or appreciation over doctrine is given to the State.

a) Religious communities as registered associations:

As it has been said, a religious community can choose to organize as a civil association and therefore register in the Register of Associations once it has fulfilled the requirements of the Civil Code (minimum number of 7 mem-

---

[222] Article 140 of the Basic Law and art. 137 (4) of the Constitution of Weimar Republic.
[223] Article 140 of the Basic Law and art. 137 (5) of the Constitution of Weimar Republic.

bers, bylaws containing the association's aims, name and address...)[224]. Once registered, they acquire legal personality so that they can, as the legal organization they are, conclude contracts, be registered as the owner of buildings etc. Registers of associations contains all registered groups without any further specification whether they are religious or not.

However, it is important to differentiate between regular associations and religious ones because some rights can only be enjoyed by religious communities, for instance, the provision of religious instruction at publicly maintained schools. This matter will be considered by the competent public authorities and in case of dispute it would be settled by state courts. Assessment of whether an association is a religious community within the meaning of the Basic Law is based on the association's self-perception and also on certain criteria developed in Constitutional Law literature and, above all, by Decisions of the Federal Constitutional Court (*Bundesverfassungsgericht*). This High Court has developed a definition of the term religious community on the basis of a definition already provided under the Weimar Constitution (WRV): "Communities which bring together all members of a religious confession within a defined geographical area for general performance of the tasks required by their shared confession".

There is no minimum size prescribed for religious communities, and these are not obliged to adopt a certain legal form. However, according to the jurisprudence, the term religious community, enshrined in the Basic Law, requires four main features:

1) It must be comprised of natural persons who can be identified as members of the respective church.

2) Certain level of organization. Several persons need to be connected to dedicate themselves to the joint exercise of their religion for a longer period.

3) The main aim of a religious community is exercising a common faith. Other purposes, for instance cultivation of culture and traditions, do not constitute the main target of a religious community. They may be a secondary purpose of a religious community, because the exercise of faith must be the key feature.

---

224 (§§55 ss. [Civil Code] Furthermore, there should be provisions on granting and terminating membership, on fees to be paid by the members, no the constitution of the board and on the convocation of the members assembly (§58). It is the board's duty to deposit a registration request at the Magistrates´Court, which is obliged to register the association if the specified formal requirements are fulfilled. The only control of the association's aims is to prevent that they don't contravene criminal law, constitutional order or the spirit of international friendship (article 9 (2) BL).

4) One difference between religious communities and religious associations could be that the first are fully dedicated to all the tasks their faith entails (exclusive dedication to exercise of faith). By contrast, a religious association is only dedicated to some aspects of religious life.

In order to cooperate with the State a religious group must have clear rules regarding their representative body so that the State can be sure that they are authorized to take binding decisions on behalf of their community. Regarding Muslim communities existing in Germany, it has not yet been established whether or not they have the degree of organizational structure required for qualifying as a religious community. No Muslim organization has yet been acknowledged as a religious community under public law, although a number have applied for this status.

b) Religious communities as public law corporations.

Article140 of the Basic Law, read together with Article 137 (5) of the Weimar Constitution, stipulates that the status of a public law corporation is guaranteed for those religious communities that were recognized as such before the entry into force of the Weimar Constitution (1919). It also declares that other religious communities shall be granted public law corporation status upon their application if their constitution and the number of their members "give assurance of their permanency". The decision on applications for public law corporation status is incumbent on the Federal *Länder*.

According to the practice established by the *Länder*, the requirements to become a public law corporation are as follows:

- Established organization (statutes, constitution as an association)

- Certain level of permanency: as a general rule they must have been active in Germany for at least 30 years.

- Certain number of members: around 1-2 per thousand of the overall population.

- Active participation in local community life

- Sufficient funding.

Furthermore, a religious community applying for public law corporation status needs to abide by the law, which means that it must also guarantee that its future conduct does neither jeopardize the basic constitutional principles described in Article 79 (3) of the Basic Law, nor the basic rights of others protected by the State, or the fundamental principles of Ecclesiastical law also enshrined in the Basic Law. But that does not mean that a specific loyalty of that community to the State is required[225].

If religious groups or communities professing a philosophical creed accomplish these requirements they are entitled under the Basic Law to be granted public law corporation status by the competent Federal *Länder*. If two or more religious communities established under public law unite into a single association, this association will also be a corporation under public law[226].

The status of a corporate body under public law confers certain prerogatives and privileges. The most important one is the right to levy church taxes on their members instead of relying on voluntary contributions: the State is entrusted with this task and also with the transfer of these revenues to the respective Church/religious community. The churches will reimburse the administrative expenses to the State. In practice, the *Länder* use the income tax as the standard to determine the church tax. Tax liability is about 8 to 9 per cent of the income tax: the respective percentage is determined by the churches.

Religious communities which are organized as corporate bodies under public law are also granted exemptions from taxes, charges and fees; they can also have the option of defining the status of their staff members on the basis of either civil law or public law – as public servants of their own kind.

Religious communities organized as corporate bodies under public law are not part of the State organization and are not subject to any State supervision; instead, they are corporations in their own right, they are recognized under constitutional law and they enjoy special privileges. Above all, the corporate body status is not the precondition for a community to be allowed to organize itself and to act as a religious community or to exercise the rights conferred upon all religious communities, such as participating in religious instruction offered at schools, operating social institutions/ facilities, or providing chaplaincy services in public institutions (e.g. in the health care sector or in prisons). A widely held erroneous view is the assumption that only those religious communities that are public law corporations obtain state recognition while other religious communities do not.

Religious communities existing traditionally as corporations under public law are: Protestant Churches (Land Churches, Congregations and Unions), Roman Catholic Church (dioceses, parishes, unions, in instances also communities of religious orders), Jewish congregations, Old Catholic Community,

---

[225] This was stated by the Federal Constitutional Court referring to Jehovah's Witnesses case, 2000

[226] Article140 of the Basic Law read together with Article137(5) Weimar Constitution.

"Old Lutherans" (Autonomous Evangelical Lutheran Church), Baptists and Mennonites (Christian Anabaptists).

Religious communities that were granted this status either after the entry into force of the 1919 Constitution of the Weimar Republic (WRV) or after the entry into force of the 1949 Basic Law are the following: □Liberal Protestant Churches (inter alia Pentecostal Assemblies, Salvation Army); Orthodox Churches (Greek-Orthodox Metropolitanate of Germany, Russian Orthodox Church Outside Russia, Russian Orthodox Church - Moscow Patriarchate, Romanian Orthodox Church); Land Unions of Jewish Congregations, Central Council of Jews in Germany (*Zentralrat der Juden in Deutschland*), various Jewish congregations and/or Israelite religious congregations; New Apostolic Church; Jehovah's Witnesses; Community of the Seventh-Day Adventists; Apostolate of Jesus Christ, a breakaway community from the New Apostolic Church (*Apostelamt Jesu Christi (AJC)*); Church of God, a liberal Protestant (Pentecostal) Church(*Gemeinde Gottes)*; The Christian Community (Lutheran, antroposophy) (*Christengemeinschaft)*; St. John's Church, based on his Revelations (*Johannische Kirche)*; Christian Science (*Erste Kirche Christi, Wissenschaftler*); Union of Liberal Theology Congregations in Germany (*Bund Freireligiöser Gemeinden Deutschlands (BFGD*) ; Liberal theology communities or congregations formed at the Land level; Liberal religious communities: Humanist Congregation of Liberal Protestants (*Humanistische Gemeinde Freier Protestanten*); Liberal Unitarian Congregation (*Unitarische Freie Religionsgemeinde*); Church of Jesus Christ of Latter-Day Saints (Mormons); Freethought Union of Bavaria (*Bund für Geistesfreiheit Bayern*).

Exemption clauses under general employment law are, in principle, applicable to all churches and religious communities. As German law introduced obligatory civil marriage in the 1870s (*Kulturkampf)* religious weddings do not have the effect of civil marriages.

Regarding special burial grounds, only churches and religious communities with the status of public law corporations are entitled[227].

---

[227] MÜCKL, S. : "Religious entities as legal persons-Germany" in *Churches and other organizations as legal persons*, Peeters 2007,p. 113

II. ISLAM IN GERMANY

1. What kind of recognition does Islam have?

Most Muslim organizations in Germany have the legal status of registered associations under the general association law. They do not meet the criteria of religious communities so far, let alone of corporations under public law. But still it is a matter of controversy whether these associations are religious communities in the sense intended by the constitutional law, which is a requirement for having religious teaching in public schools. The only exception is the Alevite Community in Germany, which –meeting the criteria of a religious community according to the German Basic Law– is partner of the *Länder* Nordrhein-Westfalen, Hessen, Baden-Württemberg and Bayern as well as Berlinand Hamburg in providing Alevite religious education in public schools. Various other court cases are pending[228].

Donations to religious communities and charitable associations are tax deductable up to a certain amount and this also applies to Muslim associations. Charitable organizations are in general exempt from corporation tax, trade tax, real state tax and inheritance tax. Muslims organizations can receive public funding for cultural activities, like any other charitable organization[229].

2. The Muslim population.

Initial Muslim presence in Germany follows a pattern similar to other European countries. First Muslims communities to settle in Germany were migrant workers that began to arrive in the 60s through recruitment agreements signed with Morocco, Tunisia and Turkey[230]. The so called guest workers became long term residents from the 1970s onwards, bringing their families with them and thus transforming the social structure of the Muslim community. A second migration wave in the mid 1970s brought an important number of asylum seekers from Iran and Afghanistan and in the 1990s Muslim from the ex Yugoslavia also arrived in Germany.

---

[228] In 1998, the High Administrative Court of Berlin established that the Islamic Federation in Berlin (*Islamische öderation Berlin*) is a religious community, and the Alevy Community in North Rhine-Westphalia has similarily been recognized as a religious community. ROBBERS, G. "Germany" in V.V.A.A. *Yearbook of Muslims in Europe..op cit.* p. 143.

[229] Ibidem.

[230] GOLDBERG, ANDREAS: "Islam in Germany" in HUNTER, SHIREEN (ed.): *Islam, Europe's second religion. The new social, cultural and political landscape*, Preaeger, 2002, p. 29-50.

Due to the lack of a general-central register of religious communities only approximate statistics about the number of Muslims in Germany can be provided on the basis of nationality. A recent survey funded by the Interior Ministry estimates that about 4 million people in the country are Muslim, around 5% of a total population of 82.3 million inhabitants[231]. Regarding their background, the main part (2.561.000) come from Turkey, 550.000 form the East of Europe, 330.00 from the Near East, 280.000 from North Africa, 186.000 from Asia, 70.000 from Iran, 78.000 from the rest of Africa and Central Asia[232]. The number of naturalized Turkish has also increased since the amendment of the law in 1999 so that Muslims with Turkish background are estimated to be 75% of the Muslim population living in Germany.

Muslim communities are mainly located in urban areas especially big cities such as Berlin, Hamburg, Köln and Frankfurt. Before the fall of the Berlin Wall in 1989 there were no Muslim population in the East of Germany and even though some Muslims moved to the eastern industrial cities in the 90s, Muslim population in the eastern part of the country continues to be very small.

Most German Muslims are Sunni (80%), although 17% are Alevi, 3% Shiite and Ahmaddiyyan[233].

Other estimates are based on the organizational and legal structure of churches, basically those who have obtained the public law corporation status. Catholic Church has about 25.7 millions of followers (31 % of the total population) and the Protestant *Landeskirchen* about 25.3 millions of inhabitants (30 %), Orthodox Christians, about 1.4 million (1,2 %) and Jewish, about 200.000[234].

3. Representative organizations of Islam.

According to the poll "*Muslimisches Leben in Deutschland*" about 20 % of Muslims living in Germany are members of a Islamic-religious association such as mosque associations.

---

[231] The survey was released in Berlin by the Interior Ministry on June 22nd, 2009. The poll surveyed 6.000 households with 17.000 residents.

[232] Source: official data from the Spanish Embassy in Berlin (2009).

[233] Source: official data from the Bundesministerium des Innern, 2007.

[234] *2008 Report on International Religious Freedom. Germany*, US Departent of State. http://www.state.gov/g/drl/rls/irf/2008/108448.htm (accessed 20/07/2009).

Turkish Muslim organizations tend to be well organized and most of them work within the framework of more than 10 umbrella organizations[235] that already exist. The biggest one is the Turkish-Islamic Union for Religious Affairs (*Diyanet İşleri Türk İslam Birliği*, DITIB) which was created in 1985 as a result of the Turkish parliament's decision to establish religious centres for Turkish immigrants in Europe. It has around 150.00 members and comprises about 870 mosque organizations[236]. DITIB is headed by a diplomat from the Turkish Embassy in Berlin and imams of the mosques associations belonging to the DITIB are approved and paid by the Turkish State to serve the Turkish community abroad. It is under the guidance and supervision of the Turkish Religious Affairs Office (*Diyanet*) [237] and is regarded as its representative in Germany.

In opposition to the lay approach of the DITIB, other Turkish organizations were created in Germany, among which are the VIKZ and the *Millî Görüş*.

The Union of Islamic Cultural Centres (*Der Verband islamischer Kulturzentren*, VIKZ)[238]founded in 1973 is part of the Süleymanci brotherhood (290 local branches) and about 20.000 members[239].

The *Millî Görüş* (*Islamische Gemeinschaft Millî Görüş* -IGMG-)[240], already present in Europe as an informal network since the 1970s, emerged in Germany as a Diaspora association of the members of *Millî Selamet Partisi*[241]. IGMG is the main member of the umbrella organization Islamic Council for the Federal Republic of Germany *Islamrat* (*Islamrat für die Bundesrepub-*

---

[235] GOLDBERG, ANDREAS: "Islam in Germany" in HUNTER, SHIREEN (ed.): *Islam, Europe's second religion. The new social, cultural and political landscape*, Preaeger, 2002, p. 29-50.

[236] Although is commonly believed that DITIB is a formal representative of Turkey in Germany, some of their members claim that they only have an informal agreement with the Turkish government.

[237] *Diyanet* is the Turkish Religious Affairs Office (*Diyanet İşleri Başkanliği*), created at the beginning of the 20th century by Kemal Atatürk within the new framework of separation between religion and state.

[238] http://www.vikz.de/

[239] FETZER, JOEL S. and SOPER, J. CHRISTOPHER: *Muslims and the State in Britain, France and Germany*, Cambridge University Press, 2005.

[240] http://www.igmg.de/

[241] The *MillîSelamet Partisi* is the political party created in 1972 by Necmettin Erbakan when the former *MillîNizam Partisi* was banned by the Turkish Constitutional Court. Since then various bans have resulted in the reestablishment of the party under different names (*Refah Partisi, Fazilet Partisi* and *Saadet Partisi*). In the mid 1970s, Erbakan published a manifesto called *MillîGörüş* (The National View) explaining his ideology.

lik)[242], founded in 1986. It has 26.500 members and around 274 mosque associations.

Other Turkish organizations currents active in Germany are the *Nurculuk*[243] (a mystical movement associated with the Naqshbandiyya Sufi order that promotes educational centres for the youth) the Turkish Islamic Union in Europe (12.000 members and 125 associations) or the followers of Fetullah Gülen (actively involved in education as well) with around 70 local associations.

The Central Council of Muslims in Germany (*Zentralrat der Muslime im Deutschland*, ZMD) was founded in 1994, although it has a longer organizational tradition, and comprises Muslim organization with different ethnic and religious backgrounds such as Bosnian, Arabic, Albanese and Turkish as well. It has around 12.000 members and it gathers 19 umbrella organizations with their mosque associations[244].

The Alevite community, the majority of whom stems from Turkey as well (a large parte of them of Kurdish background), has two umbrella organizations, of which the biggest one is the 1986 founded association "Alevite Federation of Germany" (*Föderation der europäischen Alewiten* (AABF)[245] with about 20.000 members and 120 organizations.

In 2006, the German Minister of the Interior, Wolfgang Schäuble, launched the German Conference on Islam as a long term process of dialogue involving representatives of the state and the Muslim communities. Its goal is to improve religious and social integration of Muslims in Germany as well as to prevent extremism. The German Conference on Islam constitutes a discussion process at all levels of the German state (federal state, *Länder* and local communities) that strives to achieve a broad consensus on respecting basic principles of social and religious policy. In its first period (2006-2009) the dialogue was structured through 4 working groups that met every two months: German social system and value consensus, Religious issues and the German understanding of the Constitution, Media and private sector as bridge-builders, and Security. The plenary session was made up of 30 permanent representatives: 15 state representatives (Federal Government, *Länder* and local governments), 15 representatives of the largest Muslim organizations in Germany and Muslim individuals who were invited personally. The German Islam Conference is now an established and well accepted dialogue mechanism and will be continued in the current election period.

---

242 http://www.islamrat.de/
243 http://www.jamaatunnur.net/
244 http://www.zentralrat.de/
245 http://www.alevi.com/

After the establishment of the German Islam Conference four of the main Muslim umbrella organizations (The Turkish-Islamic Union for Religious Affairs (DITIB), the Central Council of Muslims in Germany (ZMD), the Union of Islamic Cultural Centres (VIKZ), and *Islamrat* decided to create a coordination platform and established in 2007 the Coordination Council of Muslims (*Koordinierungrat der Muslime in Deutschland* KRM). The KRM is based on internal rules of procedure according to which the four member associations rotate the presidency between them at six-monthly intervals although the sole right of veto rests with the DITIB.

There are also secularist Muslims' associations, such as the Secular and Lay Islamic Citizens in Hesse, a small initiative that advocates for the rights of Muslims from a non-confessional approach.

4. Mosques.

There are approximately around 2600 Muslim places of worship in Germany[246], 150 of these being classic mosques (with dome and minaret)[247] and more than 100 building projects. According to official data, around 500 of them are linked to the *Milli Gourus* movement, 300 to the Suleymanci brotherhodd and 700 to the DITIB[248]. The oldest mosque is the *Ahmadiyya* Mosque in Berlin, which was built in 1924. Another kind of worship place are cem-houses used by the Alevis who don't attend mosques. There are around 110 of these worship places (cems)

---

[246] Source: official data from the Interkultureller Dialog und Deutsche Islam Konferenz Alt-Moabit

[247] *2008 Report on International Religious Freedom. Germany*, Bureau of Democracy, Human Rights, and Labor, Secretary for Democracy and Global Affairs, 2008. http://www.state.gov/g/drl/rls/irf/2008/108448.htm (accessed 20/07/2009).

[248] Data provided by the German Interior Ministry at the 6th meeting of the European Policy Planners' Network on Countering Polarisation and Radicalisation, held in Madrid the 12th of March, 2010.

5. Imams.

There are no official accounts of imams in Germany. In theory, each of the roughly 2,600 mosques in Germany has its own imam. Probably, only some of them act as full time (or professional) imams. The number of volunteer or part-time imams is bound to be much higher. This is so because most mosque communities could hardly afford to pay a full-time imam. Most of the full-time imams come from abroad. In 2007 the number of imams was estimated in 2.250[249].

Various States second imams to care for Muslim migrants living abroad, also in Germany (e.g. Turkey, Morocco, Egypt, Bosnia and Herzegovina). Approximately 700 imams in Germany have been seconded by the Religious Affairs Board of the Republic of Turkey (*Diyanet*). They work in mosques run by the umbrella association Turkish-Islamic Union for Religious Affairs (DITIB).

6. Chaplains.

Article 140 of the Basic Law, read together with Article 141 of the Weimar Constitution, authorizes religious communities to provide religious services and pastoral work in the Armed Forces, hospitals, in prisons or in other public institutions, to the extent that the need for such religious activities exists.

Pastoral work for Muslims has so far only been carried out only in some public institutions, such as prisons. The main reason is that the formal requirements are not sufficiently met so that it has not been possible to make the respective agreements between those running public institutions (the Federal Government, the Federal *Länder* and the municipalities) and Muslim organizations. As we have said above, it has not been clarified whether some Muslim associations constitute religious communities as defined by Article 140 of the Basic Law, read together with Article 141 of the Weimar Constitution.

There are 195 prisons in Germany that hold 75.056 prisoners but not reliable statistics about how many of the prisoners are Muslims.

However, as prison inmates are generally entitled to religious care in line with the freedom of religion enshrined in Article 4 of the Basic Law (as for instance stipulated in Section 36 of the Act on the Legal Status of Soldiers; Sec-

---

[249] Official data from the Bundesministerium des Inner.

tions 53 to 55 of the Prison Act), it is necessary to better cater for the needs of Muslim prison inmates. For this reason, the competent bodies in the Federal Government, the Federal *Länder* and in the municipalities have meanwhile worked out various forms of pastoral care for imprisoned Muslims together with the prison service.

There are about 700 Muslims in the armed forces, but no military chaplaincy equivalent to that provided for other religions has been yet established[250].

7. Islam in schools.

Teaching of Islam in German public schools falls within the constitutional right to religious education. Islam is being taught in different *Länders* and since 2000, different ways of providing Islamic education have been tried to test new possibilities for a religious education for Muslims in Germany.

While in North Rhine-Westphalia, Bavaria and Lower Saxonia it is the State who organizes the religious education, in Berlin and Baden-Württemberg Islamic organizations are involved in the whole process. As an exception, in Berlin the so-called "Turkish Federation" gained responsibility for religious education for pupils of Turkish-Muslim origin in evening courses at state schools. This federation provides religious instruction for about 4.300 Muslim students while the Cultural Centre of Anatolian Alevis teaches Islam to around 200 pupils. Also in Berlin, Turkish consulate offers Muslim instruction under their auspices[251].

Bremen has recently started to provide Islamic culture classes from a non confessional perspective (*Islamkunde*) as a state pilot project without the participation of the Islamic lobby. In many cases Islamic education is provided in classes of Turkish language for migrant children[252]. But the intention is to replace these classes for Islamic instruction in German.

Bavaria, since 1988 has offered Islamic courses during Turkish languages classes. But the tendency is to replace those courses for Islamic courses in German. In Lower Saxony Islamic instruction is provided in Turkish and

---

[250] ROBBERS, G. "Germany" in V.V.A.A. *Yearbook of Muslims in Europe...op cit.* p. 147

[251] *Ibidem* p. 145.

[252] DASSETTO, F., FERRAI, S. and MARECHAL, B.: *Islam in the European Union: What's at stake in the future?*, Policy Department Structural and Cohesion Policies, European Parliament, Brussels, 2007.

Arabic for students that have those mother tongues. In 2006-2007, about 1000 students attended Muslim religious instruction coordinated with the main Muslim associations of the *Land.* In North Rhine-Westphalia, Muslim instruction is also given in during language classes in Turkish, Arabic, Bosnian and Albanian for students of that origin. About 700 teachers of Turkish, Arabic, Bosnian or Albanian languages in public schools dedicate two of the five permitted hours of language study to Islamic instruction. Since 1999, there have been experimental courses in Islamic studies in German in which about 8.700 students participated.

A similar situation exists in Rhineland-Palatinate where language courses in Turkish, Bosnian, Arabic and Albanian are permitted to include Islamic instruction. In this *Lander* an experimental religious teaching project has been introduced in elementary schools in cooperation with Muslim associations[253].

This is also the case of Schleswig-Holstein, but in this *Lander* teachers are employed by the Turkish Republic via the Consulate General in Hamburg, and the *Lander* has no influence on the curriculum[254]. In 2007-2008 Islamic courses were introduced in some elementary schools in cooperation with Muslim organizations[255]. In Saarland, Islamic instruction is also given in the Turkish language classes.

Since 2008, pilot project of Alevi religious instruction in public school have been offered in Bavaria, North Rhine-Westphalia and Hessen. In Baden-Württember, Islamic instruction has been provided in German since 2006-2007 in twelve elementary schools, ten of them Sunni and two Alevi[256].

To face the need for the education of teachers of Islam, four universities (University of Muenster, University of Frankfurt/Main, University of Erlangen/Nuremberg and University of Osnabrück) have meanwhile started to establish several chairs of Islamic religious instruction and Islamic Religion. This process continues. Only recently the Wissenschaftsrat (German Council of Science and Humanities) which is the main advisory body to the Federal Government and the *Länder*-Governments recommended the establishing of broader Islamic-theological study programs at state universities.

---

[253] Among others, with the Turkish Women's Initiative, Christian-Islamic Discussion Circle and a Muslim scholar working as voluntary imam at a mosque. *Vid.* ROBBERS, G. "Germany" in V.V.A.A. *Yearbook of Muslims in Europe...op cit.* p. 146.

[254] ROBBERS, G. "Germany" in V.V.A.A. *Yearbook of Muslims in Europe...op cit.* p. 145.

[255] Among others, the Turkish Community Schleswig-Holstein, the Islamic Religious Community Schleswig-Holstein and DITIB. *Ibidem*

[256] *Ibidem.*

Regarding the participation of Muslim students in physical education, the German High Administrative Court (*Bundesverwaltungsgericht*) declared in 1993 that pupils may not be forced to attend coeducational courses in physical education (including swimming lessons) if they refuse to do so on religious grounds. In these cases schools have to offer separate physical education for girls and boys, or, if this is not possible because of organizational problems, to free them from attending the course. There is no general account of cases like this. While Muslim organizations list numerous cases, a survey conducted by the Intercultural Council (*Interkultureller Rat*) in 2007, where all Ministries for Cultural Affairs in the 16 German *Landër* were asked about this issue, proved that there had only been few cases and regulations in most German states are pragmatically oriented[257].

Another field is the attendance of class excursions. The High Administrative Court of North Rhine-Westphalia decided in a case in the year 2002 that a Muslim girl could not be forced to attend school excursions with overnight stays if she feels extremely uncomfortable with the circumstances[258].

As for the headscarf, Muslim students at schools and universities are in general free to wear headscarves in the classrooms. The question whether school teachers should be allowed to wear religious symbols opened with the case of Fereshta Ludin[259] Following this case, the Federal Constitutional Court (*Bundesverfassungsgericht*) stressed in a final decision in September 2003 the need to treat all religions equally; likewise it stated that the existing law did not constitute a sufficient basis for prohibiting teachers from donning headscarves.

The decision of the Supreme Court was followed by wide discussions. As a consequence of this, 8 of the 16 *Länder* parliaments (Baden Wurttemberg,

---

[257] Nevertheless, the decision of the High Administrative Court is still on debate. Up to now there are still cases reported where girls (or boys) are forced to attend mixed courses in physical education. If they refuse to do so, they would have to accept low grades for not having participated. This is for instance the case in Berlin where all students – without exception - are obliged to attend sports and even swimming classes.

[258] KARAKAGOSLU, Y.: "*Educational responses, or the lack of them, to the needs of Muslim Communities, with a special focus on Germany*" Keynote Speech in ODIHR- Assessment Meeting: "Combating Intolerance against Muslims in the Field of Education"3-4 June 2008.

[259] Fereshta Ludin is a young Muslim teacher of Afghan origin who as a teacher claimed the right to wear an "Islamic dress" in her school in Baden-Württemberg. According to the Ministry of Cultural Affairs of the *Länder*, the headscarf was at variance with basic Christian values and constitutional secularism alike because it was in opposition to the principles of freedom of thought and equality between sexes. The teacher emphasized in several interviews that she would always defend those two principles, but it was her own decision to wear it as a personal symbol of what Islam meant to her. She also stated that she did not consider it a way of inducing Muslim girls to wear a headscarf.

Saarland, LS, Hessen, Bayern, Berlin. Bremen, Northerhein-Westfalen) have established the ban for teachers and another two *Länder* (Brandenburg., Rheinland pfalz.) have started to prepare a 'law against specific religious symbols worn or used by teachers in public schools'. In four of the eastern *Länder* and in Hamburg and Schleswig Holstein there is no law against the wearing or the showing of religious symbols in state schools planed[260].

8. Muslim schools

There is a primary school in Berlin (Islamic primary School), a secondary school in Munich (*Islamisches Zentrum München*) and the King-Fahd-Academy in Bonn, the latter being financed by Saudi-Arabia and not accepted as a regular school in Germany. According to German law, private schools that comply with the law requirements can receive funding from the State.

---

[260] The current laws on teachers "faith-neutral dress codes" at state schools differs slightly from state to state. In 2004, Hessen extended its law against specific religious symbols (except Christian signs and symbols) on all state personnel, i.e. not only teachers. In Berlin, a law against all signs of religiosity which allow identifying persons as members of a specific religious group (no exception mentioned) came in force in 2005. The law includes personnel at schools, courts and police departments. Personnel at kindergartens are treated differently. In case parents utter objections against the kindergarten teachers wearing religious symbols or signs, a mediation process would have to be conveyed. Measures have to be undertaken to secure the positive and negative religious freedom for both parties, if the objection remains. The Berlin law also includes the constitution of an antidiscrimination office that already started its work. In 2005, Bremen established that not only teachers but also students in teacher training programs have to accept that the veil is absolutely forbidden in classrooms. There is still a debate about whether this legal restriction is in line with article 9 of the German Basic Constitutional Law (freedom of choice in education).

III. TRAINING CENTRES FOR IMAMS[261]

The training of religious staff concerns the right of religious communities to self-government (Article 140 of the Basic Law, read together with Article 137 (3) of the Weimar Constitution), a provision which mirrors the obligation of the State to observe neutrality. The Constitution authorizes religious communities to "regulate and administer their affairs independently". This authorization covers all facilities attributed to a religious community, for instance, organizing a mosque, religious education, customs and traditions, chaplaincy, and the training of imams.

Religious studies at universities, though, come under the competence of the Federal *Länder*. Universities need a religious community, as a contact point, to determine the contents of such studies. Due to the lack of Islamic religious communities having being granted that legal status, each Federal *Länder* has established interim solutions which are particularly designed to enable the training of Islam teachers.

- State initiatives:

Since 2002, imams hired by the *Diyanet* to go to Germany take part in a six-month course where they learn German and get familiarized with German history, geography and political system before leaving Turkey. The course takes about six months and is conducted by the Goethe-Institute, Germany's culture institution abroad. The Federal Ministry of Interior is planning to extend the existing training programme for imams from Turkey, which includes language skills and regional and cultural studies.

Some Federal *Länder* (e.g. Berlin) and some municipalities (e.g. Munich, Stuttgart) also offer language and regional and cultural studies for imams, some of which are financed from federal funds.

Furthermore, since 2004, there have been dialogue seminars for imams belonging to the Turkish-Islamic Union for Religious Affairs (DITIB) in Germany, designed to bring imams together with Christian cooperation and discussion partners to strengthen their dialogue and communication skills. The Federal Ministry of Interior asked the Federal Agency for Civic Education to conduct this project together with the DITIB and partners from the Christian churches. In 2007, the project was extended to other Muslim organizations and

---

[261] The Federal Government has not commissioned any research on imam training. One of the latest studies dealing with the issue is the research project called "*Gesellschaft gemeinsam gestalten. Islamische Vereinigungen als Partner in Baden-Württemberg*" (Shaping society as partners. Islamic associations as partners in Baden-Württemberg), which was funded by the Robert Bosch Foundation and concluded in 2008.

support is provided to civil society projects designed to provide regional and cultural studies for imams.

- Education programs in Universities:

At German universities, there is a great number of Islamic Sciences/Middle Eastern studies institutes which tend to provide education on oriental languages and religious studies as well as on Islamic theology. Several chairs of Islamic religion and/or for the training of Islamic religion teachers have also been created in four Federal *Länder*.

The University of Münster was the first German university that developed a course on Islamic religious teaching in 2005 to qualify teachers for Islamic religious education. Through the Centre for Religious Studies (CRS), created in 2001, a Master's degree course in "Islamic theology" is also offered[262].

In March 2006, the University of Erlangen-Nürnberg created the professorial chair of "Islamic religious teaching" as part of the "Interdisciplinary Centre for Islamic Religious Teaching". An extension course on Islamic religious teaching was set up the same year including the following subjects: Arabic, Koran, the doctrine of Islam, History of selected Islamic cultural spheres, Traditions of thought and law, Islam in Europe and Germany, Teaching religion, and Religious sciences

A similar professorial chair on Islamic Religious Teaching Theory was created at Osnabrück University in 2008 in order to offer a Masters program to train Islamic religious teachers. The MA is called “Islamic Religious Education” (*Islamische Religionspädagogik*) though by 2007 only four students had enrolled and many unqualified applicants from Turkey had to be rejected from the program.

Since 2003, Frankfurt University has a chair for "Islamic Religion" (now: “Institute for the study of Islamic culture and Religion”) endowed by the Religious Affairs Board of the Turkish Republic in Ankara. The University offers a course that leads to a Masters degree..

- Training courses offered by Muslim organizations

For years, the Cologne-based Union of Islamic Cultural Centres (VIKZ) has trained their own Imams and has set up its own training system in Germany. It has been designed for young Turkish nationals who undergo training

---

[262] The professor of the University of Münster, Muhammad Sven Kalish, has faced criticism from Muslim associations because of his questioning of the nature of the Qur´an.

at the association's centres in order to work in their communities once they have concluded their training.

Training programs have also been developed at institutions as DITIB or *Muslimische Akademie*[263] and programs at several other smaller institutions like the Berlin based Buhara Institute[264] are also being set up.

[263] http://www.muslimische-akademie.de/

[264] In 2009, the *Institut Buhara*, linked to a sufi movement, opened a privately funded school to train imams called Berlin's Centre for Education, Training, and Culture. It offers a six-year education program for German Muslims in order to train imams. It has capacity for 68 male students. http://institutbuhara.com/

GREECE

I. RELIGION AND STATE

1. Administrative bodies that have contact with denominations.

According with the Constitution, all Greeks are equal before the Law (Article 4.1 of the Constitution), irrespective of religious creed. Article 3 of the Constitution does refer to Church and State relations, acknowledging Eastern Orthodoxy as the "prevailing" religion in the land. The main actors in Greece's legal environment, as concerns intercultural and inter-religious relations are Parliament, political parties, the Administration, academic institutions, religious bodies and organizations, NGO's etc.

The General Directorate for Cults of the Ministry of Education and Religious Affairs is the main agency of the Administration that deals with religious entities based in Greece. This comprises three departments:

- Department for Ecclesiastical Administration, dealing only with the Orthodox Church of Greece.
- Department of Ecclesiastical Education and Religious Instruction, concerned with Theological Faculties and the (optional, since 2008) teaching of Catechism in secondary schools
- Department for Relations with Other Religions and Denominations It is the official interlocutor of non- Orthodox religious groups active in Greece.

The official participation of the Hellenic Republic in international events in the field of religion, intercultural dialogue, freedom of religion and belief, humanitarian aid activities by religiously-affiliated agencies etc. falls within the competencies of the Ministry of Foreign Affairs (E2 Directorate, established in 1837). Much of this work, however, is done directly by the interested Churches and other religious denominations themselves, the State only playing a subsidiary role, mainly when asked to.

Integrated Action Plan for the smooth adaptation and social integration of third country nationals legally residing in the Greek territory" (ESTIA Programme, Law 3386/2005) promotes - among others - the cultural diversity of the Greek society through measures and activities that encourage interaction between the Greek Culture and the Cultures of the countries of immigrants as well as through the development of intercultural orientation in the structures of the country.

A special Unit for Multicultural Issues is functioning since 2003 within the Ministry of Culture (Presidential Decree 151/2003). Furthermore, "European Fund for the integration of third country nationals" is another useful means that fosters intercultural issues among third country nationals and the host society, through targeted measures and activities, such as programs of intercultural training for civil servants dealing with third country nationals or issues related to them[265], training programs for Intercultural Mediators, as well as a series of other activities that contribute to the development of interculturalism.

2. Recognition of religions.

The Constitution (article 13 paragraph 1) guarantees the inviolability of freedom of religious conscience, specifying that "the enjoyment of civil and individual rights does not depend on the religious convictions of each person".

In Greece, there is no registration system for religious entities. Nevertheless, opening a place of worship requires a number of documents, mainly from the Urban Planning Authority and the Ministry of Education and Religious Affairs. However, recent jurisprudence has stated that such documents cannot be interpreted as surrogate acts of registration. The current system is to be revised with a view to bringing it up to modern national and European legal standards[266].

There is no specific system through which recognition is officially dispensed upon any religious entity. The reference, in article 13, paragraph 2[267] of

---

[265] E.g. for the staff serving in Immigration Offices in the competent Ministries, regional and local authorities, in hospitals, in Prison Establishments, in Juvenile Probation Officers' etc.

[266] Even though, some authors, like Ioannis Konidaris, former Secretary General of Cults, maintained that permits for a place of worship could be considered as "an image and informal register of the religious entities that have requested and were granted a permit to found places of worship in Greece". Among the requirements asked in order to obtain such a permit were:

a) A certain number of believers which, according to the Supreme Administrative Court of Greece (the Council of State), is 7 persons;

b) A confession of faith, which ensures not only that the religious entity is a known religion but also that its doctrine does not contradict public order or morals principles;

c) A shepherd. *Vid.* KONIDARIS, I. "Religious entities as Legal Persons-Greece" in *Churches and other organizations as legal persons.* Peeters 2007, pp. 116-117.

[267] Art. 13.2 "*All known religions shall be free and their rites of worship shall be performed unhindered and under the protection of the law. The practice of rites of worship is not allowed to offend public order or the good usages. Proselytism is prohibited*".

the Constitution, to the concept of "known religion", refers to any religion whose beliefs are being taught publicly and has no secretive forms of worship and of course, does not transgress public order, including statutes against obscenity. According to officials from the Ministry of Education and Religious Affairs, the reference to proselytism in the same paragraph is a "legal fossil", whose permanence is due to a technicality. Proselytism has not been prosecuted as a criminal offence in Greece for many years now, following instructions by the Ministry of Justice rendering inoperative the relevant penal statutes.

Religious entities enjoy one of these legal statuses: Legal Person of Public Law, Legal Person of Private Law, or associations under the Civil Code. So, recognized religions can be juridical persons of public law or they can have the status of private law.

According to its Charter (Law 590/1977), the Orthodox Church of Greece and each of its divisions, namely dioceses, parishes and monasteries, are Legal Persons of Public Law. The same applies to the religious entities of the Ecumenical Patriarchate on Hellenic territory, in Epirus, Macedonia (including the Monasteries of Mount Athos), Thrace, Crete and the Dodecanese Islands. The Church of Greece is organized according to the synodical system. This is a fundamental administrative institution for every Orthodox Church, and is found both at central and local levels. The supreme authority is the Holy Synod of the Church of Greece with the Archbishop of Athens as its President and the serving Bishops and Metropolitans (senior Bishops, equivalent to Cardinals) as its members.

The Central Israelite Council and the Israelite Communities are also Legal Persons of Public Law. Moreover, according to Law n° 2456/1920, when a Jewish entity is set up in any city with more than 20 Jewish families and a synagogue can be recognized as a Legal Person of Public Law.

The status of the Muslim minority in Thrace was established by the 1923 Lausanne Treaty. The said minority's rights and religious freedoms are governed both by the relevant provisions of the 1923 Lausanne Treaty and by the contemporary universal and regional human rights conventions in force. Subsequent laws – such as Law 1920 / 1991 (regulating the status of the Muftis) and Law 3536 / 2007 (establishing 240 seats for religious faith preachers and teachers at the three Mufti Offices in Thrace[268]) – and a number of concrete measures have been enacted and / or undertaken aiming at strengthening the integration of the Muslim minority into the society.

---

[268] The Mufti Offices (in Comotini, Xanthi and Didymoteicho) are also legal persons of public law. More specifically, they are public services. KONIDARIS, I. "Religious entities as Legal...*op. cit.* pp. 115.

The status of the Catholic Church in Greece is being currently modernized, upon the lines of current national and international standards, in application of article 13 of the Constitution on freedom of religion.

As with most legal orders based on Roman law, Greek law does not grant any form of special status to other religious communities, inasmuch as their legal personality is concerned. Therefore, the general rules of national legislation, in particular the Civil Code, apply in all such cases (associations, corporations etc.).

At any rate, a comprehensive settlement is sought, mainly for Protestant denominations, even if the "Charters" of many of these (in particular of non-Episcopal Churches) differ a lot with juridical systems based on Roman law, like Greek one. Normally the legal form they adopt is legal persons of Private Law.

II. ISLAM IN GREECE

1. Legal recognition of Islam.

Greece has long been acquainted with Islam, be it through her ties with the Arab world or through the presence of the Muslim minority in Thrace. According to the Greek Constitution (art. 3) the dominant religion is Greek Orthodoxy. Islam enjoys the status of a recognized religion.

By virtue of the provisions of the 1923 Lausanne Treaty, certain rights for the Muslim minority in Thrace were established (i.e. minority education and the maintenance of charitable foundations called after *wafks*).

In Thrace there are three Muftiates in the districts of Xanthi, Komotini and Didymoteicho. The three muftis, which are designated by decree-law, on the proposition of the Minister of Education and Cults, have jurisdictional competence over their believers for ten- year tenure (law nº 1920/1991). Apart from their religious duties, the three Muftis act as judges (*kadi*) with jurisdiction over certain family and inheritance matters among Greek Muslim citizens, members of the Muslim minority in Thrace. In accordance with the Greek legislation, members of the Muslim minority in Thrace have the option to address themselves either to the Muftis or to the civil courts. In order to reconcile Islamic law with the Greek public order and international obligations assumed by Greece, in particular, in the field of gender equality and children rights, Article 5 (3) of Law 1920 /1991 provides that the courts shall not enforce decisions undertaken by the Muftis contrary to the Greek Constitution. The Muftis function as public authorities, financed by the State[269].

The jurisdiction of the mufti is exercised over all the ministers of the imams and Islamic religious leaders of his district. Next to each Mufti, there are three main Management Committees, looking after property belonging to the religious communities *(waqjs)* in Xanthi, Komotini & Didymoteicho respectively, apart from the Committees of the smaller pious / charitable foundations throughout Thrace.

The *wakfs* of Thracae and of the Dodecanese are administered by those management committees under the supervision of the local authorities and the government. There is a law on the *waqfs* of Thrace (3647/2008) which provides elections of these committees but it has not been implemented so far.

The Greek state looks after the maintenance of schools for the Muslim minority, as well as after the two *madrasas* and the school teachers in Thessaloniki.[270]. The Greek State looks after the maintenance of schools for the Muslim minority, as well as after the *madrasas* and the school teachers in Thessaloniki[271].

2. The Muslim population.

After the Greek-Turkish war of 1919-1922 a population exchange took place under the Lausanne Convention (1923) and 450.000 Muslims left Greece for Turkey. As an exemption, 92.000 Muslims with Greek citizenship remained in Thrace (Turkish and Bulgarian (Pomaks) speakers) and 26.000 Albanian-speakers in Epirus (these were forced to flee to Albania at the end of German occupation in 1945). In 1947, when the Dodecanese Islands were annexed by Greece, about 12.000 Muslims became Greek citizens. Today, Greek Muslims are mainly concentrated in Thrace[272].

---

[269] For the question about who is competent to appoint the mufti, see the sentence of the European Court of Human Rights in *Serif versus Greece (14 December 1999-Case No: 38178/97)*

[270] By virtue of Law 3554/2007, the Muslim Wakifs were exempted from submitting the tax declarations on income, land property and major land property *of previous years,* and, consequently, their accumulated registered debts, fines and existing mortgages were written off. Furthermore, as of 2008 onwards, the Muslim Wakifs are also exempted from paying the major land property tax for those properties that are being used for their pious / charitable purposes. By virtue of Law 3647/2008 on the administration and management of Muslim Wakifs in Thrace, the members of the three main Management Committees are to be elected, which constituted a long standing demand of the Muslim minority.

[271] PAPASTATHIS, C.: "State and Church in Greece" in *State and Church in the European Union.* Second Edition, Nomos, Baden-Baden 2005, pp. 136.

[272] TSITSELIKIS, K.: "Greece" in *Yearbook of Muslims in Europe...op. cit.* p. 152.

The Muslim minority in Thrace consists of 3 distinct components, namely of Pomak, Turkish and Roma origin. In 2004, official sources estimated the Muslim minority in Thrace to be around 100.000 people[273]. Furthermore, a small number of Greek Muslim citizens live in the islands of Rhodes and Kos (Dodecanese islands).

As a result of significant migration flows, mainly during the last twenty years, there are also Muslim migrants living in Greece (principally in Athens). Muslim immigrants come from Africa, Asia and the Balkans[274]. The estimated Muslim population in 2008 was 350.000 (3, 1% of the total population of 11.000.000)[275]

3. Mosques.

According to official sources, there are about 300 mosques in Thrace, two on Kos and one on Rodos. Until now, the growing Muslim community in Athens has no proper purposed-built mosque though already in 2006 the Government passed legislation (law 3512/2006) providing for the establishment of a mosque in the central Athens neighbourhood of Votanikos[276]. Law 3512/2006 provides for, inter alia, the engagement of two of the most Muslim representative communities in the new Islamic mosque to be built. According to the bill, the new Athens mosque should be run by a non- profit organization staffed by Greek state officials and members of the capital's Muslim communities. The head imam will be appointed by a government-backed committee and be paid by the Ministry.

Some estimates claim that there could be about 80 Muslim worship places in greater Athens (also in Thessaloniki and other cities)[277] . The largest makeshift mosque in the city is in district of Moschato. The Moschato Islamic Cultural Center opened in 2006 funded by a Saudi donor and, as the rest of the Islamic worship places outside the Northern region of Thrace, it doesn't have a house-of-prayer permit.

---

273 KTISTAKIS, I and SITAROPOULOS, N.: *Executive Summary GREECE*, European Group of non-governmental experts in the field of combating discrimination on the grounds of racial and ethnic origin and religion or belief, Community Action Programme to Combat Discrimination, June 22nd 2004.

274 DOKOS, T. and ANTONIOU, D.: "Islam in Greece" in HUNTER, S. (ed.): *Islam, Europe's second religion. The new social, cultural and political landscape*, Preaeger, 2002, p.175-189

275 TSITSELIKIS, K.: "Greece" in *Yearbook of Muslims in Europe...op. cit.* p. 153.

276 Prior to this bill, Parliament approved the building of a mosque and Islamic Cultural Centre in the outskirts of Athens in 2000. A heated debate followed the presentation of the project with strong opposition from certain sectors of the Orthodox Church, some member of the Parliament and local authorities.

277 TSITSELIKIS, K.: "Greece" in *Yearbook of Muslims in Europe...op. cit.* p. 155.

4. Imams

As explained before, the three appointed Muftis in Thrace are public servants, operating as Judges and thus remunerated by the State. The three Muftis hold Ph.D. Degrees in Theology from Islamic Universities. Muftis are appointed by the Greek administration through a procedure in which prominent members of the minority are consulted.

According to the Law 3536 / 2007 regarding the appointment of 240 imams to serve in the mosques of Thrace, these imams should be contracted by the government[278], but the act has not been implemented so far, so the 240 Imams hired in each mosque of Trace are appointed and paid (out of the *waqf* income) buy the three Mufti Offices in Thrace. These imams are to perform their duties at the mosques of the Muslim minority and to teach Islam to Muslim pupils. These 240 imams will be employed by the Ministry of Education and Religious Affairs and are currently in the process of being appointed and registered on the Emoluments List of the Civil Service.

Most imams have been trained in the two religious secondary schools in Thrace, whereas some of them have continued their tertiary studies in Theology in Islamic Universities through scholarships granted by the Greek Government.

Religious leaders from third countries, mainly Turkey, visit Muslim communities in Greece on especial occasions such as the Ramadan.

In addition to the imams in Thrace, a number of 50 to 60 imams offer their religious services in worship places in Athens and other regions of the country[279]. However, there are no official imams to officiate at religious functions outside Thrace. Members of the Muslim community in other regions have to rely on Thrace imams for official religious rites.

5. Islam in schools and Islamic schools

Articles 40, 41, and 45 of the Treaty of Lausanne guarantee the right of education for the Muslim minority in Greece. According to the law, Thrace has secular bilingual minority schools and two Quranic schools funded by the State. There are 194 minority primary schools[280] that provide lessons in both Greek and Turkish. More than 400 Muslim teachers are working in these

---

[278] This bill has been criticized by the Islam minority which stated that is against art. 43 of the Peace Treaty of Lausanne that protects the religious freedom of the Muslim Turkish Minority

[279] Source: official data from the State Security Division of the Hellenic Police.

[280] The minority schools are an especial category of public schools in the Northern region of Thrace for the Muslim minority. According to other estimates there are 208 elementary schools in Thrace. TSITSELIKIS, K.: "Greece" in *Yearbook of Muslims in Europe...op. cit.* p. 155.

schools[281]. In 1999, half of the teachers were graduates of the Special Pedagogical Academy of Thessaloniki[282], 82 were graduates of secondary education schools (i.e. Gymnasiums and Quranic schools), 90 were graduates of Turkish schools and 9 were Turkish nationals appointed for a set period of time according to the provisions of exchange of teachers between Greece and Turkey contained in the 1968 Bilateral Cultural Protocol.[283]. As we will see later, there are also two High Schools and two Theological Schools. Islam is only taught in minority schools[284].

In the 2006-2007 school year, optional Turkish Language courses have been made available in public schools. Affirmative action measures have also been taken to facilitate the admission of children of the minority into universities and technical colleges, such as a 0.5% quota on the total number of admissions. This last measure is also coupled with an exemption from the mandatory base grade of 50% in each subject of the university entrance exams.

More than 100 Qur'an courses are offered outside school hours by private minority groups, and on Kos (Platani), the local imam has also been offering Qur'an courses. Since 1979, there is a foreign school run by Libya ("7th April School") for pupils from Arabic countries and provides Islamic religious education[285]

---

[281] Source: official data from the Greek Ministry of Foreign Affairs. http://www.ypex.gov.gr/www.mfa.gr/enUS/Policy/Multilateral+Diplomacy/Global+Issues/Human+Rights/MUSLIM+MINORITY+OF+THRACE.htm. Last updated: 24 May 2007 (accessed 26/07/2009).

[282] The Special Pedagogical Academy of Thessaloniki offers Muslim Theology courses to train teachers of Islam for the Thrace region minority schools. The Greek Ministry of Education and Religious Affairs set up the Muslim Theology Departments within the Academy.

[283] Source: official data from the Greek Ministry of Foreign Affairs: *The Muslim Minority of Greek Thrace*, June 1999. http://www.hri.org/MFA/foreign/musminen.htm (accessed 27/07/2009)

[284] DASSETO, F., FERRARI, S. And MARECHAL, B.: *Islam in the European Union: What's at stake in the future?*, European Parliament, Brussels, 2007, p. 120.

[285] TSITSELIKIS, K.: "Greece" in *Yearbook of Muslims in Europe...op. cit.* p. 156.

III. TRAINING CENTRES FOR IMAMS

Two minority secondary religious schools of Thrace offer special Islamic education to its students who, upon graduation, are entitled to work as imams. The schools are located in Komotini, in the Prefecture of Rodopi and at the other at Ehinos, in the Prefecture of Xanthi. They provide bilingual education.

These are state supported schools (funded primarily by the State and also partially out of *waqf income)* and their curricula, as any other public secondary schools, are instituted by Ministerial Decree. Degrees granted by these schools are equal to the ones dispensed by Greek Orthodox religious schools[286]. They follow the normal curriculum of secondary education schools to which Islamic education is added following the *madrasa* approach. The curriculum in Greek (30 hours per week) is taught by Greek Universities' graduates and it includes: Greek language, mathematics, physics, chemistry, biology, history, geography, basic political principles and gymnastics.

All teaching material is the same as the one used in public secondary schools. The Islamic religious curriculum (8 hours per week) is taught by Arab Universities' graduates (7 from University of Medina in Saudi Arabia and one from University of Al Azhar)[287]. Subjects comprise: Islamic Religion (Islamic Law, Sunna and Methodology for imams), Quran, Arabic and Islamic history.

Teaching material for this curriculum have been specially tailored by the Greek Muslim teachers

Studies at these two religious schools last for six years. During the first five years students are examined internally by their teachers. In the final year students participate in national exams which are directly under the supervision of the Ministry of Education and Religious Affairs. One third of the students are females.

Students who graduate from the two religious secondary schools receive a degree which is equivalent to a secondary level Greek baccalaureate. It is recognized both in the private and public sector. Students have the right to participate in the national exams in order to assert entrance to Greek Universities. Last but not least, graduates have the right to work as Imams.

The Greek Ministry of Education and Religious Affairs is also working towards introducing continuous training for existing Imams.

Islam is offered also for non –Muslim students as a subject in the theological schools of Greece over one or two semesters (Universities of Athens and Thessaloniki –Special Pedagogical Academy-).

---

[286] Article 4, Official Gazette/ Issue 136 of June 23, 1998.

[287] Source: official data from the State Security Division of the Hellenic Police.

Greece is also hosting major international educational events in the framework of inter - religious dialogue. The last of such event held in Athens was in December 11 - 14, 2008, organized by the Ecumenical Patriarchate, as a Seminar for inter - faith training for young Christian and Muslim religious leaders from E. U. member - states, Eastern Europe, Central Asia, North Africa and the Middle East, in partnership with various Muslim Institutions.

HUNGARY

I. RELIGION AND STATE

1. Administrative bodies that have contact with denominations.

Hungary has a Roman Catholic majority (65 % of the population) with a rather strong presence of Protestantism (25 %). Before Communist takeover, the Catholic Church had traditionally a great impact on both society and governmental politics. Trying to diminish the influence of the Catholic Church, the communist regime nationalized large lands of their property (1945). Schools and educational institutions attended by Catholic Church were taken over by the State (1948). Gradually, in the seventies relations between Church and State began to be more stable, especially after the agreement between Hungary and the Vatican[288]. In the process of the important changes that took place in 1989-90 the constitutional regulation of the Church was very soon on the agenda. The first task to be done was restoring Religious Freedom. The Constitution of 1990 besides recognizing that Churches and State are separated and that State is neutral before religious items, it enshrines the right of every person to freedom of thought, conscience and religion. The Act No. 4 of 1990 on the Freedom of Conscience and Religion and on Churches implemented that fundamental right.

The State Office for Church Affairs (*Állami Egyházügyi Hivatal*) dissolved in 1989 without a legal successor. Subsequently, State contact with churches adopted many forms. For the time being, the Administrative body that has most contact with denominations is the Secretariat for Church Relations (*Egyházi Kapcsolatok Titkársága*) under the Ministry of Education and Culture[289].

---

[288] PACZOLAY, P. (2008): "The Hungarian Constitutional Court's Rulings on Freedom of Religion" in *Legal Aspects of Religious freedom* (International Conference, 15-18 September 2008) Ljubljana, p. 123

[289] In July 2009 the Director of the Secretariat for Church Affairs was András Csepregi.

2. Recognition of religions.

As an expression of freedom of religion, enshrined in the Constitution, people, no matter if they are Hungarian or foreigners, can constitute a religious group without any kind of authorization or approval by the State. The free exercise of religion (in private, public or in community) is not bound to any kind of legal form.

According to the Act IV of 1990 on the Freedom of Conscience and Religion and on Churches, Religious groups can be registered as such but it is not compulsory. Both registered and non registered groups enjoy the fundamental right to religious freedom. This Act does not differentiate between churches, congregations or communities, according to their social significance or their number of members. The colloquially used phrase "historic churches" is not based in that Act[290].

Regarding the legal structure, denominations can adopt, according to the civil laws (Act IV of Civil Code of 1959), the form of a civil association having at least ten members. But if they prefer being registered as a church, hundred members are required. Registration (both for associations and for churches) is carried out at county courts.

All registered churches are equal before the law. They have the same rights and the same obligations. Nevertheless, some legal differences may be possible in the framework of the principle of equality if those differences are reasonable and proportionate. As the Constitutional Court stated: *"treating the Churches equally does not exclude taking the actual social roles of the individual Churches into account"*. Consequently, external, social differences between religious communities can be taken into account by the legislator, if these are of relevance. Differentiation would be arbitrary and unconstitutional if the aspect taken into consideration by the legislator was irrelevant.

The 2001 national census provides some information on membership of religious communities. According to this last census, the four largest denominations (the Catholic Church (54, 5%), the Reformed Church –Calvinists- (15,9%), the Lutheran Church (3%) and the Alliance of Jewish Communities (0,1%) often receive

---

290 CSEPREGI, A. (2008): *"Facts about the relationship of State and Church in Hungary"* in *Legal Aspects of Religious freedom* (International Conference, 15-18 September 2008) Ljubljana, pp. 358-360.

special attention, which does not necessary mean that they had a privileged status[291].

Requirements for Registration of religious entities:

The Act IV of 1990 on the Freedom of Conscience and Religion and on Churches determines the requirements for a church to be registerd by the court upon request of at least 100 people.

The registration of churches is done by the county courts in the same way as associations, political parties or foundations. It is necessary to underline that religious communities are not "recognised by the State; they are just "registered" by the State. In the process of registering the church, the court is only authorized to examine whether formal requirements are fulfilled and whether church acts in accordance with the law. The court is not authorised to examine or assess the dogmas or principles of faith of a religious group founded for aiming religious purposes. Thus the requirements to be fulfilled are highly formal.

Churches registered prior to 1990 were re-registered automatically. Other religious communities wishing to be registered need to fulfil the following requirements:

- To submit an application with the names of at least 100 individuals (founders);

- To present a Charter containing at least: the name of the religion, its headquarters address, its internal organisational structure, and internal units of the church that enjoy legal personality.

- Administration system of the church

- A statement, made by the founders, declaring that their organisation has a religious character and that its activities comply with the Constitution and the law.

The status of "churches" is neither that of a public law corporation nor that of an association. Churches enjoy legal personality as *sui generis* entities. Their internal organisational units, such as institutions or parishes, are also legal entities if the "charter" of the church provides so. No further State registration for these minor units is required. "Independent organisations of churches set up for religious purposes" (such as religious orders) are also legal entities, but they need to be regis-

---

[291] SCHANDA, B: "Religious entities as legal persons –Hungary" in *Churches and other organizations as legal persons* Peeters 2007, pp. 119-123.

tered by the court. In this case a declaration by the competent church organ would be enough[292].

Benefits of Registering:

a) Church autonomy, which mean that State cannot interfere their internal actions or organization[293]. They are also not bound by the principle of democratic internal structure, while associations or political parties are.
b) Churches are exempt from fees and local taxes and enjoy a variety of tax benefits. The same tax benefits enjoyed by other non-profit-making organizations, such as associations or foundations.
c) Income tax payers have the right to assign 1 % of their income tax to a church of their choice. Another 1 % of the income tax may be assigned to a non-governmental organization (which may be affiliated to a religious community, registered or not).
d) Registered churches have the right to offer optional religious education in public schools. Certainly only the larger denominations are likely to make use of this right. This optional religious education does not become part of the school's curriculum.
e) Churches can found and maintain schools, institutions of higher education, health or social care institutions and can also engage in economic activities, under special funding and taxation regimes.

Among the other legal consequences of breaching the law, the church that acts illegally can be deleted from the register of churches. In recent years the number of registered churches in Hungary has been steadily increasing.

According to APEH (Hungarian Tax Authority) statement on the disposal of 1% of the Personal Income Tax in 2009, 169 churches received it. Apart from these, there were also churches, which either did not take advantage of the tax donation system or did not have technical numbers so far. Based on unofficial data the number of registered churches is close to 190[294].

---

[292] SCHANDA, B.: "Religious entities as legal persons...*op. cit.* pág. 121.

[293] Whereas a resolution of an association can be brought before a court (they have the power of striking it down if these internal actions are unlawful or violate the charter of the association), a resolution of a bishop or a synod cannot be challenged before state courts. *Ibidem.*

[294] CSEPREGI, A.: "*Facts about the relationship of State...op. cit.* p. 361.

II. ISLAM IN HUNGARY

1. Legal recognition of Islam.

The first encounter of Hungary with the Muslim world was in sixteenth and seventeenth centuries, when Ottoman Empire ruled over a part of the country. Two centuries later, in 1878, the Austro-Hungarian occupation of Bosnia was the next major encounter with Muslims. Some years later, in World War I alliance with Turkey led to the recognition of Islam by the Hungarian Parliament in Act 17 of 1916.

Nowadays, Islam has the same recognition as other registered faiths. The Hungarian Constitution and Act IV of 1990 guarantee that the State and church operate separately in Hungary and that the State is neutral with regard to issues of faith. On the other hand, separation and neutrality does not preclude the State's prerogative to recognize the specific characteristics that differentiate the various churches from other types of social organizations, associations and representative organizations. There are 3 Islamic communities registered as churches, and according to the mentioned Act, all registered churches have the same right and obligations (see I. 1, d)[295].

2. The Muslim population.

Nowadays, most Hungarian Muslims have a Turkish or Arabic background. The 2001 National Census, the latest demographic survey available, contained an optional question on religious affiliation. According to that census, 3.201 Hungarian residents declared themselves to be Muslim. But according to other estimations, over the 10.035.000 people living in Hungary, there are almost 20.000 Muslims, (0, 3% of the population)[296].

The majority of these people live in Budapest, but there are also Islamic communities in Pécs, Szeged, Debrecen, Miskolc. A considerable part of the

---

[295] LEDERER, G.: "Hungary" in V.V.A.A. *Yearbook of Muslims in Europe* Edited by NIELSSEN, J.S.; AKAGÖNÜL, S.; ALIBASIC, A; MARECHA,B.; MOE,C; Leiden-Boston, (2009) p.161.

[296] Source: official data from the Spanish Embassy in Budapest

Muslims arrived in Hungary during the 80's for university studies (medical, engineer, economist).

While in Western European countries Muslim immigration is a significant and sensitive political issue, in Hungary the low figures of Muslim immigration and the neutral opinion of the inhabitants towards their religion makes the issue of minor importance.

Three registered Islamic communities are operating in Hungary. Each one has its own legal identity and administration. The members of these communities are mostly immigrants from the 80's, who already have established a family. Other followers of these communities are younger Muslims studying at Hungarian universities and businessmen. There is also an increasing number of converts, mainly by marriage.

3. Muslim representative organizations.

There are three registered Muslim communities in Hungary:

- Hungarian Islam Community (*Magyar Iszlám kôzösség* –MIK-[297]) founded in 1988 by Balázs Mihálffy. It defends a very modern and non extremist concept of Islam. It cooperates with the Turkish Hanif Cultural Foundation[298];
- Association of Muslims in Hungary (*Magyarországi Muszlimok Egyháza* – MME- founded in 2000 and led by people of Arab origin. It is associated to the Federation of Islamic Organizations in Europe (FIOE).
- Islam Association (*Iszlám Egyháza* -IE[299]) split from MME in 2003

Both MME and IE receive financial support from the Arab Gulf States, while MIK does not. There are two *tariqas* in Budapest, the *Süleymanci* and the *Fethüllahci*. In cooperation with MIK the *Süleymancis* also have a centre in Pécs[300].

[297] www.magyariszlam.hu
[298] www. hanif.hu
[299] www.iszlam.hu
[300] LEDERER, G.: "Hungary" in V.V.A.A. *Yearbook ... op. cit.* p.162.

4. Mosques. Imams, and chaplains

There are some Ottoman historical buildings but not purpose-built mosques in Hungary. Eleven Islamic places of worship can be found, seven of them are in Budapest. The number of imams is estimated to be more or less equal to that of the places of worship.

There aren't Muslim Faith Leaders engaged by the public sector but the opportunity is open for all the registered churches in Hungary if the need emerges.

There are 15.032 prisoners in the 30 prisons in Hungary. About 500 of those prisoners are Muslims, but none of the 32 chaplains in prisons, which are financed by the State, is Muslim: 17 are Catholics (8 full time and 9 part time), 15 protestants (8 full time, 7 part time), 1 Jew (part time). Nevertheless, MIK has regularly organised some visits to Muslims inmates in prisons.

5. Islam in public schools. Islamic private schools.

At the request of the parents of the registered Islam communities in Hungary, Islam can be taught in public schools run by the municipalities. Any other registered religious community has the same right.

Religious instruction in public schools is not a part of the school curriculum and therefore teachers of religion do not belong to the school staff. The grades in religious instruction are not included in school reports. Religious organizations decide freely on the content of the religion classes as well as on the supervision. The teachers of religion are employed by their churches; however, the State provides funding for the churches to pay their salaries.

There are 3.989 primary and secondary public schools, 870 private schools and 336 church schools: 187 Catholic schools, 120 Calvinists, 23 Evangelists and 6 Jews.MIK, MME and IE offer lectures on Islam and Arabic language courses

III. TRAINING CENTRES FOR IMAMS

As far as we know, there are no training centres for Imams in Hungary neither is there any strategy or any specific programmes for the training of imams who come from abroad. There is no legal approach or written policy relevant to training Muslim faith leaders and no private research about it has been developed yet. Nevertheless, oriental languages and cultures are taught at several Hungarian universities, e.g. Eötvös Lóránd Tudományegyetem (ELTE) in Budapest.

IRELAND

I. RELIGION AND STATE

Although the Irish constitution originally contained a clause (art. 44) which made explicit mention to the special position of the Catholic Church in Ireland, it has been removed by referendum in 1973. The e Constitution guarantees religious freedom and has accepted the principle of the separation between church and State, with the exception of education (the State will fund denominational schools). The Constitution forbids the endowment of religion and also to impose any penalties for religious belief.

Article 44.2.5 of the Constitution states:

"Every religious denomination shall have the right to manage its own affairs, own, acquire and administer property, movable or immovable, and maintain institutions for religious or charitable purposes."

This means that religious denominations are given *carte blanche* in framing their constitutions and rules and therefore such matters are not supervised by the State. Any church or religious groups are free to organise economic enterprises on the same terms as any group of private individuals. They are equally free to establish social welfare institutions such as hospitals, orphanages or charitable organisations. Religious organizations are eligible for charitable status, which allows for some tax exemptions.

There is no a definitive, whole or unified register of churches in Ireland, nor is there a requirement that they be registered *qua* church. Nevertheless, in order to fulfil certain and specific roles (in relation to marriage), to comply with specific legislation (education and planning law) or to avail themselves of certain advantages (exemption from rates) churches are required to register. Those which are registered companies are, of course, registered in that respect.

For example, under Irish Marriage law' marriages conducted by churches (with certain limited exceptions) have to take place in registered buildings, usually churches or meeting houses. For the purposes of the solemnisation of marriages, a religious body may nominate solemnisers of marriages who will be included on a Register of Solemnisers. Most of the primary and secondary schools in Ireland are still mainly denominationally based: individual office holders (usually bishops) or churches (the Presbyterian Church, the Methodist Church, the Religious Society of Friends, the Jewish Community or the Islamic Foundation of Ireland). The Minister for Education enters the names of such patrons on a register[301].

There are several state agencies with enforce equality on behalf of minorities, for example the Grand Racial and Intercultural Office (GRIO). Indeed, the GRIO has intervened in two cases in which passport of Muslim women were refused because they wore hiyab. The cases were resolved in their favour.

Structure of religious organisations

Under modem Irish law, all churches and religious groupings stand upon the same footing. Since no church is established by law, they all have the status of voluntary associations. Churches and religious groups do not automatically have legal personality; in general their legal status is that of unincorporated associations. The Companies Acts provide machinery under which they could acquire corporate status, but this does not appear to have been taken up. There is no legal procedure for making churches and religious groupings corporate bodies under public law. As a result of this lack of legal personality, church property is normally vested in trustees, in some cases for a parish, in others for a diocese (or their equivalents)[302].

---

[301] COTON, P.: "Religious entities as legal persons-Ireland-" in *Churches and other organizations as legal persons*, Peeters 2007, p. 134.
[302] CASEY, J.: "State and Church in Ireland" in *State and Church in the European Union.* Second Edition, Nomos, Baden-Baden, 2005, p. 192-195.

II. ISLAM IN IRELAND

1. Legal recognition of Islam.

Islam, as all other religions, does not need not to be 'recognised' by the State. In general terms the State engages with the Muslim community in the same way as it does with other faith communities in Ireland. In policing terms, the Garda Síochána (the Irish police) cooperates with the Muslim community through initiatives and policies of the Garda Racial and Intercultural Office and through its General Community Policing Policies.

2. Muslim population.

According to the 2006 Census, the Muslim community is the third largest faith community in Ireland, behind Catholics (3,681,446) and Protestants (125,585). Around 32,539 Muslims were estimated to be living legally in Ireland out of a total population of 4,239,848 (0.76%) inhabitants. Ireland's Muslim community is diverse in terms of nationality and ethnicity: out of these 32,539 Muslims, 9,761 have Irish nationality, 10,649 are of Asian origin and 6,909 come from Africa[303]. In the past, Muslims from the Middle East and North Africa tended to predominate whereas in recent years the population includes more Muslims from South and Southeast Asia, sub-Saharan Africa and China.

The majority of the Muslim population is Sunni and the Shia community is estimated in 2000 people[304], but there are also small communities of Deobandi[305] and Barelvi followers.

The majority of Muslims live in Dublin County and city, but the Islamic community living in Cork is the second largest of the country. There are not

---

[303] Source: Central Statistics Office of Ireland: *2006 Census. Principal Demographic Results*.

[304] *The Muslim Community in Ireland. Challenging Some Of Myths & Misinformation*, National Consultative Committee on Racism and Interculturalism.

[305] The *Deoband* Islamic movement began at *Darul uloom Deoband* in India, where its foundation was laid on 30 May 1866.The movement began to gain significant strength in the early 1900s with graduates from *Deoband* playing key roles in establishing similar institutions in other parts of South Asia.

many Muslims in the political arena, but in May 2007 a group called Muslim Community Lobby was establish to encourage Irish Muslims to participate in democracy[306].

3. Muslim representative organizations.

The first Muslim organisation in Ireland, the Dublin Islamic Society was formed in 1959 by a group of Muslim students and in 1983 it became the Islamic Foundation of Ireland (IFI)[307]. They established Ireland's first mosque in 1976.

The Islamic Cultural Centre of Ireland (ICCI)[308], a Sunni institution, was founded in 1996 with financial support from the United Arab Emirates. Its imam, Sheikh Hussein Halawa, manages both the mosque and the only registered Muslim school attached to the Centre.

The Ahul Bait Islamic Cultural Centre (the only Shia institution in Ireland) was founded in 1998 in Dublin and is managed by Sayyed Ali Abdullah.

There are also other bodies such as the Muslim Association of Ireland (mainly focused on education), the Cork Muslim Society[309], the Galway Islamic Society, the Limerick Mosque, the Federation of Islamic Student Societies, the Waterford Islamic Society and the Supreme Muslim Council of Ireland[310].

The most recent Muslim organization established in Ireland is the Irish Council of Imams, which was set up in 2006. It represents around 14 imams in Ireland (see 5)

---

306 www.muslimcommunitylobbyireland.blogspot.com
307 www.islamiinireland.com
308 www.islamireland.ie
309 www.corkmosque.org
310 According to some authors, this organization set up by Shikh Shaheed Satardian was not successful in their aim to establish themselves as an umbrella organization due to the unpopularity of Satardaian with the main organizations. He made published criticism of ICCI and its supposed links with Muslim Brotherhood. MONTGOMERY, V.: "Ireland" in V.V.A.A. *Yearbook of Muslims in Europe* Edited by NIELSSEN, J.S.; AKAGÖNÜL, S.; ALIBASIC, A; MARECHA,B.; MOE,C; Leiden-Boston, (2009) pages 170-172,

4. Mosques.

There are four purposed-built mosques in Ireland and an undetermined number of prayer halls in most of the main Irish counties. The main mosques are:

- The Islamic Cultural Centre of Ireland (Sunni). It was founded in 1996, with financial support from the United Arab Emirates in Dublin. Its imam is Sheikh Hussein Halawa. It offers facilities for daily prayers, religious celebrations and education through the Muslim National School. It has a library, a mortuary, a shop and a restaurant.

- The Islamic Foundation of Ireland (Sunni). Fit was founded in 1983 and its imam is Sheikh Yayha Al Hussein.

- The Ahul Bait Islamic Cultural Centre (Shia). It was founded in 1998 in Dublin and is the only Shia centre in the country. Its imam is Sayyed Ali Abdullah

- The Ballyhaunis Mosque (Sunni). It was built in 1986 and it was the first purposed built mosque.

5. Imams.

There are no official statistics about the number of imams. The Irish Council of Imams, an umbrella organization of Islamic institutions in Ireland, was created in 2006 by 14 imams. When it was founded it was chaired by Imam Hussein Halawa, from the Islamic Cultural Centre and its deputy chairman was Imam Yahya Al-Hussein, of the Islamic Foundation of Ireland. Council members include representatives from Cork, Galway, Limerick, Waterford, Meath, and various Dublin mosques. Among the aims of the Council are: to facilitate cooperation, consensus and a united approach, to embark on social and educational programmes for imams and to encourage positive integration into the Irish society[311].

---

[311] Declarations of Sheikh Al Faituri, Cork´s imam mosque for the Irish Times: Mary Fitzgerald, "Ireland's Muslims forging an identity" in *The faces of* Islam, The Irish

6. Chaplains.

There are 16 prisons in Ireland. In 2006, 9700 people were sent to prison. The average daily number of people in prison is 3191. There are no statistics about the religious background of prisoners.

All prisons and places of detention have either full or part-time Roman Catholic Chaplains (2006 there were 21 full-time Catholic chaplains and 2 part-time). Muslim prisoners' needs are met by local Muslim leaders who are not engaged by the public sector though Muslim counsellors are generally allowed to perform their duties in hospitals and prisons.

The Irish Defence Forces also have a chaplaincy service with currently 15 chaplains serving in it. Chaplains in the Army as well as in prisons are paid by the state[312].

Community schools are also required to appoint a chaplain (to be nominated by the competent religious authority) who is to be employed outside the normal teacher quota, to receive a salary equivalent to that of a teacher and to be a member of the full-time staff.

7. Islam in public schools. Islamic private schools.

The vast majority of schools are Catholic, subsidised by the Ministry of Education and Science.

There is a registered Muslim school, The Muslim National School in Dublin, which is partly funded, in the same way as other registered schools, by the Ministry of Education and Science. It was established in 1990 and offers primary education for 245 pupils. There are other Muslim schools which are open part-time, normally at the weekends.

Times,13/10/2006. http://www.irishtimes.com/focus/gageby/underthecrescent/identity.htm (accessed 28/07/2009).

312 There was a meeting in Sarajevo on 28. April 2009 on "Islamic military chaplaincy". The proceedings "ZBORNIK RADOVA SA OKRUGLOG STOLA "IMAMSKA SLUZBA U VOJSCI"" has been edited by "Vojno Muftijstvo" (that is the office of MUFTI for the armed forces) in the Ministry of defence of Bosnia and Herzegovina.

There are no official figures of pupils in Ireland by religion.

III. TRAINING CENTRES FOR IMAMS

Ireland does not have any institutions or organisations providing training for Muslim faith leaders. Imams and visiting imams from time to time hold meetings on particular topics at mosques.

ITALY

I. RELIGION AND STATE

1. Administrative bodies that have contact with denominations.

In Italy, the Administrative bodies which are competent for religious matters are:

- Office for Institutional Relationships, Division for Relationships with Religious Creeds, under the Prime Minister Bureau, that, according to the Law August 23rd 1988, n. 400, has a specific competence concerning the stipulation of agreements with non-Catholic creeds (art. 8 Italian Constitution).

- Central Direction for Religious Creeds (Ministry of Interior). The Central Direction for Religious Creeds (*Direttore Centrale degli affari dei culti)*[313] is located under the Department for Civic Liberties and Immigration (*Dipartimento per le Libertà Civili e l'immigrazione*). The Central Direction for Religious Creeds has competence to control the observance of laws regulating religious matters in order to accomplish the right to religious freedom (art. 19 of the Italian Constitution), and to maintain relationships with the central bodies of the Catholic Church and other denominations.

The Central Direction for Religious Creeds is divided into four offices:

a) Office for the Policies of Religious Creeds and for External Relationships (*Ufficio polithiche dei culti e relazioni esterne*). Among other things, this office pursues some comparative studies about the situation of religious creeds in other States.

b) Division for Matters Concerning Catholic Creed (*Affari del culto cattolico)*[314], which is competent for relationships with the Catholic Church deriving from the Concordat Law.

c) Division for Matters Concerning non-Catholic Creeds (*Affari dei culti acattolici)*[315]. Since some years that Division is steadily increasing its importance because of the proliferation of new religious communities, which is basically an effect of migration.

---

[313] In Januarz 2011 the Preffetto was Tiziana Giovanna Costantino.
[314] In January 2011, directed by Viceprefetto Graziella Forti.
[315] In January 2011, directed by Viceprefetto, Maura Curcio.

d) Division for Legal Matters Concerning Religious Bodies (*Affari giuridici degli enti di culto)*[316].

2. Recognition of religions

Even when Constitution safeguards liberty and equality of the individual in religious matters, the system of cooperation between the State and denominations, also enshrined in the Constitutions, allows differentiating between four types of religions, depending not only on the amount of rights recognized by the Agreements (*intese*) or bylaw but also on the way to get juridical personality.

Article 19 of the Constitution recognizes the right to associate with religious aims. Any group with religious purposes may be founded and operate within the legal system without the need of any authorisation or prior registration. The only limits are respecting public order and common decency. For these purposes denominations may choose between various types of legal capacity[317]:

a) Associations under common law:

- Non-recognized associations (*associazione non riconosciuta*[318]).

It is the easiest way to attain legal capacity. Those groups just have to declare before a notary their will to create an association, to have independence in property matters, ability to receive donations, take legal actions, etc. This model is also used by political parties and trade unions. Non-recognized associations don´t have to submit their constitutive act or statute to any form of State control.

- Recognised associations *(associazioni riconosciute)*, according to the Civil Code[319].

These associations obtain legal personality through registration in the Prefectura, provided they fulfil a socially useful purpose and have sufficient economic means.

---

[316] In January 2011, vacant.

[317] FERRARI, S. (2005): "State and Church in Italy" in *State and Church in the European. Union* Second Edition, Nomos, Baden-Baden, p. 209-230; and "Entities religieuses come personnes juridiques- Italie" in *Churches and other organizations as legal person,* Peeters, 2007, p. 139-147.

[318] arts. 36-38 Civil Code.

[319] arts. 14-35 and Dpr. 10 February 2000, No. 361.

b) Recognized associations according to the Law of June 24th 1929, n. 1159, conceived specially for groups with religious aims[320].

Actually, they don't represent the general denomination but bodies of those denominations (place of worship, institutions, etc.) which, after presenting their act of constitution and their bylaws, may be acknowledged by the state (Ministry of Interior, State Council, and Ministries Council) as religious entities. This official acknowledgement confirms the legal nature of that group.

Even if ministers of cult of these recognized associations can celebrate marriages according to the law of 1929, the main consequence of this procedure of recognition is that these religious groups have the same tax privileges than non-profit organizations. Even if they are subject to a certain control by the Government (State authorities can replace the administrative bodies of the associations by a State commissioner and also cancel their decisions), this official acknowledgement or recognition is the basic precondition to apply for an agreement with the State (art. 8.3 of the Italian Constitution)[321].

---

320 The First Commission of the Chamber of Deputies is currently discussing a new parliamentary bill with "Rules Concerning Religious Freedom". Its aim is the accomplishment of the constitutional principles in matters of freedom of conscience, religion and creed, and the abrogation of the above-mentioned Laws of 1929 and 1930 on the so-called "allowed creeds". The bill contains six items: I: concerns the general principles, i.e. the meaning of the right to religious freedom; the freedom of religious creeds and their independence; the ministers of religión;2: regards the procedure for registration in the register of religious creeds and the modifications to statutes; 3: concerns the rights of the religious creeds which are registered (burial, social security, religious buildings); 4: contains provisions on religious marriage with civil effects; 5: contains provisions on the procedure for the stipulation of agreements; 6: contains final and temporary provisions. CURCIO, M.: "Administrative and Financial Maters in the Area or Religious Freedom and Religious Communities" in *Legal Aspects of Religious freedom* (International Conference, 15-18 September 2008), Ljubljana, 2008, p. 379.

321 Religious Communities recognized according to the Law of 1929 (S. Berlingó - G. Casuscelli, *Códice del diritto ecclesiastico,* Milano, Giuffré, 2003): Chiesa ortodossa russa in Roma (1929), Comunita armena dei fedeli di rito armeno gregoriano (1956), Assemblee de Dio in Italia (1959), Ente Patrimoniale dell'Unione Cristiana Evangélica Battista d'Italia (1961), Chiesa evangélica luterana in Italia (1961), Chiesa ortodossa russa a San Remo (1966), Fondazione dell'Assemblea Spirituale Nazionale dei Baha'i d'Italia (1966), Movimento evangélico intemazionale Fiumi di Potenza (1971), Centro islámico cultúrale d'Italia (1974), Congregazione cristiana evangélica italiana (1976), Chiesa di Cristo di Milano (1977), Ente patrimoniale dell'Unione italiana delle Chiese cristiane avventiste Del giorno(1979), Chiesa cristiana millenarista (1979), Congregazione cristiana dei Testimoni di Geova (1986), Chiesa del Regno di Dio (1988), Chiesa cristiana evangélica pentecostale (1988), Unione buddhista italiana (1991), F.P.M.T, Italia - Fondazione per la preservazione della tradizione Mahayana (1999), Ente Consulta Evangélica (1999), Chiesa cristiana evangélica indipendente «Berea» (1999), Unione Induista Italiana (U.I.I.) Sanatana Dharma Sangha (2000), Ente patrimoniale della Chiesa di Gesü Cristo dei

It must be underlined that even if just “denominations′ bodies” can obtain legal capacity according to Law No. 1159 of 1929, only “denominations” can conclude agreements with the State (Art 8 Constitution).

c) Denominations with Cooperation Agreement (*intese*).

So far, six denominations have come to sign Cooperation Agreements with the Italian State (Valdensians, Adventists, Assemblies of God, Jews, Baptists and Lutherans. These denominations are no longer subject to Law No. 1159 of 1929, which has been replaced in their cases by the far more favourable provisions contained in their respective cooperation agreements (*inteses).* Those agreements have passed to Parliament in order to become ordinary laws. However, the legal capacity obtained on the basis of these laws is maintained by the six described denominations.

The two main privileges that grant those *intese* are:

- Right to have religious teaching in public schools
- Two main tax benefits: regarding the income and donations tax.

1) Quota of 8% of the Income tax (IRPEF: *imposta sul reddito dellepersone fisiche*)

   Any person liable to taxation can in his/her annual declaration decide, by ticking the respective box, if their quota of 0.8 % of income tax goes to:

- Italian State: for extraordinary measures against famine in the world, natural disasters, aid to refugees or the conservation of cultural monuments.
- Catholic Church: for the worship needs of the population, the support of the clergy, welfare measures benefiting the national community or third world countries.
- Denominations which have signed an agreement with the Italian State.

The 0.8 *per mille* of those who have not declared their preference is distributed among the different recipients in proportion to the choice made by the citizens that have declared their option. Anyhow, the Christian Evangelical-Baptist Union has declined to take part in the distribution of the 0.8 % of IRPEF. The Valdensians, Pentecostals and Adventists have taken two decisions: on the one hand, to relinquish their proportion of the 0.8 % IRPEF equivalent to the "choice not

---

Santi degli ultimi giorni (1993), Ente cristiano evangélico dei fratelli (1997), Associazione cristiana ortodossa dei Santi Agapito Martire e Serafino di Sarov(1998), Ente della Chiesa della fratellanza nella realizzazione del Sé (1998), Sacra arcidiocesi ortodossa d'Italia ed Esarcato per 1'Europa meridionale (1998), Istituto Italiano Zen Soto Shobozan Fudenji (1999), F.P.M.T, Italia - Fondazione per la preservazione della tradizione Mahayana (1999), Ente Consulta Evangélica (1999), Chiesa cristiana evangélica indipendente «Berea» (1999), Unione Induista Italiana (U.I.I.) Sanatana Dharma Sangha (2000).

expressed". On the other hand, they decided that the rest of the money (the 0.8 % of IRPEF) should be used for social and humanitarian purposes because they believe that financing of the Church and the maintenance of the clergy is an internal affair that should rely exclusively on donations by their members.

These financial flows must be destined to the above mentioned purposes.

The religious creeds have to produce each year a statement of account and send it to the Central Direction of Religious Creeds of the Ministry of Interior.

2) Deductions from donations

Donations bestowed by citizens to a religious body (that goes to the Central Institute for the Support of the Clergy or similar institutions of other denominations) can be deducted from their taxable income up to 1.032.91 Euros.

d) The Catholic Church

The Catholic Church has signed with the Italian State the so-called Revision Agreements of *Villa Madama* of 1984 (international treaties) which have been implemented by an Additional Protocol (1985) and several laws and decrees.

As it has been said, Catholic Church in Italy has public law legal capacity, even if it is in no way comparable to the bodies which belong to the State organisation. If anything, it may be compared with foreign States which are public law subjects in Italian law[322].

---

[322] FERRARI, S.: "State and Church in Italy" in *State and Church... op. cit.* pág. 216.

II. ISLAM IN ITALY

1. Recognition of Islam

The Islamic Cultural Centre of Italy was recognised in 1974 as a religious community under the 1929 Law, but so far Islam has not signed a cooperation agreement (*intesa*) with the Italian State due to the fact that no Islamic body currently represents Italian Muslims. Some attempts have been made over the past years to sign a cooperation agreement but in vain.

On 10 September 2005, the Consultative Council for Italian Islam (*Consulta per l'Islam italiano*)[323] was set up through an order of the Interior Minister. It had a consultative role in discussing the status of Islam in Italy and the process of reaching a cooperation agreement with the State. With that aim, it deals with in-depth research, prepares studies and formulates recommendations and proposals for the Interior Ministry, with a stated goal of developing the dialogue between the State institutions and Muslim communities and identifying the best ways to integrate harmoniously the latter in the Italian society.

This advisory body was chaired by the Interior Minister, who selected its members among scholars, experts, as well as individuals of Islamic faith and culture.

In 2007 the government published a charter of shared values for citizenship and integration, prepared by the Minister of the Interior (decree of 23rd April 2007 of the Minister of Interior) and presented to the members of the Consultative Council to reaffirm the values of a secular state and religious freedom. A declaration of Intentions (*Dicharqazione di intenti per la federazione dell'Islam italiano)* prepared by representatives of Muslim groups and academics was presented in March 13th 2008 with the aim of preparing the way for a valid interlocutor with the State in order to reach an agreement.

The Consultative Council of Italian Islam has been replaced in February 2010 by the *Comitato per l'Islam italiano,* an advisory body created by the Ministry of Interior (Roberto Maroni) composed of 19 members of different nationalities and all of them experts in Islam world (journalists, professors, representatives of Islamic communities etc.).

---

[323] More about the Council for Italian Islam, the Decree of constitution and its members (in Italian)...see:
http://www.interno.it/mininterno/export/sites/default/it/temi/religioni/sottotema003.html.

2. The Muslim population.

Muslim presence in Italy dates back to the 9th century when the Muslim Empire conquered parts of Sicily and the south of the Peninsula[324]. But it was not until the 20th century that important numbers of Muslim people settled in the country. As other Mediterranean countries, Italy began to receive economic migration later than its northern European neighbours. It was not until the 1980s that migrants from Morocco, Sub Saharan Africa, some Middle Eastern countries and Albania began to arrive. The diversity of countries of origin as well as the amount of people arrived in a short period of time, added to the high number of irregular migrants and the geographical dispersion, are some of the features that shape the way in which Islam is institutionalizing in Italy[325].

According to the number of followers Islam is the second religion of Italy. Out of a population of 59 million inhabitants[326], 1.3 millions are estimated to be Muslims, the majority of whom live in the north (Piedmont, Lombardy, Veneto, Emilia Romagna…).

Although the Moroccan community appears to be the most numerous, ethnic diversity within the Muslim population makes it difficult to acknowledge a particular national group as representative of Islam.

Religious marriages have civil effects if they are celebrated by a catholic priest (art. 8 of the Agreement of 1985 between Italy and the Holy See), by a minister of a denomination that has signed an agreement with the State or by authorized by the Italian Ministry of Interior to perform a religious ceremony (arts. 7-12 of Law nº 1159 of 1929). So far, this permit has not been given to any Muslim "minister" so religious weddings celebrated according to Islam has not legal validity. In order to get, the Muslim couple should go through a civil ceremony in addition to their religious marriage

---

324 ALLIEVI, S.: "Islam in Italy" in HUNTER, S. (ed.): *Islam, Europe's second religion. The new social, cultural and political landscape*, Preaeger, 2002, p. 77-95.

325 *Ibid.*

326 Source: official data from the Istituto Nazionale di stadistica, June 2008.

3. Muslim representative organizations

A minority of Italian Muslims belong to religious associations, the best known of which are:

- *L'Unione delle Comunità ed Organizzazioni Islamiche in Italia* (U.CO.II) (Union of the Islamic Communities and Organizations in Italy. It was created in Ancona in 1990 following the steps of the Union of Islamic Students of Italy (USMI). It has links with the Muslim Brotherhood. They have been active as editors and in 1993 the published *Il musulmano.* They have also supported the translation of the Koran to Italian.

- The Islamic Cultural Center in Italy (CCII), set up in 1995 in Rome is supported by the Islamic World League. They have built the Mosque of Rome, the largest mosque in Europe, funded, mainly, by Saudi Arabia. It is the only Islamic association that has been recognized as a religious community under the Law of 1929 (Decree of the President of the Republic of January 21st 1974 (n° 212).

- World Islamic League –Italy[327]. The World Islamic League was created in Mecca in 1962. One of its targets was supporting Sunni Islam throughout the world. As an NGO it is member of some international organizations (ONU, UNICEF, and UNESCO). In 1997 a branch was opened in Italy. Its president is Abdallah bin Salih al Obeid.

- CO.RE.IS, *Comunità Religiosa Islamica* (Islamic Religious Community). It is made up of Italian converts. It has its seat is in Milan and ten branches in seven different regions of Italy. In 1993, Abd al Wahid Pallavicini, converted to Islam in 1951, founded the *Associazione Internazionale per l'Informazione sull'Islam*, which was transformed into the CO.RE.IS in 1997. From the outset, his actions were marked by the strengthening of inter religious dialogue, especially between Judaism, Christianism and Islam. In 1997 they signed a cooperation agreement with the ISESCO (Islamic Educational Scientific and Cultural Organization). In 1998 they presented a proposal for an agreement between the Islamic Community in Italy and the Italian Republic. The CO.RE.IS also manages al-Wahid Mosque, which was opened in Milan in 2002. One of the main projects undertaken in recent years has been the Academy of Islamic Studies, also in Milan. Together with the al-Wahid Mosque, the Academy would complete a large complex for the needs of Islam in Italy and

---

[327] http://www.lega-musulmana.it

Europe, a project that has been undertaken in cooperation with the *Institut des Hautes Études Islamiques* (IHEI), active in France since 1986[328].

- UMI, *Unione dei Musulmani d'Italia* (Union of Italian Muslims). One of its aims is to involve Muslims in Italian politics. Its leader is Adel Smith, famous for his provocative speeches .

- AMI, *Assemblea Musulmana d'Italia* (Italian Muslim Assembly and the Cultural Institute of the Italian Islamic Community). It was created in 1982 by a group of Italian converts and immigrants in Naples. Now it has its seat in Rome[329], but its importance has recently decreased.

There are also many other smaller organizations like the Organization of Young Muslims in Italy (*Giovani Musulmani d'Italia* – GMI-)[330]

4. Mosques, imams and cemeteries.

There are no official figures about mosques in Italy but there is a great deal of worship places. In 2007 some researches spoke of 735 mosques[331]. Anyhow, Italy has experienced a significant growth in terms of mosques: from 351 in 2000 until 735 in the first semester of 2007 (39 of them opened in the first semester of that year).

There are three big mosques: in Segregate (Milan), in Rome and in Catania (but this one is infrequently used. There is one under construction in Colle Val d´Esla (close to Florence, despite political opposition, mainly from the Northern League. In April 2008, the city of Bologna scrapped plans for a new mosque, saying Muslim leaders failed to meet certain requirements, including making public its source of funding. Many Muslim reports show difficulties in building a mosque and obtaining funding.

By January 2009, 263 imams were estimated to work on Italian Islamic worship places, 55% of Moroccan nationality[332].

---

[328] http://www.coreis.it
[329] www.amimuslims.org/
[330] http://www.giovanimusulmani.it/home/
[331] Report of the Security and Information Department -Dipartimento per les informaziones per la sicurezza.
[332] Source: official data from the Italian government.

In some municipal cemeteries, like in Florence, Turin and Milan, plots for Islamic burials have been reserved. There is also a Muslim cemetery in Trieste which was established when the city still belonged to the Austro-Hungarian Empire. In 2008, a proposal to create a Muslim plot in some cemeteries in the municipality of Arezzo (Tuscany) was approved, despite a strong opposition of the neighbours[333].

5. Chaplaincy

According to the Constitution (art. 8.3) ministers of religious denomination without cooperation agreement (Islam included) have access to prisons, hospitals or to the army to give spiritual assistance to prisoners or patients upon request.

Regarding religious counselling in prisons and hospitals, Muslim counsellors are allowed to give assistance to prisoners or patients who seek it[334] but their salaries are not fund by the State. As for the Army, the only chaplains in the Italian Army are catholic priests.

Regarding health service, the Hospital of Florence (Careggi) has an agreement with the local Muslim community to visit Muslim patients. There is also a prayer room in Turin hospital, open to patients of all religions.

6. Islam in schools

Only the Catholic Church and the other 6 denominations with agreement have the right to teach their religion in public schools.

According to a decree nº 239 of 1930, religious communities without an agreement with the State may use the classrooms for classes of religion culture if there are substantial numbers of pupils of that religion and when places of worship are not available around. This option has not been taken up by Muslims.

---

[333] S.: "Italy" in V.V.A.A. *Yearbook of Muslims in Europe* Edited by NIELSSEN, J.S.; AKAGÖNÜL, S.; ALIBASIC, A; MARECHA p 186-7.

[334] This right is based on Articles 5-6 of the Royal Decree of February 1930 for the denominations recognised according to Law 1159 of 1929 and on the basis of the general legal provisions for the other denominations.

According to the Constitution (art. 33) organization and private citizens have the right to found schools without State funding[335]. No Islamic schools have been established under this article but there are some Islam schools that have been founded by foreign governments like Libya, Egypt and Tunisia.

There are also sine cases of illegal Muslim schools[336]

III. TRAINING CENTRES FOR IMAMS

Training courses were organized for imams and leading figures in mosques in 2007 and 2008 in the cities of Turin and Brescia on the initiative of U.M.I. (Union of Muslims in Italy) and U.CO.II (Union of the Islamic Communities and Organizations in Italy), respectively.

The two courses organized in Torino by U.M.I. counted with the cooperation of Morocco's Ministry for Islamic Affairs. No partnership has been established with any Italian University yet for the development of this kind of education. Actually, the U.CO.II. Course was organized by an NGO dealing with training. The teachers were mainly representatives from Islamic communities, religious authorities and university teachers, also from abroad.

The contents of these training courses were the study and understanding of the sources of Islam, the contents of sermons, knowledge of the cultural, political and social aspects of Western countries (Italy in particular), relationship between East and West with regard to traditional values, and the problem of Muslim representation.

---

335 FERREIRO GALGUERA, J.: "La financiación de la enseñanza privada en Italia II", in *Suplemento de Humana Iure de Derechos Humanos. Persona y Derecho*, 1999 (pp.377-477).
336 The Ministry of Interior have reported 88 non authorised Islamic schools COGLIEVINA, S.: "Italy" in V.V.A.A. *Yearbook... op cit.* p. 185-6.

LATVIA

I. RELIGION AND STATE

1. Administrative bodies that have contact with denominations.

The overall supervising body for religious issues is the Board of Religious Affairs (under the supervision of the Ministry of Justice). The Head of this Board is appointed by the Ministry of Justice and ratified by the Cabinet of Ministers[337].

The main functions of the Board of Religious affairs are:

- Maintaining relationships between Government and religious organizations.
- Coordinating government policy in religious issues and advising the Ministry of Justice in religious items.
- Registering religious organizations and its institutions, as well as the amendments they introduce in their statutes and changes in their organization.
- Advising religious organizations in order to observe the law.
- To advice the Ministry of Finance about religious organizations who apply for public interest status.
- Advising Migratory institutions when for missioners from abroad ask for residence e permit.

Additionally there are two advising councils on religious issues in Latvia: The New Religions Consultative Council (NRCC) and the Ecclesiastical Council (EC).

---

[337] There are 8 persons working there. It has a separated budget. In 2008 was 73.000 LVL. Vid. MACUKA. J.: "Administrative and Financial Maters in the area of religious freedom and religious communities in Latvia" in Legal Aspects of Religious freedom (International Conference, 15-18 September 2008) Ljubljana 2008, p. 384.

- New Religions Consultative Council (NRCC) meets on *ad hoc* basis and is not a decision-making authority. It consists of representatives of municipal institutions, law enforcement authorities as well as officials representing the fields of education, culture and social affairs.
- Ecclesiastical Council (EC) is an advisory body chaired by the Prime Minister and consists of representatives from the major traditional religious groups.

2. Recognition of religions: Register of congregations and churches.

The Latvian government does not require the registration of religious groups in order to exercise the fundamental right of freedom of belief[338]. They could also adopt the form of an association and so they would be regulated by the Law on Public Organizations and Associations. But according to the Religious Organizations Act of September 7th 1995, only register religious groups can profit of certain rights and privileges, such as having a separate legal entity status for owning property, conducting financial transactions or allowing tax benefits for donors. Registration also eases the rules for public gatherings, and only registered churches (and so with religious association status) may establish theological schools or monasteries.

A church can freely establish a religious entity, but the State will only recognise this entity as such after registration (that is, after it has become a legal entity)[339]. Even though, non-registered religious groups have the right to conduct services, religious rituals, ceremonies and to carry out charitable work, provided that such activities remain in compliance with the law[340]. A religious group cannot have an economic target as its main activity. If the income of a religious organisation from business activities during one calendar year exceeds 500 minimum monthly salaries (based on the minimum monthly salary set by the Government for the respective period), the religious organisation must establish

---

338 Article 150 of the Criminal Law prescribes a penalty for committing direct or indirect restriction of the rights of persons or of their freedom to choice on the basis or attitudes of such persons towards religion (excepting activities in the institutions of a religious nomination) as well as for committing violation of religious sensibilities of persons or incitement of hatred in connection with the attitudes of such persons toward religion or atheism.

339 Article 11 of the Law on Religious Organisations, 7 September 1995: "Non-traditional religious communities and associations acquire the rights of a legal personality on registration of their statutes"

340 Article 277 of the Criminal Law of the Republic of Latvia prescribes a penalty for unlawful activities of religious organisations and their members

its own business which shall be registered according to the competent legislative acts[341].

One of the functions of the Board of Religious Affairs is to register new congregations, churches (religious associations) or dioceses. The Law on Religious Organizations does not permit simultaneous registration for more than one church (religious association) in a single confession. The Board of Religious Affairs must examine the documents submitted for registration within one month and notify the applicant accordingly.

Latvia is a multi-confessional country, where the three largest denominations are the Catholic, the Lutheran and the Orthodox Church. In general, there are about 170 different denominations and religious groups. Under Article 7 of the Law on Religious Organizations, a congregation may be established by at least 20 Latvian citizens or persons who are registered as legal residents and have reached 18 years old (which includes every person who has legally crossed the border[342]).

The legal status of legal entities in Latvia is defined by the Civil Law[343], but the registration procedure is regulated by the Law on Religious Organizations of 7 September 1995. Other public organizations (except trade unions and businesses, which are subject to a different law) are regulated by the Law on Public Organizations and Associations.

The Law on Religious Organizations recognizes three types of religious organizations: church congregations, religious associations (churches) and dioceses.

a) Congregations

An authorised person of that religious community may apply for registration to the Board of Religious Affairs and presenting the written authorization entitling him/her to handle matters concerning to registration. The application must be accompanied by:

---

[341] Article 15 of the Law on Religious Organisations. Religious organisations may own movable and real property but they are prohibited from mortgaging church buildings or ritual artefacts (art. 16).

[342] BALODIS, R.: "Religious entities as Legal Persons-Latvia- in "Churches and other organizations as legal persons" Peeters 2007 pág. 150-

[343] which stands that blasphemy is a misconduct Article 1415 "Unsanctioned and indecent activities if their aim is contrary to religion, law or good morals, or they are aimed at avoiding law, cannot be the subject matter of a legal transaction and any such transaction is void."

- List of Twenty persons aged 18 or over (founders), registered in the Latvian Citizens Register, including their full names, addresses, identification numbers and signatures.

- The Charter (constitution, regulations)

- A summary from the minutes of the foundation meeting

- The document proving payment of stamp duty on registration of the congregation.

b) Religious association (church)

A minimum of ten registered church congregations belonging to the same denomination can establish a religious association (church). The application must be accompanied by:

- The list of at least ten registered congregations (founders of the church) confirmed by their respective religious leaders

-The Charter (constitution, regulations)

- An extract from the conference (synod) minutes recording the foundation meeting of church, its administrative institutions, etc. congregation

- The document proving payment of stamp duty on registration of the congregation.

c) Dioceses

A religious association (church) may take the decision of establishing a diocese. A diocese shall be a territorial and administrative unit of a certain organizational structure of a religious association (church) in accordance with the canonical rules of a particular denomination, which is overseen by a bishop (at this moment only the Catholic Church has dioceses). The application to register a diocese must be accompanied by:

-The Charter (constitution, regulations)

- The decision of a religious association to create a diocese

- Information regarding the leaders

- Document proving payment of stamp duty on registration of the conger gation.

In accordance with the Law on Religious Organizations (Article 7.1.) and for the purpose of reaching goals set by their respective charters, registered religious organizations may create not-for-profit institutions: educational institutions for ecclesiastics, monasteries, missions, deaconate institutions and similar organizations.

Any institution established by a religious organization functions in accordance with existing legislative acts, its charter and regulations approved by the respective religious organization. Religious organizations may create, reorganize or dissolve these institutions according to their internal rules.

II. ISLAM IN LATVIA

1. Legal recognition of Islam

The Board of Religious Affairs distinguishes between traditional religious groups (those that were present during the first period of the independence of Latvia, 1918 -1940) and non-traditional religious groups[344]. Islam is considered as non-traditional religion group.

There are currently 14 different Muslim congregations in Latvia that due to internal disputes have not been able to form a religious association yet.

2. The Muslims population

The majority of Muslim population are settlers and descendants of settlers from the Soviet period. They moved to the Baltics from the Soviet Central Asian republics like Uzbekistan, Kazakhstan, Tajikistan and Azerbaijan[345].

The total population of Latvia on 1st January 2007 was approx 2,270,000 people. There are no official figures relating to the number of Muslim inhabi-

---

[344] Regarding Latvia´s State relation with religious organizations, it can be said that the Government entertains special relations with the following denominations: Evangelical Lutheran, Roman Catholic, Orthodoxies, Old-believers, Methodists, Baptist, Adventist of Seventh day and Judaism. These denominations have certain rights regarding religious marriage, chaplaincies in government institutions and teaching their religion in public schools.

[345] http://www.islammuslim.lv/

tants, but non-official statistics estimate the number of Muslims in Latvia to be about 5,000[346]. But, less than 1,000 are practising.

3. Muslim representative organizations

As explained before, in Latvia there is no body that represents Islam or a group of Muslim entities at a community level. Information from the Institute of Latvia mentions the following Muslim communities in the country:

1. Muslim Congregation of the City of Riga IDEL (founded in 1996).
2. Latvian Islamic Community (founded in 1998).
3. Muslim Community of Riga CORÁN (founded in 1998).
4. Muslim Community of Riga IMAN (founded in 2002).
5. Daugavpils Islamic Centre IDEL (founded in 1996).

4. Mosques and Imams.

There are no purposed-built mosques just a few prayer halls in private homes where some Muslims occasionally gather for communal prayer.

According to a report by the Latvian Islamic Community, in 1996 there were two imams in the country[347]. At present, there is one official Muslim faith leader in Latvia (Sudanese origin, lives in Latvia since the end of 1980's). Besides, other imams from Tatar and Latvian origins also play an important role within the Muslim communities.

The imams who currently practise in Latvia received their training basically in St. Petersburg and Kazan (Russia).

---

346 DASSETO, F., FERRARI, S. and MARECHAL, B. (2007): *Islam in the European Union: What's at stake in the future?* Brussels, European Parliament. http://www.libertysecurity.org/article1582.html

347 http://www.islam.lv/

5. Chaplaincy.

Muslim faith leaders are engaged in the public sector however they are not paid by the State and their activities are not official, which means they may develop their counselling activities in prison or hospitals upon invitation. No training has been organized and no concerns or problems have been detected.

The work of other religious organisations at public institutions is mainly carried out through the Chaplaincy Service, that, in 2002 had 17 Lutheran, 10 Baptist, 7 Pentecostal, 4 Seventh Day's Adventist and 1 Old Believer Orthodox chaplain. Chaplaincy is the only approved profession in Latvia where ministerial status and recognition from the church is required.

Chaplains' activity is financed and given material and technical support by the appropriate state or self-governmental institution within its regular budget, or by the relevant religious organisation. The Regulations govern the work of the chaplaincy service in the Republic of Latvia provide that:

- "Chaplains of custody institutions" give ecclesiastical service to the personnel of places of imprisonment, conviction or confinement, morally support and advise on religious and ethical questions, and make arrangements for moral education. The structure of chaplaincy service at places of confinement is determined by the Board of the Places of Confinement in agreement with the Board of Religious Affairs. All prisoners may see a clergyman tête-à-tête once a month".

There are 15 prisons, but the Prison Authorities plan to reduce this number in the next few years. According to statistics from the Prison Service, the prison population on 1st January 2008 was 6548. There is no information on the number of Muslim prisoners.

"National Armed Forces Chaplains" provide ecclesiastical service for the personnel of the National Armed Forces. They are given service ranks and are subordinated in administrative questions to their unit commander. For issues related to chaplaincy activity they depend on the Chief Chaplain of the National Armed Forces, and for questions connected with religion to the spiritual leader of their denomination.

- "chaplains of airports, sea-ports and land transport terminals" render ecclesiastical service to the personnel of airports, sea-ports and land transport stations, giving moral support and necessary advice on religious questions within their competence.

- "chaplains of institutions of medical and social services" render ecclesiastical service to the personnel and clients of institutions of medical and social services, giving them moral support and necessary advice connected with religious questions within their competence.

Only the following religious organizations can nominate persons as chaplains: the Board of the Latvian Evangelical Lutheran Churches, the Riga Archdiocesan Roman Catholic Curia, the Latvian Orthodox Churches, the Latvian Old Believers Church Central Council, the Latvian Associated Methodist Churches, the Latvian Baptist Community Association, the Seventh Day Adventist Latvian Community Association, the Riga Jewish Religious Community and the International God Latvian Trinity Community Association[348].

6. Islam in School.

According to statistics from the Latvian Education Ministry, there are 945 public schools in the country, but there is no official information about the number of private or subsidised schools.

According to the Muslim Community in Latvia, in 1996 there were about 100 Muslim students, mainly with Pakistani, Chad and Sudanese background. The Muslim Community also comments on the positive attitude of the university authorities towards these students where they have been given a place of worship.

The Law on Religious Organizations (1995) stipulates that only representatives of traditional denominations (Christian and Jewish) may teach religion in public schools to students who volunteer to take classes. Islamic education (formally a "non traditional" religion) is not offered in public schools, but some history of Islam is taught within the history curriculum. Muslim congregation of Riga and Daugavpils provided Islamic education for young people at weekend schools.

---

[348] BALODIS, R.: "State and Church in Latvia" in *State and Church in the European Union* Second Edition, Ed Nomos, Baden-Baden 2005. pag. 274.

III. TRAINING CENTRES FOR IMAMS

There are no imam training centres in Latvia. Only churches (religious associations) may establish theological schools or monasteries and due to the fact that Islam is not an official church, there are no training possibilities for Muslim faith leaders in Latvia.

The only form of Islamic education is Koran and Arabic classes given by the mosque in Riga.

Academic courses on the Middle East (especially Arabic language) are regularly offered at the University of Latvia (Department of Modern Languages).

LITHUANIA

I. RELIGION AND STATE

1. Administrative bodies that have contact with denominations

Lithuania has taken up a model of Church-State relations that is similar in some ways to other countries in Europe, but with certain unique features as well. On the one hand, Lithuania has quite a rigid system of State recognition of religious communities which is based largely on the historical longevity of religious communities in the country. Nevertheless, separation between churches and State is established in the Constitution of 1992. The State supports religious communities though funds and people involved in religious communities are scarce.

There are few institutions that deal with some aspects of religious affairs but there is no institution specialized in State-Church relations. However, there is a Section of Religious Affairs and Legal Registration of the Department of Registers under the Ministry of Justice which is the competent body for registration of religious communities. Currently this Section has two employees which are responsible for the following tasks:

- Registration of religious communities and associations.
- Acting as an intermediary towards granting legal personality to the traditional religious communities and associations in Lithuania.
- Providing the Parliament of Lithuania (called Seimas) with recommendations.
- Monitoring religious community's activities. If they suspect that those groups are breaking the law or are acting against the public order, the Ministry of Justice is responsible for issuing a warning or taking the issue to court.
- Coordination of State-Church relations and informing about the activities of new religious movements.

Other institutions, that have some competences in the realm of state - church relations, are:

- The Advisor to the Government Office on religious affairs. This post, created straight after Lithuanian independence from the Soviet Union, had the duty of coordinating activities of different ministries related to Catholic Church and other traditional religious communities and associations.

- Ministry of Defence organises chaplaincy services for military personnel.
- Ministry of Education and Science is responsible for coordinating religious education in public schools, approving the programmes, etc.

In 2000 an inter-ministerial commission was formed to coordinate the activities of the different ministries, share information and take necessary actions in the sphere of religious activities and also those of spiritual and esoteric groups[349].

2. Recognition of religions

In addition to the Constitution, the activities of religious communities and associations are regulated by the Law on Religious Communities and associations of the Republic of Lithuania (1995), (hereafter LRCA) which, besides defining some concepts[350]:

- Establishes the freedom of religion and belief
- Regulates religious instruction and religious ceremonies in public schools
- Details registration procedures for traditional religious communities and associations and other religious communities and associations
- Sets out the provisions regarding the activities of religious communities and associations
- Sets out the provisions regarding the closing down of religious organisations, both voluntarily and initiated by the State upon certain conditions
- establishes three categories of religious organisations:
    - traditional religious communities and associations
    - State recognised religious communities and associations
    - other "non traditional" religious communities and associations;

---

[349] GLODENIS, D.: "Administrative and Financial Maters in the area of religious freedom and religious communities: case of Lithuania" in *Legal Aspects of Religious freedom* (International Conference, 15-18 September 2008) Ljubljana 2008 , pags. 392-3.

[350] Article 2 of LRCA, states that a religious community is a unit comprising a group of individuals seeking to implement the aims of the same religion. An association has to be composed of no fewer than two religious communities having a common leader-ship. A religious centre is the covering body of a religious association.

a) Traditional religious communities and associations

The Law specifies the religious denominations that are considered a part of the historical, spiritual and social heritage of Lithuania and therefore are traditional religious communities in Lithuania. Article 5 of the LRCA names 9 traditional religious communities and associations: Roman Catholic, Greek Catholic, Evangelical Lutheran, Evangelical Reformed, Russian Orthodox, Old Believers, Judaism, Sunni Muslim and Karaite.

According to article 10 of LRCA, those traditional religious communities have legal personality and they don't have to register their statues or documents. But, the law on Religious Communities and Associations does not name particular organisations that the State recognises as traditional, it only names those 9 confessions in general

Specific religious community can apply to the Ministry of Justice to be registered in the Register of Legal Entities under the umbrella of one of those 9 "traditional religious communities or associations". In that case it is up to the Ministry of Justice to decide whether the applicant religious community belongs to one of those traditional religions or not. The Ministry of Justice either accepts the claim of the new religious community or rejects it.

In this regard, there have been some problems that affected the Old Believers Church, the Evangelical Reformed Church and the Jewish communities. After the split experienced by Old Believers Church in 1995, the faction that maintained control over the Supreme Council of the Church refused to recognize the other faction as a valid Old Believers' Church. The Ministry of Justice would refuse to register the faction as well. Although the Old Believers Church basically unified in 2002, a small faction (Vilnius Old Believers Church) continued to exist and to represent its case in courts quite successfully: it was registered as a traditional religious community in late 2007. Finally, the main Church agreed to recognize the faction as an independent Old Believers Church.

The Evangelical Reformed Church of Lithuania has experienced a split in 2001. One year later the split church asked for registration as a traditional religious association under the name of *Unilas Litluumiae Synod of Lithuanian Evangelical Reformed Church*. The Ministry of Justice accepted and the older church tried to challenge its decision appealing to the Supreme Administrative Court of Lithuania. This court backed the decision of the Ministry of Justice in 2004[351]

[351] Another decision of the Ministry of Justice regarding registration of a religious community as a traditional religious community is being challenged in court at present by Kaunas Jewish Religious Community. The administrative district court ruled in favour of the minority in 2008 and, since its ruling was appealed against, the Supreme Administrative Court is to take the case. The new draft Law on Religious Communities and Associations is to

b) State recognised religious associations

Other (non traditional) religious associations may be granted State recognition as being a part of Lithuania's historical, spiritual and social heritage if they are backed by society and their instruction and rites are not contrary to laws and morality. State recognition denotes State backing of the spiritual, cultural and social heritage of religious associations. The Lithuanian Parliament of the Republic of Lithuania (*Seimas*) grants State recognition. The Law on Religious Communities and Associations details (art. 6) the procedure.

Religious associations may request State recognition after a period of no less than 25 years from their initial registration in Lithuania. As the State recognition implies State support for historical, social, cultural and spiritual heritage of the religious association, education action of a particular religious association applying for recognition is also examined. The Lithuanian Parliament, *Seimas* will grant recognition only if their religious teaching does not violate public order or good morals and if the religious association in question has public support[352].

The Ministry of Justice provides a conclusion to *Seimas* regarding the status of a state recognised religious association. To date, the Ministry of Justice has prepared conclusions regarding five religious associations, all of which have been present in the country for much more than the 25 years required: The Union of Evangelical Baptist Communities of Lithuania; United Methodist Church of Lithuania; Union of Evangelical Faith Christians (Pentecostals) of the Republic of Lithuania; New Apostolic Church of Lithuania and Seventh Day Adventist Church.

Four out of these five were positive conclusions (doubt was cast regarding the New Apostolic Church). Since the State recognition of religious associations is decided at a political level after the conclusion leaves the Ministry of Justice, the process has suffered from excessive delays. Only Baptist and Seventh Day Adventist churches have succeeded in pushing their requests to full parliament vote (both successfully) in 2001 and 2008 respectfully[353].

---

change the regulation in such a way as to grant the previously registered religious association the power to decide whether the newly created one is to be considered traditional religious community or not. GLODENIS, D.: "Administrative and Financial...*op. cit.* pag. 402

[352] By Article 1 of the 12 July 2001 Seimas of the Republic of Lithuania Resolution "On Granting State Recognition to the Baptist Union of Lithuania", the state recognition was granted lo the Baptist Union of Lithuania, *vid.* RUSKYTĖ, R: "Legal Aspects of Religious Freedom" in *Legal Aspects of Religious freedom* (International Conference, 15-18 September 2008) Ljubljana 2008 , p. 176.

[353] GLODENIS, D.: "Administrative and Financial...*op. cit.* p. 404.

c) Other religious communities and associations

The third category is formed by religious communities and associations that have become legal persons once they have enrolled the Register of Legal Person under the Ministry of Justice according to the rules of registration established in the Civil Code and the Law on Religious Communities and Associations.

Registration of religious communities and associations is not compulsory. However, unregistered religious communities are not subjects of law. There are some requirements to be fulfilled by a religious community or by a religious association in order to be registered under the Ministry of Justice:

- Membership list: in order to be registered a religious community must present at least 15 adult members, citizens of Lithuania, while a religious association can be registered if it unites at least two communities.
- Initiative meeting protocol, Statutes or their correspondent documents: The statute or corresponding documents must include the name of the community, its main office, activities and religious purposes, organisation, structure and authorities, procedures of amendment of the statutes, order of joining or seceding from the community; members' rights and duties, distribution of its property following its liquidation etc..
- A religious centre can be registered when established according to the internal statutes of the religious association

The Ministry of Justice may refuse to register statutes of religious communities and associations if:

(1) Necessary data are not provided;

(2) The activity of the religious community/association violates human rights, freedoms of others or public order;

(3) When an organization with the same name have already been regis tered[354]

There have been fewer issues regarding registration of other (non-traditional) religious communities. Although some "controversial" religious groups were registered right after the independence of Lithuania from the Soviet Union (Word of Faith Charismatic Church, Jehovah Witnesses, Unification Church), the Ministry of Justice refused registering Osho Ojas Meditation Centre in 1997 and 1998. It was argued, that in essence it was not a religious community, and its practices could violate rights and freedoms of individuals. After the subsequent refusal in 2004, the Centre appealed the decision of the Ministry to Supreme Administrative Court. This Court affirmed that in denying registration of Osho Ojas Meditation Centre, Ministry of Justice had not been neutral. According to the principle of neutrality of the State before religions, the Minis-

---

[354] KUZNECOVIENE, J.: "Religious entities as Legal Persons –Lithuania-in *Churches and other organisations as legal persons* Peeters 2007, *pag. 158.*

try of Justice must accept what the organisation says about their own creed in case there is no unanimous opinion in the scientific community whether a particular group is religious or not. It also stated that the possible threat to health and rights of others was not a valid ground for refusal registration due to the lack of proves showing that the Centre had violated public order or rights and freedoms of others.

In 2007 there were in Lithuania 1.058 religious communities and associations that belonged to traditional denominations; and 168 religious communities and associations had enrolled the register of Legal Entities. They belonged to 23 denominations[355].

II. ISLAM IN LITHUANIA

1. Legal recognition of Islam.

Under the Law on Religious Communities and Associations, Sunni Islam is considered to be one of the nine traditional religions that comprise a part of the historical, spiritual and social heritage of Lithuania. They are related to Lithuania's small Tatar Muslim community. The current representative spokesperson of Muslims before the public authorities is mufti Ramazanas Jakubauskas.

Shia Muslims are excluded from the circle of traditional religions and, in case a Shia Muslim religious community apply to be registered, they would be registered as a non-traditional religious organization.

Until now, no Muslim communities or associations have been recognised as 'state recognised" (b) and no Muslim religious community or association has been registered as a non-traditional religious group (c).

2. The Muslim population

Tatars have been living in Lithuania (the eastern part of today′s republic of Lithuania) since the fourteenth century when they started settling in what was the territory of the Grand Duchy of Lithuania as soldiers and immigrants. Most of the other Muslims are descendants of immigrants from the Muslim Central Asian and Caucasian republics who settled in Lithuania during the Soviet period.

---

[355] GLODENIS, D.: "Administrative and Financial Maters…*op. cit.* p. 400-

The total population of Lithuania is 3,366,400 people. According to the census of 2001, which included a question on religious identity, only about 2860 (0, 08% of the population) professed Islam. These figures might have changed significantly because of immigration. The total number of Muslims could be around 7.000[356].

3. Muslim representative organisations

There are about ten registered Muslim organizations in Lithuania but, so far, only the historical Muslim association headed by the Lithuanian Muslim Spiritual Centre – Muftiat- (*Lietuvos Musulmonu Sunitu Dvasinis Centras – Muftiate-*) is recognized as traditional. Established in 1998 in Vilna, is dominated by Lithuanian Tatars. The Mufti is elected for a five-year term by representatives of local Muslim congregations. The Muftiate have close relations with the Turkish government.

Another organization is the Arab dominated Kaunas-based Lithuanian Muslim Youth Society (*Letuvos musulmonu jaunimo bendrija*) which also has educational and cultural aims as translating and publishing religious literature or engaging in religious education of Youth Muslims[357].

4. Mosques, imams and cemeteries

A century ago there were over a dozen purpose-built mosques, but today only four of them remain. But only one of them, the Kaunas mosque, is regularly used. There is also a prayer hall adjacent to the Muftiate in Vilnus.

There are four known local Muslim leaders who are all of Tatar origin. One was educated in Lebanon, two in Russia, and one is self-educated. These leaders serve in the traditional Muslim communities.

A dozen of Muslim cemeteries have remained and some still are on use (in Nemezis, Raiziai, outskirts of Vilnus and elsewhere).

---

[356] RACIUS, E.: "LITHUANIA" in *Yearbook of Muslims in Europe...op cit.* pag. 206,
[357] *Ibidem* p. 207.

5. Chaplains

There are 15 prisons in Lithuania and the prison population is estimated in 7866 inmates. There are no figures on the number of Muslim prisoners.

There are 45 Catholic priests who serve as chaplains appointed by local bishops and paid either by the prison itself, or by the Diocese.

The pastoral care of Catholics serving in the army is regulated by an Agreement between the Holy See and the Republic of Lithuania. According to this document the Holy See has established a Military Ordinary responsible for the pastoral care of the Catholics serving in the Army. In cooperation with the Minister of Defence, the Military Ordinary appoints a Vicar General. The Vicar General is also the Head Chaplain of the Army.

The Penitentiary Code of the Republic of Lithuania states "the administration of all penitentiary institutions should provide conditions for the performance of religious rituals for persons who are serving the penalty of deprivation of liberty. Clergy of all confessions should have the right to visit penitentiary institutions without any restrictions".

Clergy may visit inmates at their request at times agreed with the Administration. Representatives of religious communities and associations having legal personality may visit places of detention with the permission of the competent officials.

Muslim faith leaders engage very infrequently in chaplaincy, and they do so at the request of inmates. They are not paid by the State and nowadays there are no programs of chaplaincy training for Muslim leaders.

6. Islam in schools

There are 1472 public schools in Lithuania, 23 subsidised schools and one private school. There are no statistics on the number of Muslim pupils.

Religious instruction is given in most public schools of Lithuania. In the year 2007-2008 the total number of children that attended ethics or religious instruction in public schools (these two are mandatory but interchangeable) was 495,370 of whom 53.5% attended religious instruction. Of those attending religious instruction lessons, 98% opted for Catholic teaching. Religious instruction is provided by teachers who receive their training in public universities.

As there are not private primary or secondary schools run by Muslims, Islamic religious instruction is provided in weekend schools. There are around eight of theses[358].

---

[358] *Ibidem* 208.

III. TRAINING CENTRES FOR IMAMS

There are no imam training centres in Lithuania. There are, however three seminaries for the Catholic faith: Vilnius Seminary, Kaunaus Seminary and Telšiai Seminary.

Academic courses on Islam and the Middle East are offered at Vilnius University (Institute of International Relations and Political Science, and the Centre of Oriental Studies) and the Lithuanian Military Academy.

LUXEMBOURG

I. RELIGION AND STATE

1. Administrative bodies that have contact with denominations

The institution responsible for relations between State and religious communities is the Ministry of State through the Denominations Department.

2. Recognition of religions: Convents with State

Each religious community has the right to establish and practise its religion freely and does not have to ask for authorisation from the authorities to do so. In Luxembourg we can difference between religious groups (those that have signed a Convention with the State and those who haven't) and other kind of religious entities (specially, charities).

Religious communities can adopt three forms:

a) Religious groups with a Convention

Those religious groups are recognised by the State through a convention that provides them the status of legal persons of public law.

The Constitution foresees that relations between religious communities and the State can be regulated by Agreements. Such conventions are optional and do not establish a hierarchy between communities. They offer the religious communities the opportunity to receive a financial support from the Government. This may not impede the community's full right of freedom of religion.

To benefit from a convention with the State, a religious community must fulfil four conditions:

- Being a universal religion recognised or at least known at worldwide level
- Being recognised or similar by at least one other Member State of the EU
- Respect for public order

- Being supported by a representative community of local residents
- Having a deep historical presence and a significant number of members.

Only Catholic Church, Israelite Communities, the Reformed Protestant Church, the Protestant Church, the Hellenic Orthodox Church, the Anglican Church and the Orthodox Roman and Serbian Churches have signed conventions with the State.

b) Denominations that have not signed a convention can take the form of either non profit associations (being legal persons of private law) or associations *de facto* (with no legal personality).

c) Infra religious entities that belong to a denomination (ex: charitable institutions depending on a Church) share its legal personality, but they can also adopt an autonomous legal person, for example non profit organizations, foundations or even commercial associations.

There is no legal established procedure to register religious communities. The registration refers to religious groups which have signed a Convention with the State. The criteria for the establishment of a convention were informally being set by the Government and the Parliament in 1998. The four conditions above mentioned have been already described. Religious communities don't need to have written statutes or an internal regulation in order to sign a convention. The convention establishes the denomination's head or main representative whose name has to be notified to the State.

Recognition by the State means above all financial benefits: the salaries of the denominations ministers are paid out of the State budget. They don't have other benefits, as the right to celebrate marriages with civil effects or the right to have private cemeteries (with the exception of the Israelite denomination). Their ministers of cult are not exempted from general labour law. Religious public education is reserved to the Catholic Church due to the limited number of other denominations′ congregations.

Religious entities not recognised by the State may as well be consider as "leading to an objective of general interest" so that tax exemption is justified as stated in the Tax and Income Law (art. 161, paragraph 1, nº 1). Non recognised religious entities can develop any activity as legal persons of private law (sign contracts, have properties, hire employees...). Only if they are neither legal persons of private law nor of public law will they be limited in those activities[359].

---

[359]PAULY, A.-KINSCH, p.: "Entites religieuses comme personnes juridiques- Luxaembourg "in *Churches and other organizations as legal persons"* Peeters 2007, pags. 164-7.

II. ISLAM IN LUXEMBOURG

1. Legal recognition of Islam

As explained before, the Muslim community does not need any authorisation to exercise freely its religion. It has the same constitutional rights than any other religious community and is treated the same way, whether it has a convention with the government or not.

The Government and the representative body of the Muslim community are on negotiations to conclude a convention.

2. The Muslim population

There are no official statistics on the number of religious entities or its members. Since the enactment of a law in 1979 the State has been precluded from collecting data concerning an individual's confession or membership of a religious group. However, it is assumed that the majority of the population consider themselves to be Catholic. There are a few thousand Protestants (Lutherans, Calvinists and members of Free Churches), about 1,000 Jewish and there are also groups of Orthodox and Anglicans. In the Portuguese sector there are a large number of Jehovah's Witnesses. Several thousand people are considered to be of no denomination, and the remainder of the population belongs to other non-formally-recognised religious groups. It is rather difficult to estimate the strengths of the various confessions in the population due to the large number of foreigners living in Luxembourg.

The majority of the Muslims in Luxembourg arrived in Luxembourg in the 1990s as refugees. The European Values Studies survey estimated the percentage of Muslims in 0,7% in 1999[360] and 2006 US Department of State *Report on International Religious Freedom*[361] gave the number of 9.000 Muslims, 65% of whom come from the Balkans.

---

[360] *European Values Studies* data about Luxembourg has been published in *Les valeurs au Luxembourg-Portrait d'une societé au tournant du 3e millénaire*, directed by M. Legrand, ed. Saint Paul, Luxembourg, 2002.

[361] *International Religious Freedom Report 2006*, US Department of State. http://www.state.gov/g/drl/rls/irf/ (accessed 20/06/2009)

3. Muslim representative organizations

As the Muslim community is composed of various organisations, the government asked for the creation of a unique structure that could be representative of the whole community in order to their future official recognition by a Convention. For this reason the Muslim community created the Assembly of the Muslim Community of the Grand-Duchy of Luxembourg (*Assemblée de la Communauté Musulmane du Grand-Duché de Luxembourg*) also referred to as the "Shoura". At present, the Shoura represents four different Muslim communities active in four different parts of the country.

4. Mosques, Imams and cemeteries

The *Centre Culturel Islamique de Luxembourg* reports the existence of at least five mosques in Mamer, Bonnevoie, Esch/Alzette, Niedercorn and Wiltz[362].

The projected convention between the government and the Muslim community foresees five imams and one Mufti.

Outside the conventional framework, the number of persons acting as Muslim faith leaders is estimated not to exceed 20. Up to now, all Muslim faith leaders come from abroad. The great majority come from Bosnia but some are French with a foreign background.

There are no Muslims private cemeteries in Luxembourg but there are plots in the Merl cemetery of Luxembourg City, for Islamic burials.

5. Chaplains

Muslim chaplains will be paid by the State once the convention with the Muslim community will enter into force.

The convention does not foresee any disposition related to training but some control mechanisms are included. The Shoura elects the Mufti but the election has to be confirmed by the Minister. In case of displacement of the

[362] www.islam.lu

Mufti by the Shoura, the decision has to be notified to the Minister. The Shoura must also notify the five imams to the Minister. In Schrassig prison, Islamic prayers can be organized and the imam visits regularly.

III. TRAINING CENTRES FOR IMAMS

There are no public institutions or organisations that provide training for Muslim faith leaders in Luxembourg. .

The Islamic centres offer religious training (initial training) to children and adults. The religious training provided by the Islamic centres has no official recognition.

Education in Islam is part of the basic instruction provided by the Institute for Higher Education of Teachers of Religion. There are also some projects about interreligious dialogue including Islam launched by the Archbishop of Luxembourg[363]

[363] BESCH, S.: "LUXEMBOURG" in *Yearbook of Muslims in Europe...op. cit.* pag. 215

MALTA

I. RELIGION AND STATE

The Constitution of Malta states that all persons have freedom of conscience and enjoy the free exercise of their respective mode of religious worship. All religions are recognised as long as they function within the parameters of the law.

Article 2 of the 1964 Constitution of Malta states that: "*The religion of Malta is the Roman Catholic Apostolic Religion*" and so underlines the duty and the right of "the authorities of the Roman Catholic Apostolic Church "to teach which principles are right and which are wrong". Moreover, according to this article, "Religious teaching of the Roman Catholic Apostolic Faith shall be provided in all State schools as part of compulsory education"[364].

Besides the strong presence of the Roman Catholic Church and its multiple associations, in Malta there are a number of persons, mostly expatriates, who follow other Christian creeds including Anglican, Protestant, Evangelist and Orthodox. Other inhabitants, mostly of foreign origin, together with a few locals, embrace religions such as Islam and Judaism. There are also followers of others beliefs.

---

[364] This was not the original text of the 1964 Constitution. It is the text negotiated with the Vatican in 1974 to which the Nationalist Opposition in Parliament gave its assent, even thought it criticised the text as not clear and not precisely worded. This substitution was effected by Act LVIII of 1974 *vid.* MISFUD BONNICI, U.: "State and Church in Malta" in *State and Church in the European Union* Second Edition, Ed Nomos, Baden-Baden 2005. pp. 355.

II. ISLAM AND TRAINING CENTRES FOR IMAMS

The majority of the Maltese are Roman Catholics, i.e. up to 95% of Malta's 400,000 inhabitants. The Muslim community is composed of approximately 3,000 persons (0.75 % out of the total population) the majority of which are of foreign background and a few Maltese converts. Almost a third of the local Muslims have become naturalised Maltese citizens.

In 1984, the World Islamic Call Society (WICS) in Tripoli, Libya, established the Islamic Centre, Paola which apart from the mosque, it contains a conference hall, a library, offices, a playground, and the Imam´s residence. The Imam is appointed by the WICS, his appointment is endorsed by the Maltese state. This imam[365], who has diplomatic status, represents the local Muslim community before the authorities.

In addition to the mosque, there is a small number of Muslims who follow the *Jama'at al Tabligh*. Such worshipers are from different Muslim creeds and ethnical backgrounds. Their common denominator is their Muslim faith.

Apart from the official mosque at Paola, Muslims use five other unofficial places of worship. Maltese prisons have spaces reserved for Muslim worship. A space has also been allocated for interfaith worship at the Mater Dei Hospital.

There is an old cemetery in the town of Marsa built in 1874 at the expense of the Ottoman government. Between 1996 and 2006 Muslim burials took place at the Catholic cemetery at Paola (Maria Addolorata Catholic cemetery). Meanwhile, the Maltese government allocated a piece of land adjacent to the Islamic Centre in Paola for burial purposes[366].

There are 169 public schools in Malta, which are open to students of all religions. In addition there are 134 private schools of which 82 are Catholic, 51 non confessional and the Muslim 'Miriam Al Batool' school which caters for approximately 200 students. Roman Catholic religious education is compulsory in state schools. Muslim students are given the option of either attending or following alternative subjects. This situation has prompted the Muslim community to establish in 1997 the 'Miriam Al Batool' school within the area of the Islamic Centre, Paola which operates on a strictly charitable basis. In addition, the Libyan Secretariat for Education maintains the Al Fateh Libyan School at

---

[365] At this moment, the imam is Shekh Muhammad el-Said, of Palestinian origin

[366] The first burials there took place in 2007 ZAMIT, R.: "MALTA" *in Yearbook of Muslims in Europe...op.cit.* p. 232

Ta'Giorni, St Julians. This school is open to Arab students and follows the Libyan educational curriculum. Classes are in Arabic[367]

Given the small Muslim community there are no Imam training centres in Malta. However, WICS does promote courses to cultivate Imams and callers (Du'āt) especially through their missionary work overseas and their religious university based in Tripoli, Libya.

Academic courses on Islam are offered at the University of Malta in the Faculty of Arts (Department of Arabic and Near Eastern Studies).

---

[367] *Ibidem* p. 233.

POLAND

I. RELIGION AND STATE

1. Administrative bodies that have contact with denominations

The Department of Denominations and National and Ethnic Minorities operating under the Ministry of Internal Affairs and Administration is the Administrative body responsible for relations with religious communities.

According to the Regulations of the Department of Denominations and National and Ethnic Minorities (art. 1), the Department is composed of 5 Divisions, but strictly religious matters constitute the scope of activity of the Divi sion for Churches and Religious Organizations and the Division for the Church Fund.

Among the goals of the Division for Churches and Religious Organizations we can mention the following:

1. Preparing draft regulations on religious problems and relationship between the State, the Catholic Church and other churches and religious organizations;
2. Keeping a register of churches and other religious organizations, including preparing draft decisions of the Minister of Interior and Administration on the entry in the register. Also preparing certificates and copies from the register;
3. Preparing draft ordinances of the Minister of Interior and Administration on granting legal status to organizational units of the Catholic Church and other churches;
4. Maintaining relations with the representatives of the Catholic Church and other churches and religious organizations;
5. Preparing information and analysing religious problems;
6. Conducting administrative proceedings in property cases concerning churches.

The scope of activity of the Division for the Church Fund includes regulating matters related to the Church Fund and cooperating with the Social Insurance Institution on matters concerning the insurance of clergymen. In particular:

a) Preparing draft decisions for the minister (or draft agreements) on granting subsidies for:
- Reconstruction, restoration and renovation of sacred buildings of historical value.
- Charitable work of the Church.
- Educational activity of the Church.

b) Keeping a register of applications submitted for subsidies.

c) Keeping a register of settlements of subsidies granted.

d) Cooperating with the representatives of the Catholic Church and other churches.

e) Preparing a preliminary budget estimate in cooperation with, among others, the Social Insurance Institution[368].

2. Recognition of religions

According to the principle of religious freedom enshrined in the Constitution (art. 53), it is possible to conduct religious activity and propagation of beliefs without any notification to the State as long as those activities don't break the law. Nevertheless, according to legal regulations, if churches or other religious associations opt for the way of recognition, there are three ways to be recognized by the State.

- An international Agreement (the case of Catholic Church)
- Statues regulating relations of the State to the particular churches and religious associations
- Enrolment in the Registry of churches and other religious associations.

Polish legislation does not grant churches or faith associations the status of a Public Law corporation. All registered denominations are subjects of private law. The public law status of the Catholic Church was definitely denied in a judgment of the Supreme Court in 1958.

The differences between churches and faith communities are marked by the method of registration, but all registered religious entities enjoy the same rights

---

[368] RADAJEWSKI, M.: "Administration and financial matters in the area of religious freedom and religious communities" in *Legal aspects of religious freedom (International conference 15-16 September 2008)* Ljubljana 2008, p. 409.

from a legal perspective. Churches and faith associations can belong to these groups:

a) Church or religious communities who got legal personality according to a special law that rules the relations between that religious group and the State. Within this group we can differentiate between:

1. Catholic Church, under the Concordat between Poland and the Holly See of 28 July 1993

2. Fourteen other churches and religious associations operating on the basis of separate status regulating their relation to the State. These comprise the oldest and the largest religious communities (with the exception of Jehovah Witness which, even though is the third largest community, does not operate on the basis of a special law, but on the basis of the Law of 1989).

These churches (with the date of the law in brackets) are the following: Eastern Old Rites Church (Ordinance of the President of the Republic, 22 March 1928), Muslim Religious Association in the Republic of Poland (MZR) (21 April 1936), Karaim Religious Community (21 April 1936), Polish Autocephalous Orthodox Church (4 July 1991), Augsburg-Confession Church in the Republic of Poland (hence-forth, the Lutheran Church) (13 May 1994), Protestant Reformed Church (13 May 1994), Protestant Methodist Church (30 June 1995), Baptist Christians Church (30 June 1995), Seventh Day Adventists Church (30 June 1995), Polish-Catholic Church (30 June 1995), Jewish Religious Communities (20th February 1997), Catholic Church of the Mariavites (20th February 1997), Old Catholic Church of the Mariavites (20th February 1997), Pentecostal Church (20th February 1997).

b). Registered denominations

Until now 154 religious associations have been registered on the basis of the May 17th 1989 Law on the guarantees of the freedom of conscience and confession which created a general framework for all churches and religious associations in Poland and provides for the procedure of registration of religious associations.

Since 1998 Law, a group of at least 100 Polish citizens with full legal capacity can apply for the registration of a church or religious community.

The registration body is the Division of Churches and Religious Organisations, under the Department of Denominations and National and Ethnic Minorities (Ministry of Interior and Administration).

The application must contain these requirements:

- a list of at least 100 petitioners
- Declaration of religious aims, principles, doctrine and ritual practice
- Address, representative bodies and statutes.

In the case of registration of other minor religious entities (dioceses, parishes and other church entities), their legal personality may be obtain in one of three ways:

- A statute on relations between the State and the given denomination names specific entities having legal capacity.
- The same statute includes lists of different kinds and categories of entities units. They are created according to the internal law of a denomination, namely, Canon Law for the Catholic Church.
- The church or religious community submits an application to the Ministry of Interior which will issue an ordinance that will be published in the Official Journal of the Republic of Poland.

In most cases, statutes contain a general list of types of entities and some specific entities as well. If a church wants to create an additional entity that was not listed or was not mentioned individually, it must submit an application to the Minister of Interior and Administration.

Since May 17th 1989 Act, 171 churches and religious associations have been registered and 54 applications were refused in the period 1993-2002.The Minister checks, inter alia, on whether the aims and the doctrines of a church or religious community are likely to endanger public order, public security, morals or are contrary to the right of others (this is one of the reasons why Raelians´application, who were the first group to claim the cloning of a human being in 2002, was refused. "Lacking the features of a religion" might be another cause of refusal).

The rejected applicants can appeal to the Administrative Court and subsequently to Chief Administrative Court (NSA). Only in one case the Court has suspended the decision of the Minister and asked for the opinion of experts[369].

---

[369] RYNKOWSKI, M. (2005): "State and Church in Poland" in *State and Church in the European Union* Auflage, pp. 419-438) and of the same author "Religious entities as legal persons-Poland" in *Churches and other religious organizations as Legal Persons*, Peeters, 2007, pp. 177-182.

II. ISLAM IN POLAND

1. Legal recognition of Islam

All Muslim communities, which have regulated their legal status can exercise the rights guaranteed by Polish Constitution, especially art. 25 (equality of citizens before the law, autonomy before the State), and art. 53 (right to teach religion in schools).

Muslim Religious Association in the Republic of Poland (MZR) was founded in 1925 as an officially autonomous organization representing all Muslims in Poland. A Mufti was elected by a democratic vote. It was recognised by the State, by the April 21st 1936 Act, about the relations between the State and the MZR. This law gave Islam an official recognition and the MZR the legal status of a religious association recognised by law. The law established, among other things, that the Mufti, imams and muezzins would be paid by the State. The 1936 Act was not revoked by parliament after the World War II or after the democratic changes of 1989, though the Constitution (1977) overruled some of its regulations (financial support from the State, the official seat in Vilnius and the obligation for the Polish Muslims to belong to MZR). The law still gives the MZR the right to teach Islamic religious education in schools and provides for teachers to be paid by the State[370]. According to the legislation, the State does not fund directly religious denominations, but they can obtain public funds for specific projects.

Other Muslim religious organizations have been registered in the register of churches and religious associations according to the 1989 Act.

2. Muslim population.

Over a population of 38.116.000 inhabitants, 30.000 more or less (0, 04% of the total population) are estimated to be Muslims.

Polish Muslims are divided into two groups: the first one with Tatar origin settled in Polish – Lithuanian Commonwealth from the 14th to 18th centuries. They are about 6000 and they live mainly in the east part of Poland. The

---

[370] NALBORCZYK, A.-GRODZ,S.: "Poland" in V.V.A.A. *Yearbook of Muslims in Europe* Edited by NIELSSEN, J.S.; AKAGÖNÜL, S.; ALIBASIC, A; MARECHA,B.; MOE,C; Leiden-Boston, (2009) pp. 268-269.

main Tatar centres are in Kruszyniany and Bohoniki. Tatar communities are also in Warszawa, Gdańsk, Białystok and Gorzów Wielkopolski, Bydgoszcz and Poznań. Other groups are students, traders who came in the eightees from the Araba countries (Iraq, Palestine, Syria, Yemen...) and frome the Balkans. There were also refugees that came mainly from Chechnya, Afghanistan, Pakistan, Bangladesh and Iran.

3. Muslim representative organizations.

There is one Muslim associations recognised by law and 3 Muslim registered associations according to the 1989 Act: Muslim Religious Association in the Republic of Poland (*Muzulmanski Zwiqzek Religijny* -MZR)[371], with seat in Białystok, got legal personality according to the Law of April 21st 1936. MZR unites mostly Sunni Muslims with Polish citizenship of Tatars origin. They have around 4.000 members and 8 centres, with imams mostly of Polish origin.

Three other Islamic communities were registered according to the 1989 Law

- Muslim League in the Republic of Poland (*Liga Musulmanska w Rzecypospolitej Polskief* –LM-), Sunni, established in 2001 and registered January 6th 2004[372] with seat in Warsaw, and several hundred members. There is no data on imams but their main faith leader comes from Palestine.
- Two Shí'i organizations:
  - Association of Muslim Unity (*Stowarzyszenie Fednosci* Muzulmanskiej), registered January 31st 1990. It has its seat in Warszawa. The main faith leader is Polish (Zbigniew Zuk).
  - Ahl-ul-Bayt Assembly in the Republic of Poland (*Islamskie Zgromadzenie Ahl-ul-Bayt*) , registered December 17th 1990. It has its seat in Brwinowo.

There is no a specific body which officially represents the Muslim in Poland. Currently the Ministry of Interior and Administration is working on a new act, regulating cooperation between Muslim representatives and the government.

[371] http://www.mzr.pl
[372] http://www.islam.info.pl

4. Mosques, Imams and chaplains.

According to the Spanish Embassy in Warsaw, in Poland there are 3 mosques (in Bohoniki, Druszyniany and Gdansk) and about 12 small prayer halls.

There were 13 Muslim faith leaders in Poland in 2005. Their countries of origin are: Palestine, Algeria, Syria, Jordan, Morocco and Egypt[373]. There is also a Mufti elected by the council of imams in 2004, Tomasz Miskiewitcz.

There are three Muslim cemeteries opened in eighteen century (in Bohoniki, Druszyniany and Warsaw). There are plots reserved for Muslim burials in Gdansk.

According to the Freedom of conscience and beliefs Act (May 17th 1989), to grant "freedom of conscience and beliefs", churches as well as different religious associations are allowed to fulfil their obligations in the army, prisons or hospitals. Muslim faith leaders are allowed (according to June 6th of 1997 Act) to perform their service in the 85 prisons upon the specific agreement, signed between the imam and the director of prison.

There is no information about Muslim faith leaders cooperating with the army, prisons or hospitals.

5. Teachers of Islam in public school and Islamic private schools

Churches and religious associations have the right to establish and operate schools kindergartens, and other educational institutions (art. 21, Law of 1989). The proportion of confessional schools is relatively small, and they educate only about 1% of the total number of pupils.

According to the Ordinance of the Minister for National Education of 1992 about religious instruction in schools, religious instruction of any given confession should be offered upon request of at least seven or more the students or their parents. If the number of children of a specific confession is between three and seven, religious instruction should be offered in cooperation with the religious community. The curriculum should be approved by the religious authorities. There is Islamic religious instruction in public schools in Bialystok and in nearby Sokólka[374].

---

[373] According to data provided by the MZR.

[374] NALBORCZYK, A.-GRODZ,S.: "Poland" in V.V.A.A. *Yearbook...op. cit.* p. 272.

According to our research, there are 32.473 public schools in Poland, 6.499 private schools funded by the State, and 534 private (315 of them are faith schools, mostly Catholics).

III. TRAINING CENTRES FOR IMAMS

There are no public institutions providing training for Muslim faith leaders in Poland. Most of the faith leaders are coming from different Muslim countries to work in Poland and imams of Polish origin (like the Mufti of Muslim Religious Association in the Republic of Poland, who studied in Syria, Sudan and Saudi Arabia) are sent by their communities abroad to obtain the proper education.There are no specific programmes or procedures concerning training for Muslim faith leaders coming from abroad to Poland.

However, there is one informal section of the *Institut Européen des Sciences Humaines* - IESH with seat in Białystok. The Białystok centre provides mainly a theological education through the following courses: history and activity of the Muslim organisations, Arabic, interpretation and recitation of the Quran, etc.

In the Polish section of the IESH future imams will be trained via the internet, the telephone or any other way that facilitates the communication with the lecturer and the correction on a current basis of the Arabic pronunciation or recitation of the Quran. The registration forms are sent to all Islamic Centres in Poland.

The section in Białystok mentioned above is connected with the Centre of IESH in France, but there is no information about the financing sources of the courses. The main seat of the informal section of IESH in Poland is in the French city Chaetau Chinon[375].

There are 46 centres for religious leaders training of other faiths: 41 Catholic seminars, four Protestant Seminars and one orthodox[376].

---

[375] *Institute Européen des Sciences Humaines* – IESH is a private educational Institution, established in 1990, at the initiative of Union of Islamic Organizations of France (UOIF).
[376] Source: Spanish Embassy in Warsaw

PORTUGAL

I. RELIGION AND STATE[377]

1. Administrative bodies that have contact with denominations

According to the Decreto-Lei n.º 308/2003, of 10 December 2003, the Commission for Religious Freedom (*Comissão da Liberdade Religiosa* - CLR) is independent from the Parliament and from the Government and functions as an advisory body regarding issues relating to the application of the Religious Liberty Law.

The Commission is composed, aside from its President, (currently the ex-Prime Minister and ex-President of the Republic, Dr. Mário Soares) of representatives of the Islamic Community of Lisbon, the Israeli Community of Lisbon, the Portuguese Episcopalian Conference, the Portuguese Evangelical Alliance and other experts nominated by the Ministry of Justice.

2. Recognition of religions: the Register of collective religious entities

Churches and religious communities may acquire legal personality through their inscription in the Registry of Collective Religious Entities (*Registro das Pessoas Colectivas Religiosas* -RPCP-) under the Ministry of Justice.

The decision to officially recognize a religious community is adopted by the Ministry of Justice, once it has been considered by the Commission for Religious Freedom.

The Registry of Collective Religious Entities (RPCP) sits within the framework of the National Registry of Collective Entities (*Registo Nacional de Persoas Colectivas*) as is set out in the Decreto-Lei nº 134/2003, f. June 28th 2003.

---

377 This text should be take into account the following legislation changes: the Decree-Law 251/2009 of 23 September regarding religious assistance in the Armed Forces and the Security Forces; the Decree-Law 252/2009 of 23 September concerning religious assistance in prisons and the Decree-Law 253/2009 of 23 September concerning religious assistance in hospitals and other facilities of the National Health Service.

Religious entities of any legal form, including unincorporated associations, have to register in the National Register of Collective Entities within 30 days of their constitution, or the beginning of its activity. They must provide the following information: identification number, name, head office address, legal form, main activity, and date of constitution.

In the case of religious corporations, the application is presented with the statutes and other documents that are necessary for registration:

a) The name, which should allow to distinguish it from any other religious communities existing in Portugal;
b) The constitution, institution or establishment in Portugal of the organisation corresponding to the church or religious community or the deed of the constitution of association or establishment and, eventually, the recognition of the religious corporate body;
c) The registered head office in Portugal;
d) The religious aims;
e) The goods or services that complete or will complete its patrimony;
f) Composition, competence and operational rules of the organisation;
g) Provisions to apply in case of dissolution of the corporate body;
h) Appointment procedure of their representatives;
i) Member of the representative bodies and their functions (article 34 of the RLA).

Registration of churches or religious communities of national, regional or local scope when they have not been created or recognised by the above religious corporations, requires also documentary evidence of:

- General principles of doctrine and religious practices and acts of worship, particularly the rights and duties of the believers of the church or religious community, as well as a summary of the abovementioned elements.
- Their existence in Portugal, with particular emphasis on the facts that can prove the social presence, religious practice and their presence in Portugal.

Registration can only be rejected through: lack of legal requirements, documents forgery as wall as violation of the constitutional limits of religious freedom.

Registration becomes mandatory after a year has passed since the delivery of the application for registration, if in the meantime a notification letter of rejection of the registration has not been sent to the applicant.

Religious entities may take one of the following legal statuses: unincorporated associations; private corporations; religious corporations; churches and religious communities settled in the country or canonical legal persons:

a) Unincorporated associations:

According to the fundamental right of religious freedom people can get together with religious aims. No approval of the authorities is required.

b) Private corporations

Until the Decree 134/2003 which regulated registration of religious entities, all legal persons with non-Catholic religious aims had the status of private corporations. Before that Decree, 597 religious groups had been registered in the Register of religious denominations and non-Catholic religious associations of the Ministry of Justice, which was to be abolished. Such associations could request to be converted to a religious entities (if they complied with the requirements) within a time limit of three years, from the entry into force of Decree 143/2003, namely until December 1, 2006.

Those religious entities that did not opt for this change remained registered in the National Register of Collective Entities as private associations. They have the same collective rights of religious freedom as unincorporated associations.

c) Registered religious entities

According to the Religious Liberty Law (*Lei da Liberdade Religiosa* (LLR) - Law n.º 16/2001 religious churches or communities that prove an organised social presence and religious practice in Portugal, and also declare their doctrines and their personal and patrimonial organisation, can be registered as religious corporations. They must have a national, regional, or local character.

Once registered, they can create or recognise other types of religious corporations and obtain their registration, namely:

- Institutes of consecrated life and other institutes, with the character of associations or foundations, established or recognised by the churches and religious communities in the pursuit of their religious purposes.
- Federations or associations of religious corporations.

The advantages of becoming a registered religious corporation rather than being unregistered are:

- they have public recognition of their collective rights of religious freedom
- they benefit from tax exemptions, but not from State subsidies;
- they may provide religious teaching in public schools;
- they may participate in the broadcasting time for churches and other religious communities on the public television and radio service;
- they have the right to be heard in respect of town planning and
- Their ministers are certified by the State and are included in the national social security system.

In 2005, from 76 non catholic religious corporations, 35 had converted of former non Catholic religious private associations and 41 were formally newly constituted[378].

d) Churches and religious communities settled in the country

Registered churches or religious communities that have existed and have been organised in the country for more than 30 years (or less, if it is a church or religious community founded abroad more than 60 years before) can be considered by the Government as settled or rooted in the country. This status allows those churches to several forms of collaboration with the State such as:

- celebration of civil marriages according to their religious rites
- collaboration in management or advisory bodies of the sector(Committee of the Broadcasting Time of the Religious Confessions and Committee of the Religious Liberty);
- cooperation agreements with the State
- Tax benefit of voluntary consignment by individual taxpayers of 0.5% income tax.

e) Canonical legal persons

The 2004 Concordat recognises, with the same words as 1940 Concordat, the legal personality of the Catholic Church (personality under International law). It also recognises the legal personality of the Portuguese Bishops Conference.

The 2004 Concordat establishes that the recognition of civil legal personality for entities that are 'juridical persons' under canon law depends on the notification of the competent State authority, which is the National Register of Collective Entities (*Registe Nacional das Pessoas Colectivas*). Within this register is located the National Register of Religious Corporations. A part of the database of the National Register of Corporations is entitled 'Catholic Religious Corporations', distinguishing those with the legal nature of religious corporations (8.265 in September 2005) from those with the legal nature of civil associations (366 in September 2005).

The State, according to the 2004 Concordat (Article 9,2), "recognises the legal personality of the dioceses, parishes and other ecclesiastic jurisdictions as soon as the act constitutive of its canonical juridical personality is notified to the competent State body[379].

---

[378] DE SOUSA E BRITO, J.: "Religion entities as legal persons-Portugal "in *Churches and other organisations as legal persons"* Peeters 2007, p. 185.

[379] DE SOUSA E BRITO, J.: "Religion entities as legal persons-Portugal... *oc. cit* pp... 183-188.

II. ISLAM IN PORTUGAL

1. Legal recognition of Islam

Islam is recognised in Portugal in the same way as other religions, such as Christianity, Hinduism, Buddhism or Judaism.

In 2006, the Islamic Community of Lisbon (CIL) became a registered community and as it was founded in Portugal more than 30 years before, got the condition of religious community settled in the country.

2. Muslim population.

Portugal has a population of 10.8 millions of inhabitants out of whom there are about 50,000 Muslims (0.5%), mainly Sunnis (45,000) and some 5,000 Shiite (mostly Ishmaelite). Out of the 50,000 existing Muslims, around 4,000 are of Middle Eastern origin and 12,000 from the Indian Subcontinent, mostly Pakistani and Bangladeshi. A lot of them come from Mozambique.

3. Muslim representative organisations

In Portugal, there is no official spokesperson of the different Islamic associations but the Islamic Community of Lisbon (*Comunidade Islâmica de Lisboa* - CIL)[380] is very representative, since it has traditionally coordinated, at a national level, the representation and activities of several mosques and places of worship.

The Lisbon Central Mosque is an association of religious, social and cultural character, which organizes religious and cultural activities on a national scale. Its leader has been, for many years now, the well known businessman Abdool Karim Vakil.

There are other relevant centres as well, namely those of:

- The Islamic Community of Palmela (*Comunidade Islâmica de Palmela* - CIP) – founded in 1997, guided by *Rachid Daoud Ismael* (also known as

---

[380] http://www.comunidadeislamica.pt

Sheik Rizwan) who is also the founder and responsible authority for the Islamic School of Palmela (*Colégio Islâmico de Palmela*). Founded in 1998, the above mentioned private school, working at an adjoining section of the Palmela Community – and also known as School *Darul Ulum Al-Islamiat* or Islamic School (*Colégio Islâmico).*

- The Islamic Centre of South of the Tagus river, (*Centro Islâmico do Sul do Tejo* – CIST) at Laranjeiro) in which there is also a small Koranic school. They are rather dynamic. After the Lisbon Community and jointly with Palmela (at the same side of the river, to the South) it is perhaps the most relevant Islamic community in Portugal.
- The Islamic Community of Odivelas. Its headquarters is located at the Aisha Siddika Mosque. It is well known for its faith community and international contacts.
- The Cultural Islamic Centre of Oporto (Centro Cultural Islâmico do Porto – CCIP) which has one of the main Mosques of the North of Portugal and constitutes a reference for many believers and places of prayer in that part of the country.
- The Coimbra Mosque. It is placed in the country's central region.
- In Algarve (south), there are several prayer centers of a more informal type, with a fluctuating number of members.
- The Shiite Community and the Ishmaelite communities.

Besides these examples, there are other Islamic communities, of reasonable dimension with the capacity of attracting and mobilizing believers in different parts of Portugal. These places are functioning legally, having been recognized by the Portuguese competent authorities. We can also mention some Islamic associations as the Youth Association of the Islamic Community (*Commissao de Jovens da Comunidade Islâmica de Lisboa)*

There has always been a positive relationship between the authorities and the Lisbon Mosque (headquarters of the Lisbon Islamic Community), which has been, for many years now, the venue "par excellence" for public ceremonies attended by main Political Representatives[381]. These events usually occur from an ecumenical standpoint and as a clear intent from both the State and the Portuguese Islamic Community to reinforce the role and visibility of Islam.

---

[381] Just after the 11th September 2001, there were public appearances of both High level figures of the State and the main Islamic Community leaders, who also participated in common prayer sessions with a diversity of religious participants (Jews, different Christian denominations, Hindu and Buddhist leaders).

In regional centers such as Laranjeiro, Palmela, Oporto and others, Muslim communities have ties with local authorities, and even with security or local police forces.

4. Mosques and Imams

There are 7 traditional mosques in Portugal: six of them in the Lisbon area (Central Mosque of Lisbon, Benformoso mosque; Aicha Siddika Mosque in Odivelas; Hajrak Hamza mosque in Sacavem; Laranjeiro mosque; Barreiro mosque) and one in Coimbra.

There are also several oratories: ten of them in the Lisbon area (Portela, Povoa de Santo Adriao, Forte da Casa, Colina do Sol-Pontinha, Fetais-Sacavem, Santo Antonio dos Cavaleiros, Cacem, Buraca, Carnaxide y Vialonga) 3 in Alentejo (Ëvora, Estremoz y Redondo), 5 in Algarve (Faro, Portimao, Armaçao de Pera, Quarteira y Albufeira), 4 in the north of Portugal (2 in Porto, 1 in Sanguedo y 1 in A Ver o Mar), one in the central region (Leiria) and one in Madeira (Funchal).

The official numbers relating to mosques and other places of prayer legally recognised indicate around thirty facilities from north to south of Portugal, including Madeira – the only island to have a known mosque, in Funchal.

There are around thirty active imams in Portugal. The great majority of imams who lead the religious practices in the already mentioned worship places come from Pakistan although many of them are now Portuguese nationals and other originate from Mozambique.

A lot of small prayer halls are used by immigrants from Guinea Bissau and led by Guinean imams. These are quite influential among the believers of their nationality, who currently form a relevant part of the local Islamic community.

Regarding the Maghrebian community (mostly Moroccans), there are not known legal religious associations constituted by members of this community and they do not use to attend the "official" mosques and prayer rooms.

Despite the outline of the current situation, other data and indicators point out, not exactly to the proliferation of prayer places, but rather to the existence of several clandestine prayer facilities, generally operating in private houses or apartments, private parking lots or other type of buildings.

5. Chaplains

The Religious Freedom Act (nº 16/2001) grants (art. 13) the Islamic and other communities the right to exercise religious freedom in special situations such as in the army, in prisons or in hospitals). In practice, there are no imams working in such institutions on a regular basis.

6. Islam in public school. Islamic private schools

The Religious Freedom Act (art. 24) grants the right of registered religious communities to offer religious teaching in public school if there are enough pupils (it has been implemented in at least 10 students) and it is required by their parents Religious are hired by the State, in accordance with the guidelines given by the representatives of their religious community.

There are some Islamic private schools:

- School *Darul Ulum Al-Islamiat* or Islamic School (*Colégio Islâmico)* combines the classes of Portuguese official curriculum (both at the elementary and secondary levels, up to the 12th grade) with the Islamic religious teachings.

In the first case, and concerning the teaching of the Portuguese official curriculum, the school benefits from the official recognition by the educational authorities of the Education Ministry just like any other elementary or secondary public school. In fact, the school is publicly acknowledged for its demanding standards, and for the high level of education of its pupils.

- The Islamic Centre of South of the Tagus river, (Centro Islâmico do Sul do Tejo – CIST) at Laranjeiro, in which there is also a small Koranic school, is quite important and dynamic.

III. TRAINING CENTRES FOR IMAMS

There are no official training programs for imams coordinated by the Portuguese State.

Prayer leaders are people who are nominated as such, according to the rules of their religious community (article 15 of the Religious Liberty Law). Islamic religious leaders receive their training in Islamic Schools (*Dar-ul-Ulum*). According to the Law of Religion, each faith community can nominate their ministers and establish foundations for seminars or schools, or any other cultural or religious institutions, without interference from the State or from third parties.

This means that, even though at State level there are no programs or initiatives for Imams training, there may be similar projects within the religious communities themselves (for instance, within CIL or CIP).

Nevertheless, the Islamic School of Palmela (CIP) can certify its students up to the level of hafiz, so if the students want to pursue their education they usually travel to the United Kingdom. Upon their return, and according to the level that they might have attained there, they will be recognized by the Portuguese Islamic appropriate authorities and certified to the level they reached.

Some imams have not received a good theological instruction. Quite often, they just lead prayers because they are just the oldest and most respected member of the community. We have not detected the existence of training programs for Muslim faith leaders who come from abroad.

ROMANIA

I. RELIGION AND STATE

1. Administrative bodies that have contact with denominations

There is a State Secretary for Religious Affairs[382] under Ministry of Culture and National Patrimony

2. Recognition of religions

The Constitution does not provide the status of national church for any denomination. All denominations have the same legal status and the Law no.489/2006 on Religious Freedom and Status of Denominations acknowledges the important role (spiritual, educational, social-charitable and cultural) of the Romanian Orthodox Church and of other churches and denominations. Denominations are considered social partners and factors of the social peace. There are 18 denomination specifically recognised in that law[383].

---

[382] http://www.culte.ro/Index.aspx In January 14th the State Secretary was Adrian Lemeni.
[383] 1. Romanian Orthodox Church.
2. Serbian Orthodox Bishopric of Timisoara
3. Roman-Catholic Church
4. Romanian Church United with Rome, Greek-Catholic
5. Archbishopric of the Armenian Church
6. Russian Old-Rite Christian Church of Romania
7. Reformed Church of Romania
8. Evangelical Church of Romania
9. Evangelical Lutheran Church of Romania
10. Unitarian Church of Transylvania
11. Union of Christian Baptist Churches of Romania
12. Christian Church of the Gospel in Romania
13. Romanian Evangelical Church
14. Pentecostal Union – The Apostolic Church of God of Romania
15. Adventist Seventh-Day Christian Church of Romania
16. Federation of Jewish Communities of Romania
17. Muslim Denomination

The existence of denominations is explicitly enshrined at constitutional level (art. 29.3) stipulating that they are free to organize themselves in accordance with their own statutory rules, under the conditions set out by the law. Religious communities are free to choose their association structure: denomination, religious association or religious groups. Denominations may set up and organise their own structures according to their statutory rules.

According to the Law no.489/2006 on Religious Freedom and Status of Denominations, recognition by the State as a denomination is acquired through a Government Ordinance, following a proposal submitted by the Ministry of Culture and National Patrimony. It is granted to those religious associations that, through their activities and number of worshipers, provide guarantees of sustainability, stability and public interest.

Freedom of religion can also be exercised in religious associations or in religious groups.

A religious association is a private-law legal entity, made up of individuals who adopt, share and practice the same religion. It receives legal entity status by registering in the Registry of Religious Associations, which shall operate at the Clerks' Office of the Trial Court where the association's head office is located. Religious associations can establish subsidiaries according to their bylaws.

A religious group is an association which gathers individuals who freely adopt, share and practice the same religion. It doesn't have a distinct legal entity status

On proposal from the Ministry of Culture and National Patrimony, the Government can, through Government Ordinance, withdraw the status of recognized denomination when the activities of the entity seriously threatens public safety, order, health, morality or the fundamental human rights and liberties of other people. The dissolution of the religious association shall be pronounced by the competent court for the same reasons.

The use of funds obtained from their own sources (denominations and religious communities) shall not be subject to auditing by the State.

Denominations and religious communities enjoy the protection of the civil law. Their acts and relations must comply with the law. Likewise, third

18. Religious Organization Jehovah's Witnesses

parties rights generated by legal relationships with religious legal entities are protected[384].

Denominations and Religious communities are organised and function according to their own bylaws, elaborated according to their confession, canons and traditions.

Every denomination has a national leadership or representation body. Religious groups shall elect and appoint their staff, according to their bylaws. The heads of the denominations are confirmed, upon request, through Decree of the President of the Republic.

Denominations may have their own religious courts for matters of internal discipline, according to their bylaws and internal regulations. The State acknowledges the quality of bodies of ecclesiastic jurisdiction to every denomination, as decided by the Romanian Constitutional Court in a recent decision (no.640/10 June 2008). By virtue of the principle of free access to courts - article 21 of the Constitution-, each person, religious association or community may apply the competent court to review a decision rendered by the religious jurisdictions.

II. ISLAM IN ROMANIA

1. Legal recognition of Islam

Islam is one of the eighteen religious denominations recognized by the Law no.489/2008. Moreover, the Government Ordinance (GO) no.628/2006, on acknowledging the statute of the Muslim cult, stipulated the functioning and organizing rules of the Muslim cult. According to this GO, the Muslim cult consists of all the Muslim believers, including the autochthonous (the Turkish-Tatar minority) and the foreign residents.

---

[384] BĂRBĂTEANU, V. & SULIMAN, D.: "Constitutional Jurisprudence in the area of freedom of religion and beliefs" in *Legal aspects of religious freedom (international conference 15-16 September 2008)* Ljubljana 2008, *pags*. 229-242.

2. The Muslim population

There are about 21.700.000 inhabitants in Romania. Almost 85.000 of them (4%) are Muslims. Nevertheless, Islam has existed for 700 years in Northern Dobrogea, a region on the Black Sea coast which was part of the Ottoman Empire for almost five centuries (1420-1878). After the Russian-Romanian-Ottoman War (1877), Romania became independent ant the Treaty of Berlin (1878) acknowledged Dobrudja as a Romanian territory. The law on religious denomination issued in 1923 lists the Muslim faith among the recognised "historical faiths". The Communist regime (1948-1989) tried to impose atheism and limit the impact of religious creeds. In 1967 the Muslim Theological Seminary was closed.

Today, the Muslim population in Romania is represented by the autochthonous Turkish-Tartar community (about 60.000 members) and foreign residents (approximately 25.000 people).

3. Muslim representative organizations

The Muslim community from Romania is represented by the *Muslim Cult Mufti Office in Romania* (MCMR*)*[385], which is the traditional representation body, acknowledged by the Romanian state. After being elected by the Synodal Council, the mufti is confirmed by a decree of the President of the Republic. The present mufti is Murat Yusuf.

The Synodal Council (*Consiliu Sinodal)* headed by the Mufti, takes decisions regarding the functioning and organization of the Muslim community. The Synodal Council is comprised of the mufti, four members appointed by the Democratic Union of The Turkish-Muslim Tatars in Romania (*Unieunea Democrata a Tatarilor Turco-Musulmani din Romania* –UDTTMR-), four members nominated by the Turkish Democratic Union of Romania (*Uniunea Democrata Turca din Romani* –UDTR-, the principal of the Kemal Ataturk Muslim Theological and Pedagogical High School (*Leceul Teologic Musulman si Pedagogic Demal Atatürk)* and fifteen cleriks. The UDTTMR and the UDTR are two of the nineteen political parties and cultural association representing ethnic minorities in the Romanian Parliament. According to the Romanian Constitution, the Turkish-Tatar minority from Romania is granted representation in the Romanian Parliament (two sits in the Chamber of Deputies).

---

[385] http://www.muftiyat.ro/

Apart from the traditional representation body, the communities of foreign residents are represented by foundations and associations (regulated by GO no.26/2000 on associations and foundations).

In some cases, Muslim associations and foundations function on the basis of an approval issued by the Ministry of Culture, Religious Affairs and National Patrimony, preceded by a preliminary consultative approval of the Mufti Office. The following could be mentioned: the Islamic and Cultural League in Romania (*Liga Culturala si Islamica din Romania*)[386], the Crescent Islamic Cultural Center Foundation (*Fundatia Centrul Cultural Islamic* Semiluna)[387], the Taiba Romania Foundation (*Fundatia Taiba)*[388], the Association of Muslims (*Asociatia Musulmanitor*)[389], at the same address as the Taiba Foundation, the Romanian Muslim Foundation, Foundation for Islamic Services, etc.

Some of these organizations are financially supported by various international Islamic entities (Saudi Arabia Islamic Bank, Taibah International Aid Agency, World Assembly of Muslim Youth, World Association of Muslim Youth – RYAD etc.) whose objectives are to promote and strengthen Muslim communities worldwide.

The most active of them appears to be the Taiba foundation, with a lot of activities, among them a weekly two-hour television program. Under the law on denominations (489/2006), all Islam NGOs, associations and foundations must be re-confirmed with the endorsement of the mufti[390].

4. Mosques

In Romania there are 3 major mosques (one in Bucharest and two in Constanta) and other 61 smaller prayer facilities – called *geamias* – belonging to the Turkish-Tartar community and recognized by the Mufti office. Most of them were built in the XIX century, before or after the Independence War against the Turks.

---

[386] http://www.islam.ro/
[387] http://www.scoala-araba.ro/
[388] http://www.islamulazi.ro/
[389] http://www.asociatiamusulmanilor.ro/
[390] The mufti considers that many of these associations are harmful because of their radical views VAINOVSKI-MIHAI, I.: "ROMANIA" in "*Yearbook of Muslims in Europe*"...*op.cit.* p. 289.

Also in the recent years, a number of prayer rooms have been established mostly by migrant Muslims. There are about 77 places of worship[391].

The muftiate owns 108 cemeteries.

5. Imams

According to the specific profile of the community they serve, Muslim religious leaders/Imams can be divided in several distinct categories:

For the Turkish Tartar autochthonous community:

- employees of the Mufti Office: approx. 62 imams, organized by MCMR, graduates from the Medgidia Muslim Seminar presently transformed in National High School "Mustafa Kemal Ataturk" from Medgidia or from Islamic theological institutions from abroad (Turkey, Jordan, Egypt).Employees of MCMR are paid according to Law no.142/1999 on state's support for clergy remuneration. The employed personnel may also benefit from the wage support granted by the Mufti Office for their services or the social cases (religion classes or religious assistance in penitentiaries)
- Employees of Turkish Islamic NGOs, trained in Turkey (and sometimes in Romania).

For the foreign communities the religious services are provided by the Muslim associations and foundations that set up prayer rooms and hire imams from abroad. Most of these individuals have attended religious training abroad (in Turkey, Jordan, Syria, Egypt or Iran).

6. Chaplains

Religious groups have been supported by the State and can provide religious assistance within the army, hospitals, detention facilities, private homes and orphanages.

Religious assistance has been organized for the military staff, through a protocol signed by the Ministry of National Defence and the main denominations –Orthodox Church, Greco-Catholic Church, Roman-Catholic Church and

---

[391] http://www.culte.ro/DocumenteHtml.aspx?id=1745 (accesed January 14th 2011)

Evangelical Alliance from Romania– taking into account the general exigencies of the military system, as well as the particularities of the military units.

Religious assistance is also offered in penitentiaries, reformatory units and reintegration units, in basis of a protocol signed with the Ministry of Justice. In penitentiaries and reformatory units chaplains are hired by contract. In other re-education units, religious assistance is assured by the priests of the local constituencies.

Even though chaplains are not employed in the public sector, the state pays the amount of the social security that corresponds to the employer.

A program for religious assistance to the detainees of Muslim religion in penitentiaries, initiated by the Islamic and Cultural League from Romania is undergoing. Lately, several times a year, the Taiba Romania Foundation has been organizing meetings and book donations for Muslim detainees (during main religious celebrations).

According to official sources, only 2 imams had been offering lately religious assistance to the Muslim detainees. On request of an inmate, the mufutiate can assign an imam to visit him in the prison at the muftiat´s expense. The same applies to patients in hospitals.

Religious assistance to hospital patients is assured in basis of a protocol signed with the Ministry of Health.

7. Islam in schools

According to the law, public education is non confessional. Religious education is mentioned in the Constitution and granted by the law. According to the Law on Education (Law 84/1995 of July 24th) religion is a subject that has to be taught according to the exigencies of every denomination. A national curriculum is set for the legally recognised denominations, including Islam. National curricula for religion are set by each denomination and submitted first to the Ministry of Culture and National Patrimony and then to the Ministry of Education for approval. In public schools, religion is taught at the request of each student, depending on personal option and with the parents' and legal tutors' consent. People are exempted from attending religious education classes if they declare themselves to be non-religious.

The school authorities are entitled to check whether these classes are fully accomplished. The final grade obtained is mentioned in the student's annual report.

Religious symbols are accepted in schools. The High Court of Cassation and Justice has rejected the request of some organizations concerning the banning of the religious symbols in schools.

III. TRAINING CENTRES FOR IMAMS

Religious education in general

The training of the religious staff is assured through the theological universities, some of them assimilated to the State Universities, and also through the seminars organized at the graduate and post-graduate levels, some of them assimilated to the public system of education.

The training of the religious leaders– including Muslims – is regulated by Law no.489 / 2006, and GO no.628 / 2008.

According to Law no.489 / 2006, denominations have the right to set up and administer religious education institutes. Religion teachers, as well as other specialists, need to perform their religious activities in compliance with the law.

Each cult is free to establish the type, level, number and curricula for its own education institutions, in compliance with the law. Denominations elaborate their own curricula programs for the *pre-university theological education and religion teaching*. These are overseen by the Ministry of Culture and National Patrimony and approved by the Ministry of Education, Research, Youth and Sport.

The curricula *programs for university studies* are drafted by the universities, and overseen by the religious authorities and approved by the university senates.

According to GO no.628/2008, the Mufti Office cooperates with the institutions of the state competent in the field of religious education and organizes seminars on Koran (*Kur'an Kurslari*).

There is no Islamic higher education institution in Romania for Imams training, just a project to set up an "Islamic Faculty of Theology". But in 2008 the legislative procedure was stopped.

In 1996 an Islamic secondary school "Mustafa Kemal Ataturk" High School (*Liceul Tologic Musulman si Pedagogic Kemal Atatürk)* was opened in Medgidia, a city with a sizable Turkish and Tatar population, which is now functioning with the support of the Turkish government. At present it works on the basis of bilateral agreements between Turkey and Romania. A similar institution existed before the Communist period in the same town (the Medgidia Muslim Seminary) and it was closed in 1967.

The "Mustafa Kemal Ataturk" High School from Medgidia provides only initial theological training. It works along with MCMR and its diplomas are acknowledged by the Ministry of Labor, Family and Social Protection and the Ministry of Education, Research, Youth and Sport. Just a few of its graduates carry out religious activities, within the Mufti Office or NGOs. A small number of graduates also undertake university studies in Turkey[392]. Some teachers are Romanians and some come from abroad (namely Turkey). Some classes are also taught by employees of the Mufti Office.

The Government does not have any specific policies and programs for training Muslim spiritual leaders coming from abroad. Diplomas issued abroad are subject to the recognition by the Romanian Ministry of Education after endorsement by the mufti[393]. The approval, which is for one year, is issued on the basis of an interview, the documents attesting studies and qualification, as well as the program of activities that are to be undertaken. The Mufti Office does not get involved in their religious training.

There are also various private structures (foundations), which provide general religious education for young people such as: the Islamic Services Foundation of Romania, TUNA Foundation, the Islamic and Cultural League of Romania, the Crescent Islamic Cultural Center Foundation (*Fundatia Centrul Cultural Islamic* Semiluna) and the Taiba Romania Foundation (*Fundatia Taiba).*

The graduates of the religious private courses organized by Turkish foundations are also sent to Turkey to attend short-term seminars and lectures. Those who would like to study non-theological universities can benefit of material support (accommodation and meals), carrying out – along with their university studies - religious courses in specialized centers.

---

[392] The Mufti, himself, studied in the Turkish city of Samsun

[393] "In 2007, disputes emerged after the mufti refused to endorse diplomas obtained from Islamic theological institutes in Jordan, Saudi Arabia, Syria and Sudan. The mufti officially requested the Ministry of Education not to recognise diplomas obtained by seven Tatars on the ground that thesy have studied a radical form of Islam and recognition of their diplomas was denied". VAINOVSKI-MIHAI, I.: "ROMANIA" in "*Yearbook of Muslims in Europe"...op.cit.* p. 291

Diplomas issued by the religious initiation seminaries / courses organized under the aegis of Islamic organizations that are not accredited by the Ministry are not officially recognized.

The teachers that work in private religious centers in Romania (foundations and associations) are mainly graduates of local religious courses, Imam Hatips (religious high schools) as well as in theological universities from Turkey and Arab states (Egypt, Syria, Jordan)

There are also many examples of self-educated individuals.

In terms of curricula, religious initiation courses include the studying of the Koran and the Hadith, religious practice, Islamic law (Shari'a), the Halal code and Muslim behaviour. Some courses, designed for the Turkish Tartar community, include teaching Turkish language. General curricula includes also writings of important Islamic scholars, often supported by video lectures, brochures, religious practice handbooks (interpretations according to each doctrine).

Religious courses organized by private centers are mainly held in the afternoon. The teaching method implies memorizing Koran passages, listening to audio-video lectures and explanations given by instructors.

The Turkish NGOs take care of the permanent training of their activists. A small number of employees belonging to the Mufti Office are, at the same time, activists of some Arab foundations (e.g. Taiba) and attend training programs abroad with the help of these organizations.

However, religious training in Romania is realized only at initial level. In order to undertake more thorough studies and to be accredited as future imams it is necessary for them to take part in courses organized abroad, usually in Turkey, Jordan, Syria, Egypt, or Iran.

SLOVAKIA

I. RELIGION AND STATE

1. Administrative bodies that have contact with denominations

The public institution that basically have contact with denomination is the Department of Church Affairs under the Ministry of Culture.

The Ministry of Culture established on January 1997 the Institute for State-Church Relations[394], which deals with research of relations between the State and churches and also promotes cooperation and dialogue between State and registered religions.

2. Recognition of religions

There is a Register of Religious Entities under the Ministry of Culture of the Slovak Republic (SK). The Constitution of SR guarantees the right of each individual or society to manifest their religion or faith, without exceptions, whether it is a registered or the non-registered religion (religious society - RS).

A religious group can just associate freely without any approval of the authorities. It can also get legal personality as an association registering as such in the Ministry of Interior under the condition that the religious activity is not the main and only subject of activity of a civil association. Citizens have right to establish civil associations which can provide charitable or educational activities. Registration authority for this purpose is under Ministry of interior affairs.

But, a religious group can also register as a religion under the Ministry of Culture. As we have said above, in Slovakia the competent body to register religious groups is the Ministry of Culture. In order to be registered there, and so being recognized by the State as a religious entity, the applicant group must fulfil the legal conditions obligatory for registration (Act no. 308/1991).

One of those requirements is the declaration of oath comprising at least 20.000 adult members with permanent residence in SR and with the Slovak citizenship. The names of these members have to be registered too.

The Ministry would deny or subsequently cancel the registration if it finds that the establishment or the activity of the religious entity is illegal or

---

394 http://www.duch.sk/?lang=en In January 31st the director of the Institute was Michaela Moravčíková who I would like to thank for her useful help in this research.

contrary to the citizens' security, public order, public health, public morals, principles of humanity and tolerance, or the rights of others.

Registration means that the State acknowledged that group as a registered religious entity (REE) that will spread religious and moral ideas in the society. Apart from recognizing the status of legal entity, registration entitles the group with certain privileges, for example:

- Financial contribution to the salaries of their clergy and to the central bodies, and partly for running the religious centres
- Tax benefits: for example, exemption from real property tax for sacral buildings
- Right to teach religion in public schools.
- Establish church schools partially funded by State contributions
- Celebrating marriages according to their internal norms: those religious marriages would have the same legal effects than civil ones.
- Right to provide pastoral care in the army, prisons, hospitals, police etc.
- When regulating relations between RREs and religious staff internal norms will be prior to Labour Code
- Reservation of conscience alleged by their members in certain fields if they are employees.
- Right to access to public media.

According to a provision of the Law on religious freedom and the position of churches and religious societies, religious entities officially operating in Slovakia when the law entered in force (September 1989), -in other words, those who were active under the communist era-, were automatically considered as registered. So they did not have to prove that they had at least 20.000 members in order to be registered. This threshold is so high that only 3 religions have succeeded in overcoming it after the law took into force: Jehovah's Witnesses (registered in March 1993), The Church of Jesus Christ of Latter-day Saints in the Slovak Republic (Mormons), in 2006, and the Baha'i Community in 2007. Besides, in 2001 the New Apostolic Church was registered additionally, after it had submitted relevant documents about the State consent to the performance of its activities within the territory of the SR before Act n° 308/1991 Zb. came into force[395]

Besides those, the other currently RREs (15) simply transferred their status from the previous regime. As there were cases in which some groups tried to misuse or take illegal advantages of the procedure of registration the Act was reviewed in May 1st 2007. It was the response of Parliament to the unsuccessful effort of the Atheist Church of Non-Believers that applied for registration. The current Act not only requires 20.000 sympathisers but 20.000

---

[395] MORAVCIKOVA, M.: "Religious Education and Denominational Schools in the Slovak Republic". In ASLAN, E. *(ed.) Islamische Erziehung in Europa / Islamic Education in Europe*. Wien-Köln-Weimar, Böhlau Verlag, 2009. p. 459

members of the church. Mormons and Baha'is had proved during registration procedure that they had got a minimum of 20 000 sympathising supporters.

A decision of the Ministry denying or cancelling the registration of a religious entity may be appealed against at the Supreme Court of Slovak Republic.

At 2009, the following churches had the status of a registered church (the number of adherents is based on the census carried out in 2001 when total number of inhabitants was 5 379 455):

REGISTERED CHURCH OR RS	N° OF ADHERENTS	Percentage of TOTAL POPULATION
Roman Catholic Church	3 708 120	68.9 %
Evangelical Church of Augsburg Confession	372 858	6.9 %
Greek Catholic Church	219 831	4.1 %
Reformed Christian Church	109 735	2.0 %
Orthodox Church	50 363	0.9 %
Jehovah's Witnesses	20 630	0.4 %
Evangelical Methodist Church	7 347	0.1 %
Christian Corps	6 519	0.1 %
Apostolic Church	3 905	0.1 %
Baptist Church	3 562	0.1%
Seventh Day Adventist Church	3 429	0.1 %
Church of Brethren	3 217	0.1 %
Jewish Religious Congregations	2 310	0.0 %
Old Catholic Church	1733	
Czechoslovak Hussite Church	1 696	
New Apostolic		

Church in Slovakia		
The Church of Jesus Christ of Latter-day Saints Slovakia		
Bahai Community		

Source: Department of Church Affairs, Ministry of Culture of SR

II. ISLAM IN SLOVAKIA

The state recognizes Islam as any other religion, but not as a registered religion because the Muslim community in Slovakia has not reached so far the 20.000 members required for registration. Some Muslims, before the amendment of the Act on Freedom of religious faith and the position of churches and religious societies was passed[396], tried to establish an umbrella organization (Islamic Religious Community) to be registered. However, they did not succeed[397]. Islamic communities can get a juridical personality as associations, foundations or non-profit organizations.

The current population of the Slovakia is 5, 38 millions of inhabitants. About 5000 of them are Muslims (according to the 2001 census 1212 persons declared themselves as Muslims). The Muslim community is mainly comprised of foreign students at Slovak universities and of former students who stayed in Slovakia and founded new homes and families in the country. They come from a wide range of countries (Afghanistan, Yemen, Turkey, Pakistan, Algeria…). Therefore it can be said that the Islamic community in Slovakia has a quite high financial and academic standard. A lot of them are part of various Muslim associations.

In the years 2001 – 2003 there were up to thirty Muslim associations registered as civil associations. The following entities are considered as having the greatest influence on the Muslim community:

The Islam Foundation in Slovakia (*Islamská nadácia na Slovensku (INnS)*. Established in 1999, is generally regarded as an official institution of the Muslim community[398].

The General Union of Muslim Students (*Všeobecný zväz moslimských študentov (VZMŠ)* founded in 1933 as a civil association.

---

[396] Act n° 201 from March 29, 2007, changing and amending the Act n° 308/1991
[397] MORAVCIKOVA, M.: "Religious Education…*op. cit.* pp. 460.
[398] www.islamweb.sk

The Association of Friends of the Islam Literature (*Združenie priateľov islamskej literatúry (ZPIL)*

The Muslim Community in Slovakia (*Komunita muslimov na Slovensku - KMS-*)

Direct dialogue between the representatives of these associations and the government representatives has not taken place yet.

There are no purposed-built mosques. Muslims gathers in rented buildings according to the freedom of association and religious freedom which is also recognized to non registered religions. There is a burial place assigned for Muslisl in the municipal cemetery of Bratislava (*Sláviçie údolie*).

The number of imams in the country is low. Imams are mainly former Slovak students or persons who lived and worked in Slovakia. They are mainly from a Syrian and Algerian origin, but also some from Pakistan. Foreign imams visit the Muslim community predominantly on special occasions (e.g. in Ramadan).

As Islam is a non-registered religious group, Islamic marriage ceremonies don't have civil effects.

There is none institutionalized Islamic chaplaincy in prisons, hospitals, social and health institutions. Neither Imams nor Islamic organizations are entitled to receive salaries or subsidies from the State.

In Slovak penitentiary institutions there are rooms to be used for religious ceremonies. In general, the issue of providing the spiritual services to the accused and the convicted people is stipulated in the general norms concerning the execution of custody and the execution of imprisonment, an in internal regulation – the decree of the Director General of the Corps of Prison and Judiciary Guards of the Slovak Republic (CPJG).

In prisons, inmates have the right to get their meals, according to their religion. There are 8234 prisoners in the 18 existing prisons in the country. There are no figures about how many of them are Muslims.

Nevertheless, Muslim prisoners have access to religious literature (available in the libraries of these institutions). Confessional literature is delivered by religious societies and organizations or by private correspondence.

At present, there is no Muslim clergyman in the CPJG institutions in Slovakia (as we have already pointed, Islam religion is not registered in the Ministry of Culture). Generally, there is a central authority, which appoints and nominates the clergymen. The candidates for the clergymen are vetted and the admission procedure takes place in compliance with law.

Primary and secondary schools in Slovakia provide lessons in Religious Education, which are organised by registered churches and religious communities. As Islam is not a registered denomination, Islamic religious education is not taught in state schools.

There is no private Muslim school only one private Muslim kindergarten in Bratislava[399]where Islam is taught. In other schools, pupils have access to Islam only within the framework of civics in elementary schools, or society teaching in Gymnasiums and high schools, or during ethics lessons, however, only in the case the teacher decides to do so[400].

Private's schools in Slovakia are mainly Catholics and Protestants.

III. TRAINING CENTRES FOR IMAMS

Training institutions or organizations for Muslim Faith Leaders do not exist in the Slovak Republic and there is no strategy or any specific programmes for the training of imams who come from abroad.

---

[399] Supported by the Embassy of the Great Socialist Popole´s Lybian Araba Jamahiriya in Bratislaba.

[400] The teacher can choose 30% of curriculum and 70% is stipulated by the Ministry of Education. *vid.* MORAVCIKOVA, M.: "Religious Education...*op cit.* pp. 462

SLOVENIA

I. RELIGION AND STATE

1. Administrative bodies that have contact with denominations

The Government Office of the Republic of Slovenia for Religious Communities[401] is the main administrative body that has contact with religious communities. It has a large list of tasks, which are set out in the Religious Freedom Act of February 2nd 2007[402], such as:

- monitoring the position of registered churches and other religious communities;
- providing professional assistance and inform registered churches and other religious communities on regulations, other acts and measures affecting their activities;
- conducting the procedure for registration and keep the Register of Churches and Other Religious Communities in compliance with the Religious Freedom Act;
- Issuing certificates on the legal personality of registered churches and other religious communities[403].

The Government Office has 6 employees, director included, and an annual budget of 2,497.679 EUR (2007)[404].

---

[401] Official Gazette of the RS, N° 26/91

[402] Official GAzette of the Republic of Slovenia n°14/07

[403] See art. 30 of Religious Freedom Act, 2 February 2007

[404] CEPAR, D.: "Administrative and Financial Maters in the area of religious freedom and religious communities" in *Legal Aspects of Religious freedom* (International Conference, 15-18 September 2008) Ljubljana 2008 (pag. 438).

2. Recognition of religions: registration in the Office for Religious Communities.

The 1991 Slovenian Constitution provides inter alia the fundamental right of religious freedom and separation between State and denominations. All religious communities enjoy the same rights and are able to exercise their activity freely. The Religious Freedom Act of 2007 replaced a Communist-era law on religious communities. According to the new law, a church or other religious community is a voluntary, non-profit association of persons who share the same religious belief, established with the purpose of public and private profession of this religion and having its own structure, authorities and autonomous internal rules, and also its own religious services or ceremonies[405].

Religious communities can be founded without any approval of the authorities, and they can pursue their activities freely within the limits of general legal order. If religious communities want to acquire legal status, they are required to register their establishment within the Government Office for Religious Communities. They could, of course, opt for other civil law status such as associations, trusts or foundations if they satisfy the prescribed criteria for these institutions. In that case they would have the legal status as "non-religious" institutions. This legal status is necessary to buy or rent premises, open bank accounts, purchase goods, sign contracts in their name etc. But they are not entitled to the same special rights and benefits as registered religious communities, such as tax exemptions, state contributions and other special rights. So, religious groups normally only register as non religious associations when they cannot fulfil the statutory requirements for registering as a religious community[406].

A church or other religious community may be registered in the Register of Churches and Other Religious Communities if it fulfils 2 major requirements:

a) Having at least 100 adult members, citizens of the Republic of Slovenia or foreigners with permanent residence in the country

b) It should have been active in Slovenia for at least the last ten years.

The application must be submitted by its representatives, and shall contain the following information:

---

[405] Art. 7.1 of the Religious Freedom Act, 2 February 2007

[406] PREPELUH-MAGAJNE, U.: "Religion entities as legal persons-Slovenia "in *Churches and other organizations as legal persons,* Peeters 2007, p. *139-14.*

- Name of the church or other religious community written in Latin letters. This name has to be different from other already registered names in order to avoid misleading.

- Address of the seat in the RS

- The stamp bearing the name of the church or other religious community that it will use in legal transactions[407] .

The Register is under the Government Office for Religious Communities. They decide on the applications for registration of a church according to the procedure established in the Religious Freedom Act. In doing so, they may lean on the opinion of experts.

Besides maintaining the Register, the Government Office for Religious Communities also issues certificates of their establishment and cessation. The Government Office, however, cannot evaluate or examine the creed or the dogma because it would be against principle of separation between State and Church. At the moment, there are 43 religious communities in the Register of Churches and Other religious Communities. They are legal personalities under private law[408].

A church or other religious community can be removed from the Register by the competent authority in these cases: if the church or religious community decides it, if the church or religious group is found guilty on criminal offences, if the data or enclosures contained in the application are false, if activities of the church or other religious community have been prohibited by a judicial decision.

The State may conclude agreements with the registered churches or other religious communities. Such agreements shall be concluded with the supreme authority of the church or religious community in the RS. So far, agreements have been concluded with: Holy See, Evangelical Church, Pentecostal Church, Serbian Orthodox Church, Islamic Community and Buddhist congregation Dharmaling.

---

407 When lodging the application for registration, the applicant shall pay administrative charge in accordance with the law regulating administrative fees. (article 13 of Religious Freedom Act, February 2nd 2007.

408 http://www.uvs.gov.si/en/registered_churches_and_other_religious_communities/

II. ISLAM IN SLOVENIA

1. Legal recognition of Islam

As mentioned above, religious communities can be founded without any approval of the authorities, and can pursue their activities freely within the limits of general legal order.

If religious communities want to acquire legal status, however, they are required to register their establishment with the Government.

There are two Islamic organizations in the Register of churches and other religious communities: the Islamic Community in the Republic of Slovenia and The Muslim Community of Slovenia.

The Government of the Republic of Slovenia and the Islamic Community in the Republic of Slovenia signed an "Agreement on the Legal Status of the Islamic Community in the Republic of Slovenia" July 9th 2007. It was signed by Nedžad Grabus, Mufti and President of the Meshiahat of the Islamic Community in the Slovenia and Lovro Šturm, Chairman of the Commission of the Government of the country for solving open issues of –religious communities. It was the fifth cooperation agreement signed between the Government and a religious community.

2. The Muslim population

The first encounter of Slovenes with Muslims was as member of the Ottoman army. In World War I, Bosnian Muslims fought for the Habsburg Empire on Slovenian soil. During the 1950s a significant wave of migrants arrived from the other parts of the Social Federal Republic of Yugoslavia. After its independence in 1991, the new Republic of Slovenia received thousands of refugees from Bosnia[409].

According to the last Census (2002), the total population was 1,964,036 of which 47,488 were Muslims (2.4%), 41,305 of whom live in urban areas, the remaining 6,182 in rural areas. Census data on (ethnic) nationality.

---

409 MOE, C. : « SLOVENIA » in *Yearbook of Muslims in Europe...op. cit.* p. 311.

3. Muslim representative organizations

There are two Islamic organisations in the Register of Churches and Other Religious Communities:

- Islamic Community in the Republic of Slovenia (*Islamska skupnost v Republiki* Sloveniji)[410]. This community, established in 1976, is the most representative Islamic organization. It is a branch of the Islamic Community of Bosnia-Herzegovina, and stands for Sunni Islam of the Hanafi School.

- The Muslim Community of Slovenia[411] (*Slovenska muslimanska skupnost*) is a smaller community. It was registered in 2006 by Osman Dogie, the former mufti of the Islamic Community in the RS who broke away after some conflicts before his re-appointment[412].

4. Mosques, cemeteries and Imams

There are no purpose-built with mosques with a minaret in Slovenia. Since 1968 Muslims are sought to build a mosque in Ljubljana. After years of strong opposition of some social groups, which included an anti-mosque referendum initiative, at the end of 2008 a new urban area plan provided for a definite location for an Islamic Cultural Centre and a mosque and the Islamic Community in the RS bought most of the land from the city.

There are 15 oratories where Muslims pray most of which belong to the Islamic Community in the Slovenia.

There are not Islamic cemeteries, but a few local cemeteries have allotted sections for Muslim burials (e.g. Jesenice, Maribor, Krsko, and Trzic)

According to Religious Freedom Act of 2007, "a religious employee of a church or other religious community is a member of a registered church or other religious community who is dedicated in his/her religious community exclusively and fully to the religious-ritual, religious-charitable, religious-educational and religious-organizational activities in accordance with the order, regulations, required qualifications and powers of the supreme authority of

---

410 http://www.islamska-skupnost.si/
411 http://www.smskupnost.si/
412 MOE, C. : « SLOVENIA » in *Yearbook of Muslims in Europe...op. cit.* p. 313.

his/here church or other religious community"[413] According to figures from the Islamic Community in the Republic of Slovenia, there are 12 imams in Slovenia.

5. Chaplains

Prisons: Article 24 of the Religious Freedom Act sets out the right of prisoners to regular individual and collective religious spiritual care. According to the Slovenian Ministry of Justice, there are 12 prisons and one Young Offenders Institute. The prison population of Slovenia is estimated in 1337 prisoners but information on the religious denomination of prisoners is not collected.

According to figures obtained by the Government Office for Religious Communities, there is only one chaplain for all faiths, provided by the Ministry of Justice. The area of religious spiritual care at the Prison Administration of the Republic of Slovenia is covered by the coordinator for the religious spiritual care of imprisoned persons, who is responsible for arranging visits by representatives of religious communities upon request of inmates. Prisons are regularly visited by representatives of religious communities. Liturgies or other events are organised in prisons on major religious holidays or special occasions. Religious literature is available in prison libraries or delivered to inmates on their request.

Army: Members of the Slovenian army during their military service have the right to religious spiritual care in compliance with the rules on the military service and defence of the country. Religious spiritual care for members of the Slovenian army, employees of the Ministry of Defence and their family members, regardless of their religious affiliation, is provided by the Military Vicariate. The vicariate consists of a military vicar, a deputy vicar for the Catholic Church, a deputy vicar for the Evangelical Church in the Republic of Slovenia, military chaplains, pastoral assistants and an administrative clerk. Members of the Military Vicariate regularly provide religious spiritual care with their presence among soldiers, by organising pilgrimages, family meetings, giving the sacraments, holding liturgies for the homeland, holding lectures and other activities (Article 22 of the Religious Freedom Ac).

---

[413] Article 7.2.

Police:State is obliged to provide religious spiritual care for police officers who wish, in the circumstances that make the exercise of their religious freedom difficult (Article 23).

Hospitals/social welfare institutions

Residents of the above institutions have the right to regular individual and collective religious spiritual care. If there are a sufficiently large number of patients of the same religious belief in the public hospitals, the ministry responsible for health provides for the employment of the necessary ministers of cult. Hospitals and institutions providing institutional care are obliged to provide the premises and technical conditions for religious spiritual care. Religious employees who provide spiritual care shall be given access in accordance with the legislation and the rules of individual institutions.

There are 27 hospitals in Slovenia, 22 of them have chapels and hold regular masses. In February 2008 the National Commission for Medical Ethics positively evaluated the initiative from hospital chaplains that patients to ask the patient about their wish for spiritual care when they arrive at the hospital. Religious spiritual care is provided in all 78 social welfare institutions for the elderly. Some 52 nursing homes have a chapel or other premise dedicated exclusively to religious spiritual care, while 54 also use other premises for religious spiritual care, which are specially arranged for such occasions[414]. Nevertheless, Muslim institutional care in state institutions has not yet been implemented.

6. Islam in schools

Religious education is not taught in public schools. Religious communities can establish education institutions, residence halls for pupils and students and other similar institutions. In those places the can freely perform educational activities in line with their own statutes in accordance with the constitutional and legal order of the Republic of Slovenia. The State will co-finance the activities of these private institutions in line with equivalent programmes in public institutions. Institutions which were established before 1996 receive 100% funding from the State to cover salaries and material costs, and those which have been established since this date receive 85% funding.

---

[414]*http://www.uvs.gov.si/en/thestate_religious_freedom_and_religious_communities_in_the_republic_of_slovenia/)*

According to the Government Office for Religious Communities, at the end of 2007, there were 336 nursery schools, 20 of which were private, and 15 were Catholic.

There are 447 primary schools. This includes one Catholic school which opened in September 2008.

There are 163 secondary schools, 6 of which are private: 4 Catholic and the remaining 2 are not religious. Three out of the 4 Catholic schools were established before 1996, hence receive 100% financial support; the other one receives 85% of its expenses. The other two non-religious private schools receive 85% of financial support too. There are no Muslim private schools. But Islam is taught in classes outside schools organised by the Islamic Community in the RS. According to the Ministry for Education and Sport, in the period 2007/8 there were 91,554 secondary school pupils. Of them, 1,748 were pupils of religious centres (1.9%). There are no figures on the number of Muslim students. The religion of pupils in centres is not collected.

III. TRAINING CENTRES FOR IMAMS

There are no imam training centres. According to the Muslim Community of Slovenia, imams go to Sarajevo for their training (Faculty of Islamic Studies of the University of Sarajevo).

With regard to other religions, the only higher education religious institution is the Theology Faculty at the University of Ljubljana.

According to the Slovenian Office of National Statistics, in 2007/8 there were 99,021 students in higher education in Slovenia. Of them, 835 were pupils from the Theology Faculty (0.8%). The faculty is 100% funded by the State, through grants from the University of Ljubljana.

SPAIN

I. RELIGION AND STATE

1. Administrative bodies that have contact with denominations

In Spain, relations between public authorities and religions used to be coordinated from the General Department of Relations with Denominations under the Ministry of Justice. That General Department was composed of one Director and two deputy directors: a deputy director for promotion and coordination of religious freedom[415] and deputy director of the Register of Religious Entities.

The General Department of Relations with Denominations was terminated in July 2nd 2010 suppressed. Religious Affairs were take on by the new General Department of International Cooperation and Relations with Denominations. This department only has one office dedicated to religious affairs: the deputy director of Relations with Denominations[416] which is also responsible for the Register or Religious Entities (hereinafter RRE)[417].

However, there are other ministries that deal with religious affairs: for example, the Ministry of the Interior deals with spiritual guidance in prisons, the Ministry of Finance deals with funding or tax benefits for some religious groups, and the Labour Ministry handles the social security funds of priests, imams, rabbis, and other faith ministers.

Other bodies that are engaged with religious communities are:

- The Advising Commission for Religious Freedom (*Comisión Asesora de la Libertad Religiosa)*, a consultative body appointed by the Ministry of Justice. The Commision's purpose is to undertake studies, reports and proposals for all those issues applicable to the Basic Law, with particular emphasis in the preparation and reporting of Cooperation Agreements.

---

[415] I held this post from January 1st 2006 until May 15th 2010

[416]http://www2.mjusticia.es/cs/Satellite/es/1215197982464/Estructura_C/1215328727702/Detalle.html

[417] Royal Decree 1203/2010 September 24th which implements the new basic structure of the Ministry of Justice (BOE September 25th 2010)

- The "Pluralism and Living Together" Foundation (*Fundación Pluralismo y Convivencia)*, a public Foundation created in December 2005 by decision of the Council of Ministers at the proposal of the Ministry of Justice. With a budget of 5 million Euros in 2010 their main objective is to support cultural, educational and social integration projects presented by religious communities which have signed a Cooperation Agreement with the State (this excludes the Catholic Church which has its own specific funding from the State).[418]
- Office of relations with the Holy See (*Area de relaciones con la Santa Sede)* under the Sub-Secretary of Foreign Affairs and Cooperation (Ministry of Foreign Affairs and Cooperation) which is dedicated to items related to the Holy See.[419]

According to the Spanish constitutional framework, relations between public authorities (at the national, autonomous and municipal levels) and religious groups should be developed within two juridical principles that function as if they were two juridical coordinates: the principle of secularism (or that of the non-confessional State) and the principle of cooperation:

c) Secularism, or the principle of the non-confessional State, is a legal principle established, with certain nuances, in the constitutional law of all European Union countries. Secularism is a concept based on two principles: the separation between church and State and the neutrality of public powers regarding religious matters.

d) The principle of cooperation, also observed by some European Constitutions (Austria, Germany, Italy…), is a peculiarity of the Spanish Constitutional system. Because of the constitutional duty of the public powers to take into account religious beliefs of Spanish society and to maintain cooperation relations with the Catholic Church and other religions,[420] the Spanish Constitutional Court has qualified our Church-State relations system as "positively secular."

---

[418] http://www.pluralismoyconvivencia.es/

[419] But also with the embassy of the Order of Malta and some other items like Pious Charitable Deed of Holy Places (*Obra pía de los Santos Lugares)* See FERREIRO GALGUERA, J.: "Los órganos de la Administración española encargados de la relación jurídico-técnica con la Santa Sede: la Dirección General de Asuntos Religiosos y la Subdirección de relaciones con la Santa Sede" in *Iglesia Católica y Relaciones Internacionales* Ed. Comares, Granada 2008 pp.280-291. See also Royal Decree 1748/2010, December 23rd , which implements the basic structure of the Ministry of Foreign Affairs and Cooperation (BOE January 14th 2011).

[420] Art. 16.3 Spanish Constitution: "No religion shall have a state character. The public authorities shall take into account the religious beliefs of Spanish society and shall consequently maintain appropriate cooperation relations with the Catholic Church and other confessions".

This mandate for Cooperation was undertaken by the adoption of Cooperation Agreements with the Catholic Church in 1979 in the juridical form of international treaties, as well as Agreements with the other three religions that, at the time that the agreements were signed (1992), had been declared by the Administration as "deeply rooted" denominations (Muslims, Jews and Protestants). Afterwards, those agreements were validated by the Parliament as ordinary laws.

2. Recognition of religions: The Register of religious entities

The Spanish Constitution recognises the fundamental right of religious freedom not only for individuals but also for groups and communities. The only limits to manifestations of religious freedom (whether of individuals or groups) are those necessary for the maintenance of public order which is protected by the law.

Law 7/1980 of 5th July of Religious Freedom Act implements this concept of public order. When speaking about limits of religious freedom this Act enshrines two kinds of limits:

1) Respect for the fundamental rights of others and

2) Public Order, a juridical concept which has three dimension: public security, public health and public morality.

To be entitled to religious freedom, groups do not need to adopt any special legal form. But they do have the option to enroll in the Register of Religious Entities which is the responsibility of the Ministry of Justice. Once they are registered, religious groups have the guarantee of having legal representation as religious entities.

Requirements for enrolling in the Register of Religious Entities[421]:

- Registration shall be made by request of the respective religious entity. This written application must be accompanied by a reliable document containing notice of the foundation or establishment of the organisation in Spain as well as the following information:

a. Entity name (in such way as to be appropriate to distinguish it from any other religious group) and its address.

---

[421] According to Royal Decree 142/1981, 9th January on the organisation and function of the Register of Religious Entities.

b. Declaration of religious purposes which cannot go beyond the limits established in the Religious Freedom Act, which includes the respect for the fundamental rights of others and public order.
c. Rules of procedure for the organization and their representative bodies including their powers and requisites for valid designation thereof.

Royal Decree 142/1981 establishes that four types of religious groups are adequate to be enrolled:

- "Churches, denominations and religious communities"
- Their respective Federations
- "Religious orders congregations and their institutes
- Religious associations which have been constituted as such under the Ordinance of the churches and faiths they are linked to. In this case they are obliged to attach a certificate from the Superior Body of their church in Spain[422].

According to the Constitution, the relationship between the public powers and religious groups may be implemented in a metaphorical area formed by two coordinates: the principle of non confessional State (*laicidad o aconfesionalidad*) and the principle of cooperation. In other worlds, all relations between public powers and denomination should respect those two principles. The principle of non confessional state is based on two pillars: separation between churches and State and neutrality of the State before religious affairs. With regard to the principle of cooperation, the Constitution gives two mandates to the public authorities:

- To take into account the religious beliefs of the Spanish population and
- To maintain the resulting relations of cooperation with the Catholic Church and other denominations.

The Constitution does not state how relations of cooperation between the State and religious denominations should be developed. However, the Parliament "answered" that open question at two different moments. The first was five days after the Constitution was implemented (January 3rd, 1979), when the State of Spain signed 4 Cooperation Agreements with the Holy See (which have the legal form of international treaties) on these 4 subjects:

- Economic Affairs (tax benefits…)

[422] By virtue of the Royal Decree 589/1984 of 8th it is also possible to register foundations belonging to the Catholic Church. For the time being, a Royal Decree allowing the registration of foundations belonging to other denominations with Cooperation's Agreements has not been developed, which would be recommendable in order to reinforce equality.

- Legal Affairs (juridical personality, civil effects of marriage, chaplains in public institutions)
- Educational and cultural affairs
- Religious attendance in the Armed Forces and the military service of clergymen and members of religious order (the latter has no effect nowadays because military service is not compulsory anymore and Spain has a professional Army)

The second moment was when the constitutional mandate of cooperation was implemented, as in the above mentioned Religious Freedom Act of 1980. According to article 7, the State may establish Cooperation Agreements with those registered religious entities which, due to their domain or number of followers, have obtained the classification of a "deeply rooted" (*notorio arraigo*) denomination. Such agreements are also subject to approval by an Act of Parliament.

The Catholic Church did not need to obtain the classifiacation of a "deeply rooted" denomination, because it was obvious and besides it is somehow set out in article 16 of the Constitution where Catholic Church is specifically mentioned. In 1984, Protestants Churches and Jews Community were granted the classification of "deeply rooted" denominations by the Advisory Council of Religious Freedom[423]. Muslims received the classification of a "deeply rooted" denomination in 1989. 1992 brougth three subsequent agreements into effect: those signed between the Spanish State and the Protestant Churches, the Jewish Community, and the Islamic Community of Spain respectively. As set out in the Religious Act, these agreements were approved by Parliament as Laws 24, 25, 26/1992 of November 10th

Legal form religious groups adopt?

According to Spanish law, denominatios may adopt one of these legal forms:

1) **Non registered** religious entities:

Religious entities need not to register in order to act freely or to be entitled to religious freedom. The Constitution guarantees the right of religious freedom for all religious communities, whatever legal form they adopt, without other limitation than respect for fundamental rights of others and public order. The Law on Religious Freedom refers in article 2 to several manifestations of the

---

[423] Even when there is a lack of legislation in this item, so far the classification of "deeply rooted denomination" has been granted by the Advisory Council of Religious Freedom

religious freedom of individuals and communities. Among others, these include the rights of religious groups to: held worship celebrations, commemorate feast days, celebrate marriage rites, impart religious teaching, establish places of worship, appoint and train ministers of cult, spread the group's creed, maintain relations with their own organisations and with other religious denominations, and provide religious assistance in public institutions (Army, prisons, hospitals..).

Registering in the Register of Religious Entities (RRE) is not the only way for a religious group to become a legal entity. Religious entities may also opt to constitute an association under the Law of associations[424]. In this case, the requirements would be to submit an agreement between at least 3 individuals and also a charter (in a public or private document) approving the organisation and operation of the association. If they opt to be a civil association, they can also enrol either in the National Registry of Associations in the Ministry of Interior (if their sphere of activity is within the whole country) or in any of the registers of associations in the 17 Autonomous Communities existing in Spain, if their sphere of activity is located only within one of those Autonomous Communities.

In any case, intervention or approval by a public authority is not necessary for a group to be entitled with the fundamental right of religious freedom.

2) Religious entities **enrolled in the Register of Religious Entities** (hereinafter RRE).

Religious entities can also register in a special nation-wide register: Register of Religious Entities (RRE), under the Ministry of Justice, provided the applying religious entity fulfils the requirements above described, verified by the public authority (General Department of International Cooperation and Relations with denominations). The most controversial of those requirements is the declaration of religious purposes. According to our Constitutional Court, Administration should not assess religious purposes. Thus, registration can only be refused if the aforementioned requirements are not met by the religious group or of it is legally proved (for example a by a legal sentence) that this groups uses activities or methods or seek for illegal targets or goals.

There are 12.251 catholic religious entities registered in the RER (comprised congregations, religious associations, and religious institutes -parishes are not included-) and 2.765 non catholic religious entities (comprised religious entities, federations and religious associations) [425]

The immediate effects of registry in the RRE are:

---

[424] Organic Law 1/2002, March 22th, on the right of Association.
[425] Accesed January 17th 2011.

- Enjoying of legal personality as religious groups
- Organizing themselves with complete autonomy (a democratic organization is not compulsory for religious entities, as it is in regular associations)[426]
- being able to include clauses safeguarding religious identity (particularly important in matters of labour relations), and
- Exemption for ministers of cult from the requirement to have a residence permit in order to reside in Spain.

3) Religious groups registered in the RRE that have being classified as **"deeply or firmly rooted"** according to their domain and followers.

If the Advisory Commission for Religious Freedoms grants a registered religious group the "deeply rooted" declaration two main further legal effects will be offered:

- The right to have a representative in the Advisory Commission of Religious Freedom and
- The possibility of reaching a Cooperation Agreement with the State.

4) Religious groups who have been registered in the RRE, who had got the "deeply rooted" status and have signed a **Cooperation Agreements** with the State:

At this point, we may distinguish between the agreements signed with Catholic Church, on the one hand, and the four cooperation agreement signed with the official bodies of Protestants, Jews and Muslims on the other.

Coopertion Agreements **with Catholic Church**:

The Holy See reached Cooperation Agreements with the Spanish State in 1979, five days after the Constitution came into force, but before religious freedom Act was even projected. These four specific Agreements, which have a legal status of International Treaties, contain more privileges than those reached by the Protestants, Muslims and Jews in 1992. Among others, in the Agreement concerning economic affairs, the State promises to collaborate with the Catholic Church in order to obtain "its adequate economic support", and it draws a system that has been implemented by further norms and which nowadays stands mainly on the possibility of all tax payers to allocate a percentage of the income tax – currently 0, 7%- to Catholic Church. Every year, when tax payers prepare their income tax they can expressly opt between assigning the 0.7 of their net tax

---

[426] Article 2.5 of the Organic Law 1/2002, March 22nd, on the right of Association: "Internal organization and functioning process of associations must be democratic, fully respecting pluralism..."

payable (the amount of their income they have to pay to the State) to Catholic Church and/or to other social services, through NGOs[427].

Other important benefit regards to religious education in public schools. The Agreement on Educational and Cultural Affairs foresees an educational system in which teaching of catholic religion must be offered by all public schools (and also private schools funded by State "concertados") although it is voluntary for the students.

Other benefit refers to chaplaincy; According to the system established in the Agreements concerning religious attendance in Armed Forces and Legal affairs, implemented as well by several norms, Catholic religious assistance in public establishments is regulated and paid by the State.

Coopertion Agreements **with Islam, Judaism and Protestantism**

Once the respective Federations that represented Muslims, Protestants and Jews received their "deeply rooted" status from the Advising Council for Religious Freedom, the three denominations negotiated three different but extremely similar Cooperation Agreements that, as soon as they were reached, they were passed as laws in the Parliament (Laws 24, 25 and 26 of November 10th 1992). Some of the special rights enshrined in the Cooperation Agreements were:

- Legal definition (juridical status) of places of worship and religious ministries,
- Civil effects of weddings celebrated according to their religious rite,
- Spiritual guidance in public establishments,
- Right of parents to demand religious education for their children in public schools
- Tax exemptions on specific assets (more or less the same exemptions the Catholic Church has, except for the perception of a percentage of the income tax –so far only prescribed for Catholic church-)[428],
- Celebration of religious festivities and protecting their cultural and historical heritage.

The benefits of the Agreements only affects to those religious communities that belong to the federations or Commission that have signed those Agreements with the State. These bodies are:

- Federation of Evangelical Religious Entities of Spain (*Federación de Entidades Religiosas Evangélicas de España* –FEREDE-) which has 1073 registered religious communities under its umbrella organization (1015 religious entities, 40

[427] We have to take into account that one of the NGOs that can enjoy of this taxpayers option is Caritas, an NGO belonging to Catholic Church through which this institution develops the main part of their social service

[428] FERREIRO GALGUERA, J.: "Financing of churches and religious societies" in *Financing of churches and religious so cities in the 21st Century* Ed. Institute for State-Churches Relations. Bratislava 2010. pp. 195-209.

local federations, and 18 religious associations depending on a religious entity). There are 668 registered Protestant communities which do not belong to FEREDE, thus do not enjoy of the benefits of the Cooperation Agreement.

- Federation of Jewish Communities of Spain (*Federación de Comunidades Judías de España* –FCJS-) which has 14 registered religious communities under its umbrella (13 religious entities, 1 nation federations –FJCS-. There are 10 Jews religious communities that do not belong to FCJS, and so they do not enjoy of the benefits or the Cooperation Agreement.

- Islamic Commission of Spain (CIE) we will see below in more detailed

II. ISLAM IN SPAIN

1. Legal recognition of Islam

As we have just said, in 1992 the Islamic Commission of Spain signed a Cooperation Agreement with the Spanish Government, (Law 16/1992 November 10th). The Islamic Commission of Spain (hereafter CIE) was then formed by two organizations: the Islamic Communities Union of Spain (UCIDE) and the Spanish Federation of Islamic Religious Entities (FEERI). Nowadays there are 878 Islamic communities registered in the RER,[429] but only 576 are under the Cooperation Agreement umbrella, in other words, just 576 belong to CIE : 500 of them are part of UCIDE (478 religious entities, 14 federations and 8 religious association) and 75 to FEERI (72 religious entities, 1 federation – FEERI- and 2 religious association). There is only one religious entity which does not belong to any of those two organizations but belongs to CIE.[430]

[429] Accesed January 17th 2011

[430] January 17th 2011.

2. The Muslim population.

Spain has a population of 47 million[431]. Approximately 1.4 million are Muslims (approx 2.5 % of the population). 30% of them are Spanish and 70% are immigrants. Based on estimates, the latter's backgrounds are as follows: they largely come from Morocco (754,114: 639,451 of them without Spanish citizenship) but they come also from Algeria (60,008:53,649 of them non citizens), Pakistan (56,511: 54, 379 of them non citizens) and Senegal (59, 578; 57,335 of them non citizens)[432]. They mainly live in Catalonia, Andalusia and Madrid.

3. Muslim representative organisations

There are 878 Islamic communities registered in the RER, but only 576 of them are under the umbrella of the Islamic Commission of Spain (*Comisión Islámica de España* –CIE-). This organization is composed of two distinct groups: the Islamic Communities Union of Spain (*Unión de Comunidades Islámicas de España* –UCIDE-) and the Spanish Federation of Islamic Religious Entities (Federación *Española de Entidades Religiosas Islámicas* –FEERI-).

As has been already said, the CIE represents 576 out of the 878 Islamic communities registered in the RER. Nowadays there are five other local federations (in Catalonia, Madrid, Valencia, Baleares Islands and Murcia) that don't belong to the CIE but want to join the Islamic Commission of Spain, so as to enjoy the rights promised by the Cooperation Agreement of 1992. Negotiations are on-going in order to change the bylaws of the CIE which were adopted in 1992 right after the Cooperation Agreement was signed.

---

[431] 47.021.031 official data according to Royal Decree 1612/2010 of December 7th

[432] http://www.ine.es/jaxi/tabla.do (accesed January 14th 2010)

4. Mosques

According to Article 2 of the Cooperation Agreements, Mosques are buildings that are used exclusively and regularly for prayer, religious education and training, and spiritual guidance. Mosques are certified as such by the Islamic community in question, with the endorsement of the Islamic Commission of Spain.

There are 12 mosques with minarets in Spain: two in Madrid, one in Valencia, three in the autonomous community of Andalucía, four in the autonomous city of Ceuta and two in the autonomous city of Melilla.

According to a report published in 2006 by *Observatorio Andalusi* (UCIDE) there are about 332 prayer halls whereas other reliable sources claim that more than 800 oratories exist[433]. Registering mosques in the Register of Religious Entities (RER) is voluntary. In July 2009 there were just 176 mosques registered in the RER: 113 in communities under the CIE's umbrella and 57 in other communities that are thus not entitled to the benefits of the Cooperation Agreement (e.g. exemption of property tax).[434]

According to the Cooperation Agreements, Muslims have the right to their own Islamic cemeteries but are also entitled to plots for Muslim burials in municipal cemeteries.

Currently there are five private Muslim cemeteries in Spain: three in Griñón, Sevilla and Granada built by General Franco after the Spanish Civil War (1936-1939) as a reward for the Moroccan soldiers that fought on his side, and two in the autonomous cities of Ceuta and Melilla.

There are plots reserved for Muslims tombs in municipal cemeteries in Barcelona, Manresa, Tarrasa, Valencia, Zaragoza, Benalmádena (Málaga), Palma de Mallorca, Las Palmas de Gran Canaria and Logroño.

---

433 National Intelligence Service (*Centro Nacional de Inteligencia* –CNI-)

434 There are 2568 registered places of worship that belong to Evangelical churches, 22 synagogues, 757 worship places of Jehovah's witnesses, 120 temples of Mormons and 24 Buddhist places of worship.

5. Imams

According to Article 3 of the Cooperation Agreement with CIE Islamic religious leaders and imams who lead prayers, oversee religious education and training, and provide spiritual guidance must be in possession of a certificate stating that they fulfil these duties. The certificate must be issued by the Islamic community to which they belong, with the endorsement of the Islamic Commission of Spain.

Imams are covered by the Social Security system with a status akin to that of employees. Their respective Islamic communities assume the rights and obligations of employers under the Social Security system (as stipulated in Article 5)[435]. But in December 2009 there were only 109 imams that had been registered for Social Security.

Imams and Islamic religious leaders are entitled to the right to secrecy (as stipulated in Article 3.2): under no circumstances may religious leaders and imams "be forced to reveal information disclosed to them in the exercise of their duties as prayer leaders, preachers and spiritual counsellors, by virtue of the privilege of confidentiality conferred on them by law."

6. Chaplains

Prison inmates are entitled to receive spiritual guidance from imams or persons duly appointed by the Islamic communities, subject to the authorization of the Islamic Community of Spain (as per Article 9). These must be authorised by the prison authorities and must meet certain requirements, such as not having a criminal record.

There are 87 prisons in Spain, 14 of which are under the *Generalitat* of Catalonia; the other 73 depend on the Spanish Ministry of Interior. Altogether there are approximately 73,876 prisoners (10,351 of them in Catalonia).[436]

---

[435] The respective Islamic communities will shoulder the rights and obligations of employers under the Social Security system. Royal Decree 176/2006 of February 10th sets out the terms and conditions of inclusion in the social security system of religious leaders and imams of the communities that are members of the Islamic Commission of Spain.

[436] 58, 496 male inmates 5,029 women. Source Ministry of Interior (May 2009).

While all of the 140 Catholic prison chaplains are paid by the State, the 250 Protestant chaplains and 2 Jewish chaplains do not receive any state salary because their respective Cooperation Agreement has established that the chaplaincy expenses will be covered by their respective churches.[437] This is not the case for the Cooperation Agreement with Islam (CIE) where it is stipulated that expenses for spiritual guidance shall be covered in a way agreed upon by both the representatives of the CIE and the prison establishments (Article 9.3). In addition, an agreement was reached on July 12th 2007[438] stating that Muslim chaplains will be paid by the Ministry of Interior, provided they gather a group of 10 or more prisoners. Nowadays there are 12 imams in such an agreement, offering religious counselling to the 6,746 Muslim prison inmates of foreign origin -basically from Morocco (5,421 inmates), Algeria (985), and Mauritania (103).[439]

7. Islam in public schools

Muslim pupils are entitled, upon request, to receive Islamic religious instruction at pre-school, primary, and secondary level public schools and state-subsidised private schools, provided, in the latter case, that said instruction is not in contradiction with the ideological nature of the state-subsidised private school in question (as per Article 10).

In 2010-2011, there were 45 Islamic teachers in primary level public schools, all of them in 5 autonomous provinces (Andalucía (16), Aragon (3), Canary Islands (1), Basque Country (1), Ceuta (10), and Melilla (11). Precisely these five autonomous provinces are the only ones (out of the existing 17) in which payment of religious teachers in publish schools has not yet been decen-

---

[437] Royal Decree 710/2006 of June 9th implements the right of inmates of prisons to receive spiritual guidance established in the Cooperation Agreement with Muslims, Jews and Protestants. Article 11 of this royal decree rules that funding of this spiritual guidance shall follow the regulation established in the respective Cooperation Agreement.

[438] Convenio de Colaboración del Estado con la CIE para la financiación de los gastos que ocasione el desarrollo de la asistencia religiosa en los establecimientos penitenciarios de competencia estatal de 12 de julio de 2007.

[439] Source Ministry of Interior (May 15 2009)

tralized from the central government[440]. Thus the employer of these teachers is still the Ministry of Education of the central Government[441]. .

In the Spanish Education System there are three types of schools: public, private with partial funding from the state (*concertados*), and private. To date, there are no private nor *concertado* Islamic schools within the legislated education system.

III. TRAINING CENTRES FOR IMAMS

In Spain there are 51 public universities (one of them is an open university –UNED-) and two are international universities (Menendez Pelayo and Universidad Internacional de Andalucía), 17 private universities (one of them is an open university: Oberta de Catalonia) , and 7 Universities belonging to the Catholic Church.

Spanish law (according to the Cooperation Agreements of 1992, and Organic Law 6/ 2001 of December 21st) gives denominations which have signed Cooperation Agreements in 1992 the possibility of creating university centres for theological studies where their religious ministers can be trained and receive state-recognized certification. So far, only the Catholic Church has university theology centres but the Spanish Government is obliged under the above mentioned University Act to implement this right for Protestants, Muslims and Jews. This remains something to be done in the future.

With regard to training centres for imams, there are Islamic studies courses offered by two universities (one of them is a private university, but both of them are on-line universities) and two courses organised by two Islamic organizations (Islamic Council of Catalonia and Islamic Federation of Murcia). These organizations, which to date do not belong to the Islamic Commission of Spain, organise courses which currently receive no state recognition.

---

[440] The education system is decentralized. But payment of these teachers is yet to be decentralized in these five autonomous provinces.

[441] That means that in autonomous provinces with a large number of Muslim pupils like Madrid, Catalonia or Valencia there are no Islamic teachers paid by the state even when there are many classes with more than 10 students. This is a case in which the right of the parents is recognised by the law but it is not being implemented.

National University of Distance Learning[442]

The department of Ecclesiastical Law of the National University of Distance Learning (hereafter UNED) has organised, alongside with the Pluralism and Living Together Foundation (a public foundation which belongs to the Ministry of Justice) a course called "Islam and Democratic Principles."

It was held from January to June of 2009 in Madrid, as an online course offered on weekends. Most of the teachers were from Spanish Universities. It was targeted at imams and Islamic community leaders. That year there were 47 students (42 of them with a scholarship from the Foundation for Pluralism and Living Together). The main focus of the first year is not theological studies, although one of the four thematic blocks offered dealt with Islamic and Religious Culture. This was taught by Riay Tatary, one of the two general secretaries of the Islamic Commission of Spain (president of the UCIDE). The other three parts also dealt with subjects of sociological and juridical nature: 1) Religious facts and fundamentals 2) Islam in Spain 3) Islam and Spanish Law. Students received a diploma so far only recognised by this university.

In 2010 this course was taught again, not only in UNED-Madrid (to 21 students) but extended to the UNED delegations of two other cities, Valencia (22 students) and Tarrasa (18). In September of 2010, UNED (Madrid) held the second course (Legal and Sociological aspects of Islam in Spain) for those who had completed the previous one in 2009. This course included one section on Islamic Theology. It was held from September to December of that year

The University Camilo José Cela

This private university organised a course in 2009[443] entitled: "Islamic religion and culture."[444] It is an on-line course the primary objective of which is to train specialists in Islamic culture and religion, under the guidance of academic experts. Mansur Escudero, a convert and former general secretary of CIE (former president of FEERI) was one of the course's founders.[445]

The course is composed of the following modules: 1. Spanish History and Culture 2. The Koran and Mohammed 3. The Legal Framework of Islam in Spain, 4. Islamic Thought 5. Islam and Democracy.

The students get a diploma of "expertise in Islamic religion and culture" which so far is only recognised by that university.

---

442 http://www.fundacion.uned.es/cursos/derecho/diploma-actualizacion-profesional/islam-principios-democraticos/index.html

443 Nevertheless it is its 4th edition, because a similar course was offered previously at UNED

444 See: http://www.ciberuniversidad.com/islam

445 Unfortunately, Mansur Escudero died in October 3rd 2010, while praying in his house of Almodovar del Campo (Córdoba) at the age of 62, same age the Prophet Mahomet had when he died.

Islamic Council of Catalonia

The Islamic Council of Catalonia is a Federation of Muslim entities living in Catalonia. This umbrella organization still does not belong to the Islamic Commission of Spain (CIE), the main Islamic representative to the State.

Since 2005, the Islamic Council of Catalonia has run an imam training course (currently in its 4th edition). They use a regular methodology with teachers coming not only from Spain (the imam of Mataro, the Autonomous University of Barcelona, etc.) but also from abroad (University of Agadir, University of Fez, University of Doha). The number of students varies every year from 30-50. The diplomas received do not have official recognition.

Islamic Federation of Murcia

The Islamic Federation of Murcia is another umbrella organization that does not belong to the CIE to date so their community members do not receive the benefits of the Cooperation Agreement.

The objective of their courses is not only to give a theological training but to provide the basis of a general education as well. Teachers come from Belgium, France, Spain, Morocco, and Egypt. They offer the following subjects: The Prophets Guidance (interpreting Koran in the Western world), Spanish, Computer Science and Internet skills, Oratory, etc. So far, the diplomas received by students for these courses do not have official recognition.

SWEDEN

I. RELIGION AND STATE

1. Administrative bodies that have contact with denominations

Under the *Riksdag* (Swedish Parliament) and the Government, the Ministry of Culture is responsible for the legal and financial matters regarding the religious communities (ordinance 1996:1515). The task of the Ministry is to provide the Government with drafts on legislation and budget.

Under the Ministry of Culture there is a "Swedish Commission for Government Support to the Religious Communities"[446] (*Samarbetsnámuden för statligt stöd till trossamfund* SST-)[447] Its task is, according to provisions laid down in the Act on support to religious communities and to the Ordinance on Government grants to religious communities (1999:974), to decide on these State subsidies. In other words, SST is the authority, under the Ministry of Culture, that provides religious minorities with state funding and describes its grants as being divided into three categories:

- An organisational grant enabling parishes to hold religious services, offer pastoral care and provide education
- A working grant to support specific areas of public interest (hospital churches or theological training
- Projects grants to stimulate new forms of cooperation and adjustment of buildings for disabled persons[448]

Economic support from the State is based on the idea that denominations are good to society. Nevertheless, it is the government who decides which religious communities are to be entitled to state grants. In order to re-

---

[446] http://www.sst.a.se/

[447] Ordinance (2007:1192) with Instructions for the Swedish Commission for Government Support to the Religious Communities (Sw.*Förordning med instruktion för nämnden för statligt stöd till trossamfund*)

[448] http://www.sst.a.se/inenglish.4.7f968fc211eeec933de800011945.html

ceive these economic aids, denominations must observe the principles of democracy, respect for human rights and “Swedish values”[449].

The Swedish Commission for Government Support to Religious Communities has an annual budget of five million Euros (included in the budget of the Ministry of Culture) and has six employees.

Under the Government, the Legal, Financial, and Administrative Services Agency also carry out activities in the realm of religious communities. The Agency registers the religious communities who apply for registration and also decides on the matter of right of religious communities to officiate marriages. In addition, the Agency has a lot of other activities. It has 184 employees.

2. Recognition of religions

The Church of Sweden is by all means the biggest denomination in Sweden. It amounts to over 7 million members, corresponding to about 75% of the population. Five different religious groups are next, the Swedish Mission Covenant Church, the Pentecostal Movement, various Orthodox Churches, the Roman Catholic Church, and various Muslim denominations.

On January 1st 2000, with the amendment of 1973 Constitution, the State-church system in Sweden changed. The Evangelical-Lutheran Church of Sweden is no longer the Church of the State, but a registered denomination. Registering is not compulsory but it grants the registered group a legal status. According to the law on religious communities (1998: 1953), denominations must have legal personality as an idealistic (non-for-profit) association before being registered[450].

Nonetheless, religious groups are free to act in other legal forms than registered denominations, such as an association or a company or a foundation. They can even choose not to have any legal personality at all. The Constitution enshrines the right of all citizenships to practice their religion, alone or in the company of others, and to organize public worship. Of course, any denomination (registered or not) must comply with civil and criminal law. The Act of Denominations and the Church of Sweden Act are the two mains Acts of Par-

---

[449] LARSSON, G.: “Sweden” in V.V.A.A. *Yearbook of Muslims in Europe* Edited by NIELSSEN, J.S.; AKAGÖNÜL, S.; ALIBASIC, A; MARECHA,B.; MOE,C; Leiden-Boston, (2009) pp. 332-3.

[450] Companies, economic associations or foundations cannot be registered. Section 7 Denominations Act (1998:1593).

liament in the field of religion. The Act of Denominations recognizes the Church of Sweden the status of registered organization and gives other churches and denominations the opportunity to become registered as well and so to acquire legal personality as a denomination.

The special benefits that registered organizations have, besides granting them a legal status, are, among others, the possibility of using the tax system for collecting their membership fees and the right to officiate marriages. Only the registered denominations that fulfil some requirements are entitled to exercise these rights. Up to now, beside the Church of Sweden, about 50 churches and denominations have been registered.

In order to be registered, denominations should fulfil some requirements like to present statutes or by-laws, which establish the purpose of the denomination, the decision-making procedure, and a board or a corresponding body[451]. It is not demanded that denominations have a democratic organization to be registered but they must have basically religious purposes. A denomination is defined as a community for religious activities, of which an integral part is to arrange divine services[452].

As it have been said, only registered organizations are entitled to use the taxation system for levies from its members. A denomination could get this right through a government decision, but only if it fulfils some requirements as "contributing to the fundamental values on which the society lies, being maintained and strengthened, being stable" and having its own vital power"[453]. To be allowed to use the tax system a denomination must comply with the constitutional values, such as combating all types of racism and other forms of discrimination as well as violence and brutality; they must also work to develop equality between women and men, and to work for the integration of its members, so that they can participate in the life of the society. Finally, denominations must be opposed to any anti-democratic sentiments in society. Besides the Church of Sweden, this right to use the tax system for levies from its member has only been granted to seven churches and denominations. Buy if denominations opt for the use of taxation system to collect levies from its members, the State will automatically reduce the economic support that the religious group can receive from the State.

Denominations, even those not registered, can also be granted other State subsidies. This is due to the fact that the system of State subsidies was established a long

---

[451] Section 7 Denomination Act (1998:1593).

[452] Section 2 Denomination Act (1998:1593). Thus, the Swedish Humanist Association, an organization for atheists, wasn't accepted for registration. FRIEDNER,L.: "Religious entities as legal persons- Sweden- in *Churches and other organizations as legal person,* Peeters, 2007, *p.* 217-221.

[453] Section 16 Denominations Act (1998:1593).

time before the new framework of State and Church relations, and some of the denominations that were already granted State subsidies did not want to register. The systems are now coordinated, so that, as we have just underlined, a denomination that wants to use the tax system receives less in direct subsidies[454]. At the moment there are 22 denominations receiving state subsidies. The Church of Sweden receives no subsidies under this legislation. There are five Muslim religious communities which are registred within the *Kammarkollegiet* (Agency of Legal, Financial and Administrative Services) as legal persons[455]. This five Muslim organizagions have receive subsides from the SST during those years in organizational grants, in project grants, in educational grants and to soupprt spiritual care within the medical/hospital sector[456]

A registered denomination can also be granted the right to officiate marriages, provided it is a stable denomination and has an organisation system that "can be taken for granted that the provisions concerning weddings and connected measures will be complied with"[457]. About 40 denominations have been granted this right. The Church of Sweden has this right according to the Marriage Code[458].

Another benefit of being registered is right of denominations to hold private cemeteries, if "there are special reasons and it can be assumed that they can keep the cemetery and fulfil the obligations incumbent on a possessor of a cemetery"[459]. So far, only a few private cemeteries in Sweden are held by denominations. The Church of Sweden is responsible for the public cemeteries in most parts of Sweden. It is only in Stockholm city and the town of Tranas that the local councils (municipalities) are responsible[460].

---

[454] Section 9 Denominations State Subsidies Ordinance (1999:974).

[455] The Union of Islamic Cultural Centres in Sweden (IKUS), The United Islamic Communities in Sweden (SMF), The Swedish Islamic Communities (SIF), ISC and SMUD.

[456] To see the grants in 2009, http://www.sst.a.se/bidrag/utbetaldastatsbidrag2009.4.8c40fa126730d3c5b800026659.html

[457] Section I Act on officiating marriages within other denominations than the Church of Sweden (1993:305).

[458] Chapter 4, Section 3 Marriage Code.

[459] Chapter 2. Sections 6-7 Funeral Act *(begravningslagen)* (1990:1144).

[460] FRIEDNER, L.: "Religious entities as legal persons- Sweden.. *op.cit.* p. 220.

II. ISLAM IN SWEDEN

1. Muslim population.

Large number of Muslims started to arrive in the 196s and 1970s. According to unofficial estimates, the number of Muslims in Sweden could range from 350.000 to 400.00[461], representing around 2-3, 5% of a total population of 9,283,722[462] inhabitants. This estimate is not supported by hard data as it is against the law to collect personal data on religious believe and official bodies are not allowed to maintain records that include such a sensitive data.

The Muslim population in Sweden is very heterogeneous and, according to several researchers, it can be organized in seven geographical groups considering the country of origin. Turkish Muslims, the first big Muslim group to establish in the country in the 1970s, were estimated to be around 22.000-25.000 people, in 2000[463], Arabic-speaking Muslims are best represented by Iraqis (mostly refugees that started to arrive in the late 70s), Lebanese and Palestinians. In 2000, they constituted about 1/3-1/4 of Swedish Muslim population with around 90.000 people. Iranians started to arrive in the mid 80s as refugees and its number amounted to 52.000. African migrants, a great part also refugees, are mainly from Somalia (16.000) and Ethiopia (12.000). Muslims from Pakistan constitute a small group of less than 4.000 people. Finally, Muslim communities from the Balkans began to arrive as labour migrants and through the family reunification process, though since the 1990s an important number of them are refugees.

On the other hand, and although the size of so called second-generation Muslims is even more difficult to estimate, several studies believe it to be around 100.000.

The majority of the Muslim population is Sunni. There's a small shia community, some Ahmadyyans among the Pakistanis and Alevis with Turkish background. There are also a growing proportion of Swedish converts (between

---

[461] Centre for Dialogues. Muslim Youth and Women in the West: *Source of Concern or Source of Hope?* Report of the conference organized by the New York University Centre for Dialogues: Islamic World-U.S.-The West at the Salzburg Global Seminar. Salzburg, Austria, May 15-17, 2007. p. 106; *Muslims in the EU: Cities Report* ,The Open Society Institute, 2007.

[462] According to official data published the by Statistics Sweden the 31/05/2009: http://www.scb.se/ (accessed 09/07/2009)

[463] ANWAR, M, BLASCHKE, J. and SANDER, A.: *State Policies. Towards Muslim Minorities. Sweden, Great Britain and Germany*, Berlin: Edition Parabolis, 2004. All following estimates of the number of Muslims per ethnic group have been taken from this study.

1000-3000)[464]. Muslim communities are mainly located in the cities of Stockholm, Gothenburg and Malmö[465].

2. Muslim representative organizations

Although until the 90s, the Muslim communities were organized along ethnic and linguistic criteria, the construction of proper mosques during the last decade and the gradual institutionalization of Islam has helped the process of developing a different sense of identity that encompasses the diversity of the Muslim population of Sweden.

There is a wide range of Muslim organizations claiming to represent the different communities. The first national wide Muslim umbrella organization is the United Islamic Parishes in Sweden (*Förenade islamiska församlingar i Sverige*, FIFS)[466], created in 1974. It later split because of internal divisions and in 1982 a new national organization emerged: the Swedish Muslim Federation (Sveriges *Muslimska Förbund*, SMF). Both of them represent mainly Arab communities and have set up coalition organizations within the years to better unite forces in order to deal with public authorities[467].

This two umbrella organizations (FIFS and SMF) have been able to cooperate under another umbrella organization. The Muslim Council of Sweden (*Sveriges muslimska råd*, SMR)[468] is an umbrella organization founded in 1990 that currently claims to have 9 member organizations (about 100,000 members) representing 80% of Muslims organizations: Young Muslims of Sweden (*Sveriges Unga Muslimer*), United Islamic Parishes in Sweden (*Förenade islamiska församlingar i Sverige*), Muslim Association of Sweden (*Sveriges Muslimska Förbund*), Bosnian Islamic National Association in Sweden (*Bosniska Islamiska Riksförbundet i Sverige*), Islamic School Foundation (*Stiftelsen Islamiska Skolan*), Islamic Information Association (*Islamiska Informations-*

[464] ROALD, A.S.: "From `people's home' to multiculturalism': Muslims in Sweden", in Y.Y. HADEN (ed), *Muslims in the West: From Sojourners to Citizens.* (Oxford: Oxford University Press, 2002) p. 102

[465] LARSSON, G. *Sweden, Muslims in the EU: Cities Report. Preliminary research report and literature survey*, Open Society Institute, 2007, p. 14.

[466] http://www.fifs.se/

[467] HUNTER, SHIREEN: *Islam, Europe's second religion: the new social, cultural, and political landscape*, Westport, Conn : Praeger, 2002. p. 129-131.

[468] http://www.sverigesmuslimskarad.se/insider.html

föreningen), Islamic Relief , *Politi Islami Asambly* (PIS) and the Muslim Scouts of Sweden (*Sveriges Muslimska Scouter*) .

The current chairperson of the organization is Helena Benaouda, who succeeded Mostafa Kharraki. Some people think that at least some members of SMR have ideological influence by the Muslim Brotherhood.

Other relevant Muslim organizations or federations are the Union of Islamic Cultural Centres (*Islamiska kulturcentunionen* created at the beginning of the 1980s, influenced by the Süllemancy movement; the Swedish Islamic Assemblies (SIF) founded in 2002; the first umbrella organization for Shiite communities, the Islamic Shi´as Communities in Sweden (*Islamiska Shiasamfunden i Sverige* –ISS-)[469], or the Bosnian *Bosnien-Hercegovinas Islamiska Riksförbund* (1999).

Some of these organizations also belong to the Islamic Cooperation Council (*Islamiska Sammarbetsradet*) which is the only Islamic organization that receives funding from the State[470] through the *Nämden för Statligt Stöd till Trossamfund* belonging to the Ministry of Culture.

3. Mosques, imams and cemeteries

When a Muslim organization applies for permission to build a mosque building permit has to be granted by the city hall. There are six purposed built mosques in Sweden, four of them (Sunni), in Malmö, Upsala and in Stockhol (2), one in Trollhättan (Shi´a) and one Ahmadi mosque in Göteborg (built in 1975, is the oldest one in Sweden). There are plans to build mosques in Eskilstuna; Jönköping, Väkjö, Umeä, Göteborg and Örebro, and there is a mosque under construction in Skövde[471].

According to official sources, there are 55 imams that belong to the five Islamic communities registered in Sweden, and about 115 working outside these five organizations[472]. Since there are no imam education centres in Sweden, imams usually go abroad to received special training. In some cases, imams are sent to Sweden by foreign institutions (such as the Turkish *Diyanet*).

---

469 http://www.shiasamfund.se/

470 FIFS, IKUS, ISS, SMF and SIF.

471 LARSSON, G.: "Sweden" in V.V.A.A. *Yearbook of Muslims in Europe…op. cit.* p. 335.

472 Source: official data from the Swedish Ministry of Education and Research

Nevertheless, some Islamic religious leaders don't have any formal education at all. The lack of a degree from a university or a theological centre could be a problem for foreign imams applying for a working permit as "clerics" due to the requirement of providing a degree accepted by Swedish authorities. So far, only the degrees from the Turkish seminars held by the Dyanet are recognized by the Swedish authorities.

According to statistics from 2000, 111 municipalities provide burial ground for Muslims. Law does not forbid Muslims been buried in a shroud instead of in coffin, as it is required by them, and in some local offices it is specifically permitted being buried in that way (e.g. Malmö)[473]

4. Chaplaincy

Some imams are acting as chaplains in the 55 prisons existing in Sweden (around 5.500 prisoners) but there are not official figures. Nevertheless, this work is being done mainly on a voluntary basis, because so far there are no imams employed by the State in the health service, prisons or armed forces. However, some imams receive grants from the SST and the Swedish Prison and Probation Service in order to perform this social service to religious freedom.

5. Islam in schools

Religion is a compulsory subject in Swedish public schools though it is taught in a neural way, from a secular approach focusing on the study of world religions. Pupils should not be indoctrinated into any specific religious doctrine through religious classes. So, Islam or any other religion should be presented as one religions among many others existing in the world.

There are 7.994 schools in Sweden from which 596 are private. Since the school reform of 1992, it has become much easier to receive support and economic subsidies from the State to create independent school. The majority of private schools belong to the Church of Sweden. In 2006 there were 66 primary

---

[473] LARSSON, G.: "Sweden" in V.V.A.A. *Yearbook of Muslims in Europe...op. cit.* p. 337.

schools promoted by denominations (54 Christians, 9 Muslims and 3 Jews)[474]. Even if they can be influenced by the doctrines of their religions, these private schools must follow the national curriculum and respect the law and principles of Swedish legislation.

According to official data, there are nine Islamic schools, all of them associated to Islamic School Foundation (*Stiftelsen Islamiska Skolan*). According to what we have above mentioned, these Islamic schools should follow the national curriculum. Referring to religious educations, pupils of these schools must learn not only about Islam or Muslim doctrines but also about other religions. The first Muslim school was established in Malmö[475].

III. TRAINING CENTRES FOR IMAMS

Although some Swedish political leaders have publicly supported the idea of imam's education[476], no training courses have taken place to date in Sweden.

In order to reflect on the issue, the Swedish government formed an investigatory committee concerning the training of imams in Sweden (Dir 2008:66). A report was published in 2009 with recommendations. The committee came to the conclusion that the State should not start an education for imams in Sweden. It would be unlikely that the Ministry of Education would start a confessional educational program for Imams, especially since the Church of Sweden was separated from the State in 2000.

Nevertheless, some universities offer courses in the History of Religions, Islam and Middle Eastern Studies and there are many researchers engaged in studies of Islam and Muslims[477].

---

[474] LARSSON, G.: *Sweden, Muslims in the EU: Cities Report. Preliminary research report and literature survey*, Open Society Institute, 2007, p. 22.

[475] LARSSON, G.: "Islamic religious education in Sweden" in ASLAN, E. *(ed.) Islamische Erziehung in Europa / Islamic Education in Europe*. Wien-Köln-Weimar, Böhlau Verlag, 2009. pp. 403-421.

[476] Jens Orback, former Head of the Board of Integration, believes that education for imams would be a useful tool to promote the Muslim's community integration. See Larsson 2007, p. 23.

[477] E.g. LARSSON, G.: "Islam and Muslilms in the Swedish media and academic research, with a bibliography of English and French literature on Islam and Muslims in Sweden" *European University Institute Papers* (RSCAS N° 2006/36, 2006)

THE NETHERLANDS

I. RELIGION AND STATE

1. Administrative bodies that have contact with denominations

The minister of Justice is officially in charge of relations between the State and religious denominations. Therefore he regularly discusses matters regarding religious items with the representative organisations. The Ministry of Justice is responsible for presenting the policy of the Dutch government regarding religion and State relationships and for ensuring that the law is upheld. In daily practise, depending on the nature of the issue concerned, the Ministry of Justice is the competent to deal with religious organizations on specific issues regarding that ministry.

The Directorate General for Housing, Communities and Integration[478] belonging to the Ministry of Housing, Spatial Planning and the Environment, is responsible for most issues regarding integration, and religion of minorities being an element of it[479].

The Ministry of Education, Culture and Sciences deals with the maintenance of religious monuments and the Ministry of the Interior and Kingdom Relations with the public order.

2. Recognition of religions

Even if it was not formulated in the 1983 Constitution, relations between Church and State in the Netherlands may follow the principle of separation. Churches, which are independent from State and so free to organize as they wish, are equal before the law. It is not though a "strict separation" in the sense that

---

[478] Since November 2008 Minister Van der Laan is responsible for the areas of Housing, Communities and Integration (WWI).

[479] The Delta Plan for Integration aims to promote the integration of minorities, increase the level of integration and bridge integration gaps. Reducing racism and discrimination is also a major part of this plan. Source: Ministry of Housing, Spatial Planning and the Environment Official website: http://international.vrom.nl/

churches and State should have not any contact. On the contrary, the principle of separation of Church and State must be interpreted in harmony with the principle of State neutrality before denominations and with the fundamental right of religious freedom.

Separation between Church and State was marked by a sharp decline of the Dutch tradition of "pillarisation", the late nineteenth-century institutionalisation of separate socio-politico-religious worlds in the interest of principle of equality. The country was divided essentially in four "pillars" (Protestant, Catholic, Socialist, and Liberal). General rules and regulations established the limits for these denominationally or ideologically based organisations and the performance of their duties, funded by the government[480].

This situation changed with the Constitution of 1983, where the basis of the new Church and State system in The Netherlands was put forward. Article 6 guarantees freedom of religious belief as well as freedom of non-religious belief[481]. The Netherlands does not recognise any particular religions as such. The founding and forming of a religious community is free.

Even though, neither the Civil Code nor any other piece of legislation provides a definition of a "church", these denominational groups are legal entities of civil law. There are several ways for religious communities to acquire legal status. The Civil Code introduces specific categories: "church" (*kerkgenootschap*), "independent unit of a church" and "structures in which churches are united".

Apart from these *sui generis* categories, religious entities can opt to organise themselves as a foundation (*stichting*) or as an association (*vereniging*). In practice, one Jewish community uses the 'church' form whereas Islamic communities tend to be organised as a foundation or as an association.

The law sets no formal requirements for the establishment of a "church". Article 2.2 of the Civil Code states merely that: "*Churches, their independent units, and structures in which churches are united shall have legal personality*". And the second section adds that they are governed by their own statutes as long as they do not conflict with the law.

So there are no requirements to register a religious community like having a minimum number of members or being approved by public authorities. A precondition, however, is for the religious communality that it expresses its will to establish itself as a "church".

---

[480] BLOM, J.C.H. *Pillarisation in Perspective*. West European Politics, 2000.
[481] See Annex I

Even if there is not a legal definition of what a "church" is, in concrete cases, the administration or, if necessary, the court, decides. Even if it has not been given any overall definitions, courts have sometimes formulated requirements needed such as, the will to constitute a legal entity of that kind, or the need of being a "structured organisation". Public authorities cannot test about theological or doctrinal aspects.

Churches may also decide to organize themselves as an independent unit or as structures to which they belong. One reason for choosing a "church" as legal form may be that it provides more freedom of internal organization than if they opt for the federation or association legal form, which are groups subject to the general law of their kind.

There are not many legal consequences beside the normal ones provided in the Civil Code. Being a "church" does not entitle neither to State subsides nor to officiate marriages with legal effects[482]. But in the employment field, churches can be considered as "spiritual offices". A public authority permit for dismissal of a holder of a spiritual office is not required. Tax benefits to organizations with religious purposes will be the same than other organizations of public interest[483].

In general terms, theoretically there is no state support to churches. Nevertheless churches have received subsides for various grounds in the recent years. For example, subsides on religious assistance in military institutions or in prisons. In this sense State supports religious freedom of persons who are held in those institutions and who can't go freely to the temples outside the Army or the prison. Government must take action when fundamental rights of its citizens are threatened. On the contrary, in institutions like hospitals or houses for the elderly, religious assistance would be paid by the general funds of the institutions.

Donations to churches as well as to a wide variety of charitable institutions are exempt from taxation.

---

[482] Religious marriages cannot take place before the civil marriage. The church minister who performs a religious wedding ceremony without verifying the existence of a previous civil binding marriage is liable to prosecution

[483] VAN BIJSTERVELD, S.C.: "Religious entities as legal persons –Netherlands-" in *Churches and other organizations as legal person,s* Peeters, 2007, p.171-176

II. ISLAM IN THE NETHERLANDS

Although the presence of Islam in Dutch's soil dates from the 20th century, relations between the Netherlands and Islamic countries started in 17th century when a free commerce treaty with Morocco was signed. In 1800 the Dutch colonization of Indonesia, the country with the largest Muslim population in the world, was formerly established. After the independence of the Dutch´s East Indies (1949) and Surinam, a large number of inhabitants of the former colony fled to the Netherlands, being the first Muslim community to establish in the country.

It was after World War I and until the oil crisis of 1973, when the Netherlands active policy of recruitment of low skilled male workers, brought a significant number of Moroccan and Turkish citizens to the European country. The recruitment process was framed by agreements with the different countries and it followed the model of "guest workers" adopted by other states such as Germany and France. The largest Muslim communities in the Netherlands today are originally from Morocco and Turkey. A large number of those from Turkey are Kurds.

From 1974 onwards, progressive restrictive policies that rendered more difficult the entry to the country led to the settlement of the so-called guest workers and their families. This fact, together with the increasing number of asylum seekers from different Muslim countries such as Pakistan, Afghanistan, Iran, Somalia and Bosnia, arriving in the 80s, would constitute the core of the consolidation of Muslim presence in the Netherlands.

1. Legal recognition of Islam

Although there's no formal recognition of religious communities, the State does recognize certain groups and provide them with State resources for education, broadcasting, and spiritual care in prisons and in the army. There is generally no difficulty in qualifying for this status, and Islam has been granted these privileges as the rest of the denominations.

2. The Muslim population.

Officially, the Netherlands do not have faith registers of its inhabitants. However some studies have estimated the proportion of the different denominations in the Netherlands. According to those studies[484], in 2005 out of the total population (over 16 million), the number of adherents of Islam with various national backgrounds was approaching 944.000, a number equalling 5.8% of the total population[485].

According to 2010 figures, out of the total population of the country (16.574.989 inhabitants) 20.3% (3.359.603) are immigrants. Out of the figure of 944.000 Muslims (research published August 27th 2004)[486], 383.957 are Turkish-Dutch, 349.005 are Moroccan-Dutch[487], and about 12.000 are native Dutch converts.

Muslim communities in the Netherlands are primarily located in the larger cities in the west of the country[488]. In the main cities as Amsterdam, Rotterdam, Utrecht and The Hague up to 30 % of the population is of non-Western origin[489].

Besides Sunni Muslims, there are also Shi´is (mainly part of the Iranian diaspora), Alevis (mainly kurds) and Ahmadis (Surinamese Muslims that belong to the Ahamdi-Lahore community). Turkish immigrants also belong to other lines like the *Milli Görüs* movement, the Nurçu and the Suleymançis.

---

484 DEMANT, F., MAUSSEN, M. and. RATH, J.(2007): Muslims in the EU - Cities Report, The Netherlands. Preliminary research report and literature survey, Open Society Institute.

485 http://statline.cbs.nl/StatWeb/publication/?VW=T&DM=SLNL&PA=70086ned&D1=0-1,17-18&D2=a&HD=090710-1521&HDR=T&STB=G1

486 Ibidem

487 http://statline.cbs.nl/StatWeb/publication/?DM=SLNL&PA=37325&D1=a&D2=0&D3=0&D4=0&D5=0-4,137,152,215,232&D6=0,4,9,(l-1)-l&HDR=G2,G1,G3,T&STB=G4,G5&VW=T

488 *International Religious Freedom Report 2008: The Netherlands*, US Department of State. http://www.state.gov/g/drl/rls/irf/2006/71398.htm (accessed 15/06/2009)

489 NIEUWBOER, J. W. :*National Analytical Study on Housing 2002*. Rotterdam: Monitoring Centre on Racism and Xenophobia (DUMC), 2003.

3. Muslim representative organizations

Muslims are still in a process of setting up a joint organisation, representative of the various Islamic communities in the Netherlands, for official contact with State authorities.[490] After the murder of the cinema director, Theo van Goh in 2004 by a Moroccan-Dutch Muslim, the pressure from the Dutch State on Muslims organizations to unite under one umbrella grew significantly. Meanwhile, the Minister for Housing, Communities and Integration (HC&I)[491] officially recognizes two representative bodies of the Dutch Muslim community. These Islamic umbrella organizations are the *Contactgroep Islam* (Islam Contact Group) and the *Contactorgaan Moslims en Overheid* (Muslims Contact Agency)[492].

The first umbrella organization to be established was the Muslims Contact Agency (*Contactorgaan Moslims en Overheid* –CMO-). It unites some Turkish organizations, like Islamic Foundation Netherlands (*Islamitische Stichiting Nederland*)[493], the Turkish Islamic Cultural Foundation (*Islamitsche Culturele Federatie* –TICF-)[494], both sections of the *Milli Görüs* movement, the Suleymanci Foundation Islamic Centre the Netherland (*Stichting Islamitisch Centrum Nederland* –SICN-*)*[495], some Moroccan organizations like the Unoon of Moroccan Mosque Organizations (*Umnie van Marokkaanse Moskee Organisaties Nederland* –UMMON-, the Surinamese Hindustani Wold Islam Mission[496], and the Shi´a association (mainly Iraqi Shi´a) *Overkoepelende Sjiitische Vereninging* –OSV-. These organizations claim to represent 369 mainly Sunny mosques and about 500.000 Muslims[497].

The second umbrella organization is the Contact Group Islam (*Contact Groep Islam* –CGI- which included Sunni, Shi´a, Ahmadiyya and Alevi Muslims with the Ducht Muslim Council (*Nederlandse Moslim Raad* –NMR-)

Three times a year the Minister for HC&I organises the Governmental Islamic Platform (IPO). During these meetings the Minister discusses integra-

---

[490] VAN BIJSTERVELD, S.C.: "State and Church in the Netherlands" in *State and Church in the European Union,* Second Edition, Ed. Nomos, Baden-Baden 2005. p.368-389.
[491] http://international.vrom.nl/
[492] http://www.cmoweb.nl/
[493] http://www.diyanet.nl/
[494] http://www.ticf.nl/
[495] http://www.sicn.nl/
[496] http://www.wimnet.org/events/taibah.htm
[497] DE KONING, M.: "Netherlands" in V.V.A.A. *Yearbook of Muslims in Europe* Edited by NIELSSEN, J.S.; AKAGÖNÜL, S.; ALIBASIC, A; MARECHA,B.; MOE,C; Leiden-Boston, (2009) p. 247.

tion and religious issues with representatives of the CGI and CMO. These meetings have an open agenda and other organizations, departments or scientists can be invited when dealing with specific issues. However, the CMO and CGI do not have much credibility among some groups of young Muslims who regard them as a mirror of the first generation and too compliant with the Government and its increasing prejudices against Muslims[498]

Besides the IPO-meetings, the Dutch government consults many other Islamic groups and Islamic key-figures regarding particular issues or situations[499].

There are other national organizations like the Sunni women's association *Al Nisa* [500]*,* and the Association of Imams in The Netherlands (*Vereniging van Imams in Nederland* -VIN- which claims 110 members, mostly followers of the rite Maliky[501]

At the local level different types of Muslim organisations can be found. In the case of Amsterdam there are mosque organisations, youth organisations, women's organisations, umbrella organisations and Muslim cultural organisations, for example, there is a Union of Moroccan Mosques in Amsterdam and Surroundings (UMMAO). [502]

There are also some radical communities that have gain strength as a consequence of the Islamophobia raising in some spheres of the politics and society. Among them *Hizb ut Tahird* which aims at uniting Muslims in a caliphate[503], Foundation Islamic Comittee of Ahlu Sunnag (*Islamitische Comité van Ahlu-Sunnah*) a Salafi foundation including As Soennah Mosque in The

---

[498] In t he elections of 2010, the Freedom Party (*Partij Voor de Vrijneia)* leaded by Geert Wilders that defend a hard Islamophobic doctrine raised from 9 seats (in 2006) to 24, thus becoming the third political party behind People's Party for Freedom and Democracy VVD (31 sits, 9 more than in 2006) and the Duth Labour Party PvdA (30 sits, it lost 3). In this Parliament Wilders party is a but ahead of the former leader Cristian Democratic Appeal CDA that lost 20 seats from 2006 (it has now 21seats)

[499] The so called *Islam in Burgerschap* (Islam and Citizenship) was a publicly funded foundation that developed initiatives and projects related to Islam, integration and participation but it has been terminated in 2008.

[500] http://www.alnisa.nl/

[501] http://www.imamonline.nl/

[502] DEMANT, F., MAUSSEN, M. and. RATH, J. *Op. cit.*

[503] http://www.Kalifaat.org

Hague[504], and El Tawheed Mosque in Amsterdam[505] have been targets of counter-radicalization politics[506].

4. Mosques and cemeteries.

A network of mosques and cultural centres serves the Islamic community. This network was organized to conform to the national system of subsidies, which funds cultural activities geared to social orientation and the promotion of equal opportunities. The first mosque was built in the town of Almelo in 1975. Since then, the number of mosques increased to 453: 245 are affiliated to Turkish organizations (particularly *Diyanet* with 140, the *Milli Görüs* -35 mosques- and the Suleymancis -38-) 159 mosques are controlled by Moroccans. The Surinamese community has 25 mosques controlled by the World Islamic Mission and a Hanafi Barelvi orientation[507]. But some Surinamese belong to the Ahmadiyya movement who has five mosques. Somalis Muslim communities have 62 mosques[508].

The Law on disposal of death (*Wet op de Lijkbezorging* -1991-) allowed Muslims to bury according their rite, within 24 hours and without a coffin. There about 70 local cemeteries which have plots reserved for Muslim burials. There are also foundations in charge of repatriations of Muslim bodies to their home countries. Foundation of Islamic Funeral Services (*Stichting Islamitisch Begrafeniswezen* –IBW-[509]provides information on Islamic burials.

---

[504] http://www.al-yaqeen.com
[505] http://www.eltawheed.nl
[506] DE KONING, M.: "Netherlands" in V.V.A.A. *Yearbook of Muslims in Europe...op. cit* p. 248
[507] The Barelvi movement started in 1880, deeply influenced by Sufism. It derives its name from Bareilly, situated in Uttar Pradesh, India, the home city of Ahmad Raza Khan (1856-1921), whose writings substantially shaped it.
[508] DE KONING, M.: "Netherlands" in V.V.A.A. *Yearbook of Muslims in Europe...op. cit.* p. 249.
[509] http://www.stichtingibw.nl/

5. Imams

Since no official registration of faith leaders exists in the Netherlands, only the number of foreign faith leaders is available through the register of residence permits. On average, 50 faith leaders per year applied for a staying permit in the Netherlands within the last five years (including Muslim faith leaders). About 85% of these applications were approved. Work permits for spiritual leaders are valid for one year only and must be renewed at the end of each period. On the basis of this work permit it is not possible for spiritual leaders to become Dutch citizens.

The Turkish Religious Affairs Directorate appoints the imams for some 200 Turkish mosques in The Netherlands[510]. On the other hand, Moroccan mosques are completely independent. UMMON represents these mosques formally.

Foreign religious leaders wishing to work in the Netherlands are required to complete an integration course[511]. Furthermore, in order to promote the integration of Muslim communities and the respect for Dutch´s democratic principles, temporary grants were issued to VU University Amsterdam, Leiden University and INHOLLAND University of Applied Sciences for the purpose of setting up imam and Islam courses in the Netherlands.

In 2008, Parliament proposed phasing out the issuance of work permits to foreign imams to increase the number and influence of locally educated religious leaders.

Regarding the working conditions, the Labour Relations Act states that spiritual officers do not need a public authority permit in case of dismissal of the office holder. Law has not considered Muslim religious leaders to have a religious office so far. Therefore imams enjoy protection against dismissal as any other employee.

---

[510] *International Religious Freedom Report 2008: The Netherlands*, US Department of State...*op. cit.*
[511] *Ibid.*

6. Chaplains

Religious assistance takes place in various types of institutions, such as the armed forces, prisons, health care institutions, institutions for young people, and homes for the elderly. In public institutions of the type, the Government nominates the church minister which has been appointed by the churches. In order to work as a Muslim chaplain in prisons or in the army it is compulsory to attend a training course set up by the government. The legal basis for chaplains varies depending on the institution: for prisons as well as for the army the legal basis lays on an Act of Parliament whereas currently there's no Law for spiritual care in health care institutions. At the present time, there are 2 chaplains working within the Armed Forces and over 20 to 30 in other institutions[512].

a) Prisons:

Imams who work in prisons are civil servant since January 2008. Before that date, they were contracted on seasonal basis. The 62 Muslim chaplains working in prisons are under the supervision of the Head of Islamic Spiritual Care in Correctional Institutions that drafts an education plan consisting of tailor made courses on a yearly basis. The courses are aimed at developing the competences and knowledge of these imams, so that they can work in the public sector. Moreover, the Prison Services offer courses to train the imams how to handle with prisoners. Some imams are also enrolled in university programs.

b) Hospitals:

A limited number of hospitals employ imams and they are paid by the hospitals not by the State. There is no Act of Parliament pertinent regarding spiritual care within the health care institutions.

c) Armed Forces:

According to official information, in 2009 The Dutch Armed Forces will recruit 3 imams. The imams recruited by The Dutch Armed Forces will follow training at the Military Academy and their salaries will paid out from the general budget for the armed forces.

---

[512] Source: information provided by Famile Arslan, member of the Government Advisory Board on Establishing Imam Education Programme, at the Expert Consultation on "The development of religious instruction and institutions in Europe" organised by the Institute of Strategic Dialogue in Madrid, March 11th 2010.

7. Islam in schools

A specific reference to religion can be found in Article 23 of the Constitution that relates to education. Freedom of education is guaranteed, including freedom to found a school, freedom of denomination and freedom to administer a school. Equal funding of public and confessional schools is also a key component of this principle.

The Dutch education system comprises both public and private schools most of which are Catholic and Protestant. Private schools have to comply with the same statutory requirements as public ones regarding the official curricula. Both categories of school are funded by the government and are visited by the school inspectors[513].

The first Muslim schools were established in the 80s in Rotterdam, The Hague, Eindhoven and Amsterdam, when the Muslim network began transmitting and the first imam training courses were set up. In 2006 there were 46 Muslim primary schools and two Muslim secondary schools in the Netherlands[514]. Due to the fact that public schools are free to provide religious education at the request of parents, some initiatives have been taken, on a very limited scale, regarding Muslim religious instruction in public schools[515]. Besides that, official curricula include education about different religions with the objective of encouraging mutual understanding and tolerance. Pupils at many schools can choose to study Arabic or Turkish as a second modern language. [516]

There has been public concern in the past years regarding the contents of Islam religious education. Studies suggest that further cooperation between Muslim schools and other public institutions are an important element for the integration of the Muslim community through education.

---

513 1917 Constitution for general elementary schools.

514 DEMANT, F., MAUSSEN, M. and. RATH, J... *op. cit.* p. 79

515 SHADID, W. A., and P. S. VAN KONINGSVELD (2006): "Islamic Religious Education in the Netherlands" in *European Education*, Vol. 38 (2), 2006, pp. 76–88.

516 DEMANT, F., MAUSSEN, M. and. RATH, J. *Op. cit.* p.90.

III. TRAINING CENTRES FOR IMAMS[517]

A relevant feature of the Dutch elaboration of the separation between Church and State is the state-funded academic education for clergymen, both at public and at private confessional universities and seminaries.

As stated in Dutch law, every person from outside the EU, who wants to start working in the Netherlands as a preacher, religious teacher or in another religious job for an institution (hospitals, prisons, the Army, or institutions based ona religious of philosophical ideology) has to follow a specific training program on civic issues.

The program lasts for 18 months and starts with a 3-week language training, which makes it possible for the religious faith leaders to conduct the remainder of the program in the Dutch language. The following year and a half the religious faith leaders will be present at six 2-day meetings and two one-day meetings in groups of 12-15 participants from different religious backgrounds in order to stimulate interfaith dialogue and integration in Dutch society. Contents include an introduction to Dutch society, and, in consultation with national Muslim organisations, other specific subjects[518]. After the program the participants have to take an exam.

Regarding training centres for imams, two types of institutions can be considered. On the public sector, two public universities and a public university of applied sciences have received start-up funding for a number of years (2005-2011) to develop and offer courses in the Netherlands on Islamic Theology and/or specific training for imams and chaplains. On the other hand, there's a private Muslim university currently working on imam's training as well.

---

[517] Although the Dutch government has no ongoing research on imam training at this moment, it did sponsor the International Institute for the Study of Islam in the Modern World (ISIM) until it's closing down in January 2009. The Leiden-based ISIM, which was established in 1998 by several Dutch universities, conducted and promoted interdisciplinary research on social, political, cultural, and intellectual trends and movements in contemporary Muslim societies and communities. As a follow-up to ISIM an inter-university graduate school was funded early 2009. Form and content of the curriculum of the graduate school will be submitted in the summer of 2009, after the Dutch government considers funding.

[518] Information from the *Fact sheet Islam in the Netherlands*, produced by the Ministry of Foreign Affairs in consultation with the Ministry of the Interior and Kingdom Affairs. http://home.deds.nl/~quip/archief/culture/Islam%20in%20Nederland.html#P114_14943

1. Public institutions

Following the Sterk[519] and Bos[520] motions, temporary grants were issued to three government-funded universities: the VU University Amsterdam, the Leiden University and the INHOLLAND University of Applied Sciences. Funding was provided for the purpose of setting up imam and Islam courses in the Netherlands. The aim of this initiative responds to the need of consolidating a large body of Dutch Muslim religious leaders and experts in Islam. Programs offered by these Universities are focused mainly in Islam in the European context from a literary and historical perspective.

All programmes offered by these universities are officially certified and recognised. Students receive Bachelors and/or masters degree qualifications which are nationally recognised. Graduates from these programmes will be able to work as Islamic spiritual servers or spiritual counsellors for the Custodial Institutions Service, in hospitals or in the Army, as social workers, teachers or policy employees.

Efforts have been made to develop partnerships with the two main Islamic umbrella organisations CMO and CGI. The CMO (Muslims Contact Agency) supports and recognises the three different imam and Islamic courses offered by public universities in the Netherlands, and it refers those of its members who would like to pursue such training to these universities. Attempts are also being made to involve the *Contactgroep Islam* (Islam Contact Group, CGI), which at present does not play an active role in any course recognised by the government, with the programme offered by INHOLLAND University of Applied Sciences.

- **Centre of Islamic Theology (Free University of Amsterdam)**

The Centre for Islamic Theology was set up in the Faculty of Theology of the Protestant Vrije Universiteit of Amsterdam[521] in September 2005 through a grant of the Ministry of Education, Culture and Science[522].

The centre offers studies focusing on three central themes: an examination of historic Islam, reflections on Islam in the modern era and the context in which Muslims live in the Netherlands. The centre has alliances with leading universities in such countries as Turkey, Egypt and Morocco

The institution offers a Bachelor's course in Islamic Theology and a one-year Master's course in Islamic Spiritual Counselling. In addition to these de-

---

519 Parliamentary Papers II 2003/2004, 29 200 VI, no. 155.

520 Parliamentary Papers II 2004/2005. 29854, no. 10.

521 http://www.godgeleerdheid.vu.nl/en/organisation/faculty-departments/center-for-islamic-theology/index.asp

522 Official data: 250,000 euros a year, from 2005 to 2011 (a total of 1.5 million euros).

grees, which are parts of the overall programme of temporarily subsidised Dutch imam and Islamic courses, the Free University of Amsterdam set up two Masters: a Master in Islamic Youth Care and a Master in Islamic Spiritual Formation in September 2008. A three-year Master in Islamic Theology that will entail training for students seeking to become imams in mosques and other institutions is currently being developed as well. As the one-year pre-Master's course, a Bachelor's programme in Religious Studies serves to prepare students for the various Islamic Master tracks.

The Ministry of Education, Culture and Science has encouraged the cooperation among the university and Muslim organizations for the consolidation of the programmes. Several mosque organisations have already indicated their willingness to cooperate in relation to work placements, while consultations are presently underway with the CMO and other mosque organisations.

In August 2008, the total number of students in the Bachelor's programme and the three different Master's tracks at VU University Amsterdam was 48 (24 men and 24 women). The majority of these students already have a religious counselling function, mostly in the prison service.

- **Leiden University**

There is an Institute for Religious Studies in this university[523]. In 2006 Leiden University launched Bachelor's and Master's programmes in Islamic Theology, in Islamic Studies and Islam in the Contemporary West[524]. As for the VU University of Amsterdam, the Ministry of Education has made a development grant available to Leiden University in order to set up and further develop the courses[525]. The contents of the BA (in Dutch) are mainly theologian and they are focused primarily on modern Islam in Europe.

The university is currently engaged in discussions with a number of Islamic umbrella organisations about setting up a course for students wishing to become imams. The partnership between the university and Muslim organisations has to be laid down in accordance with the *dúplex ordo* system[526]. This means that a one-year course in a Muslim organization is mandatory as part of the program.

---

[523] http://www.hum.leiden.edu/religion/research/

[524] http://en.mastersinleiden.nl/programmes/about/religion-and-philosophy/islam/

[525] The grant amounts to 472,000 euros a year, from 2006 to 2011 (a total of 2.35 million euros).

[526] The *dúplex ordo* system is a special statute in a law in which 'confessional' theological disciplines are separated from 'scientific' ones. GHALI, M.: "Training Imams in Europe: the challenges of develop a unifed program. Leiden University as a Study Case" in *Journal of Islam Religious Educaation and >Theology* vol. I (2010)

At present there are 34 students following the three-year BA's programme of Islamic Theory (13 men and 21 women) and another six enrolled for the Master, bringing the total number of students on the Bachelor's and Master's courses up to 40. The Masters courses are being taught in English.

- **INHOLLAND University of Applied Sciences in Amsterdam**

Since 1995, the INHOLLAND University of Applied Sciences in Amsterdam/Diemen, a practical training university, has had a program to train secondary school teachers of Islam. And in 2006, it started a four-year Imam and Islamic Spiritual Worker Bachelor's programme in September 2006[527].

The program is officially recognised following accreditation by the Dutch Flemish Accreditation Organisation (NVAO). The program is currently divided in 3 areas: Islamic social worker education, religious training for lay spiritual workers and imams.

Grants from the Ministry of Justice and the Ministry of Education support the development of the programme[528]. The contents are aimed at three related graduate profiles: Imams, Islamic Spiritual Workers and Islamic Pedagogic Workers.

The university has set up cooperation agreements with *Milli Görüs Noord Nederland* (MGNN), the *Nederiandse Islamitische Federatie* (Dutch Islamic Federation, NIF), the *Unie van Marokkaanse Moslimorganisaties in Nederland* (the Union of Moroccan Muslim Organisations in the Netherlands, UMMON), the World Islamic Mission (WIM) and the *Stichting Islamitisch Centrum Nederland* (Islamic Centre Netherlands Foundation, SICN).

Internships are a compulsory part of the third and fourth year program. The students have to spend time at a large mosque organisation and in a work setting of their choice (such as a mosque, legal institution, hospital, or the youth care sector). Arrangements concerning these internships are currently being made between the university and relevant organisations. At the same time, INHOLLAND University of Applied Sciences is in discussions with Moroccan, Turkish and Indian universities in order to give students the opportunity to spend a semester studying abroad.

The INHOLLAND University of Applied Sciences has also recently reached an agreement with VU University Amsterdam to facilitate student's mobility between both campuses' programmes.

The number of students enrolled for the 2008/2009 academic year (34) has exceeded the totals for the previous years, and brings the overall number of students taking part in the programme at the beginning of 2009 to 59. The first students graduated in 2010.

---

[527] From 2008, it is also possible to pursue these studies in The Hague.

[528] Official data: 400,000 euros in 2005 and another 400,000 euros for the years 2007 – 2010.

2. Private Institutions

- **Islamic University of Rotterdam (IUR)**

There is one private centre, which doesn't have official recognition, the so-called Islamic University of Rotterdam (IUR) which was founded in Rotterdam in 1998. This private institution offers studies on Islamic theology, Arabic language and culture[529]. The Islamic University of Rotterdam is a member of the Federation of the Universities of the Islamic World (FUIW)[530] since 1998 and has participated in numerous scientific meeting both in Arab countries and Europe.

The University comprises 3 centres: the Faculty of Islamic Sciences (one of its aims being the training of imams), the Faculty of Languages and Civilizations and the Faculty of Islamic Arts. It also has an Institute of Islam, a Research Institute, the Institute of Qur'an Recitation and the Centre for Wisdom Studies.

The IUR works in partnership with the Islamic University of Europe (also based in Rotterdam) and both institutions are currently working to acquire official recognition for its degrees. There are other private initiatives without official recognition like the Sunni institutes *Dar al Ilm* in Amsterdam and *Al Islah* in Lochem (affiliated to *Tabligh Jama'at.*

529 http://www.islamicuniversity.nl/en/index.asp

530 FUIW is a body working within the framework of the Islamic Educational, Scientific, and Cultural Organization -ISESCO-, specializing in supporting Universities and Higher Education institutions of the same level in the Islamic World and encouraging cooperation among them.

UNITED KINGDOM

I. RELIGION AND STATE

1. Administrative authorities that have contact with faith groups

All Government Departments engage with religious groups on different issues, and faith groups are engaged in consultation. For example, the Department for Children, Schools and Families engages with various faith communities and organisations regarding both state-funded and independent faith schools.

Within the Government, the Department for Communities and Local Government has lead responsibility for faith issues: advising on engagement between faith communities and national, regional and local Government; fostering inter faith activity and encouraging the development of faith-based service delivery as an important part of the voluntary sector. The Communities Minister co-chairs the Faith Communities Consultative Council, a formal representative body for faith communities which is used as a forum for consultation by many Departments. The Council meets every three months. This Inter-departmental Group on Religion and Belief acts as a liaison points between Government departments on issues to do with religion and belief.

2. Recognition of religions

In the UK there is no definition in law about what constitutes a 'religion'. Neither the national UK Government nor any of the devolved administrations (Scotland, Wales, and Northern Ireland) take a view about the formal official status of any religion, and there is no basis on which they could do so. In practice all are free to follow what they regard as a religion provided that they do not contravene any law.

Although the UK has not written Constitution, the legal tradition, and most recently the Human Right Act 1998, guarantees freedom of religion within the limits of public order as determined by the courts. However, the Church of England is the Established Church in England. Its position is underpinned by statute; the Monarch is the Supreme Governor of the Church of England (Anglican) and through the Prime Minister´s Office appoints its bishops. There are 26 Anglican bishops within the 743 members of the House of Lords, the upper chamber of the Parliament. Legislative Power approves or rejects the measures relating to church matters passed by the General Synod[531]. In practice, however, the Church of England is autonomous. The Church of Scotland (a Presbyterian church) has an analogous but not exactly similar status in Scotland.

Some religious communities tend to register as private associations or even companies under the Companies Act. But the legal structure most religious groups adopt is that of a charity, currently under the Charities Act of 2006. These groups have special tax benefits according to the general interest of their purposes. According to the Charities Act 2006, "the advancement of religion" is one of the types specifically included in the list of "charitable purposes". There is a Register of Charities created by the Charities Act 1960, under the UK Charity Commission. Recently, a Faith and Social Cohesion Unit has been created at the UK Charity Commission. It has to assess whether the groups who apply for charitable status are of public interest or at least follow mainly goals of public interest. Even those religions that have not got the charitable status might still be eligible for tax relief by obtaining a non-profit status[532]

As British law does not define what constitutes a religion, it does not hold information about the types of religious entities in the UK. There is no a specific register of religious organisations.

---

[531] FERREIRO GALGUERA, J.: "Reminiscencias del sistema de Iglesia de Estado en los países de la Unión Europea" in *Anuario de Derecho Eclesiástico del Estado* vol. XXVI Madrid 2010, pp. 208-210.

[532] For example, although the church of Scientology was refused registration with the Charaity Commission in 1999, HM Revenue & Custom agreed in 2000 that the Church is a not for profit body as such is exempt form paying VAT. See BAKER, E.-NEWCOMBE,S.: "Financing of churches and religious societies in Eengland".in *Financing of churches and religious so cities in the 21st Century...op.cit.* p.110.

II. ISLAM IN THE UNITED KINGDOM

1. Legal recognition of Islam

Islam is not recognised as an official religion but only in terms of right to religion and belief, and protection against discrimination.

2. The Muslim population.

The first Muslims arrived to the islands in the 18th century: they were "lascars" (merchant navy sailors) employed by the British East India Companies. They were later followed by Yemeni sailors employed after 1869 in Aden. They gradually began to settle in cities like Liverpool, South Shields, Swansea, Birmingham and Sheffield[533].

After World War II there was an important migration to the United Kingdom from the former colonies. Many Muslims migrants arrived during the 1960s and the 1970s.

According to the Census of April 2001, which included a question on religions for the first time since 1851, there were approximately 1.591.000 Muslims in UK, forming 2.8% of a total population of 58 million people[534]. There were about 1,540.000 in England and Wales, forming around 3% of the total population; 42.557 in Scotland, representing 0, 84 of the population in that province and 1.943 in Northern Ireland, which is less than 1% of its population. Three quarters of the Muslim population (74%) were from an Asian ethnic background, predominantly Pakistani (43%), Bangladeshi (17%) and Indian (8%). More recent arrivals have been refugees, coming mainly from Somalia and Irak. Figures based on the Labour Force Survey estimate that the Muslim population has now grown to approximately 2.4 million[535] .

At present, the Muslim population remains concentrated in urban areas; around 40% of the Muslims living in UK are settled in London, forming around 8, 5% of the capital's population. The rest is spread across other cities like Birmingham, Manchester, Bradford, Luton, Slough, Leicester and the mill towns of Northern England.

---

533 ANSARI, H.: *The History of Muslims in Britain, 1800 to the present.* Hurt. London 2004, p. 65

534 Office for National Statistics, 2001 figures: http://www.statistics.gov.uk/cci/nugget.asp?id=954 (accessed 03/07/2009)

535 Labour Force Survey (2009) , Office for National Statistics http://www.statistics.gov.uk/CCI/article.asp?ID=2309&Pos=2&ColRank=1&Rank=224

Most Muslims have arrived to UK as national of countries within the Commonwealth (former colonies) thus once they have entered in the UK they have full political rights and could vote and stand for local and national elections. During the 1970s and de 1980s, the majority acquired UK citizenship, and their children acquired it also by birth. At present the majority of Muslims in the UK are UK citizens, except for those who have arrived as refugees from outside the Commonwealth since the 1980s[536].

3. Muslim representative organisations

The UK Government does not officially recognise particular organisations or groups which claim to represent Muslim communities, but it takes a pragmatic approach to recognising Muslim organisations and to working with them on an issue by issue basis.

National and local Government have been working to broaden and deepen its engagement with Muslim organisations to better reflect the diversity of Muslim communities in the UK. To enable dialogue with underrepresented groups, the Government established the National Muslim Women's Advisory Group and the Young Muslim's Advisory Group to strengthen communication with, and provide advice on issues relating to, Muslim women and youth. The Government does not engage with any organisation which is involved in the promotion of violent extremism.

Although several attempts have been made to create a national representative body for the Muslim communities, there are currently several umbrella organisations that represent a part of the more than 3000 Muslim organisations in Britain[537]. Leading examples of these organisations are listed below:

The **Muslim Council of Britain** (MCB) was founded in 1997 following the Rushdie affair with the aim of reaching an Islamic consensus in national affairs. After a long process of consultation, MCB was established as a representative body of various schools of thought and political trends[538]. The MCB is committed to democracy. Today it lists over 500 organisations as affiliates.

---

[536] ABBAS, T.: "United Kingdom and Northern Ireland in in V.V.A.A. *Yearbook of Muslims in Europe* Edited by NIELSSEN, J.S.; AKAGÖNÜL, S.; ALIBASIC, A; MARECHA,B.; MOE,C; Leiden-Boston, (2009) p. 364-5

[537] Mehmood Naqshbandi: *Islam and Muslims in Britain. A Guide for non-Muslims*, City of London Police, 2006. According to the report: "about half [of the 3000 Muslim organisations in Britain] are primarily involved with running *masjids* and community centres. The vast majority are locally focused organisations and probably about half are registered charities, although many of these have only trivial amounts of finances. Many more have tiny memberships and are short-lived"

[538] http://www.mcb.org.uk

In 2007, Scottish Muslims created the Muslim Council of Scotland, which brings together a variety of Scotland's mosques and Islamic organizations. There is also a Muslim Council of Wales.

The **Muslim Association of Britain** (MAB)[539] was founded in 1997 by people of Arab origin. One of its aims is to campaign for British policy towards the Muslim world. E.g. it campaigned against UK involvement in the war of Irak.

The **British Muslim Forum** (BMF), chaired by Khurshid Ahmed, was set up in 2005 and has more than 350 affiliated organisations, of which 230 are mosques[540]. It represents nine sections of the Sunni Barelewi community. It was also an attempt to counter the outside influence on British Islam.

The **Al-Khoei Foundation**, the major Shi'ite group. It manages two education establishments in the UK (primary and secondary schools)

The **Mosques and Imams National Advisory Board** (MINAB) is an independent community organisation that aims to drive up standards of governance and leadership in mosques. It was founded in 2007 as a joint initiative of the Al Khoei Foundation, British Muslim Forum, Muslim Association of Britain and Muslim Council of Britain. MINAB aspires to work with and represent all Muslim traditions and schools of thought and since its inception, a range of organisations have joined the MINAB[541].

MINAB was set up following the recommendations of a national consultation with representatives of mosques, Islamic centres, Imam training institutes, leaders and scholars in 2006/07. MINAB held their first Annual General Meeting on 10 May 2009, where they elected their Executive Board which comprises 52 members. MINAB's objectives include assisting building capacity of mosques to function as community hubs, and to assist mosques in matters of governance[542].

Other organisations working at national scale are the Federation of Student Islamic Societies (FOSIS) founded in 1962 to cater for the needs of Muslim students in further and higher education across the UK[543]; the Sufi Muslim Council (SMC), the Islamic Society of Britain, City Circle, Muslim Safety Forum and the Islamic Forum of Europe.

The main Muslims organizations in Northern Ireland are the Belfast Islamic Centre (BIC) founded in 1978, the Irish Council of Imams[544] and the Islamic Student Society of Northern Ireland.

---

539 http://mabonline.net/

540 http://www.thebmf.org.uk

541 The Islamic Culture Centre (Regents Park Mosque), the Muslim College, and the Southampton Medina Mosque Trust Limited.

542 MINAB's Constitution: http://www.minab.org.uk/essential-documents/constitution

543 http://www.fosis.org.uk

544 See p. 138

4. Mosques

Whilst there are some privately-run websites that provide estimates of the number of British mosques[545], there are no official estimates. According to some statistics, there are around one thousand mosques in UK (defined in the broad sense as not only those with minarets but also those places that can be considered as prayer spaces)546.

Common services provided by British mosques include onsite worship and educational programmes, fund raising and offsite religious services. Other community resources delivered by mosques are legal advice services, accommodation, welfare, activities for senior citizens and healthy living initiatives[547].

According to several reports[548], Sunni Deobandi and Barelwi schools are the most wide spread branches among British mosques. In general the demographic makeup of local places reflects the ethnicity and country of origin of mosque congregations. Mosque management boards and trustees tend to be made up of males aged over 50 and less than 40% report having women's committees[549].

Different studies about mosques conducted by Muslim organisations have led to the development of capacity building programmes to empower mosques management committees and social cohesion[550] . Examples of these are the Muslim Council of Britain's *Mosques 100 Project*[551], the *Focus on Mosques* project launched by the Muslim Parliament, the *Management Guide for Mosques and Islamic Centres* developed by the OAK Community Devel-

---

545 http://www.lancashiremosques.com/discovery_muslims_in_britain.asp

546 See also RICHARD, G.: "Representing the city: Mosques and the planning process in Birmingham, UK" in *Journal of Ethic and Migration Studies* vol 31 nº 6 (2006) p. 1162

547 *Survey of Mosques in England and Wales*, prepared for the Charity Commission by BMG Research, February 2009

548 *Understanding and Appreciating Muslim Diversity: towards better engagement and participation*, Institute of Community Cohesion (iCoCo), April 2008; Mehmood Naqshbandi: *Islam and Muslims in Britain, A Guide for Non-Muslims*, City of London Police, 2006; Anya Hart Dyke, *Mosques made in Britain*, Quilliam Foundation, February 2009.

549 *Ibid.*

550 *Voices from the Minaret – MCB Study of UK Imams and Mosques;* Ruqaiyyah Waris Maqsood: *The Role of the Mosque in Britain*, The Muslim Parliament of Great Britain, July 2005.

551 This Capacity Building programme is part of the Muslim Council of Britain's programme to improve the sustainability of Mosques and Muslim Organisations in the UK, and was set up in 2007. More about the project in: http://www.mcb.org.uk./uploads/M100.doc (accessed 29/06/2009).

opment[552], or the *Excellence in Mosques* toolkit of the Madni Jamia Masjid Leadership Development Program.

The Government has also supported community-led capacity building initiatives in mosques, including the Beacon Mosques training programme for mosque management run by Urban Nexus and work by Demos to support young people participation in mosques.

5. Muslim faith leaders.

There are no reliable figures for the number of Muslim faith leaders in the UK, because there is no obligation for them to register. The number of Imams can be very roughly estimated as approximately 1000 (based on one imam per mosque), but this figures would not take into account the full range of faith leaders, such as chaplains, lay preachers, *Alim*(*a*) etc working in the UK. The Government does not collect figures on the number of Islamic religious leaders coming from abroad. However research has indicated that significant numbers of Imams in UK mosques either come from overseas or receive their training outside Britain, particularly from South Asia (Pakistan, Bangladesh and India)[553]. While the use of English is becoming more prevalent at Friday sermons, a significant proportion of sermons are delivered in community languages and for many Imams, English is not their first language.

Since 2004, religious ministers applying for a visa to the UK are required by the Home Office to prove certain knowledge of English[554]. The English language requirements for religious ministers and workers coming from abroad are currently being revised.

A report prepared by Faith Associates[555], in which 1202 questionnaires were sent to Islamic centres and mosques, showed that 33% of respondents had Imams with a university degree and 27% with *Dar al-ulum* qualifications.

---

552 This initiative is part of OAK´s Faith Action programme which includes services such as an organizational assessment tool to identify the organisation's capacity building needs, mentoring support and training, a toolkit for better management and strategic planning support. Source: http://www.oakcd.org.uk/page.php?id=5 (accessed 29/06/2009)

553 Research by Ron Geaves, University of Chester (2007).

554 Home Office UK Border Agency: http://www.ukba.homeoffice.gov.uk/workingintheuk/tier2/ministersofreligion/supportingevidence/englishlanguage/ (accessed 24/06/2009)

555 Ifath Nawaz and Shaukat Warraich: *Mosques and Imams National Advisory Body. Consultation Findings and Conclusions,* Faith Associates, 2006, p. 13

6. Chaplains

Muslim chaplains and Imams are engaged by institutions across the public sector, including prisons, universities, further education colleges, hospitals, police forces, the armed forces, the courts service, immigration centres and the fire service.

There is no single arrangement for appointing Muslim chaplains or Imams – they may be state employees, self-employed, volunteers or engaged on an informal basis. Arrangements for engaging Muslim chaplains and Imams vary between and within sectors. For example, in the prison service, chaplains are direct employees of the State, while in the university sector arrangements may be more informal and differ between institutions[556].

In some sectors, and particularly the Prison Service and the National Health Service, standards for recruiting Muslim chaplains, as with all chaplains, are high, and chaplains are given additional training in areas such as chaplaincy management, counselling and security[557]. Figures on the number of Muslim chaplains are only available for some sectors of the public service. Currently there are 197 chaplains (18 of which are female) working in the prisons of UK and 43 chaplains working in the NHS. They are all paid by the State. In November 2005, Imam Asim Hafiz was appointed as Muslim chaplain to the British Armed Forces.

There are a number of professional associations for Muslim chaplains, including the Association of Muslim Chaplains in Education, the Muslim Chaplains Association and the British Muslim Chaplain. Muslim chaplains also play an active role in multi-faith chaplaincy associations, such as the College of Health Care Chaplains. They may also participate in other bodies set up to help cater for the needs of Muslims in public sector institutions, such as the Islamic Religious Council and the National Council for the Welfare of Muslim Prisoners which were established in the Prison Service in 2001.

The UK Government is currently putting measures in place to support consistently high standards in chaplaincy across the public sector. The Department for Communities and Local Government (CLG) has been developing, with an external contractor and Muslim community organisations, voluntary guidance on the engagement of chaplains in public institutions, looking at how best practice by Muslim chaplains can be shared more widely. A series of con-

---

[556] According to a report commissioned by Minister of State for Lifelong Learning, Further and Higher Education , there are around 30 Muslim chaplains working in British universities, almost all of them volunteers. See: Ataullah Siddiqui, *Islam at Universities in England. Meeting the needs and investing in the future*, 2007.

[557] The Department for Communities and Local Government is currently developing with a n external contractor (Faith Matters) guidance on the role of chaplains in public institutions

sultation events are being planned to look at what can be done to support high standards in chaplaincy across the public sector and areas for future development, such as in the training available for chaplains. There is also potential for this work to be taken forward to Muslim community organisations looking at the training and development of Imams in mosques.

7. Muslim students and Islamic Schools.

Religion plays a role in education system in various ways, based mainly on the Education Act of 1944 and 1988 with some later amendments[558]. Every pupil in a maintained school has a statutory entitlement to religious education, which is a statutory part of the basic school curriculum but not a subject of the National Curriculum. Teachers can decline to teach the subject.

On the other hand, all pupils must take part in an act of collective worship, normally at the beginning of a school day. This is mainly of Christian character, but not distinctive of any particular Christian denomination. Students can be withdrawn by their parents and teachers can decline to

The national non statutory framework sets out what pupils should study in religious education from the ages of 3 to 19[559]. Each Local Educational Authority (LEA) must convene an ASC (Agreed Syllabus Conference) to produce a syllabus setting out a programme of study for pupils to be adopted by the LEA. Each LEA must also have a Standing Advisory Council on Religious Education (SACRE) that may review the agreed syllabus at any time[560] Building on the statutory requirements, it is recommended that there should be a wide ranging study of religion and belief across the key stages as a whole. Since the 1970s, Religious Education *syllabi*, set by a process under the local government, have had a multi-faith content, with since 1988 has had to include Christianity and has guaranteed a proportion of time for the main world religions, including Islam. Teachers of the subject are professionally trained teachers and do not require the approval of religious authorities, nor do they need to belong to any denomination. Pupils should develop understanding of concepts and mastery of skills to make sense of religion and belief at an appropriate level of challenge for their age. Not all religions or beliefs need to be studied at the

---

[558] FERREIRO GALGUERA, J.: "Reminiscencias del sistema de Iglesia de Estado en los países de la Unión Europea" in *Anuario de Derecho Eclesiástico del Estado* vol. XXVI Madrid 2010, pp. 216-220.

[559] It is organised in three sections form pupils of different ages: foundation stage, Key stages 1, 2 and 3; ages 14-19

[560] This in addition to the requirement on LEAs to convene a conference to reconsider tha agreed syllabus every five years.

same depth or in each key stage, but all should be studied in a way that is coherent and promotes progression.

In 2004, a large number of publicity funded schools were managed buy the Church of England (4.500 primary schools and 200 secondary schools) and the Roman Catholic School (1750 primary schools and 360 of secondary schools 2.100). There were also Jews (38), Sijs (3) and Hindu schools (1).

At the time of 2001 census, there were around 37,100 Muslims student in primary and secondary schools in the UK. About 20,000 of those children were attending the approximately 137 Muslim schools there are currently in England. Eleven of those schools receive State aid (maintained schools). The first State-aided Muslim school was Islamia Primary, a mixed school founded 22 years ago by Yusuf Islam, formerly known as Cat Stevens. There are about 130 Muslim independent schools. Like all independent schools, independent faith schools must meet the curriculum and other requirements set out in regulations. This includes the requirement to provide for the spiritual, moral, social and cultural development of pupils.

Established in 1992, the association of Muslims Schools UK (AMSUK) supports institutions to develop sustainable approaches and strategies that cultivate productive and transformative leadership with an aim to provide holistic education to all learners.

There are also an estimated 100,000 Muslim children attending evening classes at mosques[561]

[561] HART DYKE, A. (2009): *Mosques made in Britain*, Quilliam Foundation, February 2009.

III. TRAINING CENTRES FOR IMUSLIM FAITH LEADERS

Some research has been undertaken on imam training by UK academics[562]. However, there had been no in-depth research into Islamic seminaries (commonly Darul Ulums in the UK) or other training institutions for Muslim faith leaders in the UK, in part due to problems researchers have encountered gaining access to some of these institutions. In order to remedy this situation an independent review of training for Muslim faith leaders in the UK had been commissioned[563] and is was recently reported[564].

There is a wide range of Muslim education institutions providing different types of courses relating to faith leadership. The formal category of institutions includes full-time schools (11-16 or 11-19), further education institutions (post-16) and some Higher Education Institutions. The informal category includes part-time courses for women held during day-times, learning circles (*Halqas*) for men and women, web-based learning and also one-to-one learning between student and teacher. These formal and informal institutions are run by the different ethnic and denominational groups found among Muslims living in Britain.

Following the method of the just mentioned review, regarding Muslim faith leaders training we can difference between initial training and continuing professional development (CPD). The category of initial training can be also sub-divided into secondary education (the 11–19 age-ranges) and higher and further education (post-19).

---

562 Dr. Sophie Gilliat-Ray at Cardiff University, Yahya Birt, Dr Hisham Hellyer, and Professor Ron Geaves from Liverpool Hope University

563 The Prime Minister announced this Review in November 2007. Hazel Blears (Secretary of State for Communities and Local Government) appointed Dr. Alison Scott-Baumann and Dr. Mohamed Mukadam to lead the Review, which will carry out in-depth research in seminaries to assess the strengths and weaknesses of current provisions, consider international and other faith comparators, and make concrete proposals for how it could be improved. The Review was due to report at the end of 2009.

564 Finally, the Review *The training and development of Muslim Faith Leaders. Current practice and future possibilities,* published by the Department for Communities and Local Government, was reported at October 2010. http://www.communities.gov.uk/documents/communities/pdf/1734121.pdf .

1. Initial Muslim Faith Leaders Training: *Darul uloom*s and Higher Education Centres

There are 54 Muslim institutions in Britain providing initial faith leaders training. A high proportion of them are provided by the Deobandi community[565] even if, according to some reports, at most a third of British Muslims of South Asian backgrounds belong to this community, and that the majority are associated with the Barelvi community[566]

a) *Darul uloom*s

Thirty-eight of the 54 Initial Muslim faith leader's centers are secondary schools registered with the Department for Education as providing for the 11-16 age range. Mostly these secondary-type Muslim institutions in Britain are known as *Darul uloom*s[567]
They teach not only the national curriculum (core subjects as a minimum and often much more, including A-Levels and GCSEs) but also a traditional syllabus, often based on the Indian Darse Nizami syllabus[568] which focuses on the study of Arabic language, the *Qur'an, Sun'nah*, *Seerah* and *Fiqh.* (Shia Muslims centers have their own syllabus). The duration of this syllabus ranges from 5 to 8 years and upon completion students become 'Alims ('Alimahs, feminine) and are awarded the Ijaza (Certificate). As Dr. Siddiqui states in his report, they "develop a bridge to degree level studies with universities"[569]. Students who graduate from these institutions are recognised within the Muslim communities as 'Alims (Islamic Scholars) and 'Alimahs (females).

---

565 The Deobandi movement began at *Darul uloom* Deoband, India, where the foundation stone was laid on 30 May 1866. Its members played a key role in establishing similar institutions in other parts of the South Asian subcontinent during the late nineteenth century and early twentieth century.

566 The Barelvi movement started in 1880, deeply influenced by Sufism. It derives its name from Bareilly, situated in Uttar Pradesh, India, the home city of Ahmad Raza Khan (1856-1921), whose writings substantially shaped it.

567 *Darul uloom*s: Literally Houses of Knowledge. These are schools that provide an in-depth course on Islamic Sciences, popularly known as the 'Alimiyyah syllabus. In its original form it was a nine-year course for students in the 12–21 age-range and led to a degree-level qualification. The medium of instruction was originally Farsi but later was Urdu. After graduation, former students pursued careers as imams or Islamic scholars, or else as senior government administrators and officials. It was based on a set of carefully selected texts reflecting rationalist traditions developed in Iran and became the dominant system of Indian Islamic education from the eighteenth century onwards.

568 Syllabus established by Mulla Nizamuddin Sahalwi (d. 1748) in India and later developed by the Deobandi madrasa.

569 SIDDIQUI, A. (2007), *Op. cit.* p. 32.

Most *Darul ulooms* in the UK have made variations to the original syllabus, for example by cutting back on content which they considers superfluous to the need of students growing up in contemporary society. The language of instruction is nowadays frequently English rather than Urdu.

Seven of these centres are in Yorkshire, seven in Lancashire, eleven in the West or East Midlands and 13 in London and South East[570]. All of them are inspected by Ofsted

b) Higher Education Institutions

There are at least 16 institutions providing post-18 years education about Islam. Fifteen of them are colleges and one is a distance learning centres. Five are in London, five in the Midlands, one in Scotland, one in Yorkshire and one in Wales. Two others are in Cambridge and Winchester[571].

Following the Review of the Department for Communities and Local Government[572], A useful distinction may be drawn between Islamic Sciences and Islamic Studies. The former is taught from the perspective of believers and comprises traditional studies focusing on learning and interpretation of texts to clarify and enhance personal and religious practice, and the application of Islamic law. The latter is not necessarily taught from a believer's perspective and draws on a range of modern academic disciplines, including sociology, history, anthropology, linguistics, geography and politics to study the Muslim world. Broadly, Islamic Sciences is taught in Muslim institutions and Islamic Studies is taught in publicly-funded institutions.

b.1) Islamic Sciences

- The **Ebrahim College** in London was founded in 2003 by the Ebrahim al-Khalil Trust, an umbrella organisation with a mainly academic orientation, and is influenced by the Deobandi School. Its structure comprises an Islamic 6th form and madrassah, which combines A levels with an 'Islamic Sciences Programme' (ISP), and an Islamic Jami'ah (higher education institute). The Jami'ah offers an Alim course (7 years) combined with undergraduate qualifications in Islamic Studies and a final year consisting of intense hadith study (called at-Takmeel). It has also set up a BA in 'Islamic Sciences and Society' which includes modules such as Social Cohesion and Conflict Resolution

---

[570] Twenty-two of them are form males, 10 for females and six are co-educational. For more details see Appendix A of the Review *The training and development of Muslim Faith Leaders. Current practice and future possibilities, op. cit* p. 39.

[571] *Ibidem.*

[572] Review *The training and development of Muslim Faith Leaders. Current practice... op. cit.* p.p. 44-47

through Translation and on British Society and Global Politics. The College certificates are validated by British universities.

- The Cambridge Muslim College[573]

It currently offers a one-year Diploma in Contextual Islamic Studies & Leadership, This course aims to provide an intensive introduction to a range of contemporary perspectives and disciplines which will complement the students' existing Islamic education. This course is designed to to help those who already possess significant training in the Islamic sciences (for example through attendance at a *Darul uloom* as described above) to develop, articulate and implement their knowledge effectively in Britain today. Further, it aims to help students with a background in traditional Islamic sciences to go on to join mainstream higher education. Graduates of the colleges will not work only as imams and religious personnel. By providing a wide range of skills, it is hoped that the college will act as a stepping-stone for graduates to go on to higher education, or employment in teaching, journalism, diplomacy, and other career tracks where a deep knowledge of Islam will be beneficial.

In the longer term, the college will offer part-time and distance learning options, three- and four-year degree courses, and a range of non-accredited summer courses and regular study days for employers and the public. The diploma course has three interlinked objectives:

• To enable students to understand and engage with contemporary debates about the role of religion in general, and Islam in particular, in modern society

• To encourage the students to be compassionate and reliable spiritual and pastoral advisers to Muslims and others

• To equip students with practical skills to make them more effective leaders of Muslim institutions, and to enhance their prospects for further education and work.

The college is non-denominational, and accepts students from every school and tradition within Islam. It is independent of government, and is directed by the Muslim Academic Trust, a registered charity.

- **The *Al Mahdi* Institute**

The *Al Mahdi* Institute (AMI) [574] is Shia oriented and was established in 1993 in Birmingham as a non-profit charity to respond the need for an educa-

---

[573] http://www.cambridgemuslimcollege.org/
[574] http://www.almahdi.edu/

tional institute in the UK which would provide students with a structured degree course in the fields of Arabica and Islamic Sciences within a multicultural and pluralistic society. It follows the model of the curriculum taught in the traditional Islamic colleges with greater emphasis on the use of modern theories in the study of religion, theology, and language. The fact that the members of the Institute come from diverse intellectual and philosophical schools of thought is a reflection of its philosophy and mission.

The staff has been mainly trained in Iran and they use both English and Arabic as the main languages of instruction.

Programmes offered include a BA in Islamic Studies & Arabic Language, MA in Islamic Studies (with a specialisation in Social & Community Studies and practical work within Muslim communities, visits to Mosques, taking responsibilities in the performance of Muslim rituals in the community) and a Postgraduate Diploma in Islamic Studies or Arabic language.

The Mahdi Institute has links with Gloucestershire University. It also hosts an international distance learning course pursued at the Imam Sadiq University, Tehran.

- The European Institute of Human Sciences

The European Institute of Human Sciences (EIHS) [575] is located in a rural area near Lampeter, Wales. It opened in 1998 to teach Arabic language and Islamic Studies up to degree level standard. It is the UK branch of the French *Institut europeen des sciences humaines* (IESH) of the UOIF[576].

The EIHS is also a partner organisation of the University of Wales Lampeter, which accredits some of the Institute courses, and it has links with the International University of Malaysia and the International University in Islamabad. The EIHS, like its French partner in Château-Chinon, is a boarding school and has 80 full-time, residential students, most of whom come from abroad. Arabic is the primary medium of instruction but English support lessons are available. The teaching staff has been mainly trained in the Middle East. It offers three types of programmes:

Arabic Language: Arabic Language Certificate (1 Year), Arabic Language Diploma (2 Years)

Islamic Studies/Shariah: Certificate in Islamic Studies (1 Year), Diploma in Islamic Studies (2 Years), Licence in Islamic Studies (3 years). Licence for Inculcating the Holy Qur'an, M.A. and Ph.D. in Islamic Studies (coming soon)

Imam Diploma (2 years) which includes modules such as Western Society, Elocution and Public Speaking Skills, Jurisprudence for Minority Groups,

---

[575] www.eihs.org.uk/

[576] The UOIF is supported by the Muslim Brotherhood's nets in the Gulf and the Islamic World League and has tight relations with the European Council of the Fatwa and Research and the Federation of Islamic Organizations in Europe promoted by Yusuf al Qaradawi. It is one of the main umbrella organizations of French Muslims in France.

Public Relations and Communication, The Principles of Issuing Fatwa and Rhetoric. It also organises short summer courses.

- **Faculty of Asian and Middle Eastern Studies, University of Cambridge**[577]

An intensive professional training course was launched in 2009 and completed in 2010, organized jointly by the University of Cambridge and Al-Azhar University in Cairo. It was designed for young British Muslims currently studying in *Darul uloom*s and similar institutions and the aim was to build on the knowledge students had already gained through lectures, tutorials, seminars, visits, workshops and personal study assignments, and in this way to broaden their appreciation of Islam in modern contexts. The visits were not only to Muslim organizations but also to a Christian postgraduate theological training centre and a Jewish rabbinical college.

There was first a period of three months study at Al-Azhar. The Cambridge component of the course then required the students to tackle questions and issues they would not necessarily have encountered before. Themes included the role of Muslims in Britain, the challenges facing Muslims in the West, multiculturalism, British Muslim identity, gender equality, human rights, and pastoral care.

- **Khoja Shia Ithna-Asheri Community, Damascus, and University of Winchester**

The Khoja Shia Ithna-Asheri Community has a course that started in 2007 and is validated by the University of Winchester as an MA course in Islamic education. Graduates of the programme will be authorized as religious scholars in their communities (*alims* and *muballigheen*, religious scholars as educators) and also have a master's degree. In Damascus, high standards of traditional Islamic and Arabic education are provided by the Islamic Institute for Postgraduate Studies.

There are five MA modules: teaching religion; moral, spiritual and religious education; Qur'an – scripture and signifier; Islamic ethics; authority in Shia Islam; and research methods. In addition there are 16 enrichment modules delivered in English including Islam in the West, Islamic finance and the position of women in Islam. There are also 19 competency seminars on topics such as leadership skills, conflict resolution and financial management. The muballigheen course seeks to bring together in one course religious learning, vocational education (for example, leadership, management and administrative skills) and pastoral ministry.

---

[577] http://www.ames.cam.ac.uk/

- **The Islamic College in London**[578]

Islamic College in London provides a range of curricula, which at bachelors and masters level do not necessarily emphasize the distinctive nature of Shiism (except the planned MA in Shiite Studies) – the Shia focus comes at doctoral level. The master's level courses are validated by MiddlesexUniversity. These comprise Islamic Studies and Comparative Philosophy (i.e.Islamic and Western), and further courses are in preparation, for example in Islamic banking and finance, and Muslim civilization and the culture of dialogue.

The *Hawza*[579] studies provide ministerial and pastoral as well as theological training and offer a range of qualifications, none externally validated as yet. The first of these is the Diploma in Muslim Chaplaincy; the second, the Diploma in Shia Studies. Each takes two years. The students may also study the Muslim ministry course for becoming an *alim*, which they may take to a higher level in the doctoral course.

Middlesex University does not validate the faith leadership aspects, which can be studied alongside the masters and doctoral studies, but students at masters or doctoral level receive authentication for their theology through their connections with the Islamic College and the al Mustafa University in Qom, Iran.

b.2) Islamic Studies

As an academic discipline, Islamic Studies was not originally intended to contribute to Muslim faith leadership training within Britain. In recent years, however, a number of UK universities have developed programs which, amongst other things, are relevant for British Muslim students wishing to undertake leadership roles in their communities, for example as teachers and youth workers of various kinds. Such programs are taught full-time at degree level and part-time at diploma or certificate level.

In the academic year 2005-06, the course with the most postgraduate students was Arabic and Islamic Studies at the University of Exeter (53 students). Amongst first degree programs, Islamic Studies at University of Birmingham had the most students (62 students). There are other programs at the universities of Cambridge, Cardiff, Durham, Edinburgh, Glasgow, Lampeter, Leeds, Manchester, Oxford, Queen´s University Belfast and the School of Oriental and African Studies (University of London)

According to the Review of the Department for Communities and Local Government[580], a report in 2010 identified 1,101 modules currently being pro-

---

[578] http://www.islamic-college.ac.uk/

[579] The term *hazwa* is used in the Shia would to refer to the traditional Islamic school of advanced studies.

[580] Review *The training and development of Muslim Faith Leaders. Current practice... op. cit.* p.p. 48-51

vided in UK universities which could be defined as being concerned with Islamic Studies. In terms of numbers of modules, however, the greatest provision is at master level.

Forty-three per cent of students studying Islamic Studies programs were identified as Asian or Asian British.

It is strange that areas with low Muslim populations have a substantial Islamic Studies presence (e.g. Cambridge, Edinburgh, Exeter, Oxford and St Andrews) yet there are areas with a large Muslim population (e.g. Bradford), where the Islamic Studies presence is small.

2. Continuing professional development in Muslim Faith Leaders Training

Following the aforementioned Review[581], for Muslim faith leaders, as for leaders in other religious traditions, continuing professional development (CPD) is of crucial importance. It helps them to reflect on their own practice and changing circumstances, to respond to new realities and challenges in wider society. Its content may have distinctive features and emphases for leaders who received their initial training overseas.

CPD is provided for Muslim faith leaders not only through award-bearing courses such as higher degrees, diplomas and certificates but also through a wide range of short courses, modules, conferences and workshops. In the following paragraphs there are descriptions of chaplaincy and counseling courses at Markfield Institute of Higher Education; an imam training course at the Muslim College, London; a pilot faith leadership course run by the National Institute of Adult and Continuing Education (NIACE); and short courses and events run by a range of organizations and professional associations.

- **The Markfield Institute**[582] (MIHE) was established in 2000 in Leicestershire as an affiliate body of the Islamic Foundation. The Chair of the Board of Directors, Khurshid Ahmad, is also Vice President of the *Jamaat al Islami* party and senator in Pakistan[583]. Courses are structured in Postgraduate Certificate, Postgraduate Diploma, MA Degree and some of them are validated by Gloucestershire University and Loughborough University (Leicestershire). It offers different programmes including:

- The Islamic Studies programme which includes modules on Chaplaincy and Spiritual Care, Management of Mosques, Trusts and Endowments
- The Muslim Community Studies programme
- Med in Islamic education: New perspectives.
- The Islamic Banking, Finance and Management programme, with an MA validated by the University of Loughborough.

---

[581] *Ibidem* p. 51
[582] http://www.mihe.org.uk/mihe/
[583] At present the Rector is Dr.Manazir Ahsan.

It also offers short courses to provide continuous training for existing faith leaders: Training of Muslim Chaplains (since 2002), Introduction to Islamic Counselling, Certificate in Muslim Family Law, Diploma in Islamic Jurisprudence, Certificate in Islamic Finance, Diploma in Islamic Finance and Imam Training: Awareness of British Culture.

The course for Muslim chaplains provides training for chaplaincy in three areas: HM Prison Service, NHS hospitals, and further and higher education. It is the first one of its kind to be set up.

The Institute uses modern pedagogical techniques such as an enquiry based approach, discussions and debates and an academic staff mainly educated in Southeast Asia and Africa.

- The idea of setting up the **Muslim College**[584] as a postgraduate school for the training of Imams and Muslim teachers in the West was first proposed at a conference of Muslim leaders held at the Islamic Cultural Centre in London in 1978. The college was founded in 1984 by M.A. Zaki Badawi through funding of the World Islamic Call Society (Libya). It began functioning as an educational institution of graduate studies in 1987, and the first M.A. students graduated in 1990. It has a long cooperation history with Birkbeck College (University of London) that started through a series of annual public lectures and in 1992 evolved into Certificates in Islamic Studies and Arabic Language offered by Birkbeck College and taught at the Muslim College. The curriculum of its courses includes the study of both Islam and Western society and emphasises interfaith dialogue using modern pedagogical techniques such as an enquiry based approach, discussions and debates. It offers a wide range of programmes: MA in Islamic Studies, PhD in Islamic Studies, Media Studies, Imamship Training, Education and Research Methods.

- Other projects offered by private or public institutions.

In addition to the CPD programs provided by academic institutions such as those described in the preceding paragraphs, it is relevant to note that courses, conferences and seminars of various kinds are planned and offered by professional bodies and associations. The Association of Muslim Chaplains in Education, for example, has established a leadership development program for women. The Association of Muslim Lawyers and the Mosques and Imams National Advisory Board (MINAB) are currently rolling out seminars. A recent MINAB activity was a one-day workshop in which imams from various denominations came together at the Victoria Park Mosque, Manchester to engage in a non-theological leadership development program.

Local initiatives include an imam training program run by Dudley Muslim Forum with introduces topics such as studying other faiths (particularly Christianity and Judaism), international affairs, British law, counselor training, and health and safety. Also projects delivered by the Urban Nexus consultan-

---

[584] www.muslimcollege.ac.uk

cy[585], like producing and piloting a draft framework of standards to be provided to all public institutions which wish to engage Muslim chaplains

3. Distance learning courses

There are at least 6 institutions offering different kinds of distance courses on Islamic Sciences or Islamic Studies, most of them outside Great Britain[586].

The vast majority offer introductory courses to Islam (Sunni-Path, Shariah Programme, Zaytuna's Distance learning Programme, The Islamic College for Advanced Studies). Only the University of Exeter and the Open University offer modules about Islam in contemporary times. Al-Sirat offers a diploma in Arabic accredited by the EIHS.

4. Leadership programmes

There are a wide range of capacity building programmes for Muslim faith leaders being run by Muslim and other community organisations at both a national and local level.

On a national level, CLG have funded a number of faith leader training programmes through the Community Leadership Fund. 10 projects have been funded since 2007 covering a range of capacity-building measures. This has included engagement with young people, interfaith dialogue, media literacy, speaking out against extremism, strengthening moderate ideologies and developing Muslim-British identity.

CLG and the Department of Business, Innovation and Skills (BIS) have also supported the development of an accredited Faith Community Development qualification for leaders of all faiths. The qualification develops skills in 5 main areas: community leadership and relationships; safeguarding of children and vulnerable adults; equality and diversity; running an organisation and; improving engagement with marginalised groups.

---

585 Set up in 2006 to deliver projects and programs in community cohesion, urban regeneration, economic development, preventing extremism and fundraising. http://www.urbannexus.co.uk/pages/navigation/page.php?page_id=310

586 Ataullah Siddiqui, *Islam at Universities in England. Meeting the needs and investing in the future*, 2007

On the local level, local councils have supported community organisations to develop and deliver training programmes for Muslim faith leaders in their communities. Examples include:

- The Future Leaders Programme run Madni Jamia Masjid in Bradford to train young leaders who can contribute to the community development[587]. The programme is accredited by the University of Bradford and supported by Bradford Council.
- Faith Associate's Capacity Building Training for Imams in High Wycombe aimed at empowering British Imams to play a more active role within their own community. Commissioned by Wycombe District Council, the training includes modules such as effective planning and leadership, conflict resolution, handling the media, engaging agencies and UK cultural awareness. Further programmes by Faith Associates include specialist training for Youth Workers on tackling the voices and images of extremism with young Muslims.

Muslim community organisations have also commissioned and developed their own leadership training programmes. For example, The Muslim Council of Britain has set up the *Seventh Leadership Development Programme* with the aim of developing leadership capacity across the Muslim communities in the UK[588].

---

[587] Madni Jamia Masjid- Islamic Cultural and Educational Association: http://www.icea.org.uk/Events/toolkit.pdf

[588] Muslim Council of Britain: http://www.mcb.org.uk/uploads/LDP7smallfile.pdf

CONCLUSIONS

Some of the issues covered in this research can be summarized as follows:

1. Administrative bodies of the EU Member States that deal with religious organizations

Most of EU countries (24 to be precise) have specific administrative bodies that deal with religious affairs. Most of those bodies are under three kinds of ministries: ministries of Justice, ministries of Education and/or Culture, and ministries of Interior. The exact name of the ministry depends on a political decision made by the country's government.

So, according to how governments deal with religious affairs, or depending on what type of ministry is qualified to maintain relationship with churches we can classify countries as pertaining to the following groups:

- Six countries have a specific board regarding religious affairs under the Ministry of Justice: Belgium (at Federal Level), Denmark (there is also a Ministry for Religious Affairs, but for items regarding Lutheran Church), Latvia, Lithuania, Spain, Portugal (where there is also an independent advisory body called Commission for Religious Freedom)

- Nine countries concentrate religious affairs under the ministry that deals with education or/and culture:
  - Five of them, under the Ministry of Culture (E.g. Czech Republic, Slovakia, Germany – *Länder's: m*ainly under departments of Culture-, Sweden and Romania (Ministry of Culture and National Patrimony).
  - Two, under the Ministry of Education and Culture: Hungary and Austria (Ministry of Education, Art and Culture)
  - One, under the ministry of Education: Finland (nevertheless the National Board on Patents and Registration is under the Ministry of Economy and Employment).
  - One of them (Greece) under a Ministry named "Ministry of National Education and Cults"
- Four countries concentrate religious affairs under the ministry of Interior: Estonia, France, Italy and Poland. In Germany, even if the responsibility for church-state relations is mainly assigned to the *Länder,* at Federal Level the Ministry of the Interior has soe competences in this regard.

- Three Countries have a board on religious affairs under other institution different from the ones above:
    - Bulgaria (under the Council of Ministers),
    - Luxembourg (Ministry of State)
    - Slovenia (Government Office for Religious Communities)

- Five Member States have no specific body in the government for this purpose, sucha that religious affairs depend on several ministries: Cyprus, Malta, Ireland, United Kingdom and The Netherlands.

We must take into account that most of the countries which have an specifically qualified institution to deal with religious affairs also have other ministries that maintain some kind of relations with denominations regarding specific issues. For example, in Spain, besides the Ministry of Justice (where the General Department of International Cooperation and Relations with Denominations is located) there are other ministries that deal with religious affairs: the Ministry of the Interior directs spiritual guidance of inmates in prisons, the Ministry of Economy deals with funding or tax benefits of some religious groups, the Labour Ministry deals with social security of priests, imams, rabbis, and other faith ministers, etc.

Central Governments of some countries have two qualified bodies dealing with religious affairs; although usually one of them has broader capabilities, while the other more specific ones. For example in Italy, besides the two departments which are under the Ministry of Interior, there is also a "Division for Relationship with Religious Creeds" under the Office for Institutional Relationships of the Prime Minister Bureau. And in France, besides the *Bureau Central des Cultes* under the Ministry of Interior, there is also an "Adviser for Religious Affairs" under the Ministry of Foreign Affairs.

2. Registers of religious entities.

Seventeen countries have got registers of religious entities: Austria, Cyprus, Bulgaria, Czech Republic, Estonia, Finland, Hungary, Latvia, Lithuania, Luxembourg, Poland, Portugal, Romania, Slovakia, Slovenia, Spain and Sweden. Twelve of them were in the past under the Soviet Communist influence.

Romania has Registries of Religious associations which operate at the Clerk´s Offices of every Trial Court. Hungary and Bulgaria have also registers of religious entities within central or county courts).

Some Member States that don't have specific registers of religious entities have other kind of registers on items related with religion: In Ireland there are some specific registers (register for ministers that can officiate marriages, register of religious private schools under the Ministry of Education…). In Denmark the Department of Family Affairs (under the Ministry of Justice) have registered all the denominations that have fulfilled the conditions required to obtain a wedding permits. Even if in Greece there is not registration system of religious entities, according to some authors (Konidaris) permits for a place of worship can be considered "as an image and informal register of religious entities" that have obtained a permit to found places of worship.

Seven countries don't have any kind of register of religious entities: Belgium, France, Italy, Malta, The Netherlands, United Kingdom and Germany, although in the later, the ministries of Education of the Landers have Registers or public law corporations (for the denominations that have got that legal status).

3. Legal structure of denominations.

According to the principle of religious freedom enshrined by all the fundamental laws of EU Member States, religious communities (as well as individuals) can enjoy several manifestations of religious freedom (praying, gathering together on religious purposes, etc..) without any previous recognition of the state.

Religious groups have also the possibility of getting legal status as civil associations, if they wish so. But most countries' legislation also provides, for religious groups, the possibility of getting legal status as religious groups by registration. Nevertheless there are countries like the United Kingdom and Ireland, where religious groups mainly adopt the legal form of charities. Even France, where according to the law of 1905 the Republic doesn't recognize, fund or subsidize any religion, legislation provides several way for religious groups to get legal status (such as *associations cultuelles, associations diocésaines* or *congregations)*

Regarding EU Member States that recognise the status of religious groups as such (i.e. legally distinct as religious groups), we can observe some differences that led to four additional categories:

a) Countries with a "formal" State-Church system.

Some countries still maintain, although in a formal way, a National (State) Church or predominant religion. For historical reasons these countries keep close links between public powers and the main existing Church. This is the case of England, Denmark, Greece, Malta and Finland. England does not have a written constitution but in the Fundamental Laws of Denmark, Greece, Malta and Finland the National Church is mentioned:

Art.3 of Greece's Constitution mentions *"the Eastern Orthodox Church of Christ"*

Art. 4 of Danish Constitution maintains that *"The Evangelical Lutheran Church shall be the Established Church of Denmark, and, as such, it shall be supported by the State"*;

Art. 76 of the Constitution of Finland stands that *"Provisions on the organisation and administration of the Evangelic Lutheran Church are laid down in the Church Act*";

Art. 2 of Malta's Constitution declares that "*The religion of Malta is the Roman Catholic Apostolic Religion"*.

We cannot fully include Sweden anymore in this group, because since the last Constitutional Reform (2000), this country has to a very large extent cut the close ties that existed between the state and the Lutheran Church.

b) Religions recognized ***by*** law or ***according*** to the law

- Religious groups recognised ***by*** law

In certain countries, some denominations have been recognized by parliamentary law which takes historical grounds into account. This is the case of Belgium (6 denominations), Denmark (denominations existing before 1870 were recognized by Royal Decree) Lithuania (9 denominations) or Poland (15 denominations).

Apart from the so-called State-Church system countries, some constitutions that specifically recognise separation between Church and State mention specific denominations. For example, the Catholic Church is mentioned in the constitutions of Spain and Italy; the autocephalous Greek Orthodox Church and the Vakf are underlined in Cyprus Fundamental Law; and the Swedish Constitution singlesout the Evangelical-Lutheran Church of Sweden.

- Religious groups recognized ***according*** to the law

In some countries certain groups get the status of a religious entity by legal registration E.g. the ones we have seen above. In the case of Poland churches can get legal personality according to the law (15 religious groups) or by legal registration on the basis of 1989 Law (154 denominations).

In some Member States where there is no register of religious communities, religious groups are granted legal status by simply fulfilling the requirements established by law, normally, a religious freedom act. This is the case of Italy (according to the Law of 1929; but, so far, seven denominations have signed agreements with the state *–intese-* which must be transformed afterwards into the corresponding law*),* France (*associations cultuelles*), Germany (public law corporations).

- Mixed system: religious groups are officially recognized both by law and according to the law. This is the case of Austria, Denmark, Finland, Greece and Lithuania.

c) Corporation under public law and similar

In some Member States, certain denominations have obtained the status of "corporation under public law"; e.g., Germany, Austria and Greece (legal person of public law).

In Luxemburg denominations might be recognised through a Convention with the State through which they receive the status of legal persons of public law.

d) Cooperation Agreements with specific denominations.

Some countries, like Spain, Portugal, Italy and Slovenia have signed cooperation agreements with deeply rooted denominations which entitles those religions to specific legal benefits. Normally the State signs these agreements with the umbrella federation that represents that denomination and must pass a corresponding law in parliament afterwards.

Slovenia and Spain have signed a cooperation agreement with Islam.

4. Legal recognition of Islam

Islam had been recognised by a specific law in Austria, Belgium, Cyprus (the constitution recognizes the institution of *Wakf*), Greece (Treaty of Lausanne), Lithuania (Sunni Islam), and Poland (Muslim Religious Association in the Republic of Poland -MZR-). In Romania, Islam has been recognised by a governmental ordinance.

However, most countries don't recognize Islam as a global denomination but rather as singular communities. Sometimes Islamic groups are recognized as civil associations (in Slovakia, Germany, Ireland) or even as charities (UK). Sometimes they are recognized as "approved religions" (Denmark), as "*associations culturelles*" (France) or as a registered religious entities (Bulgaria, Czech Republic, Denmark, Spain, Estonia, Finland, Hungary, Latvia, Sweden).

In some countries like Spain, Islamic communities get legal personality as religious groups once they enter in the Register of Religious Entities. But apart from being registered, if those Islamic communities belong to an umbrella organization which has signed the Cooperation Agreement with the State (e.g. the Islamic Commission of Spain –CIE-), they will enjoy the legal and economic benefits of the Cooperation Agreement. Slovenia has also signed a Cooperation Agreement with Islam.

5. Islam representative bodies before the State

In some countries Islamic groups have one representative body or umbrella organization that is supposed to represent Muslims before the State. This is the case of Austria (Islamic Religious Community in Austria –IGGiÖ-), Belgium (Muslim Executive Board –EMB-), Estonia (Estonian Muslim Congregation), Finland (Islamic Council of Finland), Luxembourg (Assembly of the Muslim Community –Shura-), Spain (Islamic Commission of Spain), Slovenia (Islamic Community in the Republic of Slovenia) and Sweden (Muslim Council of Sweden). In Bulgaria, Greek-Thrace, and Romania there is a Mufti Office.

In some countries, there are umbrella organizations which are not the official representative body of Islam but they try to act as if they were. E.g. the Association of Czech Muslim Religious communities –ACMRC-, in Czech Republic or the Lisbon Central Mosque in Portugal.

Sometimes, the state makes efforts to promote and support a representative body of Islam. This is the case of France (*Conseil Francais du culte Musulman*(2003) and Germany (German Conference on Islam (2006). The German Islam Conference, which tries to institutionalize the dialogue between the state (federal state, *Länder*, local communities) and Muslim umbrella organizations, also includes prominent Muslim individuals and experts.

Finally in some UE Member States even if there is no official body representing Islam, Governments deal with more than one umbrella organizations. For example, in Denmark or The Netherlands Governments deal with two Islamic umbrella organizations. In other Member States Governments deal with several ones according to the specific items (United Kingdom, Ireland, Hungary, Italy, Slovakia and Poland)

6. Muslims in Europe

According to available data, the two countries with the highest percentages of Muslim population are Cyprus (12, 5%) and Bulgaria (12%). These figures show that Islam has long been part of the European identity. Besides those two, France is the country with the highest proportion of Muslims (6-8%) followed by the Netherlands (5.7%), Germany (5.22%), United Kingdom (3%, according to 2001 Census), Sweden (2-4%), Spain (2.5%) and Italy (2.5%).

Based on the number of Muslims, France also leads the group with 6 million followed by Germany (4.3 million) and United Kingdom (2.4 millions according to some recent reports). Poland is the country with smallest proportion of Muslim population (0.04%) followed by Lithuania (0.07%) and the Czech Republic (0.09%).

7. Imams and Mosques.

As already stated, we have chosen the term *Imam* because to date, it is a more established term than *Muslim faith leaders* even though the latter is more inclusive. For Sunni Islam, the imam is the religious leader who leads prayers in a mosque, where full-time or part-time. However, faith leadership is exercised not only at mosques but also at schools, universities, courses, conferences, youth settings, etc., and by a wide range of religious scholars (*alims and alimahs*), teachers, instructors, youth workers, chaplains, writers and opinion leaders, including many women. To focus only on imams would be to overlook important leadership roles exercised by many members of Muslim communities.

As for the number of imams, it is very difficult to obtain reliable statistics on this due such a religious status lacks official recognition. All the same, according to our calculations, the number of imams does parallel the number of places of worship (mosques and prayer-halls). Thus, Germany would be at the top of the list with 2600 places of worship and about 2500 imams; France has about 2415 mosques and prayer halls and about 2400 imams; and the United Kingdom has around one thousand mosques and prayer halls and same number of imams.

In some countries, like Belgium, Imams are paid by state funds, but only if their mosque is recognized by the regional government.

8. Chaplaincy

In regards to chaplaincy, all EU Member States recognize the right of inmates to receive spiritual aid in public institutions such as prisons, the army or hospitals. Accompanying this is the corresponding obligation of public powers to provide and promote this manifestation of religious freedom in buildings decreed by the state where inmates have objective difficulties to exercise this right. For example, there are 3 Muslim Great Chaplains in France referred to prisons, the army and hospitals. The three of them are appointed by the *Conseil Francais du Culte Musulman.*

The following statistics are available for Islamic chaplains in prisons: the United Kingdom is at the top of the list (197, of which 28 women), followed by France (69) The Netherland (62), Austria (38), Belgium (18), and Spain (12). In all countries mentioned here, Islamic chaplains are paid by the State.

9. Islam and School

There are some countries where Islam is taught in public school not from a historical point of view but from a faith-based approach, in other words, not teaching about religion but teaching the doctrine of a specific religion. This is the case of Austria (400 teachers of Islam), Belgium, and Spain (45 teachers). Those teachers are appointed by Muslim authorities but paid by the State. In Bulgaria, Islam has also been taught in public schools since 1999, and text books are prepared on the basis of curricula approved by the Ministry of Education.

In some countries, such as The Netherlands or United Kingdom, Islam can be taught in public school but from a scientific or historical point of view (teaching "about" religion). In Spain, "History of religions" is one of the options students can choose if they don't want to receive religious education.

There are also Islamic private schools throughout Europe: these are not only *madrasa*s but also primary or secondary private schools recognized by their respective educational system.

United Kingdom has around 130 schools maintained by Muslim charities (nine of them receive state funding). In the Netherlands there are 48 Muslim private schools (46 primary and two secondary schools). In Denmark there are 20 Islamic private schools, in Austria, 12 (8 nurseries, 3 primary and 1 secondary schools). There are 9 Islamic schools in Sweden, all of them associated with the Islamic School Foundation.

In Germany there are several private institutions for religious instruction and education but very few private recognized Islamic schools as for instance a primary school in Berlin ; there is also one diplomatic school in Bonn (King-Fahd-Academy in Bonn) financed by Saudi-Arabia. In France there are two Islamic private schools under a contract of association with the State (La Madersa –SaintDenis de la Réunion- and *Lycée Averroes* –Lille- financed by the State from this year), but there are other private schools.

10. Islamic Religious Leaders training centres

Some imams of rural areas do not have in-depth religious training while others who are theologically well-trained have received their training from institutions abroad that preach a strict form of Islam that creates problems with regards to adapting to the European context. More and more voices from the ranks of younger Muslims are calling for imams trained in Europe

Only 12 out of the 27 EU member states have developed some kind of training courses for Islamic faith leaders. Within the broad variety of training offered, four different categories can be outlined:

- Language and cultural courses.

These types of courses are intended for foreign faith leaders coming to work in Europe. Most of them are state initiatives that are implemented in cooperation with local Muslim umbrella organizations. These courses tend to be short or conceived of as projects with a particular emphasis on language skills, history and civic issues. The Turkish Presidency for Religious Affairs has set up various agreements with different EU governments so that the imams sent by the *Diyanet* to serve the Turkish community abroad are trained on the reality of host countries either before leaving (through courses offered by the Goethe Institute in Ankara) or upon arrival (cooperation between the Austrian Ministry of European and International Affairs and the ATIB) or the cooperation project "*Imam für Integration*" between the German Federal Office of Migration and Refugees and DITIB). Examples of this kind of training can be found in Austria, Belgium, and The Netherlands and in Germany.

- Specific training/education for future imams and chaplains.

This type of education ranges from short courses to BA and MA degrees on Islamic Theology. Most of them are offered by private Islamic institutions, but in some Member States this education is also provided in public universities. Learning is primarily focused on the study of the *Sharia*, Islamic theology and the Holy Quran, even though the majority of these institutions also include subjects about Islam in the EU, socio-political and cultural aspects about the country and sometimes public speaking skills, communication, counselling, etc. These kinds of courses are targeted at future imams who wish to start their education or to continue it in their home country in the EU. Most of these educational initiatives are private and the certificates delivered by those institutions are not officially recognised. On the other hand, in a few countries (Bulgaria, The Netherlands, Greece and Romania) institutes or programmes for the training of religious leaders are supported or even funded by public authorities in cooperation with Muslim organizations.

- Training courses for teachers of Islam.

Several countries provide religious education in public schools (e.g. Spain, Austria, Belgium, and Bulgaria). The lack of teachers with a proper degree has been a problem in recent years. To counteract this situation, several universities have launched programmes to train teachers of primary and secondary schools and for BA and MA degrees in Islamic Theology and Religious Studies (The Netherlands) as well as Islamic religious Pedagogy (Vienna University). At the same, in recent years, many universities have set up chairs of Islamic religion or Islamic religious instruction (Germany) or expanded their programmes about Islam (Denmark, the Netherlands, and Spain).

- Management and community leadership training programmes.

Examples of this kind of training for Islamic faith leaders can be found in the UK (Faith Associates, MCB…) and Belgium (CIFOP-ORACLE initiative), following the inspiration of similar projects developed in the US. This training is aimed at religious leaders and managers of places of worship and religious institutions. The objectives are usually to improve leadership capability and increase management skills in order to facilitate the process of community cohesion and integration. Stress is made on capacity building strategies with the aim of modernising existent structures.

Besides this, there are other centres for the study of Islamic Sciences where students begin their Islamic education and memorize the Qur'an(become a Hafiz). Madrasas attached to places of worship and *darul ulums* provide education based on traditional Islamic curricula from different Muslim countries. Research centres and institutes which organise round tables and seminars also contribute to the education of future imams as well as to the continuous training of current Islamic faith leaders

In this book we have tried to offer a map of the existing imams training courses in Europe, at least a map of the ones that we have detected. As explained in the Foreword, the second step of this strategy is to get closer to the existing imam centres and to political authorities of the countries where they are set in order to study more deeply how they are working, what are their virtues, their needs, their shortcomings, the desirable legal framework in which they should feet and any kind of aspects that can enrich our knowledge about this important issue. Nevertheless, although exciting, this Project belongs to the work to come.

Corrections, suggestions or comments on this research or on the two further steps to come will be more than welcome in j.ferreiro@udc.es or juanrferreiro@gmail.com

A Coruña January 24th 2011

REFERENCE LIST

V.V.A.A. (2010). *Financing of churches and religious so cities in the 21st Century* Ed. Institute for State-Churches Relations. Bratislava 2010.

V.V.A.A. (2010) *The training and development of Muslim Faith Leaders. Current practice and future possibilities.* Edited by the Department for Communities and Local Government. London.

V.V.A.A. (2010) *Religion and the Secular State: National Reports* Edited by MARTINEZ TORRON, J-DURHAM, C.W. The International Centrer for Law and Religon Studies Bringham Young University Provo 2010

V.V.A.A. (2009) *Yearbook of Muslims in Europe* Edited by NIELSSEN, J.S.; AKAGÖNÜL, S.; ALIBASIC, A; MARECHA,B.; MOE,C; Leiden-Boston

V.V.A.A. (2005) *Droit des cultes. Personnes, activités, biens et structures,* Paris, Ed. Juris Associations.

ALIBASIC, A.: "Higher education in the Balkans: A Survey" in NILSEN, J.S. (Ed) (2010) *Yearbook of Muslims in Europe* vol. II, Leden: Brill 2010.

ALLIEVI, S. "Islam in Italy" in HUNTER, S. (Ed.) *Islam, Europe's second religion. The new social, cultural and political landscape.* Preaeger (2002).

AMGHAR, S., BOUBEKEUR, A. & EMERSON, M. (Eds.) (2007) *European Islam*

ANSARI, H.: *The History of Muslims in Britian, 1800 to the present.* Hurt. London 2004,. *Challenges for Public Policy and Society* Brussels, Brussels, Centre for European Policy Studies.

ANSPAHA, K. (2008) "The Integration of Islam in Europe: Preventing the radicalization of Muslim diasporas and counterterrorism policy" in *ECPR Fourth Pan-European Conference on EU Politics,* University of Latvia, Riga, Latvia.

ANWAR, M., BLASCHKE, J. & SANDER, A. (Eds.) (2004) *State policies towards Muslim minorities: Sweden, Great Britain and Germany,* Berlin, Ed. Parabolis.

ARIGITA, E. (2004) "Al-Azhar in the Post 9/11 Era". *ISIM Review,* 14.

ASLAN, E. (ed) (2009) *Islamic education in Europe* (Vienna: Böhlau Verlag.

BALÁZS, S. (2007) "Religious entities as legal persons –Hungary" in

FRIEDNER, L. (Ed.) *Churches and other organizations as legal persons,* Peeters.

BALODIS, R. (2007) "Religious entities as Legal Persons-Latvia" in FRIEDNER, L. (Ed.) *Churches and other organizations as legal persons,* Peeters.

BĀRBĀTEANU, V. & SULIMAN, D. (2008) "Constitutional Jurisprudence in the area of freedom of religion and beliefs" in *Legal aspects of religious freedom (International Conference 15-16 September 2008).* Ljubljana.

BASDEVANT-GAUDEMET, B. (2005) "State and Church in France" in *State and Church in the European Union.* 2nd ed. Baden-Baden, Ed Nomos.

BIJSTERVELD, S. C. V. (2007) "Religious entities as legal persons – Netherlands" in FRIEDNER, L. (Ed.) *Churches and other organizations as legal persons,* Peeters.

BLOOM, J. C. H. (2000) "Pillarisation in Perspective". *West European Politics.*, Volume 23, Issue 3 July 2000 , pp. 153 – 164.

BOENDER, W. (1999) "Imams in the Netherlands: an Impression", *C.I.E. Newsletter,* 1, pp. 23-28.

-------------- (2008) "Imams in the Netherlands. Expectations & Realities" *ISIM REVIEW* 21, pp. 22-23.

BONNICI, U. M. (2005) "State and Church in Malta". *State and Church in the European Union.* 2nd ed. Baden-Baden, Ed Nomos.

BOUSETTA, H. & L.A.BERNES (2007) *Muslims in the EU: Cities Report. Belgium. Preliminary research report and literature survey.* Open Society Institute.

BRITO, J. D. S. E. (2007) "Religion entities as legal persons-Portugal" in FRIEDNER, L. (Ed.) *Churches and other organizations as legal persons,* Peeters.

CAEIRO, A. (2003) "The European Council for Fatwa and Research". *Fourth Mediterranean Social and Political research meeting organised by the Mediterranean Program of the Robert Schuman Centre for Advanced Studies at the European University Institute.* Firenze-Montecatini Terme.

CAPUTO, B. (2005) "Domestication of Space, Arab Migrants in Milan". *ISIM Review,* 16, pp. 24-25.

CASEY, J. (2005) "State and Church in Ireland" in *State and Church in the European Union.* 2nd ed. Baden-Baden, Ed Nomos.

CELADOR, O. (2007) "Régimen jurídico de las entidades religiosas en el ordenamiento jurídico británico" in *Entidades Eclesiásticas y Derechos de los Estados. Actas del II Simposio Internacional de Derecho Concordatorio. Almería 9-11 de noviembre de 2005.* Comares.

CEPAR, D. (2008) "Administrative and Financial Maters in the area of religious freedom and religious communities" in *Legal Aspects of Religious freedom (International Conference, 15-18 September 2008).* Ljubljana

CHOUDHURY, T. (2004) *Muslims in the UK: Policies for Engaged Citizens.* Open Society Institute.

CHARITY COMMISSION'S FAITH AND SOCIAL COHESION UNIT (2009) *Survey of mosques in England and Wales.* Available at: http://www.charity-commission.gov.uk/Library/tcc/pdfs/faithmus.pdf

CORONADO, A. F., GARCÍA, J. A. R., MUÑOZ, M. M. & PRIETO, P. C. P. (2002) *El Derecho de la libertad de conciencia en el marco de la Unión Europea: pluralismo y minorías,* Madrid, Colex.

COTON, P. (2007) "Religious entities as legal persons-Ireland" in FRIEDNER, L. (Ed.) *Churches and other organizations as legal persons,* Peeters.

CSEPREGI, A. (2008) "Facts about the relationship of State and Church in Hungary" in *Legal Aspects of Religious freedom (International Conference, 15-18 September 2008).* Ljubljana.

CURCIO, M. (2008) "Administrative and Financial Maters in the Area or Religious Freedom and Religious Communities" in *Legal Aspects of Religious freedom (International Conference, 15-18 September 2008).* Ljubljana.

DELGADO, V. T. (2008) New Muslim Youth Associations in Spain. *ISIM REVIEW,* 22, p. 38.

DEMANT, F., MAUSSEN, M. & RATH, J. (2007) *Muslims in the EU: Cities Report.The Netherlands. Preliminary research report and literature survey.* Open Society Institute.

DIMITROV, I. Z. (2008) "Legal settlement of the relations between the State and religions in Bulgaria today" in *Legal Aspects of Religious freedom (International Conference, 15-18 Septermber 2008).* Ljubljana.

DOKOS, T. & ANTONIOU, D. (2002) "Islam in Greece" in HUNTER, S. (Ed.) *Islam, Europe's second religion. The new social, cultural and political landscape.* Preaeger.

DUYVENDAK, J. W. & SCHOLTEN, P. *Questioning the Dutch multicultural model of immigrant integration.* Available at:

http://www.assr.nl/conferences/documents/Burgerschap-QuestioningtheDutchmodelbyDuyvendakandScholten.pdf

DYKE, A. H. (2009) *Mosques made in Britain*. Quilliam Foundation.

EMILIANIDES, A. (2007) "Religious entities as legal persons –Cyprus" in FRIEDNER, L. (Ed.) *Churches and other organizations as legal persons,* Peeters.

EVSTATIEV, S. (2006) *Islam: A Short Handbook,* Sofia, Centre for Intercultural Studies and Partnership.

FERRARI, S. (2005) "State and Church in Italy" in *State and Church in the European Union.* 2nd ed. Baden-Baden, Ed Nomos.

---------------- (2007) "Entités religieuses come personnes juridiques- Italie" in FRIEDNER, L. (Ed.) *Churches and other organizations as legal persons,* Peeters.

FERREIRO, J. (2006) "Las caricaturas sobre Mahoma y las Jurisprudencia del Tribunal Europeo de los Derechos Humanos" in Revista Electrónica de Estudios Internacionales, Nº 12. Avaliable at: *www.reei.org.*

---------------- "Financing of churches and religious societies" in *Financing of churches and religious socities in the 21st century* Ed. Institute for State-Churches Relations. Bratislava 2010.

---------------- "Reminiscencias del sistema de Iglesia de Estado en los países de la Unión Europea" in *Anuario de Derecho Eclesiástico del Estado* vol. XXVI Madrid 2010

---------------- "Los órganos de la Administración española encargados de la relación jurídico-técnica con la Santa Sede: la Dirección General de Asuntos Religiosos y la Subdirección de relaciones con la Santa Sede" in *Iglesia Católica y Relaciones Internacionales* Ed. Comares, Granada 2008.

---------------- "La financiación de la enseñanza privada en Italia II", in *Suplemento de Humana Iure de Derechos Humanos. Persona y Derecho*, 1999

FETZER, J. S. & SOPER, J. C. (2005) *Muslims and the State in Britain, France and Germany,* Cambridge, Cambridge University Press.

FRIEDNER, L. (2007) "Religious entities as legal persons- Sweden" in FRIEDNER, L. (Ed.) *Churches and other organizations as legal persons,* Peeters.

GARAY, A. (2009) "La reconnaissance des cultes religieux en France au regard de la fiscalité applicable" in *Anuario de Derecho Eclesiástico del Estado.*

GARCIMARTIN, C. : «Religioun and Secular State in Ireland », in *Religion and the Secular State: National Reports* Provo 2010

GHALI, M. (2010)"Training Imams in Europe: the challenges of develop a unifed program. Leiden University as a Study Case" in *Journal of Islam Religious Education and >Theology* vol. I (2010)

GILLIAT-RAY, S. (2010) *Muslims in Britain: an introduction*, Cambridge: University of Cambridge Press

GLODENIS, D. (2008) "Administrative and Financial Maters in the area of religious freedom and religious communities: case of Lithuania" in *Legal Aspects of Religious freedom (International Conference, 15-18 September 2008)*. Ljubljana.

GOLDBERG, A. (2002) "Islam in Germany" in HUNTER, S. (Ed.) *Islam, Europe's second religion. The new social, cultural and political landscape.* Preaeger.

HAMID, S. (2008) "The Development of British Salafism". *ISIM Review,* 21, pp. 10-11.

HEIKKILÄ, M., KNUTILA, J., SCHEININ, M. & FERRARI, S. (2005) "State and Church in Finland" in *State and Church in the European Union.* 2nd ed. Baden-Baden Ed. Nomos.

HUSSON, J. F. (2006) *Pour une formation des imams en Belgique. Points de références en Belgique et en Europe*. Brussels, Foundation Roi Baudouin.

-------------------- (2007) *Training imams in Europe. The current status*. Brussels, King Baudouin Foundation.

IFATH NAWAZ, S. W. (2006) *Mosques and Imams National Advisory Body. Consultation Findings and Conclusions*. Faith Associates.

KARAKAGOSLU, Y. (2008) "Educational responses or the lack of them, to the needs of Muslim Communities, with a special focus on Germany" Keynote Speech in ODIHR- Assessment Meeting *Combating Intolerance against Muslims in the Field of Education* 3-4 June 2008.

KIVIORG, M. (2005) "Religious entities as legal persons –Estonia" in *State and Church in the European Union.* 2nd ed. Baden-Baden Ed Nomos.

KOTIRANTA, M. (2008) "Status of religious communities" in *Legal Aspects of Religious freedom (International Conference, 15-18 September 2008)*. Ljubljana.

KRIZ, J. (2008) "Religious Freedom and State in the Czech Republic" in *Legal Aspects of Religious freedom (International Conference, 15-18 September 2008).* Ljubljana.

KROISSENBRUNNER, S. (2002) "Islam in Austria" in HUNTER, S. (Ed.) *Islam, Europe's second religion. The new social, cultural and political landscape.* Preaeger.

KTISTAKIS, I. & SITAROPOULOS, N. (2004) *Executive Summary GREECE*, European Group of non-governmental experts in the field of combating discrimination on the grounds of racial and ethnic origin and religion or belief, Community Action Programme to Combat Discrimination , 22nd of June, 2004.

KÜSTER, B. (2008) "Administrative and financial matters in the area of religious freedom and religious communities" in *Legal Aspects of Religious freedom (International Conference, 15-18 September 2008).* Ljubljana.

KUZNECOVIENE, J. (2007) Religious entities as Legal Persons –Lithuania" in FRIEDNER, L. (Ed.) *Churches and other organizations as legal persons,* Peeters.

LALOUETTE, J. & SORREL, C. (2008) *Les lieux de culte en France. 1905-2008 Record of the Symposium of the Savoie and Paris 13 Universities (17/11/2006 and 16-17/01/ 2007)* , Paris, Éditions Letouzey et Ané.

LARSSON, G. (2006) "Muslims in Swedish Media and Academia". *ISIM Review,* 18, pp. 38-39.

-----------------. (2007) *Muslims in the EU: Cities Report. Sweden. Preliminary research report and literature survey*. Open Society Institute.

LEGRAND, M. (2002) *Les valeurs au Luxembourg-Portrait d'une societé au tournant du 3e millénaire,* Luxembourg, Ed. Saint Paul.

MACUKA, J. (2008) "Administrative and Financial Maters in the area of religious freedom and religious communities in Latvia" in *Legal Aspects of Religious freedom (International Conference, 15-18 September 2008).* Ljubljana.

MALIK, A. R. (2005) *Report on Opening Session. Islam in Higher Education Conference*

University of Birmingham, Selly Oak Campus 29 January – 30 January 2005. Available at: http://www.amssuk.com/docs/pdf/Islam%20in%20HE%20Conference%20Review.pdf

MAQSOOD, R. W. (2005) *The role of the Mosque in Britain Muslim Parliament UK*, The Muslim Parliament of Great Britain, London.

MARÉCHAL, B. (2008) "The Muslim Brothers in Europe: Roots and discourse". Brill.

------------------. (2008) « Courants fondamentalistes en Belgique» in *Middle Est Review of International Affairs* (MERIA) Vol. 3, No.1

MEZŘICKY, V. (2008) "Constitutional guarantees f freedom of faith and positions of churches in the Czech Republic" in *Legal Aspects of Religious freedom (International Conference, 15-18 September 2008).* Ljubljana.

MICHEL, L., BRAHMY, B., CANETTI, C. & DELBOS, V. (2005) *Guide de la pratique psychiatrique en milieu pénitentiaire*, Heures de France.

MIKLOS, T. (2000) *Value Systems and Chances in Religion in Europe and in particular in Hungary based on the Results of the European Value System Study and Other Pieces of Research*, Budapest.

MORAVCIKOVA, M. (2009) "Religious Education and Denominational Schools in the Slovak Republic" in ASLAN, E. (Ed.) *Islamische Erziehung in Europa / Islamic Education in Europe.* Wien-Köln-Weimar, Böhlau Verlag.

MORERAS, J. (1999) *Musulmanes en Barcelona. Espacios y dinámicas comunitarias*, Barcelona, Fundació CIDOB.

----------------- (2005): "Autoritats en (re)construcció. La figura de l'imam en el context migratori" in AUBARELL, G. / MORERAS, J. (eds.): *Imams d'Europa. Les expressions de l'autoritat religiosa islàmica*, Barcelona 2005. Fundación CIDOB.

----------------- (2007) "Imames en Europa. El déficit de formación de los imames y su excesiva influencia sobre la comunidad forman argumentos erróneos en torno a la autoridad religiosa islámica". *AFKAR/IDEAS,* Invierno 2006/2007.

MÜCKL, S. (2007) "Religious entities as legal persons-Germany" in FRIEDNER, L. (Ed.) *Churches and other organizations as legal persons,* Peeters.

NAQSHBANDI, M. (2006) *Islam and Muslims In Britain, A Guide for Non-Muslims*. City of London Police.

PACZOLAY, P. (2008) "The Hungarian Constitutional Court's Rulings on Freedom of Religion" in *Legal Aspects of Religious freedom (International Conference, 15-18 September 2008).* Ljubljana.

PAPASTATHIS, C. (2005) “State and Church in Greece” in*State and Church in the European Union.* 2nd ed. Baden-Baden, Ed Nomos.

PAULY, A. & KINSCH, P. (2007) “Entités religieux comme personnes juridiques - Luxembourg" in FRIEDNER, L. (Ed.) *Churches and other organizations as legal persons,* Peeters.

POTZ, R. (2005) “State and Church in Austria” in *State and Church in the European Union.* 2nd ed. Baden-Baden Ed Nomos.

PREPELUH-MAGAJNE, U. (2007) “Religion entities as legal persons-Slovenia" in FRIEDNER, L. (Ed.) *Churches and other organizations as legal persons,* Peeters.

RADAKEWSLO, M. (2008)) “Administration and financial matters in the area of religious freedom and religious communities”. *Legal aspects of religious freedom (International conference 15-16 September 2008).* Ljubljana.

RICHARD, G. (2006) “Representing the city: Mosques and the planning process in Birmingham, UK” in *Journal of Ethic and Migration Studies* vol 31 nº 6

ROALD, A.S.: “From `people´s home´to multiculturalism´: Muslims in Sweden”, in Y.Y. HADEN (ed), *Muslims in the West: From Sojourners to Citizens.* (Oxford: Oxford University Press, 2002)

ROBBERS, G. (Ed.) (2008) *State and Church in the European Union.* 2nd ed. Baden-Baden, Ed Nomos.

ROOSE, E. (2008) “Mosque Design in the Netherlands”. *ISIM REVIEW* 21, pp. 50-51.

RUSKYTÉ, R. (2008) “Legal Aspects of Religious Freedom” in *Legal Aspects of Religious freedom (International Conference, 15-18 September 2008).* Ljubljana.

RYNKOWSKI, M. (2005) “State and Church in Poland” in *State and Church in the European Union.* Auflage.

----------------------- (2007) “Religious entities as legal persons-Poland” in FRIEDNER, L. (Ed.) *Churches and other organizations as legal persons,* Peeters.

SCHEPELERN JOHANSEN, B. (2005) *Imamuddannelse i Europa – udfordringer og perspektiver/Imam Education in Europe –Challenges and Perspectives.* Copenhagen, University of Copenhagen.

-- (2006) *Islam at the European Universities.* Copenhaguen, University of Copenhaguen.

-- (2006) "Islamic Theology at the European Universities: Secularisation, boundaries and the roles of religion." *Nordic Journal of Religion and Society*. 2.19, pp. 93-106.

SCHINKELE, B. (2007) "Religious entities as Legal Persons" in FRIEDNER, L. (Ed.) *Churches and other organizations as legal persons,* Peeters.

SERENA HUSSAIN, T. C. (2007) *Muslims in the EU: Cities Report-United Kingdom. Preliminary research report and literature survey*. Open Society Institute.

SIDDIQUI, A. (2007) *Islam at Universities in England. Meetings the needs and investing in the future*. Available at:

http://www.dius.gov.uk/higher_education/~/media/publications/D/DrSiddiquiReport

SMOCK, D. (2005) *Teaching about the Religious Other*, *Special report*, United States Institute of Peace. Available at: http://beta.usip.org/specialists/david-r-smock

SUNIER, T. (2006) "The Western Mosque, Space in Physical Place". *ISIM Review,* 18.

TRETERA, J. R. (2005) "State and Church in Czech Republic" in *State and Church in the European Union.* 2nd ed. Baden-Baden, Ed Nomos.

TYSEBAERT, M. (2008) "Administrative and Financial Maters. The situation in Belgium" in*Legal Aspects of Religious freedom (International Conference, 15-18 September 2008).* Ljubljana.

WIKTOR-MACH, D. (2008) "Muslim Organizations in Poland". *ISIM Review,* 22.

REPORTS:

European Union Agency for Fundamental Rights (2009) *EU-MIDIS at a glance. Introduction to the FRA's EU-wide discrimination survey.*

---------------- (2009) *European Union Minorities and Discrimination Survey. Data in Focus Report: Muslims.*

Greek Ministry of Foreign Affairs (1999) *The Muslim Minority of Greek Thrace*. Available at: http://www.hri.org/MFA/foreign/musminen.htm (accessed 27/07/2009)

Haut Conseil de l'Integration (2000) *L'Islam dans la Republique*. Available at: http://lesrapports.ladocumentationfrancaise.fr/BRP/014000017/0000.pdf

Metroscopia (2008) *La comunidad musulmana de origen inmigrante en España. Encuesta de opinión.*

Ministry of Refugee, Immigration and Integration Affairs (2008) *Islam and Muslims in Denmark Factsheet.*

Ministère des Affaires Étrangères (2007) *Infosynthese: La France à la loupe. Le culte musulman en France*. Paris.

National Statistical Institute (2001) *Bulgaria Census 2001 - Final Results: Population by districts and religion group as of 1.03.2001.*

National Consultative Committee on Racism and Interculturalism *The Muslim Community in Ireland. Challenging Some Of Myths & Misinformation*. Available at: http://www.nccri.ie/pdf/ChallengingMyths-Muslims.pdf

US Department of State (2002) *International Religious Freedom Report 2002. Belgium.* Available at: http://www.state.gov/g/drl/rls/irf/ (accessed 20/06/2009)

-------------------------------- (2006) *International Religious Freedom Report 2006. Luxembourg.* Available at: http://www.state.gov/g/drl/rls/irf/ (accessed 20/06/2009)

-------------------------------- (2006) *International Religious Freedom Report 2006. Denmark.* Available at: http://www.state.gov/g/drl/rls/irf/ (accessed 30/06/2009)

-------------------------------- (2007) *International Religious Freedom Report 2007. Cyprus.* Available at: http://www.state.gov/g/drl/rls/irf/ (accessed 20/06/2009)

-------------------------------- (2007) *International Religious Freedom Report 2007. France.* Available at: http://www.state.gov/g/drl/rls/irf/ (accessed 20/06/2009)

-------------------------------- (2008) *International Religious Freedom Report 2006. Germany.* Available at: http://www.state.gov/g/drl/rls/irf/ (accessed 01/06/2009)

-------------------------------- (2008) *International Religious Freedom Report 2008. Greece.* Available at: http://www.state.gov/g/drl/rls/irf/

-------------------------------- (2008) *International Religious Freedom Report 2008. Austria.* Available at: http://www.state.gov/g/drl/rls/irf/

-------------------------------- (2008) *International Religious Freedom Report 2008. Belgium.* Available at: http://www.state.gov/g/drl/rls/irf/

Statistical Service of Cyprus (2007) *Statistical Abstract* 2007. Series I, Report No 53. Avaliable at: http://www.mof.gov.cy/mof/cystat/statistics.nsf/index_en/index_en?OpenDocument

ANNEX: BASIC REGULATIONS

AUSTRIA

a) Articles of the Constitution of 1920

Article 62 [Oath]

(1) On his assumption of office the Federal President renders the following affirmation before the Federal Assembly:

"I solemnly promise that I shall faithfully observe the Constitution and all the laws of the Republic and shall fulfil my duty to the best of my knowledge and belief."

(2) The addition of a religious assertion is admissible.

Article 72 [Affirmation]

(1) Before assuming office, the members of the Federal Government render an affirmation to the Federal President. The addition of a religious assertion is admissible.

b) **Important laws**

1. Related to religious freedom of individuals and groups in general:

- The Constitutional Act on the Fundamental Rights of Citizenships (*Staatsgrundgesetz über die aügemeinen Rechte der Staatshürger* (StGG) of 21 December 1867, declared a constitutional law of the Federal State by article 149 of the Constitution of 1920, has introduced a denominationally neutral system in ecclesiastical matters. Though Art. 15 StGG conferred upon all legally recognised churches and religious societies certain rights for the first time, it did not give details of the way in which the adherents of a certain denomination may obtain legal recognition. These provisions are contained in the following.
- Law concerning legal recognition of Religious communities Recognition Act (*Anerkennungsgesetz- AnkerG-* 1874.
- The Act on Confessional Relations Communities (*BekGG*) 1988 (an amendment to the Recognition Act 1874).

2. Related to the legal status of specifically recognised churches and religious communities:

- Law of 21 March 1890 on the External Legal Positions of the Israelite Religious Society (I*sraelitenG*). In a decision from 1981 sect. 2 *IsraelitenG* was partially declared unconstitutional.

- Law of 15 July 1912 concerning the Recognition of the Adherents of Islam as a Religious Community (*IslamG*) published at the "Imperial Gazette" in the Austrian Hungarian Monarchy, After Annexation of Bosnia Herzegovina 1908.
- Concordat between the Republic of Austrian State and Holy See, June 5th 1933.
- Federal Law of 6 July 1961 on the External Legal Position of the Protestant Church in Austria (*ProtestantenG*).
- Federal Law of 23 June 1967 on the External Legal Positions of the Greek Oriental Church in Austria (*OrthodoxenG*).

Since 2003 there has been a special law for the churches of the oriental-orthodox tradition, including not only the already legally recognised churches (Armenian-Apostolic Church since Joseph II or 1973 respectively and the Syrian Orthodox Church since 1988), but also the Coptic Orthodox Church, which has been a registered denominational religious community since 1998.

BELGIUM

a) Articles of the Constitution of 1994.

-Article 19 (guarantees the freedom of worship and its public practice)

They are guaranteed the freedom of cults, the one of its public exercise, as well as the freedom to show the opinions own in any matter, without damage of the repression of the crimes committed with occasion of the use of these liberties.

-Article 20 (guarantees the so-called negative freedom of religion)

Nobody could be forced to participate in way some in the acts and ceremonies of a cult, nor to observe days of rest.

-Article 21 (guarantees the organisational autonomy of the religions)

The State will be able to take part neither in the appointment nor in the taking of possession of the cult ministers some, nor to prohibit them that they are related to its superior ones, or that publishes their writings, without damage in this last case of the ordinary responsibility in the matter of press and publications.

The civil marriage will have to always precede to the nuptial blessing, except for the exceptions that the law establish in its case.

-Article 181 (expresses the mutual independence of Church and State although this separation is not absolute)

1. The repayments and pensions of the ministers of the diverse cults will be the responsibility of the State, and the bottoms necessary will be briefed annually in the Budgets to take care of them.

2. The repayments and pensions of the delegates of the organisations recognised by the law, who offer moral attendance in agreement with nondenominational a philosophical conception, will be the responsibility of the State and the bottoms necessary will be briefed annually in the Budgets to take care of them.

The payment of remuneration and pensions applies only to ministers of the recognised religions, currently the Catholic, Protestant, Jewish, Anglican, Islamic and Orthodox religions. A legal recognition holds certain other advantages, such as the right to provide religious education in the State education system (Article 24.1, fourth indent, of the Constitution).

-Article 24.1 (guarantees the freedom of education):

The community organises non-denominational education. This implies in particular the respect for the philosophical, ideological or religious beliefs of parents and pupils.

Schools run by the public authorities offer, until the end of compulsory education, the choice between the teaching of one of the recognised religions and non-denominational ethics teaching.

-Article 24. 3 of the Constitution guarantees the right to education. It provides in its second indent:

All pupils of school age have the right to moral or religious education at the community's expense.

b) Important laws

-Special law of 13th. of June 2001 regionalising some matters (in particular article 4 concerning the recognised religions).

-Special law of 21st. of July 1844 relatively on civil and ecclesiastic pensions.

-Law of the 4th. of march 1870 concerning the temporal of religions.

-Law of 19th. of July 1974 holding recognition of Islam.

-Law of 2nd. of August 1974 concerning the salaries of some public officers and of the ministers of religions and the delegates of the laic movement.

-Communal law of 24th. of June 1985.

-Law of 2nd. of June 1998 creating the Information and advisory Centre on harmful cults and the Administrative coordination Cell concerning the struggle against harmful cults.

-Law of 21st. of June 2002 holding recognition of the non confessional movement (laic movement) and fixing the statute of their delegates.

-Law of 20th. of July 2004 creating a Commission on the renewal of the representative bodies on Islam.

-Decree of the Flemish Parliament of 7th. of May 2004 concerning the material organisation and the functioning of recognised religions.

-Decision of the Walloon Government of 27 may 2004 holding codification of the regional legislation on local administrations.

-Decision of the Council of Brussels Capital region modifying the imperial decree of 30th. of December 1809 on church administrations.

-Royal decree of 8th. of November 1998 concerning the organisation and the functioning of the Information and advisory Centre on harmful cults as well of the Administrative coordination Cell.

-Royal decree of 3th. of may 1999 recognising the Executive of the Muslims of Belgium.

-Royal decree of 4th. of may 1999 holding acceptance of the members of the Executive of the Muslims of Belgium.

-Royal decree of 25 October 2005 concerning the statute of de chaplains in the state prisons.

-Decree of the Flemish council of 27th. of march 1991 concerning the legal position of the teachers in the free subsidised schools.

-Decree of the Flemish council of 14th. of July 2004 concerning the free choice or the exemption to follow a course of a recognised religion or philosophy in the public lower and secondary level schools.

-Decree of the Government of the French community of 1st. of February 1993 concerning the legal position of the teachers in the subsidised schools.

-Decree of the Government of the French community of march 2002 concerning the teachers of religions.

-Basic law of 12th. Of January 2005 concerning the legal positions and the rights of detainees in prisons (amongst them the right of religious or philosophic assistance).

-Decree of the Flemish government of 15th. of october 1999 concerning the conditions, procedure and lasting period to have the right to broadcast religious or philosophic programmes.

-Decision of the Government of the French community of 31st. of May 2000 concerning the recognition of representative's bodies that are allowed to broadcast emissions on radio and television.

-Decree of the Council of the germanophone community of 26th. of april 1999 on the media.

-Law of 20th. July 1971 concerning the cemeteries.

-Agreement of 27th. of may 2004 on cooperation between the federal sate, the Flemish, the Walloon and German regions concerning the recognition of religions, the salaries and the pensions of the ministers of the recognised religions, the church administrations and the establishments in charge of the administration of the temporal of the religion.

-Decree of the Flemish Government of 30 September 2005 concerning the criteria for recognition of the local administrations of recognised religions.

-Ordinance of Government of the Brussels capital region of 18 July 2002 and 19 February 2004 concerning the administrations on the recognised religions.

BULGARIA

a) Articles of the Constitution of 1991

- Article 13: Religion

(1) The practicing of any religion is free.

(2) The religious institutions shall be separate from the state.

(3) Eastern Orthodox Christianity is considered the traditional religion in the Republic of Bulgaria.

(4) Religious institutions and communities and religious beliefs shall not be used to political ends.

- Article 37: Freedom of Religion and Belief

(1) The freedom of conscience, the freedom of thought, and the choice of religion and of religious or atheistic views are inviolable. The state shall assist the maintenance of tolerance and respect among the believers from different denominations, and among believers and non-believers.

(2) The freedom of conscience and religion shall not be practiced to the detriment of national security, public order, public health and morals, or of the rights and freedoms of others.

- Article 46: Matrimony

(1) Matrimony is a free union between a man and a woman. Only a civil marriage shall be legal.

- Article 53: Education

(5) Citizens and organisations shall be free to found schools in accordance with conditions and procedures established by law. The education they provide shall fit the requirements of the state.

(6) The state shall promote education by opening and financing schools, by supporting capable school and university students, and by providing opportunities for occupational training and retraining. It shall exercise control over all kinds and levels of schooling.

b) **Important Laws:**

- Religions Act, published on the 29th of December, 2002.
- Not-for-profit Legal Entities Act
- Higher Education Act.

CYPRUS

a) Articles of the Constitution of 1960:

Article 2 (For the purposes of this paragraph a " *religious group* " means a group of persons ordinarily resident in Cyprus professing the same religion and either belonging to the same rite or being subject to the same jurisdiction thereof the number of whom, on the date of the coming into operation of this Constitution, exceeds one thousand out of which at least five hundred become on such date citizens of the Republic).

Article 18
1. Every person has the right to freedom of thought, conscience and religion.

2. All religions whose doctrines or rites are not secret are free.

3. All religions are equal before the law. Without prejudice to the competence of the Communal Chambers under this Constitution, no legislative, executive or administrative act of the Republic shall discriminate against any religious institution or religion.

4. Every person is free and has the right to profess his faith and to manifest his religion or belief, in worship, teaching, practice or observance, either individually or collectively, in private or in public, and to change his religion or belief.

5. The use of physical or moral compulsion for the purpose of making a person change or preventing him from changing his religion is prohibited.

6. Freedom to manifest one's religion or belief shall be subject only to such limitations as are prescribed by law and are necessary in the interests of the security of the Republic or the constitutional order or the public safety or the public order or the public health or the public morals or for the protection of the rights and liberties guaranteed by this Constitution to any person.

7. Until a person attains the age of sixteen the decision as to the religion to be professed by him shall be taken by the person having the lawful guardianship of such person.

8. No person shall be compelled to pay any tax or duty the proceeds of which are specially allocated in whole or in part for the purposes of a religion other than his own.

Article 87.1

1. The Communal Chambers shall, in relation to their respective Community, have competence to exercise within the limits of this Constitution and subject to paragraph 3 of this Article, legislative power solely with regard to the following matters:
(a) all religious matters;

Article 110

1. The Autocephalous Greek Orthodox Church of Cyprus shall continue to have the exclusive right of regulating and administering its own internal affairs and property in accordance with the Holy Canons and its Charter in force for the time being and the Greek Communal Chamber shall not act inconsistently with such right.

2. The institution of *Wakf* and the Principles and Laws of, and relating to, *Wakf*s are recognised by this Constitution.

All matters relating to or in any way affecting the institution or foundation of *Wakf* or the *wakf*s or any *wakf* properties, including properties belonging to Mosques and any other Moslem religious institution, shall be governed solely by and under the Laws and Principles of *Wakf*s (ahkamul evkaf) and the laws and regulations enacted or made by the Turkish Communal Chamber, and no legislative, executive or other act whatsoever shall contravene or override or interfere with such Laws or Principles of *Wakf*s and with such laws and regulations of the Turkish Communal Chamber.

3. Any right with regard to religious matters possessed in accordance with the law of the Colony of Cyprus in force immediately before the date of the coming into operation of this Constitution by the Church of a religious group to which the provisions of paragraph 3 of Article 2 shall apply shall continue to be so possessed by such Church on and after the date of the coming into operation of this Constitution.

b) **Important laws**

-"The 1914 Charter of Orthodox Church of Cyprus" was modified by the 1980 Charter which is still in force.

CZECH REPUBLIC

a) Articles of the Constitution of 1993.

- Article 15

(1)The freedom of thought, conscience, and religious conviction is guaranteed. Everyone has the right to change her religion or faith or to be non-denominational.

(2)The freedom of scholarly research and of artistic creation is guaranteed.
(3)No one may be compelled to perform military service if such is contrary to his conscience or religious conviction. Detailed provisions shall be laid down in a law.

- Article 16

(1)Everyone has the right freely to manifest her religion or faith, either alone or in community with others, in private or public, through worship, teaching. Practice, and observance.
(2)Churches and religious societies govern their own affairs; in particular, they establish their own bodies and appoint their clergy, as well as found religious orders and other church institutions, independent of state authorities.
(3)The conditions under which religious instruction may be given at state schools shall be set by law.
The exercise of these rights may be limited by law in the case of measures necessary in a democratic society for the protection of public safety and order. health and morals, or the rights and freedoms of others.

b) **Important laws**

- Enumeration Law (Act No. 298/1990 Coll. and Act No. 338/1991 Coll.).

- Act no. 3/2002 Coll. of January 7th 2002 on Freedom of Religious Convictions and the legal status of Churches and Religious Societies (a list of about 150 catholic buildings returned to Catholic Church).

- Act on freedom of religion and status of churches and religious associations (approved by government on 25th April 2001).

- Act no 101 /2000 Coll., on Personal Data Protection (the complete wording announced by Prime Minister under no 525 / 2004 Coll.).

There are also several State-Church Treaties at an internal level in present Czech law:

- Cooperation Agreements between the Ministry of Defence of the Czech Republic, the Ecumenical Council of Churches in the Czech Republic and the Czech Bishops′ Conference (1998).

- The Agreement on pastoral service in prisons between the Prison Administration of the Czech Republic, the Ecumenical Council of Churches in the Czech Republic, and the Czech Bishops' Conference (1999), which replaced that of 1994.

A Cooperation Agreement between the Czech Radio, the Czech Bishops' Conference and the Ecumenical Council of Churches in the Czech Republic (1999).

DENMARK

a) Articles of the Constitution of 1953 :
- Section 4 [State Church]
The Evangelical Lutheran Church shall be the Established Church of Denmark, and, as such, it shall be supported by the State.
-Section 6 [Member of the State Church]
The King shall be a member of the Evangelical Lutheran Church.
Part VII [State Church]:
-Section 66 [Church Constitution]
The constitution of the Established Church shall be laid down by Statute.
-Section 67 [Right to Worship]
The citizens shall be entitled to form congregations for the worship of God in a manner consistent with their convictions, provided that nothing at variance with good morals or public order shall be taught or done.
-Section 68 [Church Contributions]
No one shall be liable to make personal contributions to any denomination other than the one to which he adheres.

-Section 69 [Regulation of Other Religious Bodies]
Rules for religious bodies dissenting from the Established Church shall be laid down by Statute.
-Section 70 [Freedom of Religion]
No person shall for reasons of his creed or descent be deprived of access to complete enjoyment of his civic and political rights, nor shall he for such reasons evade compliance with any common civic duty.

ESTONIA

a) Articles of the Constitution of 1992.
Article 40 [Freedom of Religion]
(1) Everyone shall have freedom of conscience, religion and thought.
(2) Everyone may freely belong to a church or a religious association. There shall be no state church.
(3) Everyone shall have the freedom, either alone or in community with others and in public or private to practice his or her religion, unless it endangers public order, health or morals.
-Article 42 [Privacy of Religion and Belief]
No state or local government authority or their officials may collect or store information on the persuasions of any Estonian citizen against his or her free will.
-Article 124 [Duty to Service]
(1) Citizens of the Republic of Estonia shall be obligated to participate in national defence, in accordance with the bases and procedures determined by law.
(2) Those that refuse service in the Defence Forces for religious or ethical reasons shall be obligated to participate in alternative service, in accordance with the procedures prescribed by law..."
b) Important laws:
- Churches and Congregations Act of 1993 established a legislative framework for religious associations as legal entities.
- Churches and Congregations Act of 2002. Replaces the 1993 CCA maintaining the basic principles of a liberal legislative framework.
- The Non-profit Organizations Act 1996.
- Cooperation Agreement between Catholic Church and Estonia ratified by the Estonian Parliament in 1999.

FINLAND

a) **Articles of the Constitution of 1999**:
-Section 11. Freedom of religion and conscience
(1) Everyone has the freedom of religion and conscience.

(2) Freedom of religion and conscience entails the right to profess and practice a religion, the right to express one's convictions and the right to be a member of or decline to be a member of a religious community. No one is under the obligation, against his or her conscience, to participate in the practice of a religion.
-Section 76. The Church Act
(1) Provisions on the organisation and administration of the Evangelic Lutheran Church are laid down in the Church Act.
(2) The legislative procedure for enactment of the Church Act and the right to submit legislative proposals relating to the Church Act are governed by the specific provisions in that Code.

b) Important laws:

- Freedom of Religion Act, nº 453 of June 6th 2003.
- The Church Act of the Lutheran Church, Act 1054 of 1993.
- The Church Act of the Orthodox Church, Act 521 of 1969, and its supplementary statute (179/1970).
- Chapter 17 of the Criminal Code (includes several provisions that protect religious entities and the free exercise of religion through criminalization).

FRANCE

a) Art. 1 of the Constitution of 1958

France shall be an indivisible, secular, democratic and social Republic. It shall ensure the equality of all citizens before the law, without distinction of origin, race or religion. It shall respect all beliefs. It shall be organised on a decentralised basis.

Statutes shall promote equal access by women and men to elective offices and posts as well as to professional and social positions.

b) **Important laws**

-1901 Law (July 1st) on the contract of association

- 1905 Law (December 9th) on separation between Churches and State

- Decree of the Ministry of Public Education, Beaux-Arts and cultes (16th march 1906)

- Law of 2 of January of 1907 on public exercise of cults.

- 2004 Law allowing the expulsion of individuals for "inciting discrimination, hatred or violence against a specific person or group of persons."

- Law of 31 December 1959 (Debré law) regulating relationship between private and State schools.

GERMANY

a) Articles of the Basic Law for the Federal Republic of 1949

- Article 4. [Freedom of faith, conscience, and creed]

(1) Freedom of faith and of conscience, and freedom to profess a religious or philosophical creed, shall be inviolable.

(2) The undisturbed practice of religion shall be guaranteed.

(3) No person shall be compelled against his conscience to render military service involving the use of arms. Details shall be regulated by a federal law.

- Article 7 [School education]

(1) The entire school system shall be under the supervision of the state.

(2) Parents and guardians shall have the right to decide whether children shall receivereligious instruction.

(3) Religious instruction shall form part of the regular curriculum in state schools, with the exception of non-denominational schools. Without prejudice to the state's right of supervision, religious instruction shall be given in accordance with the tenets of the religious community concerned. Teachers may not be obliged against their will to give religious instruction.

(4) The right to establish private schools shall be guaranteed. Private schools that serve as alternatives to state schools shall require the approval of the State and shall be subject to the laws of the Lander. Such approval shall be given when private schools are not inferior to the state schools in terms of their educational aims, their facilities, or the professional training of their teaching staff, and when segregation of pupils according to the means of their parents will not be encouraged thereby. Approval shall be withheld if the economic and legal position of the teaching staff is not adequately assured.

(5) A private elementary school shall be approved only if the educational authority finds that it serves a special pedagogical interest or if, on the application of parents or guardians, it is to be established as a denominational or interdenominational school or as a school based on a particular philosophy and no state elementary school of that type exists in the municipality.

(6) Preparatory schools shall remain abolished.

- Article 140 [Provisions respecting religious societies]

The provisions of Articles 136, 137, 138, 139, and 141 of the German Constitution of August 11,1919 shall be an integral part of this Basic Law.

- Article 141 ["Bremen Clause"]

The first sentence of paragraph (3) of Article 7 shall not apply in any Land in which Land law otherwise provided on January 1, 1949.

Appendix to the Basic Law.

Extracts from the German Constitution of August 11, 1919 [Weimar Constitution].

Religion and Religious Societies.

- Article 136

(1) Civil and political rights and duties shall be neither dependent upon nor restricted by the exercise of religious freedom.

(2) Enjoyment of civil and political rights and eligibility for public office shall be independent of religious affiliation.

(3) No person shall be required to disclose his religious convictions. The authorities shall have the right to inquire into a person's membership in a religious society only to the extent that rights or duties depend upon it or that a statistical survey mandated by a law so requires.

(4) No person may be compelled to perform any religious act or ceremony, to participate in religious exercises, or to take a religious form of oath.

- Article 137

(1) There shall be no state church.

(2) The freedom to form religious societies shall be guaranteed. The union of religious societies within the territory of the Reich shall be subject to no restrictions.

(3) Religious societies shall regulate and administer their affairs independently within the limits of the law that applies to all. They shall confer their offices without the participation of the state or the civil community.

(4) Religious societies shall acquire legal capacity according to the general provisions of civil law.

(5) Religious societies shall remain corporations under public law insofar as they have enjoyed that status in the past. Other religious societies shall be granted the same rights upon application, if their constitution and the number of their members give assurance of their permanency. If two or more religious societies established under public law unite into a single organization, it too shall be a corporation under public law.

(6) Religious societies that are corporations under public law shall be entitled to levy taxes on the basis of the civil taxation lists in accordance with Land law.

(7) Associations whose purpose is to foster a philosophical creed shall have the same status as religious societies.

(8) Such further regulation as may be required for the implementation of these provisions shall be a matter for Land legislation.

- Article 138

(1) Rights of religious societies to public subsidies on the basis of a law, contract, or special grant shall be redeemed by legislation of the Lander. The principles governing such redemption shall be established by the Reich.

(2) Property rights and other rights of religious societies or associations in their institutions, foundations, and other assets intended for purposes of worship, education, or charity shall be guaranteed.

- Article 139

Sunday and holidays recognized by the state shall remain protected by law as days of rest from work and of spiritual improvement.

- Article 141

To the extent that a need exists for regions services and pastoral work in the army, in hospitals, in prisons, or in other public institutions, regions societies shall be permitted to provide them, but without compulsion of any kind.

b) **Basic legislation related to religious freedom and religious communities**.

The Constitutions of the various *Länder* also contain provisions on religious freedom and on the relationship with religious communities. In addition, pertinent provisions are contained in ordinary (i.e. sub-constitutional) laws such as the Act on the Religious Education of Children *(Gesetz über die religiöse Kindererziehung - RKEG)*.

The two major Christian Churches and the Jewish Community (represented by the Central Council of Jews in Germany, *ZdJ*) had signed Agreements ["treaties"] with the *Länders* (which, as we have just outlined, have primary responsibility for these matters).

As regards the Roman Catholic Church, the so-called *Reich* Concordat (1933 Concordat between the Holy See and the German *Reich*) continues to be in force. Other Concordats have been concluded by the various *Länder* and the Holy See.

Also Agreements ["treaty"] between the various *Länder* and the Federation with the Protestant Church in Germany *(Evangelische Kirche in Deutschland – EKD.* See: the homepage of the Federal Ministry of the Interior (www.bmi.bund.de) (under *Themen A-Z* ("subjects A-Z"), *Kirchen und Religionsgemeinschaften* ("churches and religious communities"), *Daten und Fakten* ("data and facts"); direct links: *Verträge mit der katholischen Kirche* (Roman-Catholic Church); *Verträge mit den evangelischen Landeskirchen* (*Land* Protestant Churches) and *Verträge mit der jüdischen Gemeinschaft* (Jewish Community).

As regards to Federal legislation:

- The General Equal Treatment Act (Act to implement European Directives implementing the principle of equal treatment; *Allgemeines Gleichbehandlungsgesetz*)

- Special regulations on religious rites (e.g. provisions of the Animal Protection Act *(Tierschutzgesetz)*), to the bodies providing social institutions/facilities and to participation in the furtherance of the integration of foreigners in the Federal Republic.

- Regulations of property law in favour of religious communities are contained in the Equalization Benefits Act (*Ausgleichsleistungsgesetz)* and the Act Regulating Unsettled Property Issues *(Gesetz zur Regelung offener Vermögensfragen).*

GREECE

a) **Articles of the Constitution of 1975:**

- Article **3** (position of the Church):

1. The prevailing religion in Greece is that of the Eastern Orthodox Church of Christ. The Orthodox Church of Greece, acknowledging our Lord Jesus Christ as its head, is inseparably united in doctrine with the Great Church of Christ in Constantinople and with every other Church of Christ of the same doctrine, observing unwaveringly, as they do, the holy apostolic and synodal canons and

sacred traditions. It is autocephalous and is administered by the Holy Synod of serving Bishops and the Permanent Holy Synod originating thereof and assembled as specified by the Statutory Charter of the Church in compliance with the provisions of the Patriarchal Tome of June 29, 1850 and the Synodal Act of September 4, 1928.

2. The ecclesiastical regime existing in certain districts of the State shall not be deemed contrary to the provisions of the preceding paragraph.

3. The text of the Holy Scripture shall be maintained unaltered. Official translation of the text into any other form of language, without prior sanction by the Autocephalous Church of Greece and the Great Church of Christ in Constantinople, is prohibited.

- Article 13 (religious freedom):

1. Freedom of religious conscience is inviolable. The enjoyment of civil rights and liberties does not depend on the individual's religious beliefs.

2. All known religions shall be free and their rites of worship shall be performed unhindered and under the protection of the law. The practice of rites of worship is not allowed to offend public order or the good usages. Proselytism is prohibited.

3. The ministers of all known religions shall be subject to the same supervision by the State and to the same obligations toward it as those of the prevailing religion.

4. No person shall be exempt from discharging his obligations to the State or may refuse to comply with the laws by reason of his religious convictions.

5. No oath shall be imposed or administered except as specified by law and in the form determined by law.

- Article 33 [Installation]:

"... (2) The President of the Republic shall take the following oath before Parliament and prior to his taking office:

"I swear in the name of the Holy, Consubstantial, and Indivisible Trinity to observe the Constitution and the laws, to provide for the faithful observance thereof, to defend the national independence and territorial integrity of the country, to protect the rights and liberties of Greeks and to serve the public interest and the progress of the Greek People....".

- Article 59:

1. Before undertaking the discharge of their duties, Members of Parliament shall take the following oath in the Chamber and in a public sitting.

"I swear in the name of the Holy Consubstantial and Indivisible Trinity to keep faith in my Country and in the democratic form of government, obedience to the Constitution and the laws and to discharge conscientiously my duties".

Members of Parliament who are of a different religion or creed shall take the same oath according to the form of their own religion or creed.
- Article 105 (Mount Athos):

1. The Athos peninsula extending beyond Megali Vigla and constituting the region of Aghion Oros shall, in accordance with its ancient privileged status, be a self-governed part of the Greek State, whose sovereignty thereon shall remain intact. Spiritually, Aghion Oros shall come under the direct jurisdiction of the Ecumenical Patriarchate. All persons leading a monastic life thereon acquire Greek citizenship without further formalities, upon admission novices or monks.

2. Aghion Oros shall be governed, according to its regime, by its twenty Holy Monasteries among which the entire Athos peninsula is divided; the territory of the peninsula shall be exempt from expropriation.

The administration of Aghion Oros shall be exercised by representatives of the Holy Monasteries constituting the Holy Community. No change whatsoever shall be permitted in the administrative system or in the number of Monasteries of Aghion Oros, or in their hierarchical order or in their position to their subordinate dependencies. Heterodox or schismatic persons shall be prohibited from dwelling thereon.

3. The determination in detail of the regimes of the Aghion Oros entities and the manner of operation thereof is effected by the Charter of Aghion Oros which, with the cooperation of the State representative, shall be drawn up and voted by the twenty Holy Monasteries and ratified by the Ecumenical Patriarchate and the Parliament of the Hellenes.

4. Faithful observance of the regimes of the Aghion Oros entities shall in the spiritual field be under the supreme supervision of the Ecumenical Patriarchate, and, in the administrative, under the supervision of the State, which shall also be exclusively responsible for safeguarding public order and security.

5. The afore-mentioned powers of the State shall be exercised through a governor whose rights and duties shall be determined by law.

The law shall likewise determine the judicial power exercised by the monastic authorities and the Holy Community, as well as the customs and taxation privileges of Aghion Oros.

b) **Important laws:**

- Law 590/1977 concerning the statutory Charter of the Church of Greece.
- Law N° 2455/1920, M.L. 367/1945, L.1657/1951 (legal status of Israelite religion).
- Treaty of Lausanne (1923), Law 1920/1991 & others (legal status of Muslims).
- Law 1230/1982 concerning civil marriage, when a licence for such a marriage could be obtained by a non-Orthodox bishop for a member of his Church.
- Law 1763/1988 on army conscription which exempts all monks or novices, regardless of whether they are Orthodox or belong to another faith.

L.D. 3843/1958 on income tax and L.D. 1249/1982 on property-tax, which exempt not only Orthodox but also non-Orthodox churches and monasteries

HUNGARY

a) **Articles of the Constitution of 1990**

- Article 60 Freedom of thought, conscience and religion

(1) In the Republic of Hungary everyone has the right to freedom of thought, freedom of conscience and freedom of religion.

(2) This right shall include the free choice or acceptance of a religion or belief, and the freedom to publicly or privately express or decline to express, exercise and teach such religions and beliefs by way of religious actions, rites or in any other way, either individually or in a group.

(3) The church and the State shall operate in separation in the Republic of Hungary.

(4) A majority of two-thirds of the votes of the Members of Parliament present is required to pass the law on the freedom of belief and religion.

b) Important laws:

- Act IV of 1990 on the Freedom of Conscience and Religion and the Churches.

- Act XXXII of 1991 on the Settlement of Ownership of the Former Real Estates of the Churches (Restoration Act).

- Act 124 of 1997 on the Financial Conditions of Religious and Public Activities of Churches

- International agreements signed and ratified by Hungary: International Covenant on Civil and Political Rights, Convention of the Rights of the Child, European Convention for the Protection of Human Rights and Fundamental Freedoms with its additional protocols

- Agreement with the Holy See of 10th January 1994, on the military ordinaries, a precondition for the Government to set up an army chaplaincy.

- Agreement with the Holy See of 20th June 1997, on the financial issues concerning the Catholic Church.

Other churches have entered into contractual relations with the government, though without international dimensions: Contracts were signed on the army chaplaincies as well as on financial issues, the latter especially the agreements with the Reformed Church and the Alliance of Jewish Communities. The status of these agreements is however disputed.

IRELAND

a) **Articles of the Constitution of 1937** :

Preamble: …."In the Name of the Most Holy Trinity, from Whom is all authority and to Whom, as our final end, all actions both of men and States must be referred, We, the people of Éire…"

- Article 40 (6).

1° The State guarantees liberty for the exercise of the following rights, subject to public order and morality:

The right of the citizens to express freely their convictions and opinions.

The education of public opinion being, however, a matter of such grave import to the common good, the State shall endeavour to ensure that organs of public opinion, such as the radio, the press, the cinema, while preserving their rightful liberty of expression, including criticism of Government policy, shall not be used to undermine public order or morality or the authority of the State.

The publication or utterance of blasphemous, seditious, or indecent matter is an offence which shall be punishable in accordance with law.

The right of the citizens to assemble peaceably and without arms….

The right of the citizens to form associations and unions. ..

2° Laws regulating the manner in which the right of forming associations and unions and the right of free assembly may be exercised shall contain no political, religious or class discrimination.

- Article 44

The State acknowledges that the homage of public worship is due to Almighty God. It shall hold His Name in reverence, and shall respect and honour religion.

1° Freedom of conscience and the free profession and practice of religion are, subject to public order and morality, guaranteed to every citizen.

2° The State guarantees not to endow any religion.

3° The State shall not impose any disabilities or make any discrimination on the ground of religious profession, belief or status.

4° Legislation providing State aid for schools shall not discriminate between schools under the management of different religious denominations, nor be such as to affect prejudicially the right of any child to attend a school receiving public money without attending religious instruction at that school.

5° Every religious denomination shall have the right to manage its own affairs, own, acquire and administer property, movable and immovable, and maintain institutions for religious or charitable purposes.

6° The property of any religious denomination or any educational institution shall not be diverted save for necessary works of public utility and on payment of compensation.

b) Important laws:

- The Prohibition of Incitement to Hatred Act 1989 –makes it an offence to publish, distribute or display material which is "threatening, abusive or insulting" and intended, or likely, to stir up hatred, also against a group of persons on account of their religion.

- Irish Church Act 1869

- Irish Presbyterian Church Act 1871

- Methodist Church in Ireland Act 1915 – created a corporate body ("The Trustees of the Methodist Church in Ireland"); the Constitution of the Church was given statutory effect by the Methodist Church in Ireland Act 1928.

- Charities Act 1961 – Section 45

ITALY

a) **Articles of the Constitution of 1948** :

- Article 7 [Relation between State and Church]

(1) State and catholic church are, each within their own reign, independent and sovereign.

(2) Their relationship is regulated by the Lateran Pacts. Amendments to these pacts which are accepted by both parties do not require the procedure of constitutional amendments.

- Article 8 [Religion]

(1) Religious denominations are equally free before the law.

(2) Denominations other than Catholicism have the right to organize themselves according to their own by-laws, provided they do not conflict with the Italian legal system.

(3) Their relationship with the state is regulated by law, based on agreements with their representatives.

- Article 19 [Freedom of Religion]

Everyone is entitled to freely profess religious beliefs in any form, individually or with others, to promote them, and to celebrate rites in public or in private, provided they are not offensive to public morality.

- Article 20 [Religious Associations]

For associations or institutions, their religious character or religious or confessional aims do not justify special limitations or fiscal burdens regarding their establishment, legal capacity, or activities.

b) Important laws.

Relationships between State and Catholic Church: have been regulated first by the

- Revision Agreement of February 18th 1984 and of a related Additional Protocol between the Italian Republic and the Holy See,

- Law May 20th 1985, n. 222, with "Provisions on Ecclesiastical Bodies and Properties in Italy and on the Maintenance of Catholic Clergy Being in Service in the Dioceses"

- Decree of the President of the Republic (D.P.R.) February 13th 1987, n. 33.

- Law June 24th 1929, n. 1159, with "Provisions Concerning the Practice of Religious Rites Allowed by the State and Marriage Celebrated Before the Ministers of Religion", and the subsequent Royal Decree February 28th 1930, n. 289.

Beside the Catholic Church, there are 6 religious creeds which have stipulated agreements with the State (*intese)*, which have been acknowledged by parliamentarian laws:

1. *Tavola Valdese* (*Waldensian Table*) – Law August 8th 1984, n. 449, modified
by Law October 5th 1993, n. 409;
2. *Unione delle Chiese Cristiane Avventiste del Settimo Giorno* (*Union of the Seventh-day-Adventist Christian Churches*) – Law November 22nd 1988, n. 516, later supplemented with Law December 20th 1996, n. 637;
3. *Assemblee di Dio in Italia* (*Assemblies of God in Italy*) – Law November 22nd 1988, n. 517;
4. *Unione delle Comunità Ebraiche Italiane* (*Union of the Jewish Communities in Italy*) – Law March 8th 1989, n. 101, later supplemented with Law December 20th 1996, n. 638;
5. *Unione Cristiana Evangelica Battista d'Italia* (*Evangelical Baptist Christian Union in Italy*) – Law April 12th 1995, n. 116;
6. *Chiesa Evangelica Luterana in Italia* (*Luteran Evangelical Church in Italy*) – Law November 29th 1995, n. 520.

LATVIA

a) **Articles of the Constitution regarding religious freedom and relations between churches and the State**:

- Art. 99. Everyone has the right to freedom of thought, conscience and religion. The Church is separate from the state.

- Art. 116. Those rights of a person which are determined in Articles (...) may be limited in those cases prescribed by law in order to protect the rights of other people, a democratic state system, the safety of society, welfare and morals. On the basis of the provisions mentioned in this Article, the expression of a religious conviction may be limited also.

b) Important laws:

- Law on Religious Organisations, 7 September 1995

- Criminal Law of the Republic of Latvia

-Latvian Civil Law

- Law "On Trademarks and Geographical Indications" (Article 2 says that religious symbols fall into the group called "non-registrable marks", as well as state emblems).

- Law "On the Press and Other Public Means of Information" (Article 7 imposes a prohibition on the publication and dissemination of information advocating religious intolerance. Equally there is a ban on commercials which infringe religious sensibilities.

- Advertising Law (Article 4 prohibits in advertising express discrimination against a person due to his or her race, skin colour, gender (...) political or other convictions. Moreover it is prohibited in advertising "to exploit the effect created by fear or superstition", to a certain extent being applicable also to religious conviction. Sanctions are not of criminal, but of an administrative and civil nature.

- Radio and Television Law (Article 20 provides that commercials may not injure human dignity and religious feelings).

LITHUANIA

a) **Articles of the Constitution of 1992:**

- Article 25

(1) Individuals shall have the right to have their own convictions and freely express them.

(2) Individuals must not be hindered from seeking, obtaining, or disseminating information or ideas.

(3) Freedom to express convictions, as well as to obtain and disseminate information, may not be restricted in any way other than as established by law,

when it is necessary for the safeguard of the health, honour and dignity, private life, or morals of a person, or for the protection of constitutional order.

(4) Freedom to express convictions or impart information shall be incompatible with criminal actions - the instigation of national, racial, religious, or social hatred, violence, or discrimination, the dissemination of slander, or misinformation.

(5) Citizens shall have the right to obtain any available information which concerns them from State agencies in the manner established by law.

- Article 26

(1) Freedom of thought, conscience, and religion shall not be restricted.
(2) Every person shall have the right to freely choose any religion or faith and, either individually or with others, in public or in private, to manifest his or her religion or faith in worship, observance, practice or teaching.

(3) No person may coerce another person or be subject to coercion to adopt or profess any religion or faith.

(4) A person's freedom to profess and propagate his or her religion or faith may be subject only to those limitations prescribed by law and only when such restrictions are necessary to protect the safety of society, public order, a person's health or morals, or the fundamental rights and freedoms of others.

(5) Parents and legal guardians shall have the liberty to ensure the religious and moral education of their children in conformity with their own convictions.

- Article 27

A person's convictions, professed religion or faith may justify neither the commission of a crime nor the violation of law.

- Article 38

(4) The State shall register marriages, births, and deaths. The State shall also recognise marriages registered in church.

- Article 40

(1) State and local government establishments of teaching and education shall be secular. At the request of parents, they shall offer classes in religious instruction.
(2) Non-governmental teaching and educational institutions may be established according to the procedure established by law.

- Article 43

(1) The State shall recognise traditional Lithuanian churches and religious organisations, as well as other churches and religious organisations provided that they have a basis in society and their teaching and rituals do not contradict morality or the law.

(2) Churches and religious organisations recognised by the State shall have the rights of legal persons.

(3) Churches and religious organisations shall freely proclaim the teaching of their faith, perform the rituals of their belief, and have houses of prayer, charity institutions, and educational institutions for the training of priests of their faith.

(4) Churches and religious organisations shall function freely according to their canons and statutes.

(5) The status of churches and other religious organisations in the State shall be established by agreement or by law.

(6) The teachings proclaimed by churches and other religious organisations, other religious activities, and houses of prayer may not be used for purposes which contradict the Constitution and the law.

(7) There shall not be a State religion in Lithuania.

b) Important laws

- Law on Religious Communities and Associations of the Republic of Lithuania (4 October 1995)

- The Civil Code of the Republic of Lithuania (18 July 2000).

LUXEMBOUG

a) **Articles of the Constitution of 1868** :

- Article 19 [Freedom of Religion]

Freedom of religion and of public worship as well as freedom to express one's religious opinions are guaranteed, subject to the repression of offenses committed in the exercise of such freedoms.

- Article 20 [No Forced Religion]

No one may be forced to take part in any way whatsoever in the acts and ceremonies of a religion or to observe its days of rest.

- Article 21 [Civil Marriage]

Civil marriage must always precede the nuptial benediction.

- Article 22 [State and Church]

The State's intervention in the appointment and installation of heads of religions, the mode of appointing and dismissing other ministers of religion, the right of any of them to correspond with their superiors and to publish their acts and decisions, as well as the Church's relations with the State shall be made the subject of conventions to be submitted to the Chamber of Deputies for the provisions governing its intervention.

- Article 106 [Salaries of Priests]

The salaries and pensions of ministers of religion shall be borne by the State and regulated by the law.

- Article 119 [Provisions Concerning Religions]

Pending the conclusion of the conventions referred to in Article 22, the current provisions concerning religions shall remain in force.

b) Important laws:

- The Concordat of 1801.

- In 1998 Agreements were concluded with the following: Catholic Church, Protestant Church (the Reformed Church has had an Agreement since 1982), the Jews, the Greek Orthodox., the Anglicans, the Rumanian Orthodox and the Servo/Croatian Orthodox.

MALTA

a) Articles of the Constitution of Malta of 1964 :

- Article 2:

(1) The religion of Malta is the Roman Catholic Apostolic Religion.

(2) The authorities of the Roman Catholic Apostolic Church have the duty and the right to teach which principles are right and which are wrong.

(3) Religious teaching of the Roman Catholic Apostolic Faith shall be provided in all State schools as part of compulsory education.

- Article 40:

(1) All persons in Malta shall have full freedom of conscience and enjoy the free exercise of their respective mode of religious worship.

(2) No person shall be required to receive instruction in religion or to show knowledge or proficiency in religion if, in the case of a person who has not attained the age of sixteen years, objection to such requirement is made by the person who according to law has authority over him and, in any other case, if the person so required objects thereto:

Provided that no such requirement shall be held to be inconsistent with or in contravention of this article to the extent that the knowledge of, or the proficiency or instruction in, religion is required for the teaching of such religion, or for admission to the priesthood or to a religious order, or for other religious purposes, and except so far as that requirement is shown not to be reasonably justifiable in a democratic society.

(3) Nothing contained in or done under the authority of any law shall be held to be inconsistent with or in contravention of subarticle (1), to the extent that the law in question makes provision that is reasonably required in the interests of public safety, public order, public morality or decency, public health, or the protection of the rights and freedoms of others, and except so far as that provision or, as the case may be, the thing done under the authority thereof, is shown not to be reasonably justifiable in a democratic society.

b) Important laws:

- Education Act (Act XXIV of 1988, Chap. 327 of the Laws of Malta).
- Marriage Act (Act XXXVII of 1975 as subsequently amended, Chap. 255 o the Laws of Malta).
- Cultural Heritage Act (Act VI of 2002).
- Five Cooperation Agreements with the Holy See:
- Agreement of September 28th over a Faculty of Theology within the University of Malta
- Agreement of November 16th 1989 on religious education in public schools, implemented by Agreement of November 16th of 1989 between the Minstry of Education and the President of the Episcopal Conference of Malta
- Agreement of November 28th 1991 about trespassing properties not used for pastoral purposes from the Catholic Church to the State of Malta - Agreement of November 28th 1991 Schools of the Catholic Church

- Agreement of February 3rd 1993:recognizing civil effects to the catholic marriage, and Protocol for its implementation February 3 1993

POLAND

a) Articles of the Constitution of 1997

Article 25 (legal status of churches and religious communities)

(1) Churches and other religious organizations shall have equal rights.

(2) Public authorities in the Republic of Poland shall be impartial in matters of personal conviction, whether religious or philosophical, or in relation to outlooks on life, and shall ensure their freedom of expression within public life.

(3) The relationship between the State and churches and other religious organizations shall be based on the principle of respect for their autonomy and the mutual independence of each in its own sphere, as well as on the principle of cooperation for the individual and the common good.

(4) The relations between the Republic of Poland and the Roman Catholic Church shall be determined by international treaty concluded with the Holy See, and by statute.

(5) The relations between the Republic of Poland and other churches and religious organizations shall be determined by statutes adopted pursuant to agreements concluded between their appropriate representatives and the Council of Ministers.

-Article 53 (religious freedom and religious instruction in schools).
(1) Freedom of faith and religion shall be ensured to everyone.
(2) Freedom of religion shall include the freedom to profess or to accept a religion by personal choice as well as to manifest such religion, either individually or collectively, publicly or privately, by worshipping, praying, participating in ceremonies, performing of rites or teaching. Freedom of religion shall also include possession of sanctuaries and other places of worship for the satisfaction of the needs of believers as well as the right of individuals, wherever they may be, to benefit from religious services.

(3) Parents shall have the right to ensure their children a moral and religious upbringing and teaching in accordance with their convictions. The provisions of Article 48 (1) shall apply as appropriate.

(4) The religion of a church or other legally recognized religious organization may be taught in schools, but other peoples' freedom of religion and conscience shall not be infringed thereby.

(5) The freedom to publicly express religion may be limited only by means of statute and only where this is necessary for the defence of State security, public order, health, morals or the freedoms and rights of others.

(6) No one shall be compelled to participate or not participate in religious practices.(7) No one may be compelled by organs of public authority to disclose his philosophy of life, religious convictions or belief.

- Article 85 (military service).

(3) Any citizen whose religious convictions or moral principles do not allow him to perform military service may be obliged to perform substitute service in accordance with principles specified by statute.

b) Important laws

- Law on the Guaranties of the Freedom of Conscience and Faith of May 17th 1989.
- Concordat Treaty between Poland and the Holly See of 28 July 1993.

PORTUGAL

a) Articles of the Constitution of 1976:

- Article 35 Use of Data Processing

(3) Data processing may not be used in regard to information concerning a person's philosophical or political convictions, party or trade union affiliations, religious beliefs, or private life, except in the case of non-identifiable data for statistical purposes.

- Article 41 Freedom of Conscience, Religion, and Worship (1) Freedom of conscience, religion, and worship are inviolable.(2) No one may be persecuted, deprived of rights, or exempted from civil obligations or duties because of his convictions or religious practices.(3) No one may be questioned by any authority about his or her convictions or religious practices, except for gathering of statistical data that cannot be identified individually, nor shall anyone be prejudiced by his or her refusal to reply.(4) The churches and religious communities are separate from the State and free to organise and exercise their own ceremonies and worship.(5) The freedom to teach any religion within its own denomination and the use of its own means of public information for the pursuit of its activities, are safeguarded.(6) The right to be a conscientious objector is safeguarded in accordance with the law.

- Article 43 Freedom to Learn and Teach

(2) The State may not arrogate to itself the right to plan education and culture in accordance with any philosophical, aesthetic, political, ideological, or religious guidelines.

- Article 51 Political Associations and Parties

(3) Without prejudice to the philosophy or ideology inspiring their programs, political parties may not use names that contain terms directly related to any religion or church or use emblems which may be mistaken for national or religious symbols.

-Article 288 limits to the Revision on the Substance The laws revising the Constitution safeguard: (…) c) The separation of the Churches from the State.

b) Important laws:

- Religious Liberty Law (*Lei da Liberdade Religiosa* (LLR) - Law n.º 16/2001, of the 22nd. June 2001), complemented by:

- Decree-Law 134/2003 of 28 June, on the registration of religious legal entities;
- Decree-Law 194/2003 of 23 August, regarding fees;
- Decree-Law 308/2003 of 10 December, on the Commission for Religious Liberty (CRL).
- The Concordat of 7 May 1940, amended and confirmed by the Protocol of 15 February 1975 (Conc. 1940); the Concordat of 18 May 2004.
- Missionary agreement of 1940 between the Holy See and Portugal.
- Decree-Law 323/83 of 5 July,
- Ordinance 333/86 of 2 July,
- Law 46/86 of 14 October (especially Art. 47),
- Ordinance 831/87 of 16 October,
- Ordinance 344-A/88 of 31 May,
- Decree-Law 286/89 of 29 August (especially Art. 7),
- Decree-Law 407/89 of 16 November,
- Decree-Law 329/98, of 2 November (all relating to the teaching of religion in State schools).
- Decree-Law 79/83 of 9 February and Decree-Law 345/85 of 23 August, on chaplaincy work in prisons and young people's homes.
- Decree 58/80 of 10 October, Ordinance 603/82 of 18 June, and Decree 22/90 of 3 August (on hospital chaplaincy).
- Law 31-A/98 of 14 July (Art. 45(c)), concerning the amount of broadcasting time for each denomination on State TV).
- Law 7/92 of 12 May (on objection to military service for religious reasons).
- Several scattered provisions on the ineligibility of the ministers of religion for election to Parliament and other State and municipal functions: Decree-Law 701-B/76 of

29 September (Art. 4, Municipalities), Law 14/79 of 16 May (Art. 6(1), *Assembleia da República* and regional parliaments).
- Decisions of the Constitutional Court 92/84 of 7 November; 423/87 of 26 November, and 174/93 of 17 February.

ROMANIA

- **Articles of the Romanian Constitution of 1991:**

- Article 29: Freedom of conscience

(1) Freedom of thought, opinion, and religious beliefs may not be restricted in any form whatsoever. No one may be compelled to embrace an opinion or religion contrary to his own convictions.

(2) Freedom of conscience is guaranteed; it must be manifested in a spirit of tolerance and mutual respect.

(3) All religions shall be free and organized in accordance with their own statutes, under the terms laid down by law.

(4) Any forms, means, acts or actions of religious enmity shall be prohibited in the relationships among the cults.

(5) Religious cults shall be autonomous from the State and shall enjoy support from it, including the facilitation of religious assistance in the army, in hospitals, prisons, homes and orphanages.

(6) Parents or legal tutors have the right to ensure, in accordance with their own convictions, the education of the minor children whose responsibility devolves on them.

- Article 32.(5 and 7): Right education.

(5) Education at all levels shall take place in state, private, or confessional institutions, according to the law.

(7) The State shall ensure the freedom of religious education, in accordance with the specific requirements of each religious cult. In public schools, religious education is organized and guaranteed by law.

b) Important laws:

- Law no.489/2006, on religious freedom and the general status of denominations,

-Government emergency Ordinance no. 137/2000 - banning any form of discrimination;
- Law 84/1995 of July 24th on Education;
- Law no. 128/1999 / status of teaching staff;
- Government Ordinance 38/1997-financial support provided to the cults
- Law no. 103/1992 - exclusive right to produce and sell cult objects;
- Government emergency Ordinance no.94/2000 retrocession of the denominations' real estates;
- Government Ordinance no.82/2001 establishing certain forms of financial! support for the cult units;
- Law no. 195/2000 on military clergy;
- Law no. 142/1999 regarding the state support for the clergy's salaries;
- Decree Law no. 126/1990 - return of confiscated properties that belonged to the Greek-Catholic Church;
- Government emergency Ordinance no.21/1997 restitution of the real estates that belonged to the Jewish community;
- Government Ordinance 112/1998 on retrocession of real estates that belonged to national communities (religious cults) transferred in the Romanian State's patrimony through confiscation;
- Government Ordinance 628/2006 on acknowledging the statue of Islam.

SLOVAKIA

a) Articles of the Constitution of 1992:

- Article 1 The Slovak Republic is a sovereign, democratic, and law-governed state. It is not linked to any ideology or religious belief.

- Article 24 [Freedom of Religion]

(1) The freedoms of thought, conscience, religion, and faith are guaranteed. This right also comprises the possibility to change one's religious belief or faith. Everyone has the right to be without religious belief. Everyone has the right to publicly express his opinion.

(2) Everyone has the right to freely express his religion or faith on his own or together with others, privately or publicly, by means of divine and religious services, by observing religious rites, or by participating in the teaching of religion.
(3) Churches and religious communities administer their own affairs. In particular, they constitute their own bodies, inaugurate their clergymen, organize the teaching of religion, and establish religious orders and other church institutions independently of state bodies.

(4) Conditions for exercising rights according to Sections (1)-(3) can be limited only by law, if such a measure is unavoidable in a democratic society to protect public order, health, morality, or the rights and liberties of others.

- Article 25 (military service)

(1) The defence of the Slovak Republic is a matter of honour for each citizen.

(2) No one must be forced to perform military service if this runs counter to his conscience or religious belief. The details will be specified in a law.

b) Important laws:

- Act N° 308/1991 Coll. on freedom of religious faith and on the position of churches and religious society, amended by Act Nª 394/2000, and amended by Act n° 201/2007 March 29th .
- Act N° 192/1992 Zb. on registration of churches and religious communities. (cancelled, some parts of Law was transformed to the Law Act 308/1991, take effect from 1 May 2007)
- Law 218/1949 about the economic providing of churches and religious societies by the State.
- Act N° 163/1990 Zb. on theological colleges.
- Act N° 282/1993 Z.z. on restitution of property to churches and religious communities.
- The Basic Treaty between the Slovak Republic and the Holy See (no. 326/2001), ratified in December 2001.
- The Agreement between the Slovak Republic and Registered Churches and Religious Societies (no. 250/2002), approved in April 2002, which regulates the status of eleven non-Catholic churches and religious societies.
- The Treaty between the Slovak Republic and the Holy See on Spiritual Service in the Slovak Armed Forces and Armed Corps (no. 648/2002)
- The Agreement between the Slovak Republic and Registered Churches and Religious Society on Pastoral Service to their Believers in the Slovak Armed Forces and Armed Corps (no. 270/2005).
- The Treaty between the Slovak Republic and the Holy See on Catholic education (no. 394/2004)
- The Agreement between the Slovak Republic and Registered Churches and Religious Societies regarding Religious Education (no. 395/2004).

SLOVENIA

a) Articles of the Constitution of 1991:

- Article 7

The state and religious communities shall be separate.

Religious communities shall enjoy equal rights; they shall pursue their activities freely.

- Article 41 (Freedom of Conscience)

Religious and other beliefs may be freely professed in private and public life.

No one shall be obliged to declare his religious or other beliefs.

Parents have the right to provide their children with a religious and moral upbringing in accordance with their beliefs. The religious and moral guidance given to children must be appropriate to their age and maturity, and be consistent with their free conscience and religious and other beliefs or convictions.

- Article 63 (Prohibition of Incitement to Discrimination and Intolerance and Prohibition of Incitement to Violence and War)

Any incitement to national, racial, religious or other discrimination, and the inflaming of national, racial, religious or other hatred and intolerance are unconstitutional.

Any incitement to violence and war is unconstitutional.

- Article 123 (Duty to Participate in the National Defence)

Participation in the national defence is compulsory for citizens within the limits and in the manner provided by law.

Citizens who for their religious, philosophical or humanitarian convictions are not willing to perform military duties, must be given the opportunity to participate in the national defence in some other manner.

b) Important laws:

a) Religious Freedom Act, 2 .2.2007 (Official Gazette of the RS, Nº 14/07).

b) Legal Status of Religious Communities in the Republic of Slovenia Act – Article 20 (this Act was repealed by the Religious Freedom Act but Article 20 remains applicable).

c) Agreement between the Republic of Slovenia and the Holy Seaton legal issues (signed in Ljublljana in 14.12.2001, but ratified by the National Assembly on January 28th 2004 (Official Gazette of the RS –MP, 4/04)..

d) Act Regulating Cemetery and Burial Services and the Maintenance of Cemeteries, 1984.

e) Act Regulating the Recognition of Marriages Entered into prior to 9 May 1946. whose validity was Contested according to Former Regulations, 1949.

f) Cultural Heritage Protection Act, 2008.

g) Organization and Financing of Education Act, 1996.

h) Register of Deaths, Births and Marriages Act, 2003.

i) Relations between the Republic of Slovenia and Slovenians abroad Act, 2006.

j) Agreement on the legal status of the Evangelical Church in the Republic of Slovenia, 25 January 2000.

k) Agreement between the Slovenian Bishops' Conference and the Government of the Republic of Slovenia on spiritual care for military persons in the Slovenian army, 21 September 2000.

l) Agreement between the Evangelical Church in the Republic of Slovenia on spiritual care for military persons in the Slovenian Army, 20 October 2000.
m) Agreement on the Legal Status of the Pentecostal Church in the Republic of Slovenia, 17 March 2004.
n) Agreement on the Legal Status of the Serbian Orthodox Church, July 9th 2004.
o) Agreement on the Legal Status of the Islamic Community in the Republic of Slovenia 9 July 2007.
p) Agreement on the legal status of the Buddhist congregation Dharmaling, 4 July 2008.

SPAIN

a) Articles of the Constitution of 1978:

- Article 16.

1. "The freedom of ideology. Religion and worship of individuals and communities will be guaranteed. The only limits to its manifestations are those necessary for the maintenance of public order which is projected by the law".
2. "No one can be forced lo declare his/ her ideology, religion or beliefs".
3. "No denomination will have State nature. The authorities will take into account the religious beliefs of Spanish society and will maintain the resulting relations of cooperation with the Catholic Church and the other denominations"

b) Important laws:

- Law 7/1980 of 5th July of Religious Freedom (BOE number 177. 24th July).

- Royal Decree 142/1981, January 9th on the organisation and function of the Register of Religious Entities.

- Four Cooperation Agreements between the Spanish State and the Holy See concerning legal affairs, educational and cultural affairs, economic affairs, and religious attendance of the Armed Forces January 3th 1979.

- Laws 24, 25 and 26 of 10th November 1992 approving 3 Cooperation Agreements subscribed between the Slate and the following religious bodies:

- Federation of Evangelical Religious Entities of Spain "Federación de Entidades Religiosas Evangélicas de España" (FEREDE).

- Federation of Jews Communities of Spain "Federación de Comunidades Judías de España" (FCJE).
- Islamic Commission of Spain "Comisión Islámica de España" (CIE).

- Royal Decree 176/2006 inclusion of Imams and Islamic religious leaders under the General Regime of Social Security.

- Royal Decree 710/2006 implementing the Cooperation Agreements regarding to spiritual guidance in prisons.

SWEDEN

a) Articles of the Constitution of 1976:

- Art. 1. Every citizen shall be guaranteed the following rights and freedoms in his relations with the public institutions:

"….6. Freedom of worship: that is, the freedom to practise one's religion alone or in the company of others…."

- Art. 2. Every citizen shall be protected in his relations with the public institutions against any coercion to divulge an opinion in a political, religious, cultural or other such connection. He shall furthermore be protected in his relations with the public institutions against any coercion to participate in a meeting for the formation of opinion or a demonstration or other manifestation of opinion, or to belong to a political association, religious community or other association for opinion referred to in sentence one.

- Art. 12. The rights and freedoms referred to in Article 1, points 1 to 5, in Articles 6 ,8, and 11, paragraph two, may be restricted in law to the extent provided for in Articles 13 to 16. With authority in law, they may be restricted by other statute in cases under Chapter 8, Article 7, paragraph one, point 7, and Article 10. Freedom of assembly and freedom to demonstrate may similarly be restricted also in cases under Article 14.

The restrictions referred to in paragraph one may be imposed only to satisfy a purpose acceptable in a democratic society. The restriction must never go beyond what is necessary having regard to the purpose which occasioned it, nor may it be carried so far as to constitute a threat to the free formation of opinion as one of the fundaments of democracy. No restriction may be imposed solely on grounds of a political, religious, cultural or other such opinion…."

Chapter 8:

- Art. 6. Provisions concerning religious communities are laid down in law. Provisions concerning the bases of the Church of Sweden as a religious community shall also be laid down in an act of law.

The enactment, amendment or abrogation of such a law is governed by the provisions of Article 16 concerning enactment of the Riksdag Act.

b) Important laws

The new state-church relations in Sweden from the year 2000 have led to quite a lot of new legislation:

-Church of Sweden Act, the Act on Introduction of the Church of Sweden Act,
-the Religious Communities Act, the Act on Support to Religious Communities,
-The Ordinance on Government Grants to Religious Communities.
-The Heritage Conservation Act and the Burial Act.
-The 1993 Act on Right for Officiating Marriages within other Religious Communities than the Church of Sweden
-1994 Act on the European Convention Regarding Protection of Human Rights and Fundamental Freedoms.
-1999 Act on Fees to Registered Religious Communities, implemented in the Ordinance on Fees to Registered Religious Communities.
-1999 Ordinance on Registration of Religious Communities.
-Act on Entrusting Public Documents to the Church of Sweden or any of its Organisational Parts on Deposit, etc.
- Ordinance on Entrusting Public Documents to the Church of Sweden or any of its Organisational Parts on Deposit.
- Act on the Church of Sweden's Personnel at the Changing of Relations between the State and the Church of Sweden on January 1, 2000.
- Act on Exemption from Taxes for Pries Livelihood Resources at the Yearly Taxations 2001-2010.
-Act on the Legal Confirmation in Some Cases for the Church of Sweden's Acquisition to Property.

THE NETHERLANDS

a) Articles of the Constitution of 1983.

- Article 6 [Religion, Belief]

(1) Everyone shall have the right to manifest freely his religion or belief, either individually or in community with others, without prejudice to his responsibility under the law.

(2) Rules concerning the exercise of this right other than in buildings and enclosed places may be laid down by Act of Parliament for the protection of health, in the interest of traffic and to combat or prevent disorders.

- Article 23 [Education]
(1) Education shall be the constant concern of the Government.
(2) All persons shall be free to provide education, without prejudice to the au-

thorities' right of supervision and, with regard to forms of education designated by law, its right to examine the competence and moral integrity of teachers, to be regulated by Act of Parliament.
(3) Education provided by public authorities shall be regulated by Act of Parliament, paying due respect for everyone's religion or belief.
(4) The authorities shall ensure that primary education is provided in a sufficient number of public-authority schools in every municipality. Deviations from this provision may be permitted under rules to be established by Act of Parliament on condition that there is opportunity to receive the said form of education.
(5) The standards required of schools financed either in part or in full from public funds shall be regulated by Act of Parliament, with due regard, in the case of private schools, to the freedom to provide education according to religious or other belief.
(6) The requirements for primary education shall be such that the standards both of private schools fully financed from public funds and of public-authority schools are fully guaranteed. The relevant provisions shall respect in particular the freedom of private schools to choose their teaching aids and to appoint teachers as they see fit.
(7) Private primary schools that satisfy the conditions laid down by Act of Parliament shall be financed from public funds according to the same standards as public-authority schools. The conditions under which private secondary education and pre-university education shall receive contributions from public funds shall be laid down by Act of Parliament.
(8) The Government shall submit annual reports on the state of education to the Parliament.
-Article 4 (Additional articles)0
The following provision shall remain in force until such time as statutory measures provide otherwise: 'The stipends, pensions and other forms of income of any sort received by various religious denominations or their ministers shall continue to be paid to the said denominations. Ministers who do not receive a stipend from public funds, or who receive one that is insufficient, may be awarded a stipend or their existing stipend may be increased.'

b) Important laws

- Public Manifestations Act *[Wet Openbare Manifestaties]* (April 1988)
-Article 9 of the European Convention on Human Rights (ECHR)
-Article 18 of the Covenant on Civil and Political Rights (CCPR)
-Mass Media Act
-Labour Relations Act
-General Equal Treatment Act
-Article 218 of the Criminal Procedure Code
-Article 429 b of the Criminal Code

-Article 137 c-e of the Criminal Code
-Article 147 a of the Criminal Code
-Military Conscription Act
-*Minderhedennota*: Dutch Minority Policy, 1983
-Memorandum on Ethnic Minorities 1983

UNITED KINGDOM

a) The UK does not have a written constitution.

b) Important laws

Charities Act of 2006

Rechtspolitisches Symposium
Legal Policy Symposium

Herausgegeben im Institut für Rechtspolitik an der Universität Trier
von Bernd von Hoffmann und Gerhard Robbers

Band 1 Bernd von Hoffmann (ed.): Towards a Common European Immigration Policy. Reports and Discussions of a Symposium held in Trier on October 24th and 25th, 2002. 2003.

Band 2 Bernd von Hoffmann (ed.): Global Governance. Reports and Discussions of a Symposium held in Trier on October 9th and 10th, 2003. 2004.

Band 3 Gerhard Robbers (ed.): Reforming Federalism – Foreign Experiences for a Reform in Germany. Reports of a Symposium held in Trier on December 2nd to 4th, 2004 hosted by the Institute for Legal Policy at the University of Trier in Cooperation with the German Bundesrat. 2005.

Band 4 Gerhard Robbers / Dieter C. Umbach / Klaus-Eckart Gebauer (Hrsg.): Innere Sicherheit, Menschenwürde, Gentechnologie. Kolloquium aus Anlass des 80. Geburtstages von Ernst Benda am 22. Januar 2005 in Trier, veranstaltet vom Institut für Rechtspolitik an der Universität Trier und den Professoren Dr. Gerhard Robbers (Trier), Dr. Dieter C. Umbach (Potsdam), Dr. Klaus-Eckart Gebauer (Mainz) in Zusammenarbeit mit dem Landtag Rheinland-Pfalz. 2005.

Band 5 Bernd von Hoffmann (Hrsg.): Rechtspolitische Herausforderungen. Kolloquium anlässlich des 75. Geburtstages von Ministerpräsident a.D. Dr. Carl-Ludwig Wagner. 2005.

Band 6 Joachim Mertes / Gerhard Robbers (Hrsg.): Antworten auf den internationalen Terrorismus. Gewährleistung der Inneren Sicherheit durch Bund und Länder. Mit Beiträgen von Manfred Baldus, Wolfgang Bosbach, Paul Dubois, Rüdiger Freiherr von Fritsch, Joachim Mertes, Wolf Plesmann, Gerhard Robbers, Dieter Wiefelspütz und Heinrich Amadeus Wolff. 2007.

Band 7 Bernd von Hoffmann (Hrsg.): Universalität der Menschenrechte. Kulturelle Pluralität. 2009.

Band 8 Katharina Knüppel: Religionsfreiheit und Apostasie in islamisch geprägten Staaten. 2010.

Band 9 Johan D. van der Vyver: Implementation of International Law in the United States. 2010.

Band 10 Michael Rahe: Begriff und Bedeutung der Staatspraxis in der Rechtsprechung des Bundesverfassungsgerichts. 2011.

Band 11 Kathrin Luise Lang: Das Antiterrordateigesetz. Zusammenarbeit von Polizei und Nachrichtendiensten im Lichte des Trennungsgebotes. 2011.

Band 12 Christoph Streiß: Das Trennungsgebot zwischen Polizei und Nachrichtendiensten. Im Lichte aktueller Herausforderungen des Sicherheitsrechts. 2011.

Band 13 Bernd von Hoffmann / Gerhard Robbers (Hrsg.): Demografischer Wandel in Rheinland-Pfalz. Auswirkungen, Herausforderungen und Perspektiven. Mit Beiträgen von Heinz Georg Bamberger, Jörg Berres, Hans-Jörg Duppré, Bernd von Hoffmann, Josef Peter Mertes, Georg Müller-Fürstenberger, Gerhard Robbers, Hubert Schnabel, Rainer Wilhelm. 2011.

Band 14 Juan Ferreiro: Islam and State in the EU. Church-State Relationships, Reality of Islam, Imams Training Centres. 2011.

www.peterlang.de